XPEDITIO ROUTE
SEC ER

Inuvik

Arctic Red River

ARCTIC CIRCLE

N

Fort Good Hope

GREAT BEAR LAKE

Norman Wells

Fort Franklin

Fort Norman

Mackenzie R.

Wrigley

Yellowknife

Fort Simpson

GREAT SLAVE LAKE

Fort Providence

••••••••• author's route
———— roads

100   200 miles

rumpshire.

Date Due

FEB 18 '72		
MAR 13 '72		
MAY 1 '72		
JUL 1972		
MAY 2 3 1977		
MAR 7 - 1978		
MAR 2 4 1979		
SE 6 '86		
AP 2 7 '87		
JA 1 3 '93		
NV 0 1 '01		
DEC 0 9 '02		
MR 1 8 '04		
JE 07 '05		

Books by Constance Helmericks

WE LIVE IN ALASKA

WE LIVE IN THE ARCTIC
(*with Harmon Helmericks*)

OUR SUMMER WITH THE ESKIMOS
(*with Harmon Helmericks*)

OUR ALASKAN WINTER
(*with Harmon Helmericks*)

THE FLIGHT OF THE ARCTIC TERN
(*with Harmon Helmericks*)

DOWN THE WILD RIVER NORTH

Down the Wild River North

Constance Helmericks

Down the

Wild River North

Illustrations by MICHAEL ALLEN HAMPSHIRE

Little, Brown and Company · *Boston* · *Toronto*

Acknowledgments

THE author wishes to thank the Honorable Arthur Laing, Minister of Northern Affairs and Natural Resources, Canada, for his helpfulness in sending government statistical information. She also wishes to thank other persons in the Department for answering questions and gathering materials that contributed to the writing of this book. The invaluable assistance of Western Pacific Airlines in Canada, too, is gratefully acknowledged.

The author sincerely thanks her family for their forbearance during two years of book writing; she especially wants to thank Mr. Gilbert Barrett for helping with many of the details of assembling the manuscript.

Finally, the author wishes to thank her publishers for financing this expedition of a mother and children into the Arctic in their canoe — a daring enterprise on the publishers' part never before undertaken in publishers' annals.

Contents

PART I

The Peace

1

Some Babes in the Woods

WHEN I opened my eyes that morning the leaves outside the bedroom screens were green with glints of shimmering sunlight, and I thought, as I had for years: "Green, there's nothing like green. Lots of it. Years of it. For your soul's good, you absolutely need green."

The room where I awoke was like a bower, for just a moment. The leaves shut out the fact that just beyond the lawn on every side lay the stone city. Sunday morning. It came then, the half-expected knocking at the front door. Knock, knock, bang. Kick.

Who would dare to interrupt another person's Sunday morning reverie in such a beastly fashion? Children, of course.

The children were running wild outdoors in their pajamas, and they had locked themselves out, of course, as they came down from the roof, onto which they often climbed with singular agility from our little tree.

"Let us in, in, in," screeched Ann, who is by nature a coloratura soprano, untutored. We lived on Bean Alley, fortunately, quite off the main avenue. We lived there with our guinea pigs, who enjoyed the green grass from the door of their little house, and forty wild birds which at dawn visited at the feed pan, and with Henrietta Hen who cackled in strident tones when she laid her daily egg in the old rocking chair on the porch — all of us guarded by the watchful black dog Sylvia beside the house. There were no cages or fences or dog chains. I have always advocated freedom for chickens, dogs, and children, even if grown-ups don't like freedom, or at least seldom have it after their maturity is reached.

"Let us in, in, *in*," screeched Ann.

"Quiet, children, the neighbors!" I called automatically. Hustling the two of them, carrying Henrietta Hen, into the house, I fell back into bed and stared outward into the green leaves.

Life stretched out, dull and endlessly worry-filled for me, a civilized adult mother, breadwinner by necessity; but life asked, "What next, little girl, for you?"

"Who wants to get the family breakfast?" I called out. "I'll pay ten cents to have mine served on a tray in bed."

"I can't," said Ann, of the long golden hair, the screamer. "I'm only nine."

"Ah, but you've been in training for breakfast since you were four," I urged cleverly.

"I want to wait until I'm older."

"I'll bring your breakfast," said Jean. "But you forget that we're only children. I very much need fifteen cents."

"Oh, my dear," I said. "That's very good."

Ann brought my newspaper and nothing happened for a long time. "I can't get breakfast," complained Jean from a vague distance. "Ann won't let me. She's sitting on my head."

"*Get off her head*," I yelled out. "One of these days I'm going to take you two girls up north. Do you know that?"

From the small kitchen came bacon, eggs, toast and coffee eventually, on a tray, carried by unsteady hands. Imperfect but wonderful eatables, they represented the magnificent culmination of my special five years' indoctrination course which I recommend working mothers give their children if they, the mothers, do not have husbands that tradition dictates they have to get up for.

"Jean, go into the bathroom, please, and wash your hair."

"My hair isn't dirty, Mummy."

"Yes, it is," I argued, desiring to be alone with breakfast and newspaper. "Don't argue."

"I will so argue."

The bathroom door slammed. Jean had wanted to be a boy, and everything was irksome to her at that point.

Then Jean came out of the bathroom, wearing glasses for myopia, and it was Sunday morning, and she was fourteen. Three years had passed.

Now Jean was five feet seven inches tall, unhappily wearing a size 36 C bra, and hating herself wildly for her protuberances. But grown men passing in the street, from the age of twenty-two to ninety, turned their heads and stared, and Jean was unaware of it.

Ann was right behind Jean in age. She, who still screamed mightily when things did not go as she wished, was blessed with a shock of yellow hair and a soprano voice, and was twelve and a half now, with flat ribs much like a washboard.

"I sure wish I could take you girls into the North," I had kept saying over the years. The girls had a fair idea what I meant when I used the word North, although of course they had not seen it. They were raised on stories I told them of the North. The stories usually began like this: "It was in our fourth month of canoeing down the Yukon River . . ." or "One day five hundred miles by river north of the Yukon, up the Koyukuk . . ." or perhaps, "on the Kuparuk River we were carrying five caribou in the canoe . . ."

Poor children of today and of tomorrow. How many of you will ever again on this continent carry five caribou in your canoe?

"I think at last we are going north," I told the girls on this Sunday morning, hardly daring to believe it myself.

"What will we do with the chicken? What about the guinea pigs?" they asked instantly. "What's to become of poor Sylvia? Can we take them?" Then, as an afterthought, "What about Grandmother?"

"I don't know yet," I answered. "Give me some time to work it out."

"But, Mother, *you* are so slow. I would like to leave for the North right now," sighed Jean. "I've been ready for years."

"We have to work out a plan," I told them, "which requires money, and that's the thing I don't have right now."

I had tried a lot of plans to go places in the world with the children, only to find that women as heads of dependent families cannot be employed in overseas positions because of Rules. Eventually, I resolved to visit once more that land that I had known when I was young: the perenially young arctic wastelands. I would take the children with me, of course.

When the telephone rang I leaped through the front room, skidding nimbly over a game of marbles, and fell on the chicken, causing a flurry of cackles and feathers. "Get Henrietta *out!*" I yelled. "You know she doesn't belong in here."

"I'm treating her," said Ann stoutly. "I'm busy treating her for athlete's foot."

It was Ginnie on the phone, and she told me she had just got a new pink motorcycle. "But nothing keeps you looking younger," she boomed heartily. "You really should have one."

"I wanted to tell you about this wonderful man who's taking me to dinner tonight. He says he may be able to bring a friend . . ."

"Yes, Ginnie," I was booming back, perhaps a trifle less heartily than she, "you always give me such a lift. You've done your *hair* in St. Louis Tomater? Well, did you know that Erline did *hers* in Violet Ice last week? Do you think she can get away with it, with her shape? Yes, but she has to wear only rose or black or violet with it. She's getting rid of all the rest of her wardrobe, I guess. . . ."

"Mother's on the telephone with her horrid girl friends again," I could hear Jean say.

"And you know how they can talk," added Ann. "Mother, hurry up. You promised you would take us all in the car and look at homes where the pets can stay, and then we can go north."

I realized then that I must have a terribly split personality. Everybody is torn into a million pieces today. We have to live in the American culture and we can't get away from it. But I had a foot in two worlds, for I remembered another.

It was nearing noon when I finally got the kids and dog and the chicken and guinea pigs loaded into the car. Henrietta, who had just come from a brisk ride in the bicycle basket, was settled with many a squawk upon the rim of her familiar cardboard egg box on the front seat of the car beside me. From her elevated perch Henrietta could look out the window during her last ride. As we drove through the traffic Jean thoughtfully arranged her tail so it would hang over the box filled with hay.

In the back seat rode the children, with the guinea pigs in a small box, and dog Sylvia. The guinea pigs, the result of several breedings, consisted of the mother, called Piggie, and her three mean-tempered, sulky daughters, all of whom looked much alike with black beady eyes set close together on the tops of their heads. In their eyes no expression of conviviality with human beings lingered. Their rodent world with us had been a green, grassy world of juicy stems and blades viewed from a three-inch elevation. Yet, by some wonderful feral instinct which takes care of all creatures, they knew and gauged their activities on the lawn to the attentive guardian dog who made it safe for them to run freely out of their little house set in the bushes to nibble greedily at twilight and in early day. The pigs were not used to being picked up, and they huddled in a resentful mass of bodies.

In the back seat rode Sylvia, the large black dog who was going along for the ride but who perhaps could stay with Grandmother if we went north. Sylvia's great muscular pink tongue would occasionally lollop the hen with affection, or wrap around the neck of the driver.

Where were we going? What was it all about? The dumb animals couldn't know. We were going to put some of them into retirement. Piggie and her daughters and Henrietta were going to be placed gratis at the City Sanitation Plant, which had a collection of retired animals of children who had grown up. Here the animals lived out their retirement until they died of old age.

"They will be happy here," I said, when we handed our pets over to their kindly keepers, but I felt a little choked up. It was as Jean said: "You know, a chicken is very delicately made; it's very beautiful really. When you live with a chicken for several years you see a lot of things about her you didn't see at first. When you get to know a chicken really well, you get awfully fond of her."

"She will finally die of old age here," said Ann. I knew perfectly well that Ann's statement was a euphemism, but I let it ride. Nobody dies of old age. Either we die violently in our youth, or we die of degenerative diseases miserably, one part at a time, as old cars wear out. Henrietta, she who was such a loyal little egg layer, who had such colossal conceit, would now have to take her chances with all those other chickens and with the weather, and she would die of exhaustion outdoors during the first summer's heat, or the first winter's cold in the way that has been nature's plan since time immemorial. Dear, fragile little creature, part and parcel of our fragile security — we were never to see her again.

"Yes, she's already old and is about to die of old age, anyway, my dears," I told the youngsters as we drove away. "As a matter of fact," I added reflectively, "so am I."

"Oh, not yet, Mother," said Ann, brightly. "Not for a very long while yet."

Our car wended its way back through the traffic, one among the eighty-one million automobiles of America, which if they were placed bumper to bumper would have stretched ten times around the earth in that year 1965.

My vitality was sapped from the long responsibility of breadwinner and homemaker. This little family had to eat over two tons of food every year. Somebody had to earn the money to buy the food. Somebody had to stand in the long lines at the supermarkets and then carry two tons of food into the house and put it on the table, trying to achieve the American picture-book standards. Life was a routine of food and dishes, mopping the kitchen, sweeping the floor, defrosting the fridge. Somebody had to buy the children's clothes and run the washer. That somebody was me.

Almost every day, the clothes of little girls demanded altering or mending. Grandmother did most of that part, fortunately. The little girls required some ten to fifteen dresses each to attend school, as contrasted with the three dresses my mother owned when she was a child, and the perhaps six dresses owned by myself in my schooldays. Often the little boys tore sashes and buttons and bows off. Required also was a variety of skirts, blouses, shorts, blue jeans, stretch pants, sneakers, party shoes, bathing suits and caps, winter coats, party frocks, sweaters, handbags, gloves, shoes, slippers, and dainty underthings that would have astounded our forebears. Life had become so complex! The full-time services of a chauffeur were clearly indicated for girls who expected to have any social life or hobbies, for as cities grew, the children could no longer walk the distances these things required. Children after the age of ten, at one time of little annoyance to their elders, were now dependent upon their elders for years to come for transportation, for not only were the distances great, but the cities were unsafe.

Meanwhile each American, whether man, woman, or child, consumed on the average fifteen tons of irreplaceable earth's resources each year, yet a large percentage of people on the earth were starving, and the competition among populations merely to survive grew more acute daily.

The ideal of unlimited consumption was unfortunate for the women who were the economic heads of families, as well as for other underprivileged groups. These people could not achieve the ideal set up by the complicated American patterns of living, without undergoing the most agonizing stress. The stress permeated all aspects of life, making life utterly commercial, and emotionally meaningless for multitudes. The stress helped to destroy the innocence of childhood.

As we drove back to the little house on Bean Alley, I said, "If we find we are able to go north this spring, we will then leave the dog with Grandmother, won't we?"

"I won't go unless we take Sylvia," objected Ann.

"It's absolutely impossible to take the dog to Canada," I argued, "since we'll be traveling all summer, and next summer, in a canoe. Girls, I have told you that before."

"We can't take her. You've heard Mother explain it, lots of times, about how it is in the wilderness. The mosquitoes would eat Sylvia alive," stated Jean steadily, with an older person's insight. "Would you like that?"

"Besides, Ann," I persuaded, "what would happen to all of us if Sylvia tipped over the canoe, or maybe jumped into the river?"

"We could paddle down the river and pick her up."

"No, we couldn't, Ann. Not on those rivers."

"Look here, Ann," argued Jean emphatically. "You are more than twelve years old and it's time you got some sense. Don't you realize that whenever we came to shore along the river the savage dogs of Indians would try to kill Sylvia? Those dogs would eat her up for breakfast. And she's a short-haired dog, and could never stand the cold rains, or how about when we reach the Arctic Ocean? We have got to let the dog and Grandmother stay right where they are, where they are well off."

"A very wise decision, Jean," I commended her. But Ann looked mad and wild-eyed.

"Sylvia would die from the insect swarms and the summer rains," I told Ann, straight to the point. "And the Canadian Rivers Expedition can't carry food to feed a dog, and be successful explorers."

"Then I guess we'll have to leave her home," Ann conceded.

"Good. Well, girls, we are going to make a canoe expedition to the Arctic Ocean," I informed them. "Far as I know, nobody has written an account of a voyage down to the Arctic in modern times. Well, I don't see why you, Jean, at fourteen, and Ann, at twelve, and me of course, shouldn't be the ones to make the trip and see a few things for ourselves instead of enduring this stifling humdrum all the time."

They took this in their stride, not seeming surprised. They apparently thought I could do anything.

"We are an expedition and we are about to make an epic voyage." I waxed enthusiastic. "We'll make a trip through North America as long as Lewis and Clark made, through Indian country all the way. Peaceful Indians, though. You are about to see country that no American women or children have seen before, perhaps in all the history of the world."

"Oh, gee, let's get at it," said Jean.

"It will be a real education for you girls," I informed them. Of course that was the understatement of the year, but they had no way of knowing that, the poor dears.

They were mainly concerned with each having along her proper shampoo — Jean had an oily scalp and Ann had vice versa — and with their hair curlers, an item with which every single other girl of their general age group in America is wholeheartedly involved.

"I flew over some of the Peace River country and the Mackenzie country about fifteen years ago," I told the kids. "It's something I haven't seen by canoe, and I've often thought of it while I was washing dishes, and things. I always thought in the back of my mind I'd like to see those rivers someday. But I never imagined I'd have the opportunity to take my two daughters there."

Here in North America we have one of the last great natural wilderness areas left on earth. Although at one time I was an Alaskan for twelve years, and spent most of that time north of the Arctic Circle, it was not to Alaska that I turned now. My imagination wandered to the vast domain of interior Canada and the great subarctic hinterlands I hadn't yet seen. A person can spend a whole lifetime seeing North America's rivers and lakes and waterways, and never see them all. You get out on these rivers, and the rivers flow north to the polar sea. You can take two years getting to that polar sea by small boat or canoe, loafing along and camping, and it's a good education in geography for anyone.

"There will be people living here and there along those shores," I told the kids. "It will be interesting to meet them and see what they're like, won't it?"

Jean didn't think so. "I like animals better."

"Fine. There will be animals, too."

"Will we get to shoot some animals? Moose, bears?"

"Possibly. I doubt it. We'll plan to live mostly on canned and dried food. We'll always keep our rifles loaded, of course."

"Oh, boy," said Jean, really glad for the first time. "I've never had a loaded rifle."

"But I don't see how I can leave Dickie," sighed Ann.

"You're just lucky that your mother is an explorer," lectured Jean sternly. "Besides, Dickie never even looks your way, so you won't be leaving anything after all."

"Jean Helmericks, don't you ever dare say that. Dickie thinks of me all the time and I am never off his mind, for one teeny second, so there."

"Aw, he doesn't even think about you. He doesn't know you are alive. He likes that girl he goes with. He didn't even ask you to skate last time."

Ann burst into twelve-year-old sobs and screams of humiliation as I hushed Jean with difficulty, pulling the car into our yard with one hand while this romantic crisis exploded, and slaps and hair-pulling began. There came into my mind the Saturday nights that I had chauffeured the girls. Four trips and forty miles through traffic lights to the roller rink, that subteen mecca for romance, where the loud rhythmic rollers and lights went round and round to ponderous melodies. Well, there wouldn't be any more chauffeuring for me or any more twelve-year-old romantic heart-break, at least. I stalked into the house.

The telephone rang and a familiar melodious male voice came soothingly to my ear: Gerald, senior professor of Elizabethan liter-ature. You couldn't say he was my fiancé because we weren't en-gaged. A silly word, fiancé, so flossy and artificial-sounding. We need a better word. Sometimes I referred to him as my boyfriend. But I have never liked that word, either. I guess we have no good English word for it, whatever it is. Anyway, it was good to hear Gerald's distinguished, stuffy, kindly voice.

Gerald was glad for me that at last I was able to go north on the rivers, since it was what I had long wanted to do; and he was help-ing in many ways to iron out the minor and major problems of organizing the expedition. He and I usually spent our evenings with the children, doing seventh- and eighth-grade homework with difficulty. "I never expected I would be called upon to go through seventh and eighth grade again," he once groaned, "but it's an in-teresting challenge to see if one can do it."

"You're the type who enjoys mental labors," I told him. "I'm not that type. But I do appreciate your sitting with them at the study table and encouraging them, as you know they do suffer so these days."

"Yes," he agreed. "They do indeed suffer. They have to be much brighter than we were."

"But they're so dumb about other things in the world today, I mean the real world," I said.

As I hung up, a neighbor came across the lawn, and I let her in. "Have you heard?" she asked, frightened.

I paused, curiously alert. "What next?" a small voice warned inside, not for the first time.

"You know the lady who lives in the south duplex, just in front?" she asked. "Rents from the same landlord that we do? Last night, this prowler, see, he was wearing a stocking mask, cut through the window screen of her house. Don't let the children hear. He raped her with a knife at her throat. Her little baby girl was sleeping in the bed with her at the time. Cut this lady with his knife," she whispered, "right near the corner of her eye. She is in the hospital, completely hysterical. The officers been asking if we heard or saw anything . . ."

I sat down with my heart pounding. "It could have been any of us," said my neighbor. "You know my husband works nights. I'm often afraid. You are alone, too. Of course, you have your dog and you're armed. The police are looking, of course, but they've found nothing, yet. . . ."

The children came across the lawn. They had heard, of course, from others.

The idea of rapes at knifepoint, of shootings, holdups, and violent assaults, was not new to their not innocent childhood. Several times each had avoided possible molesters and kidnapers by practicing a continuous vigilance in which they were drilled in school as well as at home. They thrived, apparently imagining it to be an adjunct to familiar violent television shows of their times. The problems of survival for women raising children alone, besides being acute economically, were thus doubly compounded.

Through this weird "civilization" we had wended our way for some years and had luckily survived its many dangers. When anybody asked me later, "How could you dare to go alone, a woman, taking your two little daughters away to the Arctic Ocean in a canoe?" I would think of this.

It is not so difficult perhaps as some other things. If one has happened already to be an explorer, one merely returns to one's natural habitat, in a manner of speaking, training the children, of course, to take over those survival functions which require the harder labor. The question is: How do you teach American city children? Perhaps by showing and doing as you go. To Jean and Ann go the credit. I can say now that my remark to Gerald — that

I expected the children to successfully follow the track of the great explorers who preceded us one hundred and fifty years ago — was beautifully borne out. At my stage of life, alone I never could have managed it. Their magnificent physical strength and their unyielding moral courage were to pull us through.

2

The Canadian Rivers Expedition

THE children and I were driving along a vast superhighway. They took it for granted; and why not? They were born into this age, and they knew nothing else. They might as well enjoy it now while they could, I thought. It's possible that the age of the private automobile on our earth may last only a hundred years. We don't know yet if we will be able to make it last. However, I do think that their private automobiles will be the last freedom the American people will be willing to give up. Everything else will go first.

"Look over there!" I said. "See those new shoebox houses in that development?"

"Ugh! People," said Jean. "There's too many people."

"Civilization has changed since I was young."

"What makes civilization change, Mother?"

"I don't know. Nobody knows. Nobody has ever been able to control it, or direct it."

"Can they control the rivers where we are going?" asked Ann. "If they wanted to, I mean."

"Oh, yes, they can dam and control the mightiest rivers. But fortunately they haven't needed our rivers yet. But even now, the engineers have plotted hydroelectric power sites in the Arctic. Only tomorrow Canada will be selling water to our drying-up population of the south. Yes, they can control the rivers, they can harness all nature," I said. "But they can't control themselves."

The kids, in common with their generation, and even with most people in mine, had never seen a natural river in their lives, or natural lands which have never been plowed or used. All the rivers and streams have been tampered with, many of them generations ago. Most rivers are unhealthy, sunken within their banks, stinking from refuse and sludge. The American Great Lakes are fast becoming dead lakes; I felt the children should know. Long ago most of our sweet waters were drunk up and consumed. Where highways are built it is economical to direct them through the valleys. At the bottom of each valley lies a stream. In order to build a straight, fast-traveling and economical state or federal highway, the stream alongside is straightened and rechanneled. When this is done and all natural curves and turns are taken out of the stream, and it has perhaps been supplied with concrete walls, the native flora is swept away by the swift current, and no fish or small marine life, or water birds or animals will ever live there again.

However, it is very fortunate that a combination of factors has allowed much of Canada immediately to our north to remain untampered with to this day. A partial explanation may lie in the fact that there is an innate conservatism in Canadians. Another reason is that a population of twenty-two million does not produce the tax money for the "development" of their enormous country all at once.

As we drove northward I tried to tell the kids how civilization in Canada consists of a number of cities along the Trans-Canada Highway and the railroad, separated like beads on string, hanging along the northern border of the United States. Almost all of the population of Canada lives in these cities. Three hundred miles to the north, railroads and most roads end, and there is wilderness. "The wilderness of North America is your natural heritage," I told them.

I had written over a hundred letters organizing the Canadian Rivers Expedition, whose members comprised myself and my two girls. I had carefully checked out the rivers upon which we were to voyage so that the voyage could be as long as possible, covering the most area, and had chosen rivers which I thought we could handle with a reasonable degree of safety — if one can ever order that in the case of a river. There were to be two portages during the first summer around falls or rapids that were unnavigable — about which more later. I planned for the complete voyage to take two summers of camping along the way. Possibly we would be able to take lodging and stay over a winter in the North, and thus I carried along report cards to facilitate a transfer into the Canadian school system.

Of all the strange equipment which generations of *voyageurs* have carried on those rivers I suspect that report cards would rank among the most strange, but they were nonetheless relevant to our time and day.

The first big question was just where to put our canoe into the Mackenzie River system. The children didn't care a hang about the names of the rivers I studied on the maps, to begin with. Nothing was real to them in life. They accepted the fact when I decided we would be spending much of our first summer on the "mighty Peace," starting up in British Columbia in Canada's extreme northwest. Our course would take us diagonally north and east across Alberta, near or perhaps into Saskatchewan. Then, north, into the Northwest Territories. We would be able to see the very heartland of North America in this way, traveling over about eleven hundred miles of river to the halfway mark, by the beginning of fall.

Our autumn destination would be the town of Yellowknife. With a population of some four thousand souls and a School District Number 1, Yellowknife, a gold camp, lay on the north shore of Great Slave Lake, so my map informed me. One of our problems would be to get across or around Great Slave Lake, a body of water larger than Lake Ontario. There were a number of problems inherent in our trip, yet experience in the past had taught me that there are usually ways in which to surmount natural obstacles when one comes to them.

The second year of our voyage, when the water flowed again, we planned to proceed out of the west end of Great Slave Lake and go on down the great Mackenzie for 1,087 nautical miles to the little government town of Inuvik, built since I was last there. The town lies on the east side of the forty-mile-broad delta of the Mackenzie, whence the kids might possibly get the chance to see the Arctic

Ocean. This is an old stamping ground of mine, in a manner of speaking. Of course they had never seen it. But why not enjoy it now? From Inuvik, these days, airline passage out is readily arranged.

It is doubtful if many Americans have really studied the map of North America as a whole carefully enough to appreciate the size of the delightful area which lies directly north of the United States. The territories which Canada owns up that way are about 40 percent as large as the Dominion itself.

Canada's territories comprise the Northwest Territories, the Yukon Territory, and, presently under Dominion administration, Arctic Quebec Territory — although the latter is not strictly a territory and its status is unclear, because while it is Eskimo country, it still falls into the domain of the Minister of Northern Affairs and National Resources until Quebec itself is able to get hold of it. Eskimo Labrador, however, is not a territory and has attained its own autonomy as a Province. These contiguous territorial areas total about one and one half million square miles, plus the north half of Hudson's Bay (one million square miles in extent), with its islands.

Of concern to us in our voyage were Alberta and the Northwest Territories only, as I tried to explain to my girls. I wanted them to know that the NWT comprises one million square miles and is divided into three districts, politically speaking. You would think politics should make small difference where there are few people, but the few people are sensitive about it because of the peculiar ideas about freedom that people have who live in enormous open lands of unknown potential. For administrational purposes the NWT is divided into the districts of Mackenzie, Keewatin, and Franklin.

Although I had touched all of them by plane, the experience was brief and long ago. Keewatin includes Boothia Peninsula, the site of our planet's North Magnetic Pole, which moves around a bit and has to be relocated now and then. Keewatin is altogether treeless and it is predominantly rocky, with arctic rock desert, lying east of the Shield: a fascinating, little-known land. But not for the children right now. They must wait until they are older.

Franklin includes the arctic islands which stretch out near the North Pole. These also are treeless and too rigorous for canoeing because they are so solidly frozen most of the time. These islands would have belonged to the United States in 1918 except that our government turned down the financing of the expedition of Dr. Vilhjalmur Stefansson, American explorer, and so he hired out to Canada with the result that Canada owns this large area today. It is a sort of logical justice that she does, for after all the islands are a nearby stepping-stone to her present dominion; and Canadians have become the best northerners from long habituation to the grim latitudes.

Now the District of Mackenzie in the NWT, including the broad, luxuriantly wooded Mackenzie River valley, would be something that, with care, we could handle, I told the girls. Into the five-mile broad giant of a river, replete with its innumerable islands, come major rivers of America. Lovely rivers, of all kinds and descriptions. A multitude of unnamed side streams from their green summer jungles. For more than one hundred and fifty years the Mackenzie route has been the major highway into the North for all manner of boats. The reason one never heard about this giant, which rivals the Mississippi, is that it flows the wrong way for most practical men to care about it. The river flows north and freezes up early. All during the long arctic summer days, year after year, the Mackenzie River system way out north there at road's end conveys boats manned by unknown crews transporting unimportant products, probably sacks of beans, for the sparse and scattered population of the great North. Mostly, the boats carry products downstream from the south to the north, and return upstream empty.

Grandmother commenced to worry about the availability of doctors and hospitals at this point in our plans. "What will happen if one of you gets an acute appendix?" She gasped at our audacity.

"Not likely." I shrugged it off. "But even so, there are several little hospitals along our water route these days. We can renew our food supplies too." I reassured her with the statistic I dug out that along our route as we voyaged there were no less than fourteen airfields supplying regular air service at the villages, usually called forts. These are the forts left over from the old Indian days. They were established by the early traders of the Northwest Company, which later merged with the Hudson's Bay Company long before the nation of Canada was founded.

For generations the men who controlled the fur empire maintained a conspiracy of silence about their doings in that great country. Much of the history of their skirmishes for power among themselves and between themselves and the Indians is forever lost — a fascinating unwritten chapter of North American history. Indian tribes still live in these forests. In 1967 the tribes or bands in Canada at large numbered 204,796 persons in 588 bands. Having no legal rights, they were wards of the government and lived on some 2,260 reserves. However, there are no reserves in the Northwest Territories and Yukon, where the natives, frequently mixed with white blood, constitute the entire northern population of trappers and wanderers. We would be guests, then, in what is still the Indians' country, the whole one and a half million square miles of it. Here the Indians retain from birth their ancestral hunting, fishing, trapping and roaming rights, according to the last treaty made in 1921, "for as long as the sun shall shine and the rivers shall flow."

"Will we get to town in time for school?" the kids earnestly asked me. School had been out just two days, and it was June.

"I don't know," I said. "It's up to the river. We'll do the best we can."

"But we can't be late for school!" Ann whispered, shocked.

"You can't be late for your childhood and youth, either," I retorted. "When it's gone it never comes again."

"Mother, how would you dare?"

"I dare anything," I said poetically, "when the month is June and there yet remains a country which is young and green."

Our car took us through Yellowstone Park, by Jackson, Wyoming, along the chain of the snow-laced Tetons. Ann carried in her lap a small yellow stuffed animal, bearing the name Piggie. Jean was carsick and morose, and Ann's dreams when we started on our epic trip were of Saturday night at the roller rink and a thirteen-year-old boy on wheels.

"By the way, listen to me now, both of you. This is the beginning. From here on all expedition members are going to have to coordinate. Hear this. You do not, either one of you, do anything whatsoever in the woods without first having explicit directions from me, your leader. You are not to touch the canoe, fires, matches, fishing gear, rifles . . ."

"But you said we can do everything you do on the trip," cried Jean, "That's not fair. Mother, you're breaking your promise. . . ."

"Hold it," I lectured. "You will, of course, learn to handle all our equipment. All in time. But don't jump into things. Wait for instructions, do you hear me clearly? Furthermore, as I told Ann weeks ago back in town, there is to be no climbing of trees. . . ." Ann in particular thought the injunction against tree-climbing exceptionally cruel when she considered all the trees that would undoubtedly be available.

"You have to give up reckless and childish behavior if you're going to explore the wilderness," I lectured ponderously. "You are going to have to learn to think about every move you make before you make it, because in the wilds you can't afford accidents. That's how we lived twelve years in the wilds and never had an accident," I told them. "In twelve years I never cut a finger with a pocketknife, or sprained an ankle, or tipped over a canoe. You just can't do those things out there because you are completely on your own and cut off from all help." There was no particular danger in the nature of the country itself — our biggest danger would be accidents caused by ourselves.

While freezing rain and wet snow alternated, we made our way north through Montana. Once out of the isolation of Yellowstone Park we learned at Livingston, Montana, that the succession of spring rains had culminated in floods, and that a twenty-thousand square-mile area across our direct route into Canada had been closed off and declared a disaster area. Some six hundred people caught in Glacier National Park were being airlifted out, having to abandon their cars, since all bridges leading there had been washed out. We felt fortunate, for we had planned to go to Glacier National Park. We had missed losing our car and equipment by a matter of hours. There remained a problem of how to cross the swollen Missouri. Our route through Great Falls, Montana, was cut off. The newscasts had it that people were drowning in their homes along the river, while others were hanging in treetops.

It would cost us nearly a thousand-mile detour to get around the whole area. Starting off toward Billings, we learned partway there that the road was blocked, turned north to another little town, then back west, then east to Harleyton, racing back and forth across Sweet Grass County, where no information was available about which bridges across the Missouri still held.

After a while a way was found across the Missouri River on the high Robertson Bridge via Malta. "The Missouri must be very much like the Peace River, which we will navigate," I said. "We're getting near the Peace. They originate in the same kind of country, the prairie provinces. Look how it cuts its channel five hundred feet below the level of the country around us. That's what the Peace will be like, only it flows north."

"But you said we were going to be in the woods."

"Well, I don't know," I said, rather mixed up. "I think that at first the Peace headwaters start out with little clear streams way up in the Rocky Mountains of British Columbia. Then the Peace flows through the prairie, with probably a forested valley, and then gradually enters the scrub timber of the Subarctic. If you were in Russia, you'd call it *taiga*. It's characteristic of the northern part of all the Northern Hemisphere. You'll learn from the river the rules of geography that apply all over the world."

"We want to begin our river trip in the mountains," they insisted.

"We can't. Too dangerous. I made our plans so that we will navigate the Peace only after it comes out of the last canyons of the Rockies."

"Will there be wolves?"

"Yes, I should think so. It's their natural habitat."

"Prairie wolves or timber wolves?"

"Hard to tell, right off the bat. Those are some of the things we would like to find out — the habitats of the animal populations. I have always wanted to look at the country where the antelope and deer stop, going north, and the moose begin — also, to see where the caribou range starts, and to find out how far north the porcupines go. And I've often wondered about the turtles and snakes and frogs and their latitudes. Of course scientists know, but I'd like to see for myself. I would just like to see how the river flows through the different rocks and soils: to see the natural world without cities and the works of people. When we go down the Peace River and on north we ought to be able to figure out how everything is laid out here in North America, naturally. I've heard people say they would like to float down the Missouri or the Mississippi, but I think those people would be disappointed: they were born a hundred years too late. It's better now to go on the northern watershed."

All day we drove through the spring prairie of Montana, "land of the big sky," stopping occasionally so that we could hear the gay song of the meadowlark, which sings on the wing — since the girls had never heard the meadowlark before. No one who has not been there can possibly appreciate how sweet-scented the prairie winds are or how high the sky seems.

In other places, that is, places to the south, the sky seems to close right down on a person. This is true even in our Southwest now, and in Southern California; yet only recently it was all big sky country there. If you have been a frontier resident, you know that something very sad happens when man establishes vineyards, farms, factories, and dense habitation which spawns gas stations, shopping centers, beauty salons, and bowling lanes. It may be progress but somehow it lacks the old beauty, and one day you wake up and you realize that the sky has closed down, the joy has gone. The country grows small and mean and dingy, and nobody ever feels really good, not even children, because they are slowly being gassed to death by air pollution.

The clean big sky country made us feel like singing, and Jean made up a song as we drove: "I'll See You in Alberta." She hadn't ever known Alberta, of course, but it must be good. The dirt road stretched straight from horizon to horizon, unfenced. Cumulus prairie clouds hung above.

Suddenly there was a maple-leaf flag waving on a tall pole in the middle of nowhere. For almost the first hundred years that she was a nation, Canada didn't have her own flag, but used the Union

Jack. Beneath this new flag was a small, lonely building. We pulled off the road to it.

"Girls, we have reached the border. Here is Canada."

"Stop, Mother. Stop, right where you are. I've got to take my curlers off, before he sees me."

"Can't stop now."

"Vain little flirt," crowed Jean at her sister. "Don't you know Mother is tired? She can't wait for your beauty."

The Inspector — a tall, bleak, uniformed man — came out to the car. When I told him we might stay up in the Arctic for an indefinite time, he said with shaky dignity, "I think you had better come into the office."

We followed him into the tidy white office building where he waited all alone on the prairie from 8 A.M. until 10 P.M. — somewhat shorter hours in winter — on what one might presume to be a less than opulent monthly pay check. His neat white and green living quarters, exactly matching the office decor, were a few steps away, while out in back, connected by a path through some petunias planted by his wife, were two green and white matching outhouses.

There was nothing else for seventy miles in either direction, except the green and white signpost pointing with arrows: "To the United States; To Canada." No fence separated the two friendly countries.

When the Inspector heard me briefly relate our purposes he seemed quite intrigued with the entry problem our case posed. Thumbing through a heavy volume, he admitted there didn't seem to be any rule which fit us. He could give us a six-month permit to visit in Canada — that in itself was routine — but if we stayed longer up in the Arctic, our car, by being stored in Edmonton, would be committing a violation. Canada is strict about importing cars, even if the cars are in storage and have their wheels taken off.

"There is no rule that admits the car for longer than six months," he concluded bleakly, perspiring sympathetically. "I can't find a rule for it anywhere."

Ann chose that moment to push a bunch of flowers under his nose. "What kind of flowers are these, sir?"

"Hasn't something like this ever come up before?" I pressed.

"Not at the Wild Horse Entry," he said. "You should have gone through one of the main ports."

"I guess I've never gone through the main port for anything in my life," I said. "Anyhow, this time we couldn't. Floods."

"Yes, that's right," he agreed reasonably, "you couldn't."

"Do you want to look at our rifles? I'll open the car trunk."

"No, no. Not necessary. But if I were you I would go to the immigration authorities when you get to Edmonton. I'm sure they will straighten you out — somehow."

"What kind of flowers are these?" said Ann.

"I really don't know," said the Inspector with great formality. "Never thought about it, you know."

We were driving off, when the Inspector halted us with a siren.

"Oh, do I have a flat tire, or something?"

"Not at all. Sorry." His mustache twitched. "Would you mind stepping into the office again? It seems I forgot to get your address. Also, would you mind giving your name? Regulations say we have to fill it in, right here."

The girls and I drove off, feeling very Canadian, which is a special sort of feeling, and before an hour had passed on the empty gravel road Jean discovered antelope. The lovely thin agile animals were sprinkled all over the landscape in the slanting evening sun, dappled and prancing, as far as the eye could see. Under our wheels appeared one solitary prairie chicken. Of course I stopped for her and said politely, "Give our regards to all the family."

And she said plaintively, "I have just come out at the edge of the road in the evening for a few choice delicacies, including a replenishment of gravel for my craw." The kids laughed with delight. None of us had ever talked with a prairie chicken before — even I hadn't — that nearly extinct species of our ancestors' stewpots.

It was six in the evening when we left the Inspector. On we drove, since there was nothing else we could do, through empty horizons of gathering clouds and sporadic rain showers which poured down pitcher-like spouts. At a little town called Elkwater the road became a paved ribbon of narrow, burnished metal stretching into purple night between fence posts and green fields and telephone poles marching into the unknown. The road was like those narrow upsy-downsy roads of New England. It was lighted only by occasional oncoming cars and distant flickering windows of storybook farmhouse people whom you would never know.

At Medicine Hat we joined the modern Trans-Canada Highway, not long completed. The absence of traffic on it made it a joy to travel, while it too was golden in the rain and gloom of slowly advancing night. At the edge of town we stopped at a café for coffee. Into the café came an odd-looking group, out of a large, black, hearselike Cadillac bearing a Manitoba license. The women of the group parted their hair in the middle and wore it up in buns just as you see in very old pictures. Each woman wore a black head-scarf and her face was plain, without make-up. Each wore a home-made ankle-length dress with heavy black-button shoes. The men of the party looked like Biblical characters with their long beards flowing across their vests.

"Look, Mother! Are *those* Canadians?" Ann marveled at her first Canadian citizens coming out of the night.

"They must be," I said. "We're in Canada." Actually they were prosperous farming Mennonites. They spoke to me in English and expressed great astonishment that an American woman alone with two girls would be driving around at night.

At 1:30 A.M. it had been dark for some time, except for occasional weird red gas flares from open wells along the highway, when we finally stopped at Bassano, Alberta, to get off the road. There was one hotel there, which we might call the Crown's Pride.

"Mother, is *this* a Canadian hotel?" Ann gasped again ruefully, as she was rudely dragged into an unpainted, three-story, leaning semblance of a haunted house of the 1880's.

"Guess so," was all I cared to reply at the moment. And I added, "It's in Canada."

"Mother, I don't think I'm going to like Canada."

"Oh, you'll get used to it," I laughed, tongue in cheek.

Bravely the two girls heaved our luggage up two flights to the unlighted third floor, while I paid the desk clerk four dollars and quickly followed. The staircase wobbled. I only hoped the place wouldn't catch on fire during the few hours we would be there.

As we fumbled along the dark hall with a large iron key, looking for room numbers, suddenly an old man with insomnia threw open the door of his room and peered out with rheumy eyes into the glare of a bulb hung by a dirty cord from the ceiling. He looked like an ancient owl.

"Where are the bathrooms, please?" I instantly capitalized upon opportunity.

"Thataway!" He slammed the door, leaving us blinking in darkness again. Every footfall echoed as we dragged and thumped our way, until we found our room and the communal bathroom with its nine-foot tub and ancient ponderous plumbing. At last we collapsed into sagging, creaky iron bedsteads, and all lapsed into Stygian darkness and silence.

Next morning as I applied lipstick over quadruple sets of lips which were reflected back to me from the undulating tiny square of wall mirror, I asked cheerily:

"Well, kids, how do you like Canada?"

Jean said she liked it all right because there didn't seem to be many people in it, but Ann was unsure. "I've never seen anything like it," she said, struggling for an analysis. "These people, and such terrible hotels. There isn't even a decent mirror to look at yourself in."

"Well, as you can see," I said morally, "people in Canada don't waste their time looking at themselves in mirrors all the time."

"Oh, Mother, what's come over you? If that old owl we saw last night ever wasted much time looking at himself in a mirror, he'd scare himself to death."

"Ann, you shouldn't always be so vain," sermonized Jean.

Before an explosion could come and rock the Crown's Pride and its owls to the foundation, I whispered an explanation, bearing in mind that these walls had ears:

"Dear girls, I promise you that this is not representative of Canada. I'm afraid it's a kind of flophouse for old men who are down on their luck."

Breakfast was an ice-cream stand and hamburgers, just as in the United States — a treat we had not often had there, however — eaten in the car as the rain pattered.

"Wonder if it's going to keep on raining like this?" I said. "Soon we won't have any more roof overhead."

They took this calmly, as they were busy counting and fingering Canadian money at the time.

At three that afternoon we were seventy-five miles from Edmonton, a city with a population of over 300,000, and one of Canada's greatest cities — the Chicago, you might say, of the western prairie hinterlands, and a granary of wheat.

Now I telephoned into the city to my old friend Mr. R. O. Hill — "Yours faithfully for the Hudson's Bay Company" — whom I had never met but who had received some money from me as a down payment on our expedition charge account many months before. Mr. R. O. Hill did not have any first name. People often don't in Canada — only initials — that is, if you meet them only in business. R.O. was out at a meeting when I telephoned, just as executives always are in any place — just what are these mysterious meetings? — so his secretary made a reservation for our members at the MacDonald Hotel. In due course we drove up to the hotel, to find that it was a large, lovely, downtown castle, with turrets and cupolas and battlements, and with green clipped lawns whose formal flowerbeds perched high upon the bank of the South Saskatchewan River, with its trestles and bridges, and crawling traffic lanes.

"Oh, Mother!" breathed Ann luxuriously from our eleventh-floor window. "So this is really Canada!"

The first thing to do in any place in the world, I have always maintained, is to have a good meal. As I hurried at my dressing mirror the girls vanished by elevator. But they weren't merely riding the elevator to explore the hotel, I later learned to my extreme chagrin. They were running up and down eleven flights from roof to basement, and were discovered on an unoccupied floor which was undergoing repairs, having a sprightly conversation with the painters and plasterers. "Mom, do you know what? They're putting in new bathrooms!"

"Dammit, I don't care if they are," I said.

"But you didn't tell us not to!" they protested.

"Good grief," I said, "I didn't think of that. Didn't I tell you girls not to jump into strange situations without asking?"

Quite unsympathetic to the plumbing and plastering problems of the MacDonald, I herded my flock into the dining room. To-morrow was Saturday. We could perhaps wind up all the expedition shopping tomorrow, at the Bay Company down the street. Sunday we would rest, because rest is all you can do in Canada on Sunday. Monday or Tuesday we would embark for the wilds.

The MacDonald Hotel, or the Mac, as Edmontonians affectionately call it, being one of the chain of old Canadian National Railroad Hotels set up to encourage pioneering seventy years ago, is a last citadel of traditional ceremonious living, especially its Empire Dining Room. Into the hush of its tall vault two healthy stories high come elderly dowagers leaning heavily on canes, wearing ancient ratty animals around their necks, supported at times by shadowy demure nieces. Waiters who apprenticed here in their boyhood now rule mercilessly over frightened young apprentices wearing white uniforms with gold braid and gold epaulets, serving guests who are accustomed to silent, extremely leisurely courses wafted on silver tureens.

Into this rare atmosphere loud democracy, however, begins to intrude when young traveling Americans can be heard to cry like piping swamp birds, "Look, Mom! Tablecloths!"

Lovers of the atmosphere in the Mac have been jarred, moreover, when the management has been forced of late to supplement the supply of traditional hushed waiters with a bevy of chattering, clattering waitresses who were apparently hustled in from some local hash house. These aging witches were not intimidated by formal atmosphere. They galloped back and forth like Percheron horses — the kind that used to pull fire engines — through banging doors, and snatched up the silver tureens as veteran customers choked. One waitress, lounging with hand on rotund, aproned hip, badgered the old lady she served while scratching her head with her free hand. "Wal, wal, where 'ev y' been?" We heard the wait-ress all over the listening dining room. "Haven't seen yez in a long time," scratch, scratch. To our interest, as she then thwacked the customer good-naturedly over the back, this alarmed dowager shrunk down like a beaten dog into the lower depths of her bro-caded chair — thus proving that the days of pomp and ceremony are definitely on the decline in Canada.

On Saturday we met R. O. Hill, Yours truly for the Hudson's Bay Company, and some of his capitalist conspirators and we spent the day in the huge Bay Store, even being treated to a cafeteria meal there, with many loyal Bay men in close attendance upon our expedition needs. Here were the very descendants of a company which has had fabulous experience with arctic exploration, with northern living, and with river travel. These were the descendants. But they themselves had never canoed on rivers. They had never been north of Edmonton, except to inspect a store.

First, comes the canoe. It was a Chestnut, made in Canada. You will find the name Chestnut in little-read books of olden days, of expeditions long gone and vanished in the mists of time. It was a boat, really, in canoe shape, built of solid half-inch planks, with waterproof painted canvas glued over the outside. It was 20 feet long, 53 inches broad amidships, weighed 180 pounds empty, and was called a freight canoe. Its load capacity was up to 3,000 pounds freight. Not our freight, composed of fluffy sleeping bags and bulky hair curlers, perhaps, but it would carry 3,000 pounds probably if you loaded it with bricks.

This canoe was absolutely noncapsizable. It was so stable you could sit on the rim and dangle your feet in icy waters, if you wanted to. When I first saw it, as it was unloaded from its excelsior-packed and burlap-wrapped package two days later on the bank of the Peace River, I was reminded strongly of the big, stable home-made canoe in which the children's father and I, years ago, had paddled entirely successfully twelve hundred miles down the Yukon River through the heart of Alaska.

We didn't get a chance to see our canoe in the store, as it was shipped from New Brunswick. We only had pictures of it and the description. But I was very reassured: no canoe for a ten-day outing, this, but a genuine seafaring ice breaker. You could sail it. You could paddle it if you were a number of strong men. You could adapt it for an outboard motor.

Of course it was necessary to overlook the fact from the beginning that we were not a number of strong men.

At first I had thought we would only paddle: I thought it would be good exercise for the children. But when the Bay Company and the Alberta Government Travel Bureau urged that nobody go into the North without a motor at least being taken along, I conceded the point. If serious illness or accident should strike, the carefree paddler would then be glad to exchange his paddle for mechanized power that would deliver him downstream to the nearest fort within a matter of days.

The trouble is that, if a motor is taken, the weight of your canoe, what with thirty-five to forty gallons of gas hauled along in cans, is suddenly and awkwardly increased. The weight of the motor and the gas changes the picture for the canoeist and his paddle, for he is no longer able to push such a load dexterously. In fact, nobody told me this but I quickly found it out: with a boat this heavy, even empty, you have to have either very large biceps or a motor to control your direction in the current and to make landings — if you are not a number of strong men.

After months of consideration I had ordered a 9.5-horsepower outboard motor of the newest model, just what the Bay recommended. For a while I toyed with the idiotic notion of economizing on expenses by getting a secondhand or rebuilt motor. The very thought of this near misjudgment of mine is now quite dismaying to contemplate.

The modern outboard motor is more costly than its predecessor of twenty years ago but it's worth it when you intend to trust your life upon large expanses of water, all flowing north. Such motors today are nearly 100 percent dependable. Such fine motors, two-cylindered, can be compared only to the fine two-cylinder engine of the sportsman's small airplane in which he trusts himself to the frail support of sky. Water, too, can be a frail support.

After the canoe and motor came the tent. I had spent a lot of thought on this, also. Remembering fondly the tents I lived in for

years in Alaska, I wanted to acquire as nearly as possible their rep-
lica, so tried and true.

This proved to be difficult. Plain old-fashioned tents of untreated white canvas are nearly impossible to find now in North
America. The Indians like a white tent for three reasons: first,
white is the color most repulsive to mosquitoes. It shatters their
morale, if anything can. Second, a white tent is more livable for
days in camp because it conveys natural light for family activities
indoors such as reading and mending. Third, when pitched in the
endless sea of green wilderness you want to be plainly visible to all
passersby. To make yourself easily seen is customary out there.

Only Indians and Eskimos still use the old white canvas wall
tent, and this we were able to get from the Bay Company. It had
an asbestos safety vent for the stovepipe of the little traveling
sheet-iron woodstove, which we also ordered. The dimensions of
our tent were eight by ten feet, with four-foot walls. I wanted untreated canvas because in a good deal of earlier airplane camping
with lightweight nylon tents I had found that the waterproofed or
tight fabrics do not "breathe," and hence make for an unwhole-
some camp over a period of time. The untreated canvas tent-stove
combination for northern climates or for fall and winter almost
anywhere in North America is pretty hard to beat — if, again, you
are a number of strong men.

In one respect I went against the advice of the Bay Company
experts. They suggested that we cut our tent ridgepole and tent
stakes fresh at each camp, since materials would be available everywhere. But I insisted upon buying an aluminum set. My two
daughters and I were not yet the world's greatest living ax-women,
and I only hoped we wouldn't be the world's greatest dead ones. It
seemed to me that every stroke of the ax we didn't have to chop
put us that farther ahead.

Our rifles, binoculars, and the 35-mm camera were from Gerald,
and they had been brought along in the car. The rifles I selected
were a .22 — it is standard for campers anywhere — and a bolt action .30–06. As an added factor, while I was at it I selected a good
four-power scope, and a carrying sling. All instruments were

equipped with cases against the dampness of continual outdoors life.

I had been living in a city for so long that I almost, though not quite, relinquished the idea of taking arms along on the expedition at all; especially when I learned that Canadian law earnestly intends to protect game from the white man in the Territories. In the city, fed all the food we need, with every creature want cared for, insulated from the rains, the snows, the winds, the sun, and even from changes in the seasons, we seldom have occasion to visualize the environment of the one million square miles of uninhabited lands in the Northwest Territories, in which a person could conceivably be placed alone, lost or without defenses.

So I brought my guns along, all the time wondering if I would be prevented from taking them in the canoe. No one stepped forth to stop me. I had no hunting license, since hunting licenses are not issued in the NWT, and no one asked me to get an Alberta hunting license since the season of my travel was summer, when licenses to hunt are not required.

To complete our camp outfit we took the usual pots and pans and wire cooking grill; one fishing rod with line, hooks, and lures; canvas gloves and a mosquito hat with headnet for each; canned and dehydrated foods; an attaché case for maps and papers; a lightweight jacket each and an Arctic Dew Line parka each; and something I had never carried before in my younger days: a steel, snaplocking container from Army surplus that Ann, with absorbed morbidity, made up into a first-aid kit.

3

Peace River Country

THE way we got to the Peace River was this. One of the Bay's men chauffeured us three hundred and seventy-five miles northwest of Edmonton to Dawson Creek, B.C., using our car. The chauffeur was provided a room for the night at the hotel in Dawson Creek, where we stayed; then the following day he drove us thirty miles up the Alaska Highway to the place where the highway crosses the Peace, our point of embarkation. The Bay Company arranged for renewal of the permit for storage of the car beyond six months in Edmonton, or for as long as necessary.

A Hudson's Bay truck from the branch store at Dawson Creek, with two men, followed us to the Peace River with all our stuff aboard, and they and our chauffeur assembled our camp equipment in piles, and the canoe, on the bank of the Peace beside the big bridge. When the men had dumped us and our stuff and collected their wages, they drove off, taking my car back to Edmonton, three hundred and seventy-five miles, and there we were!

When I saw my car go over the hill and disappear, leaving me with a canoe and Jean and Ann out there under the sky, I must say that certain feelings of insecurity assailed me. We were dressed in our new woolen trousers and long-sleeved wool shirts, and heavy boots.

"You see, kids, I have a great surprise for you. I have named the canoe after you, in honor of your big trip. It's painted the *Jeanie Ann*."

"Why not the *Annie Jean?*" said Ann.

"Now don't start to fight over *that!*" I cried. "We have important things to think about."

"What?" said Jean. "What's there to think about?"

"Well, for one thing, we must all start right in writing in our explorers' journals each day. Right now, the first thing to do is pitch the tent, right here."

"Oh, no," they demurred, "let's get going, down the river, Mother."

"Hold on, kids. We'll have to stay here a day or two and practice with the equipment, so we'll need the tent at once, to sleep in, and in case it rains. All right, *start pitching.*"

To tell the honest truth, I was terrified when I saw the "mighty Peace River" for the first time, and for every day thereafter for a long time to come. It was enough to terrify anybody with any sense. It was not at all what I had been led somehow to believe. Just like the Missouri, it was in flood stage!

The first glimpse of that river from above on the prairie, had shown that it was a giant. It lay brown and crawling in its valley, which lay at a level varying from five to eight hundred feet below the general prairie surface. Tiny black objects whirled down the river: driftwood. Some of the drift was uprooted forest giants — enormous black spruce from the mountains of British Columbia, capable of bulldozing through the side of a house. The Peace River here was three thousand feet across.

Less than a hundred miles upstream lay Hudson's Hope, where the river tunnels through a precipitous gorge, and a great hydro-electric dam project was now being built.

For twenty miles through this gorge, long known as Portage Mountain, the Peace plunged into a terrific rapids, which, it used to be said, no manner of boat had ever ridden. Around the gorge for centuries there existed a foot trail used by Indians, and later by explorers and prospectors whose names are legend, such as Mackenzie, McLeod, Finlay, Butler, Pike, and Twelve Foot Davis. The Peace River, with the exception of one other river, the Liard, is the only river in North America to push its way eastward through the Rocky Mountain barrier.

Now at Portage Mountain, upriver from where my girls and I were to put our canoe into the river, one of the world's major hydroelectric projects was beginning to take shape. Even now being built was the Portage Mountain Dam, six hundred feet high, one and a quarter miles wide, with a base one-half mile thick rising to a crest width of forty feet — a massive, earth-fill dam which is to form the backbone of a 807 million dollar Peace River hydroelectric project. The project was planned to include the main dam; a 2.3-million-kilowatt powerhouse, larger than any now existing in the Western world; a smaller dam and a 650,000-kilowatt powerhouse 12 miles downstream from Portage Mountain; a storage reservoir or lake 230 miles long; and an extra high voltage power delivery system carrying the power 574 miles south and east to the populations. Thus the Portage Mountain Dam, scheduled for completion in 1967, in Canada's centenary of nationhood, will henceforth completely control the headwaters of the Peace, creating at one stroke also the world's largest man-made lake. Its reservoir will cover an area of 680 square miles at elevation 2,200 with a storage capacity of 62 million acre-feet of water. By contrast, for instance, Lake Mead behind Hoover Dam (Boulder Dam) holds but 30 million acre-feet. It would back up the Peace valley to the Rocky Mountain Trench near Finlay Forks for about 75 miles, thence north for a distance of about 80 miles and south for about 70 miles. Already, at the time when it was our privilege to know the Peace, the access roads had been built for the site, a 500-foot steel arch bridge was erected across the river and a ten-foot-square pilot tunnel was driven 1,000 feet under its west bank. Next came the problem of rerouting the river to lay bare 3,000 feet of the riverbed so that the dam would be built in the dry.*

As I stood on the shore now, some miles below the dam site, I saw sadly ahead the inevitable taming of a great river — a process which has been going on in all lands all over the world within the last decade. A few years from now, canoeists and boatmen would not see the same wild river we saw. They would see only another river greatly diminished from its original wild strength. A thought

* Information from the British Columbia Hydro and Power Authority, Vancouver, B.C.

came to me, "Lucky to know this great river, while there is still time."

As I gauged with horrified eyes that fast-flowing, muddy torrent carrying 450,000 cubic feet per second (according to Water Resources measurements that very day), whose flood was foam-flecked and churning with whirlpools; as I looked at those deadly irresistible, rolling waters, I realized that this was not what I had visualized for Jean and Ann at all. I had pictured a slow-moving, peaceful stream, since no official impediments to navigation had been marked. This river was as big as the Mississippi and three times as fast. The Peace carried 450,000 cubic feet at this time, while the Mississippi may vary from 75,000 to just two million cubic feet. The figures put it certainly into the Mississippi class.

An old B.C. guide had sent a message to the hotel at Dawson Creek for me. He asked that I please get in touch with him. He was driving out here thirty miles to the river to show a boat he had just completed building for his client, this very evening.

"Just what is this I hear about you goin' down the Peace River?" asked this sunburned, honest man upon his arrival. With him was a younger man who was a real estate agent and notary public in Dawson Creek. We shook hands all around.

"Mother," piped up Ann at this moment, "you look enormous in those pants."

"That's beside the point," I caroled back, and gave my attention to the two gentlemen.

"Have you had much experience on rivers?" the guide boat-builder asked, with toothless but sincere concern for our welfare.

"Yep! But it was a good many years ago. Before they were born." I pointed to the kids who dawdled at the mass of tent canvas, not knowing how to pitch it or what to do.

"They tell that you don't plan to take no man, no guide with you? Just you three ladies? That right?"

"Yep."

"I would not advise it," he said flatly. "Now, I don't mean to butt in where it is not my business, but I definitely would not advise it."

"I agree," I said. "But we don't have a man."

"That Peace River is dangerous." He enlarged upon the subject, waving his hand out to indicate the raging waters beside which we stood as dwarfs. He told us how once he had capsized in the river. Four men in the boat. He told of swimming to shore, his life preserver holding him. All the men got ashore, because shore was near, but one of the men, a doctor, died of heart failure. "The water in this river is so cold," the guide explained patiently, "that if you capsize it's six to one you're done for. You might last twenty minutes, but soon your heart will stop from the cold. If you don't drown you freeze to death." He explained that when he himself managed to make shore he had lost all use of his limbs. "Your arms lasts the longest," he advised. He added, "I wouldn't ever want to go through them few minutes again.

"Lots of men disappeared in the Peace River and never been found," he added reflectively, and I believed him.

"I can see it's like the Yukon," I said. "I think it's a worse one."

"Didn't anyone tell you it is in flood?"

The old boatbuilder squatted down upon the sand in concerned meditation, and the neat real estate man squatted down beside him. Being constitutionally unable to squat — a considerable handicap for an explorer — I sat down flatly, cross-legged on the rounded, damp rocks there, and the girls crept up, looking rather anxious and remaining unusually silent.

"Well, here comes Johnny Taylor," said the real estate man. "I myself don't think you and the children should try to go down that river right now. Let's see what Johnny Taylor says."

After saying hello all around with Johnny Taylor and his two boys, who were near my girls' ages, all squatted again, except me, and the conference continued about the state of the flood. Johnny Taylor was handsome, about forty, with high copper cheekbones and slitted, dark, dangerous eyes, a perfect Indian. He might have come out of a book.

"We was the original settlers here," he explained with a laugh. "Little village of Taylor you see right across the bridge named for my folks. I live here all my life. So you go down the Peace River, eh?"

"That's the plan," I said.

"Can you run a kicker?"

"No, we haven't learned yet," said Jean. "But the manual I have here says that even a child can run it."

"That's fortunate, isn't it?" added Ann.

The old guide heaved an audible sigh, and the Indian, Johnny Taylor, twinkled his eyes, and his handsome brow furrowed in thought. "I am going to bring over my friends who run the hotel," he said, "and I know they will want to have you to dinner. Cocktails too. They got a nice little bar."

"How nice," I said.

"You could camp here on the shore for a few days and see what happens," Johnny suggested. "You don't have to make a decision today. You got a nice tent, and food."

"I would like to look at their boat and see how seaworthy she is," said the old guide. "We could give a look at this new motor, too."

"First, we'll get their tent up," said the real estate salesman. "We want them to like our country and want to stay, don't we?" He and the two Taylor boys, who were handsome, perfect Indians like their father, immediately set to work on it.

Suddenly there were so many things to learn how to do that Jean and Ann and I found ourselves very busy with our new friends upon the riverbank. The realtor had a summer cabin here he wanted to give us the key to, but we turned down his offer.

I was glad when our canoe was pronounced seaworthy by our self-appointed guardians, although their own crafts beached nearby were thirty-foot-long, plank riverboats, and their motors, converted to remote control, were never less than forty horsepower. When I saw the size of the boats and the larger power which the knowledgeable river people actually used, I realized that there was a considerable discrepancy in size between those boats and the ones that the Alberta Government Travel Bureau recommended for a canoe trip on the Peace in their official bulletin. The bulletin had said that a nine-horse motor was "ample power to play around with" on the Peace. But the Peace River was not something you play around with at any time, according to the rivermen.

The water boiling around the pylons of the high bridge was far faster than our little motor could climb at its top power. That current today was clocked at fourteen miles an hour!

It was not as if I had not checked everything out carefully. I had written to the Mounted Police with the assumption that they kept a check on the river, only to find that nobody patrolled it, virtually nobody traveled it, and the RCMP had no interest in it, inasmuch as their concern was law enforcement, and this was limited to where the greater numbers of people are.

The Mounted Police did not give or deny permission, or venture an opinion. I was glad for that. What they did do was request that all travelers check in and out at the forts, so that a surveillance could be kept out for the sake of safety. In this way, the police who are the administrators over large areas of country have a general idea of what part of the country travelers are in at any given time.

The Forest Service, which included game surveillance, was composed of men who probably knew the most about the river and countryside of any government department; but they did not use boats, preferring instead the modern method of patrol by air.

At one time, a good many years ago, sternwheel paddle steamers fired by wood had plied the Peace River, carrying cargo, missionaries, and pioneers from rail's end. The old guide on the beach here was a descendant of parents and grandparents who were among the first farmers to press by boat and ox train into the Peace River Block, an area of 3,500,000 acres of choice land which was opened for homesteading and controlled by the Dominion. One can scarcely talk to anyone in the Peace River country today who does not bear one of the famed Canadian pioneer names.

But today this great river carried no travelers aside from brief sporting excursions which usually stayed within thirty miles of each town.

The recently completed Mackenzie Highway, of all-weather gravel, today carried all the Peace River freight by truck. This highway passed large farms and scattered villages; and after the river turned northward it would run roughly parallel to our course, eighteen to eighty miles to our west. Road distance was nine hundred and thirty-seven miles from Edmonton to Yellowknife, our own eventual destination for this fall. It was a continuous road except for one ferry crossing far north.

"Please send me," I had written the Alberta Government Travel Bureau, "a road map showing every side road which comes down to the edge of the Peace River from the Mackenzie Highway, because we will be canoeing the Peace River."

I was sent a road map of Alberta, and the usual scenic and descriptive bulletins of things to see. But to my surprise the map cut off the entire northern half of Alberta, just as though many thousands of square miles of Alberta did not exist. Perhaps because up until this time there had been no interest expressed by the public, no road map existed except for its lower half. The Peace River immediately ran off our map into the north, entirely ignored by these government thinkers.

"Yet, it stands to reason," as I said to the men on the riverbank, "that there's bound to be some roads built down to the Peace River by northern farmers. I just would like to know where those roads are."

"I guess the fellows that built them roads knows, and they is probably the only ones that knows," our friends guessed.

The only maps I had were some U. S. World Aeronautical Charts and a Canadian Forest Service map used for flights.

"Nothing for piloting?" asked the old guide.

I had an excellent series of enormous parchments from the Canadian Bureau of Mines and Technical Surveys, giving the river to the scale of one statute mile to the inch. But this series did not start until below our first portage, Vermilion Chutes, six hundred miles down the river; and it was so large that it nearly filled the canoe, using up room needed for other equipment. I had mailed the second year's voyage series to Yellowknife, as we could not carry it all at once.

"Maybe we could let you have one of our Adventure Tour Charts," the real estate man offered, "to start you off with."

These charts were souvenirs which each man had saved from a trip made in flotilla with a considerable number of craft in early May of this year, starting right here at Taylor and ending at populous Peace River town. This would help us for the first one hundred and seventy-five miles, to get started anyway. The cruise had been taken to commemorate the anniversary of the explorer Alexander Mackenzie.

Gladly I seized upon one of these little bound booklets of charts, which had guided the only cruise of modern times. How glad I was for Mackenzie's anniversary! The charts resulted from the careful labors of several firms. They were: Hill Aviation of Fort St. John — aerial reconnaissance flight; Mackenzie Stationers of Fort St. John — preparation of the map sets; APECO of Canada — the machine and paper for making the map copies from field notes; and Steward, Weir and Stewart, Surveyors, of Edmonton — furnishing the published base maps.

When our friends returned to our camp for visits during the days to come, I studied my copy of the *Peace River Adventure Tour* assiduously with them, as I had never had occasion to read navagation code before. On the charts it looked easy: *F* for fast or rough water; *S* for shallow water or gravel bar, barely submerged; *B* for boulders, etc. But when I looked at the real river roaring before our tent door, the whole proposition looked pretty fishy. In a current this powerful on a river the size of the Missouri, all you need to settle your hash is to make just one mistake. If I ran onto a bar in midriver, how would an old flub like myself and two kids have the strength to push off it? More likely, the canoe would be inundated and rolled over in exactly one instant.

"I don't think you would have to worry about bars, none," the men contended, however. "Not at this flood stage. That's one good thing."

During the several visits the men brought their families, and soon many families came each evening after work, to view the swollen river and to meet the young girls and their snugly trousered mother who lived in a tent beside it. I had dinner and cocktails across the bridge at the hotel owned by the Armeneaus. Jean and Ann turned down the dinner to stay on the riverbank with its assortment of rosy roving boys and young men, who came, drawn by the campfire and the tent and the young inhabitants. The trooping youth appeared from far and wide, as apparently the news of new girls in British Columbia traveled quickly.

Jean was dumbfounded. "Mother," she said. "You know what? I'm popular with *boys!*"

"But you don't like people."

"Well, some boys are all right, I guess."

I was looking at the old guide's stricken face as he was being forced by Ann into tasting her vitamin-rich feast of full-blown dandelion blossoms which she had rolled and fried individually in desiccated egg batter.

"But you'll love it," I encouraged him. "Next time you guide tourists on a hunting trip, you'll find that they'll simply marvel at you when you feed them Anne's recipe."

The river was dropping a foot a day, leaving a pasty mud or glue which for generations in western Canada has been known as "Peace River gumbo." A famous broth, a wondrous concoction, it is taken by people both internally and externally when they live in this great land.

For drinking and cooking, we dipped our water out of the 450,-000 cubic feet per second with a bucket, then sterilized it by dropping in little white pills. The pills were developed for the use of the armed forces during World War II and since then have been used all over the world. Also, we had had typhoid inoculations.

"Don't worry about that," said Johnny Taylor reassuringly. "It looks kind of brown, but I have drunk this river all my life and it hasn't killed me yet."

"That's good old Peace River water," said the real estate man's wife, Fran. "Once you drink this water they say you will always come back to the Peace River country."

"I don't know why, but I love this river," added her husband. "It's muddy and mean, all right. But I spend every moment I can get away from the office, fooling around the river with my boat. The river's dropping fast now, and I think if you'll just wait a little longer, you'll make your trip all right — if you're careful.

"I was thinking," he said. "A bunch of us may take my new boat down to the Pouce Coupé — it comes in about thirty-two miles down the river — and you could ride along with us, maybe? Can you wait until next weekend? We have a favorite camping place down there. We could tow your boat. You could learn more about the river and you could camp with us on the Pouce Coupé, and we could see that you start off all right from there on your own."

"That's a real great idea," I said. "I've been sitting here on the edge of canceling this whole expedition, I'm so scared of the river."

"Well, I wouldn't blame you for that," said Fran. "Yet wouldn't it be a shame, after all your plans?"

So we remained on the riverbank, while the brief summer days slipped by. Meanwhile, all day and all night the Alaska Highway traffic poured whining and pounding over the gleaming metal span, and all kinds of strangers, as I have said, were drawn to visit our camp from off the Highway.

One of these strangers who came meandering by, with the sideways gait of a wandering bear, was Bum Littleton.

At the time he arrived in the afternoon it happened to be raining slightly, and we were ineffectually stoking a smoky campfire.

"I'll help you with that," the stranger said. "You got a ax?"

"Oh, yes." I smiled. "Right here." Jean ran and got it quickly.

Returning with a load of wood, he made our fire blaze up.

"That was real nice of you. What's your name?"

"Littleton's the name," he said. "Prospector, Bum Littleton. Friends just call me Bum. Just come down from Kluane Lake, that's my home, when I seen you here on the beach, God bless you."

"Say, I know that lake!" I cried. "Kluane Lake, in the Yukon! Say," I asked him spontaneously, "If you are a prospector, Bum, I'll bet you are about the only person in modern times who remembers how to build a little camp stove out of a tin can? We're getting kind of wet around here. You see the Bay Company forgot some of the parts to the stove, and so I sent the whole thing back to Edmonton — refused to accept it — and the result is, we don't have any stove at all for our tent. We need a little stovepipe, too. I would pay you something for your trouble, if you can make us a stove real quick."

"Oh, I wouldn't charge you nothing," he said. "If you would happen to have a little dinner in the stewpot, well, that would be acceptable. Very acceptable," he said.

I got the idea that he wanted the dinner right now, so we fed him quickly. The rain accelerated. Giving him money for stove supplies, and a rubber rain slicker with a hood, I sent him walking off in a downpour with Jean trudging delightedly beside him, over the bridge to Taylor. In due time the drenched duo reappeared with four-inch stovepipe lengths and a five-gallon metal can donated by a gas station. I didn't like the shape of the five-gallon can he got: it was round, and would have to be upended to cook on. We used to get the square-sided ones. They had more cooking room. But anyway, it was something. Our total cost for the stove was less than four dollars. I didn't approve of the asbestos stovepipe vent which the manufacturer had placed in the back of the tent. So three of us patched that hole over with canvas and Bum cut a new hole in the tent roof where I wanted it, just to one side of the doorway. He put in a soft tin safety which he had drilled holes through, and we sewed it fast. Then he set up the little tin-can stove, with its pipe thrust through the new vent.

The reason I liked the stove at the front of the tent is that you don't have to carry all the wood for it clear into the back, stepping over and dirtying everything else in the process. Also, with the stove in front, you can pitch your tent according to the direction the wind is blowing, and have its back to the wind. You don't want to pitch a tent with its doorway into the wind, you see. The disadvantage of having the stove placed in the back of the tent is that you are then always forced to pitch your tent facing into the wind to keep the sparks from being blown over your tent roof. Since cold wind is a real factor as you proceed north, the position of the stove and the stove's serviceability, not to mention its safety, become very important.

The trouble was that there were three things wrong with the stove. First, Bum had forgotten to get wire thread, so the tin safety was sewed to the tent with short-lasting cotton thread. Second, the cooking space on the can he got was too limited to hold more than one small pot. Third, and most important, he did not seem to know how to attach the lip of the stovepipe onto the stove; so every time a gust of wind blew, the hot stovepipe would kick off into the campers' faces, and would have to be instantly replaced with gloves, or suffocation would ensue. But at the time I was so glad to get the dampness dried out with this makeshift stove that I overlooked the fact that here, obviously, was a man completely without foresight, unable to anticipate possible future difficulties.

"Bum," I should have said to him, "you are no good and shiftless." His code of life, and the principles he lived by, were plain to see.

It was ten at night and we peeked out the tent flap upon the changing colors of the roiling flood — black and ghastly white, and cherry red. That unbelievable living flood poured past the great concrete and steel columns under the three-thousand-foot bridge, while periodically a great roar like a volcano would portend the white and cherry-red flames of a hundred-foot natural gas flare located directly across the river from us at Taylor, at the oil storage tanks and pumping stations.

Bum sat in the tent, licking his chops, and I was washing dishes, and the murderous rain poured down into black night. Bum didn't seem to have any place to go. The little tin-can stove crackled cheerily.

"Do you know how to run our new outboard motor?" I asked the girls. "You know," I added helplessly, "I was born in a generation that never learned how to read directions, and I've never learned to this day, unfortunately."

"Mother, for heaven's sake. Stop worrying. We've read the directions," said Jean complacently. "We understand them okay."

"You ought to have a man along with you on that river," said Bum, wiping his whiskery chops with a dirty handkerchief.

I was thinking: "I know it. But you are not the one I would choose." As it didn't seem kind to say this out loud, I said nothing.

Jean said, "The guys have shown me and I understand the motor pretty good, and as you know we're all gassed up. Got the right mixture of oil to gas, that's one quart of oil to five Canadian gallons after it's broken in, and we got our extra tank ready to hook right on. Everything's ready, except, well, here with this fast current there is no way to go out on the river and practice — you would be swept down the river, and you couldn't get back."

"That's right. We're underpowered."

"Ann," lectured Jean, "you better not forget and leave one of your boots on some riverbank where we camp, because we could never in this world get back and get it."

"What do you think I am, dumb?" snapped Ann.

"Well, I was just saying . . ." repeated Jean. "Half your life the whole family has been under the bed hunting for your shoe. . . ."

"I could probably go down the river a few miles with you," said Bum. "I've run motors on rivers all my life as a prospector. I could let my business wait. I say, 'God bless you and the little girls,' and I shall be glad to help you out, since you need someone to help you."

"That's really very good of you to offer," I thanked him. "All of you people around here have been so good to us, I don't know what to say."

Although I felt a personal aversion to him, he was always saving things like "God bless you," and "For Jesus' sake," and it is difficult to quarrel with a person like that.

"I think that God sent me here," he said, "to help you for a few days. I don't mind in the least."

"Are you sure you don't mind?"

"No, actually, not in the least," he said. "It is better to give than to receive. My business is not important when you think that I might be God's means of keeping some persons from drowning."

"Well, also, I hate to think of trying to do all this heavy camp work," I quickly inserted in answer to his morbid remark.

"Oh, camp work is nothing to an experienced woodsman like me," added Bum. "And I always have the greatest respect for ladies."

I looked at him closely now for the first time, as he sat there on our tent floor, with the cold rain beating a heavy tattoo on the tent roof outside and the stove heartily fed with good wood — not "squaw wood," but the kind of wood a man can get.

Up until now I shortsightedly had only seen my new stove. Here was a man of about thirty-five to forty-five years, probably. Hard to tell this individual's age — he was ageless. He always kept his hat on, but when he occasionally shoved it to the back of his head, you saw that his face was of two colors; fishbelly white above the hat brim, and weatherburned red below, with miserable-looking chin whiskers. Here was a man who, by his coloring, plainly spent his life in the open. He told us that God's open woods and fields were his home, and in summer he often just slept under the trees. His hair was probably of sandy or reddish hue, and his eyes bluey-blurred or vice versa; or, as Ann later described them, like olives in a bowl of catsup. He had a long, sharp, prominent nose which gave him a sort of hatchet face, and a look which can only be described as crafty humility.

The clothes he wore were rags. The sand-colored trousers bagged at the knees; and as he came into the tent and took off one wet pair, we saw that he wore at least one other pair underneath, perhaps more — all full of holes. His worn jacket was loose over what we thought was a potbelly. But later Ann, who always had an eye for clothes, told me this was not the case at all. The fact was that he carried his wordly possessions in a cradle on his stomach underneath his jacket. But I never guessed this, for I was in an emotional state of shock over my fear of the river and our problems of survival.

"For God's sake," said Bum, "you mustn't let anything happen to them little girls."

Of course, I was aware of this, but his bald statement made me shiver.

When midnight came in the black downpour of rain, as the hundred-foot gas flare across the river roared into the sky, I told Bum he could take one of our three new sleeping bags for the night. Then, while I took another, the girls reluctantly doubled up in the third, and we all passed into the sleep of the exhausted for a few hours.

Since in a way our lives were at stake, it didn't seem improper, so long as the prospector behaved himself, I decided. Going to bed in a whole group in a tent was a fairly familiar situation to me in my earlier life. It was sometimes necessary to sleep thus in close proximity with your guests or host, as the case may be, in order to have shelter in a savage land. You learn to dress and undress within the sleeping bag, simply peeling off the outer layers. I had experienced many episodes of this sort during two summers and a winter with the Eskimos.

I decided that when the old guide and party arrived next day, I would ask them if they would mind taking our new guide along. Bum Littleton only required a few meals for his trouble. I couldn't afford the services of a regular licensed guide, and besides, I would not have considered one, as the whole point of the trip was to make it on our own. Yet it seemed to me a reasonable improvisation to let the wandering prospector go on downriver with us a few days, to Peace River town perhaps, until we got used to the river. It was just a temporary expedient. It seemed better than my collapsing with nervous and physical exhaustion, and all of us drowning. I felt reasonably certain that our other friends would approve of our fortuitous discovery of the unemployed prospector, whose admirable turn of mind was to do good deeds in this world.

I went off to sleep with a headache, but that was of minor importance. "Dear Lord," I thought, as I drifted off, "if Thou in Thine infinite charity hast seen fit to send a man to help us on the river just to start the trip, I do now humbly thank Thee. But in this case, why, dear Lord, didst Thou send us this particular specimen?"

Next morning Bum worked stoically packing the camp stuff, and he and the kids struck the tent together and somehow got everything into the canoe, while I went off with Joan Armeneau in her car to the hotel. Joan and I got back just as our party arrived, in three cars. Out of the cars poured the holiday group, including Fran's little girl and her big doll, and the principal of the school, and some other people with Fran and her husband, the realtor, and of course the old guide who was the experienced river pilot for us all. A tremendous amount of duffle was piled into the big plank riverboat, all these people came aboard, and we came aboard with our new guide.

"Meet Bum Littleton, from the Yukon," I introduced him around, as they made room for him. Bum said a cautious, "Thank you, thank you," and tried to make himself useful with the other men.

The men shoved us off into the river, the forty-horse motor caught, and away we went down the current. The *Jeanie Ann* was pulled behind.

"Here, you," said the old pilot, addressing Bum. "Take this rope

over your shoulder and hold her fairly close to the stern, but mind
you don't ram her into the propeller."

"Thank you, thank you," said Bum, taking the rope. He seemed
too humble for a man to be. As the current caught us and we
gained momentum, heading for midriver, the rope tightened
around his neck. Jean and I jumped to get a sweater under the
grinding rope, to cushion it. We saw his face flush from the strain.
Bracing himself with every ounce of strength he had, he withstood
the force of our loaded canoe, pulled by her nose ring. "That man
really isn't as strong as I thought he was," I reflected.

It seemed strange to me that the old guide, who seemed so kind
and who was so experienced with boats, would place a man this
way for towing. A boat tows hard in this fashion. Only later I
learned that the easy way to tow a boat is to make a rope cradle by
crossing the ropes under the bow and lifting her up. This way she
towed like a dredge.

All the way down the river to the Pouce Coupé — or Moose
Café, as Jean called it — Bum stood braced with puffing, heaving
breaths, towing the canoe, and plowing a muddy furrow. I felt
sorry for him, and wondered. An hour later we were there.

We camped that night at the Moose Café River which came
into the Peace suddenly through a narrow cleft of rock and would
be hard to find if you didn't know it was there. Towing the *Jeanie
Ann*, we went up the still waters behind the cliff, deep into green
forests.

"It's all backup water from the flood," said the school principal.
"Won't be any fish, but the whiskey's good."

After a marvelous supper which Fran cooked in the woods, using
the portable gasoline stove, cupboard, and icebox which she had
secured with her trading stamps, we left the men to stand around
their blazing fire, singing and drinking and telling hunting tales.

"Mother, why can't we join them?" asked Jean. For a long time,
a wistful tomboy, she sat in the shadows and listened. Then, unnoticed, she crept off to bed. We girls heard them howling and singing around the crackling fire, from where we lay in our tents, until
late into the night. It was a good, wholesome, typical Canadian

drinking party, I explained to my girls, and this was their way of having fun in British Columbia.

Oh, no, it wasn't British Columbia at all. We had passed over into Alberta now. Well, then, it is fun in Alberta, too.

Now a beautiful feature of this Moose Café River was that in its still water we had a chance to practice with our new motor without being swept away. The gruff old guide at camp on the cutbank beneath the trees directed Bum, then Jean, then Ann, then me, as we took our turns at the throttle, passing back and forth in review before him on these tranquil deeps in the fragrant forest. He had us reload our canoe a bit so she would ride better.

"Keep your load up in front," he called. This was to allow for the acceleration of power. "If the load's too much in back, it's dangerous on a current when you come to make your turns."

"Now, when you come into shore," he directed, "always come up the eddy from downstream." How we were going to do this without being swept by, he didn't say. But to come into shore from upstream pushed by the current was dangerous and not good boatmanship. If you should hit some snag in the muddy water or crash against the shore with the current pushing you, an accident was probable. Also, the person in the bow must be poised to leap ashore at the proper moment with the tow chain and all his weight. I intended this to be my duty.

Our worst moments were going to be making shore.

Now came the time I had worried about. We had to leave this kind party of people and head out down the Peace River, if we intended to do it. Sunday morning, and the thrush singing back in the cool, green woods — and life so precious. I didn't feel ready for this test, but it was now or never.

Just before we left them there at the Moose Café River, I took the old guide aside and asked him what he thought about our new guide.

"You want my candid opinion?" he said. "Of course I don't know the man, and maybe it isn't fair to say, but I think he's a freeloader. Oh, we have lots of them in British Columbia. We have them in Alberta, too. He's looking for someone to attach himself to. He won't be any harm to you, I don't think. But he won't be any good to you, either. Since you ask me, I think you'd be better off by yourselves."

"But I'm scared of the river," I said. "Just until we get used to it, and the camp life, well, he'll come along a day or two just out of kindness and concern over us, just for his meals."

"Cheap labor can sometimes prove to be very expensive," warned the old guide gruffly.

How right he was.

4

Mother's Guide

OUT of the mouth of the Moose Café River from behind the cliff we motored timidly, escorted by the larger boat. Then, as we turned out into the bright sky of the vast open river, the other party started their slow upstream return to town, waving good-bye. Good friends of the river, how often we see your smiling faces along our journey!

The canoe rode well. But with four people in it there wasn't an inch to move about in, without crawling on hands and knees over layer upon layer of duffle.

The river was flowing south and west in a big loop, before taking off north. I'll confess that with every tremor of the water beneath us I trembled.

We started along down the rolling, oily, full flood between glorious green wooded hills under a blue sky. Our canoe traveled smoothly over what Bum called the "whirls and boils" of the river, many of them thirty and forty feet across; and slowly we gained confidence. When we shut off the motor for a while to see how she drifted, I heard an old familiar sound, called back over twenty years of memory: a soft, rather ominous, sibilant hissing sound everywhere in the water beneath us. Sand. The river was so saturated with soil in suspension that you could hear it hissing against the canvas bottom of the canoe.

When we girls picked up the three paddles to try paddling we found that the canoe would move ahead only mere inches from the bubbles made by our strokes, dig as we would. When the muddy flood turned the craft sidewise we could not right it again. What with the weight we were dragging, the out-of-balance load, and the extra man, we had zero paddle power. This was pretty disquieting to me.

We were, then, completely dependent for our very lives upon this motor. We had no control without it. If it should fail, we could not get to shore. I thought: "Dear God, we could be swept into a yard of driftwood if the motor ever stopped during the voyage ahead."

The driftwood yards lay at the heads of the big river islands. This is where all the washed-out trees and timbers pile up by thousands of tons like jumbled matchsticks caught in the seas of churning water and mud. Such traps could be a burial ground for a boat — so I wrote in my journal at the time.

From a book of old river travels I read later: "The current usually sucks under the jams with relentless power, and instances have occurred in which men and boats have been drawn under and have never been seen again. Unless the occupants can manage to spring upon the jams before their craft goes under it," advised the text, "their fate is sealed." *

And again, another reliable author: "I climbed forward to the end of the driftpile; one could feel it vibrating as the river drove into it, through it and underneath it, splitting into two channels. Let yourself get swept backwards in a canoe into one of these things and it would be the end of you; and the same applied to those lashing sweepers under the cutbanks — trapped, smashed and thrust under." †

These dangers, fortunately, diminish both as summer advances and as one proceeds down the river.

As we hurtled down the flood I observed that the north banks were largely composed of prairie, and the south banks of the river were wooded. The explorer Alexander Mackenzie, camping along

---

* Paul Leland Haworth, *On the Headwaters of Peace River* (New York, Charles Scribner's Sons, 1917), pp. 105–106.

† R. M. Patterson, *Dangerous River* (New York, Sloane Associates, 1954), p. 50.

here nearly two hundred years ago, noted in his journal basically the same topography.

He had strong young men with him, did Mackenzie, and they were traveling, not down the current as we were, but upstream when they became the first Europeans to see the mighty Peace. How did they ever come up this current?

They were experts. They knew how to take advantage of every eddy near shore, and they traveled when the river was not in flood. We forget that until well after the turn of this century men simply did without mechanized power. A man who was any kind of a man was expected to "track" or "line" his boat up the banks, and he could make perhaps ten miles a day in this manner. Thus, with a knowledge of how to paddle, how to track, and how to pole a boat, a man could go anywhere — portaging around the rapids of course.

Along this river Mackenzie met Indians who called the river the *Ungava*, and they offered to his young men the usual amenities and hospitality which the natives traditionally offer to young explorers. The Indians gave food, guide service, and the comforts of their wigwams and wives — which were gratefully accepted by the Scots newcomers. Mackenzie noted that the women of the Indians did all the camp work and were the beasts of burden, while their lords rested, smoked their pipes, and took their ease. In the beginning it was women, working with their babies strapped to their backs, who entirely carved out human habitation, such as it was, in this wilderness. Kicked, cuffed, and unthanked, women labored along these shores. The old women were left to starve when they became too old to work any more. Even the rugged Mackenzie expressed pity for the Indians' women in his journal. Things were rugged for the human species in general in those hard days.

Explorers have their guides, at least at intervals, and Mackenzie had his Indians who taught him much about the country. Much later, Ernest Thompson Seton, the naturalist-conservationist, boating down the adjoining Athabasca and down the Slave, had guides, in 1905. Now we had our guide, too, didn't we? All explorers always have trouble with their guides. Their journals routinely record it.

Mackenzie in those early days saw herds of buffalo with their

frolicking calves on the north bank. It was believed that generations of Indians camped and fired the forest in an effort to maintain the north bank as prairie for the buffalo. On the south side
were bands of elk, still existing in pockets. But soon the river turns
north in the Peace valley, people said. On both sides of the river
today scrub timber is growing patchily: white birch, cottonwood,
poplars, box elder, and other soft woods, with occasional stands of
the more valuable white and black spruce.

Part of Europe lies farther north than we were here. But Europe
is modified by the nearby ocean, whereas North America's historic
harshness to settlers lay in the immensity of its land mass, extending far from all oceans, which permitted the most severe extremes
in temperatures. Here heavy August frosts frequently ruined the
wheat and oats. Possibly the best land and warmest growing temperatures were in the valley itself, going northward as the valley
widened out and the banks slowly lowered. Settlers on the high
prairie seven to eight hundred feet above the Peace valley would
always be faced with the yearly frost hazard. Winter temperatures
ranged to fifty degrees below zero and lower.

It wasn't, then, that this river was newly explored, oh no! It was
known before John Jacob Astor, in founding the American Fur
Company, opened the Missouri to navigation in 1808. It was
named the Peace almost a century before that, when the Hudson's
Bay Company insisted on the smoking of the peace pipe between
the Sioux and Ojibwa, the Blackfoot and Assiniboin, the Dog Rib
and Copperknife, the Beavers, the Chipewyans and the Crees.

Today that old sun shone down upon the Peace River and a new
generation, that was all. And from beside the quiet, purring little
motor attached to the modified V-stern of the canoe by its two vise
clamps and two chains, came the voice of our guide mumbling a
song.

The kids and I raised our voices under the sky and sang with
him. Then as we traveled our guide regaled us with other songs
which we had never heard before: Canadian folk songs, pioneer
songs, and presently, songs of the railroad and of the open road,
and sad prison songs.

I pinched myself. "Connie," I said to myself, listening to that

whiny tenor voice, "what kind of a guide have you got anyhow?
Does he really know anything about the river, the motor, the
woods? Is he really a prospector as he said? What is he?"

I began to see that he might be a migrant field worker perhaps, or
someone of that sort. Perhaps he just woke up in a ditch near our
camp after a drunk? Perhaps he wandered into camp feeling religious and contrite? Or maybe he was an actual *bum*, just as his
name implied, who spent his life on the railroads and highways of
all North America for all we knew.

"Connie," I said to myself then in rising alarm, "how could you
be so very dumb? How exactly does it happen that on this fine day
you are traveling down this big wild, lonely Peace River, headed for
the Arctic as fast as you can go, with your poor helpless children
aboard, and this person here in the boat whom you don't know a
thing about, really?"

"In a week or two all this baggage you have will straighten out for
you," shouted Bum companionably from the stern. "If it please
God." Then he added, "They say the current slackens out and
becomes slower as we go on north."

"Have you ever been into the North?" I shouted at him.

"Only as far as Peace River town," he said. "Have always wanted
to go north, as a matter of fact."

"Mother, don't you dare take that man all the way north with
us." Ann pinched me, outraged. "Mother, I don't like that man. I
simply can't stand him."

"Why not?" I asked, curious about a child's impression.

"You can't explain it," cut in Jean. "There's just something
about him you can't stand. Those other people didn't like him,
either, don't you realize that, Mom?"

"Maybe after a day we can get rid of him," I whispered. "Soon
as we feel sure we can handle the canoe and the motor ourselves."

"He looks stupid and mean, sitting there with his hands all over
our new motor."

Indeed, he somehow did give the impression of having settled
himself there like cement.

"You can't put a man off to starve in the woods," I said to the
children. "It wouldn't be humane. We've got to look for roads on

the south shore, roads that head south. We could put him off on a road, I guess."

"Mama, I'll jump right out of this canoe, unless you promise to do that," threatened Ann, with flashing eyes.

"Okay, okay," I agreed.

Still, I was experiencing a degree of comfort in the knowledge that a man, presumably a mechanical genius of sorts, was at the helm. I was brought up in an age when it was believed that a man can do certain things that a woman can't do, that a man can somehow manage magically to make things come out all right. It was a faith I know I will always have, although future generations of women may not have it.

Funny thing, a person felt almost secure boating along out here in the mainstream. But the water along the margins of the river went twice as fast when you approached shore. Or, was that only an illusion caused by the wide distances on the river? At any rate, each approach to the shoreline caused us to recoil in panic.

Nerving myself, I asked Bum to see if he could put the boat ashore, just for a practice landing.

It was then found that we couldn't get ashore.

Along the shores the furious water rushed, tearing out earth and vegetation in wild disarray. Place after place where we thought we might find a quiet nook or indentation in the shoreline turned out to be impossible to reach. Islands as large as a hundred city blocks had their green-leaved little trees all leaning downstream. As the flood abated they were already springily righting themselves. Of course it was impossible to land wherever forest actually was standing in the river.

Bum Littleton at the tiller followed my directions as I gave them from the bow. When I told him to try a landing, he tried for it agreeably. When I changed my mind at the zero moment, he turned the canoe out into the river again. Each time we narrowly missed a death trap among the rhythmically thrashing sweepers. As the day waned I sat with the binoculars in the bow, bone-weary. Bum's shaky hand on the motor was indecisive. You could sense through the length of the twenty-foot canoe that he did not know,

any more than I did, how to get ashore. I took the motor myself for
a little, but completely lost my nerve and handed it back.

"I'll take it, I'll take it," clamored Jean.

"Down, Jean. Not now!" I cried.

"Let me! Let me!" yelled Ann eagerly.

I said that we would hunt for the mouth of a creek for harbor,
but none were to be found. I pored over the map for creek mouths.

Finally I said, "We'll have to try the islands. The sides or tail of
an island. It's our only chance."

Any traveler of big rivers will tell you about camping on the
islands. Here can sometimes be found fine stands of spruce. Spruce
stands mean high, dry ground. They mean good firewood, shelter, a
place to rest and sleep. Islands are more productive of these conditions than flooded-over brushland along the river's shores.

As the sun lingered we hunted feverishly through the islands,
carefully avoiding the woodyards at their heads, coming along down
the sides of the islands cautiously. Sweepers of trees hanging out
into the current and attached to the banks by their roots repelled
us. The speed we were going was perhaps twenty-five miles an
hour, with power. It allowed no room to maneuver in, to dare to
make shore. While a speed of twenty miles per hour is not fast as
the modern-day automobilist sees it, he can only ask himself how
he would manage if he were obliged to make his carport at such a
speed, unchecked, and leap out to tie fast.

All at once there was an opening, a little cove of the kind a
boatman dreams of, indented into the side of the heavily timbered
island we followed.

"Head in there!" I screeched from the bow, waving my hand. It
was possible that our guide's vision, or at least his comprehension,
was not good, for he did not seem to recognize the harbor. "Don't
get swept past it," I cried. "Quick! Head straight in."

He gunned the motor, and the canoe charged into quiet water,
between sheltering wharves of stranded floating timber in the
eddy. He pushed the wrong button, the motor stalled, and at that
moment I grabbed for a projecting root from the bank, and hung
on.

There seemed not to be another comparable campsite in hundreds of miles of raging river. It was one of those spots where you are able to bring the canoe right alongside a cutbank shelf just large enough to accommodate it, and you can snub her up to the root system of the bank. Since the cutbank stood only three feet above the water, one person ashore could catch the parcels that the others tossed out of the canoe, and so easily unload. This was real fine so long as timber floating in the eddy did not move and block you in, trapping you on the island. We had no choice but to take this chance.

With Bum whistling a sullen, minor tune, we started wearily at tent pitching and making camp on the warm, dry mat of spruce needles beneath the sheltering, kindly spruce trees. He was no speed artist at camp work. Doddering and puttering, he continually forgot what he was doing, as the children worked with him. Everything was in a mess. The camp work seemed interminable.

It was so warm that the camp stove would have been unendurable inside the tent on such an evening. We cooked over the open campfire, opening cans with profligate abandonment in a land where many men in earlier years starved to death. Ann buried the cans, using the short-handled lightweight camp shovel to dig a pit for them, just after Bum flung the first can into the river.

"Hey," instructed Ann, "don't do that."

He only looked at her, half angry and half amused. "This old river don't mind," he said. He added, "She just gobbles it all up. Everything you give her."

"You should be a conservationist," lectured Jean.

"You tell me I should be a *what?*" His grin suddenly seemed like a leer to me. I saw at once that it irritated him to be instructed by children.

I could hardly hush them. They were American children.

"Hey, Mom," called Jean. "Come over here and look at something. If we weren't on an island way out in the river, you would think there were cows here."

"Moose track," I said when I saw it. "There's at least one cow moose who has come over to the island to have her calf. Could be just a few yards away from us through those willows. Keep your ear open. You may hear a hoof stomp any time."

"But how does a moose get on the island?"

"She lives here, dear. This is her home. Came out here, walking across the ice last March, perhaps. This is a big island. Very typical. There's moose living right now on this island, and black bear, too. They swim back and forth from the mainland nearly any time they want to. The big game swim just like power launches," I explained.

Ann came to examine the tracks, and, not to be outdone, she picked up a black bear track in the soft loam. "Mom," she confided, "your guide hasn't even noticed these tracks around here."

"Some guide," scoffed Jean. "Ha, ha! Mother's guide. He doesn't know a moose track from a chickadee."

"Keep your voices down, children. Yes, I suppose I'll never hear the last of it. I made a mistake, I think. First he won my friendship because he arrived when it was raining, you know. And I wanted that fool stove so much. . . ."

"He lies about everything," Jean divulged. "I've caught him in a dozen lies. He said he's twenty-eight years old, too. Pooh!"

"Did he say that? That's ridiculous."

"Yes, Mother, he said he was twenty-eight. Then he said his mother was eighty-nine. He was the oldest of thirteen kids, he said, and they all lived on moosemeat. Well, I was thinking," said Jean. "His mother would have had to be sixty-one years old when she had him, and she would then have to be seventy-four years old when she had the *last* of the kids, that is, if she had one every year."

"That's ridiculous," I said.

"That's right. That's ridiculous, Mother. A man who says things like that is not reliable. All you have to do is use arithmetic and figure it out for yourself. That's the kind of problems we had in fourth grade. Can you figure it?"

"Oh, dear," I said. "I can't."

"Mother," announced Jean decisively, "follow me. I'll lead you through the bushes and show you where I've decided to sleep tonight."

"Close your eyes," added Ann playfully.

"No," I rebelled. "Do you want me to break a leg? And, Jean Helmericks, you are not going to sleep away from the camp. I'll have none of that."

"Aw, gee whiz, Mom. You always spoil everything." Ducking through the bear wallows, she dragged me in the fading light down the margin of the island quickly to a little glade, where she had already placed her sleeping bag and propped her bednet.

"Jean Helmericks," I hissed, when I finally caught up with her, "please, please stop this madness. You can sleep away from camp among the animals another night, not now. Please listen to me."

"Well, what do you want?" she asked coldly. "I've waited all my life for this, to sleep out with animals."

"Jean," I pleaded. "That man. Listen to me. I think he's awfully strange. Maybe he can't help lying. Maybe he doesn't even know he does it. He could be out of touch with reality. He could be paranoid, and well, things like that. He could be dangerous. We have found that he is full of surprises, so many suits of clothes on him and places he hides things."

"What? Old Bum? He's just a bum and a nut, Mother. He wouldn't harm a flea. He'd be scared of the fleas."

"Probably so. But how do we know for sure? I wasn't a charter member of our county mental health association for nothing," I added. "I have a healthy suspicion of everyone I meet."

"Mother, if you are worried, I'll just stay on guard out here in the bushes," she suggested.

"No, no. That wouldn't do at all. Jean and Ann, we've got to all stay together, don't you see? We've got to watch him every minute. Especially," I added with true concern in my voice, "we must not leave him alone with the boat."

There ensued a moment of silence as the gravity of our situation was borne in upon us.

"Mother, I think you are right," Ann said sensibly. "You can sleep out among the animals some other night, Jean. Listen to what Mother says. Let's hurry back to camp right now, for what would happen to us if he stole our boat in these wilds?"

"We are on an island," I whispered, panting, as I followed the energetic girls back to the tent. It was good suddenly to feel their concerted moral support. "Do you realize what it would mean if you didn't have a boat? There's no way to get off the island."

It was not pleasant to think of.

"Of course he knows that the Mounties know we started down the river," I thought. This knowledge most likely would deter anybody from a foul action. The good old Mounties. On the other hand, there do exist in this world some individuals who are so poorly balanced, who are held in check by such tenuous bonds of self-control, that even the knowledge that the Mounties will eventually catch them is not sufficient deterrent — especially should such persons be placed on some island in some river once in a lifetime where there could be an unexpected opportunity for gratifying their long pent-up malice.

He is too humble for a man to be, I had thought, almost from the first. Something is strange about a man like that.

The vague face, the mumbled songs, the clumsy boat operation, the cowardice and meanness masked by a disguise of religiosity. . . .

"Act perfectly natural, chatty, and cheery," I instructed the children, as we came up to camp, although by now my thoughts had thoroughly frightened me.

"Well, we sure got a good start down the river," I said loudly, with forced cheer, as we tramped back into camp. "Wonderful scenery, Bum. Wonderful camp we have here. Guess it's as good a time as any right now to load up the good old rifles."

Climbing into the tethered boat, Jean handed me up the rifles in their cases — hereafter often referred to as "our precious rifles" — and I got them out, and methodically opened the ammunition.

"First, for the .22," I said. "Ann, you won your marksman's medal at Friendly Pines Camp when you were ten. Here is your .22, dear. All loaded and ready to go." It was a pump action and held fourteen shots. None were in the chamber. It would have to be pumped to use it.

"Goody gumdrops! Thanks, Mother," said Ann.

"We'll share, Ann," said Jean, being agreeable for once. "I'll sleep with you and we can put it between us."

"Now for the .30–06, the big rifle for your mother," I said, opening the bolt and sliding four big shells into the magazine.

"Gee, I haven't shot much of anything since I killed my last polar bear," I lamented loudly. Actually, this was a muddled statement of the facts. I could only boast one polar bear my whole life, it happened a long time ago, and I was out of practice. But I saw that our sly guide was taking it all in. Now the guns were loaded. But with no shell in the barrel, for I have never trusted a safety catch too far. Actually, now that we were embarked down the river north, it was in fact time to load the guns, just as I said, on general principles.

The children took their sleeping bags and made their beds on the warm spruce needles in front of the tent, with their .22 between them. I laid my own bed right by, about fifteen feet in front of the tent door.

"You can sleep in the tent, Bum," I said.

He just stared at me with rheumy eyes. I explained that, since it was a warm night, our family wanted to sleep out on the ground.

I situated myself where I had an elevated pillow for my head, formed most conveniently by a forest root. In this way I had an excellent view of the tent door, and the rifle lay at hand, pointing toward the tent as though by accidental arrangement.

My neck ached from the root, but the root was a friend. In fact I hardly gave it a passing thought at the time. I intended to remain fully clothed and on guard all night long.

"Yes, Bum, you can have the tent all to yourself tonight." I yawned and stretched with elaborate unconcern. "It's so nice and warm, the girls want to sleep outside."

"Thank you, thank you," he agreed. He even stepped over to help them arrange their bednet, and sprayed the area with our spray can. "I'll just roll myself up in the boat canvas very comfortable," he said. "God bless you, and don't worry none about me."

But he did not go into the tent as I hoped he would.

The twilight of the northern summer night wore on, and the melancholy voice of the hermit thrush was heard. "That's the hermit thrush, children," I called. We lay awake listening to that melody which some bird lovers tell us is one of the rare voices of earth, more beautiful than the nightingale's. Beside our camp the wild, gurgling river sounds merged into an unreal dream. Midnight; 1 A.M. Still he did not go into the tent. He was restless for some reason. What was he thinking? Still, he puttered about in the eternal twilight, a bluish figure, ragged and stooped, his loose jacket concealing who-knew-what surprises — I can see him now — putting more twigs on the campfire, washing some ancient socks in the frying pan, hanging them up on branches, moving about. The sweet pungent smell of campfire smoke mingled with the melancholy songs of the thrushes signaling to each other at quarter-mile intervals down the line; one, two, three, four, five thrushes hidden in the trees, merging their voices into river distance, like cathedral bells.

"Will that man never go to sleep?" I thought, exasperated. Once he went down to the boat, and puttered with something. My heart pounded. What was he doing there? Would he start our motor and speed off, abandoning us on an island? I couldn't bear it. I couldn't take any chances. I sat up and called in a falsely friendly voice, "For heaven's sake, Bum, go to bed in the tent. You're keeping us all awake."

Perhaps the reason this unfortunate man prowled the night may have been that he was hoping for an opportunity to sneak a drink from a bottle of whiskey he may have been hiding from my suspicious eye. But if so, I never saw the bottle or any evidence. Perhaps, what with the loading of the rifles, he thought that he was a captive upon a river island with crazy people, who knows?

At last he gave up the day and retired into the tent where I wanted him. Snoring sounds emerged presently in a steady drone from the tent, and I keyed my light snoozing to those regular snores.

In bright daylight next morning naturally I was exhausted. I was haggard; but nobody here was not.

A pack of coyotes broke out barking and howling across on the mainland in the broad daylight. Then suddenly, silence.

"Beautiful song, isn't it?" I said.

Nobody answered. Nobody had much pep. Collecting the guns and bedding and stuff, we ate breakfast and loaded the canoe.

The children were quiet and helpful and very nice. Much nicer than they were on school mornings back home, you bet. They had stopped their nervous picking on each other a few days ago, almost the very first moment they saw the river, in fact. They were adapting to river life, and nature. They didn't ever complain. They had already faced much danger with a coolness of courage one would never have believed possible. They were perfectly happy, for once. They didn't nag or ask for a thing. They were oddly satisfied. If we never know physical hardship in nature's hard school we never really live; and this is a great pity, if we are young. I wondered why it was like that. I had learned before now, on the river, that for some reason, it was.

It was no task at all to get launched out into the wild current again. But continuing to let Bum know that we were strong was going to become harder with each passing hour. It was embarrassing to keep up the fiction that we were friends. We weren't now. We had to get rid of him. But how? How?

He no longer made any pretense of his former fawning affection for our party, or loyalty to our cause. He had his own troubles and felt unappreciated. His personality was changing as the hours passed. I had already spent one thoroughly frightened night with him in camp, and I didn't intend to spend another night like that. By tone of voice and facial expression he showed that he intended to make his bid for power to captain this expedition, to assume the role of boss and bully here, one way or another.

"You treat me like I was a slave, or something — you women," he leered resentfully as we embarked. "Don't you think I know nothing?" he growled. "Well, I'll tell you one thing, I know more than you think. Somebody ought to come along, put you women in your place."

"Jean wants to run the motor," I switched the subject. "Say, Bum, will you give her some lessons right now?"

"Jean wants to run the motor," he sneered meanly. Then, just as I had a moment of extreme uneasiness, he abruptly weakened. "Well," he drawled sarcastically, "I always said you women can run it any time you want to."

Rather sulkily he relinquished his place in the stern, and Jean slid into his position. Jean took over, frightened but brave, and I stayed with the glasses up front and piloted, remembering how to read water all over again. I hadn't seen any water in years. I had the charts up front, and of course, the rifles under the bow.

We passed Rolla Landing, once a historic steamboat landing and pioneer trail. Its lumber mill was fallen into decay. Not a soul there nowadays. At last I saw a bridge in the distance where the river narrowed. It was Dunvegan. Dunvegan had the second bridge over the Peace, tying in the northern pioneer farmlands with the south. A graveled road connected with Grand Prairie southward, and civilization.

"This is the place," I thought. "Here is my only chance to get rid of that bum."

But I'll never forget the last great fright we had there in doing so, in which every suspicion we had had about this man was now at once confirmed.

It was as though he read my mind, for when I told him we would land at Dunvegan, he pushed Jean out of the way, grabbed the motor, and accelerated. Down the river past the town we went, toward the big pillars of the bridge and the rushing water under it.

"Where do you think you're going?" Jean yelled.

He didn't answer for a moment, just swerved directly at one of the pillars of the bridge.

I can say now in retrospect that a large wave was created where the water rushed around the bridge supports. Had we gone over the crest of that wave and into the trough we would have smashed against the bridge pillar or capsized instantly. Just as I thought he was going to kill us all, he swerved out safely, and the bridge flew past. "Oh, I thought we would find a better landing downstream," he shouted to us. "Or maybe I thought that since you do not want me to guide you on this here trip, I will kill myself. Ha, Ha," he laughed without humor.

The moment had passed so quickly that tragedy, which could have happened in an instant, might almost have been ignored as a figment of the mind. Only the horrid sick feeling that we three females had in the pit of the stomach reminded us that it was real enough. Having given us one last fright at high speed under the bridge, Bum motored obediently in to shore with us. He wanted people on the shore to see that a man was at the helm when we came in, he explained.

There were just three permanent families living at Dunvegan, scattered far apart. There was a telephone, a gas station on the road, and a small store. The rest of it was a small museum employing a government caretaker, and some camp grounds for cars and trailers.

Bum knocked on the door of the caretaker's little home, and the caretaker's lean wife came to the door in the hot Peace River sunshine. Now my self-elected guide said to the woman, importantly, "I am guiding this American lady here, and we are traveling by canoe. I wonder if you will please invite us in for a cup of coffee? She may wish to rent cabins from you for her party."

"Well. Come right in. If you don't mind my house being in such a mess," she apologized.

As she politely opened her door, I found myself stumbling in with the children, under these false pretenses. I was sick. I was dazed. My only desire for the moment was just to sit down. Just rest a moment, and feel safe, and pull myself together.

My guide, whatever he was, was an expert at getting doors to open in hospitality. He had a friendly, easygoing way. We left our boots on the porch, caked with mud. We gingerly took seats in the parlor. Bum disappeared to wash up. Here was my chance.

Paddling in stocking feet, I followed my hostess into her kitchen. "We want to leave Mr. Littleton here," I told the woman quickly when we were alone. "Frankly, we don't like Mr. Littleton. He is incompetent. But he resists the idea of our being rid of him. This is why we came ashore here. In the presence of other people I want to tell him to leave. Can he easily find a ride from here south?"

The woman at her stove brushed a strand of hair from her face, and looked astonished, and then seemed quickly to pick up the feeling of my genuine alarm.

"I'll call my husband," she said in a low tone.

Yes, the wandering prospector, or whatever he was, could certainly make his way south from here, for many trucks passed daily. As we returned to the parlor another caller came in, a square-

jawed authoritative man, who might have passed for a retired policeman. He and his wife were middle-aged tourists inhabiting the
only trailer now parked in the camp. Mr. and Mrs. Grundy, as I'll
call them, were the kind of people who stand for law and order and
the conventions, the kind of people who brook absolutely no non-
sense — and I shall say that I was extremely glad at this time to
meet the Grundys. Such people take their set jaws and stalwart
character with them wherever they go to the ends of the earth, and
all good people feel secure in their very presence. Bad people had
better take care.

"Oh, please excuse my house being such a mess," said the caretaker's lean wife for the second time. "I never dreamed that I was
going to have company today." She fluttered at pouring more
coffee.

I smiled and bit my lip to keep from breaking into wild laughter
which I was sure would have been offensive and misunderstood.

"So your house is a mess? So you think you have troubles?" I
thought, as I began to relax sipping the coffee. "Dear lady, if you
only knew how good your house and your friendship looks to me
now!"

When we had all drunk coffee and washed some of the river
mud off, and everybody was assembled there, I knew that I must
speak out now and send Bum on his way — gently but firmly. I had
no desire to hurt his feelings, to hurt anyone. My intention was to
give him all benefit of the doubt, but I must release myself from
what had become a growing and fearful tyranny from this supposed "guide."

"I have decided," I told the group in clear tones, "that the children and I will pitch our tent here tonight and stay over at the
public camp grounds."

"Well, we'll be very glad to have you folks," said the caretaker
helpfully. Everyone waited. There was a stillness in the room.

"Oh, heck, Mother . . ." began Jean.

I waved her to be quiet. "Bum Littleton here has helped us on
the river this far. I wish to say thank you very much, Bum, for your
help. But now the time has come when the children and I will be
able to take over and continue the trip down the river by ourselves.

So thank you again very much, Bum. Now we will put you on the road here so that you can return to civilization and to your own work — ah, and we will say good-bye."

I saw that he took it very hard. "But listen," he argued, "I can see that you need me to go on with you for a while yet. Just for a while," he insisted.

He began to talk in grandiose terms to the assemblage of the experience he had had in the woods, and how much he had done for our party. His voice became loud and strident and excited. The assembled people, covertly watching him, lowered their eyes in embarrassment, and I think they realized right then that here was a man who was difficult to get rid of, indeed. For he seemed not to hear actually what I said at all. He just kept right on arguing his way around it, refusing to accept my statement.

"I am going to pack up a knapsack of things you will like. Let's do it right now. And you can be on your way," I said.

I then outfitted him with our extra knapsack and filled it with a half week's supply of food, with mosquito repellent, matches, pocketknife (the supposed woodsman came to us without so much as a pocketknife on him), comb and toothbrush and flashlight; and crowned it all by donating a new bright red hat to take the place of the battered old hat on his head.

He proposed that he stay to pitch our tent for us before he left, but the children wouldn't have it, nor would I. After we had it up on one of the floors under the trees, he came back hours later, hoping to share our evening meal, and in fact our evening with us, as before. "I think I'll kill myself," he said suddenly, when we declined his company.

I put a good face on it. There was no psychiatrist out here in these woods. "Oh, things will work out for you all right," I encouraged him with cheery voice. He sat down, saying, "God bless you." But this would never do. "On your feet and get going," I then told him. "Don't come back." Arguing and angry, off he went into the night.

Even so, we put in another tense night, sleeping with the rifle at hand at the lonely public camp grounds, which were empty of all people but us. It rained and the night was black, and we were afraid of the dazed, malcontent prowler who was out somewhere in the night.

We waited a couple of days at Dunvegan for the weather to clear. Occasionally on the horizon we saw a hatchet face and a familiar ragged figure walking along. We shrank from the anger in his eyes when he stared our way. He wore the same old hat — saving the new one, I guessed. He had not yet left the area. Would he never go away?

It made us nervous, seeing him always lurking around. Ann suggested that we had better watch out for him even when we canoed farther on to Peace River town, because he could hitchhike that far on the highway, if he wanted to.

It turned out that Ann was right. He did hitchhike there, and went right to the police about us! He said we were not competent to canoe alone on the river and that we ought to have a guide forced upon us by the law. If we refused to hire a guide, he told the police they should step in and stop us from going.

The authorities did not stop us, of course. Least of all would the authorities have recommended Bum Littleton, for he was not a licensed or bonded guide.

Later on northward a letter awaited us at the next fort, still insistently offering his help if we would send for him. He said he believed his services, even though he had offered them free of charge in the beginning, should be worth twenty-five dollars a day in the future. He would postpone other business, he wrote, and make our camp days gloriously free of labors. He had an idea for improving the camp stove.

"Don't you ever weaken, Mother," Ann said sternly, when we read the scrawled letter. But there was no danger of that. How could I ever forget that dreadful night on the island, "keeping guard," as Jean put it, "over a man with our guns"? And so concluded the only time we ever tried to have a guide on our river exploration into the North.

5

River Camps My Mother
Used to Show Me

OUR first day really on our own found us motoring down the great flood feeling the keenest interest in finding out what lay ahead and the rarest exhilaration at our own audacity in finding out.

We started traveling very late in the day, after 5 P.M. It was only then that the rain clouds lifted. We wanted to get away from Dunvegan and its disgruntled prowler.

"Don't stay out on the river when it gets late in the evening," the old guide had originally instructed. "Get off the river early," he had warned. Nevertheless, I felt we could count on about four hours' light yet today. It was eighty miles to Peace River town. At a motor speed of twelve miles per hour and a current estimated at about the same, we ought to be able to make it there before dark, with some margin. But life on a river is not that way. Nor is life any place that way, so far as I have found.

The people at Dunvegan had told us that there was another party of canoeists on the river somewhere ahead of us.

"Nobody saw them here," was the word. "They didn't stop. Very unusual this summer, two parties now, including you. Not many cares to make this trip, it seems."

They were two young college athletes, fellow Americans, we learned, coming down from far above, from Summit Lake and the Parsnip, the very headwaters of the Peace in the Rockies. Each fellow had his own small kayak equipped with tiny auxiliary motor;

but mostly they paddled, using two-bladed paddles as lively as waterbugs. The two were going right through, traveling fast, to the Arctic Ocean. The kayaks were perilously tippy, but I was told that these fellows were experts. They had trained their bodies to whip-cord endurance before beginning the voyage, and also rapids and fast water held no terrors for them.

"Why couldn't *we* have done that?" wailed my kids.

"Because I was too tired out washing *your* clothes and *your* dishes," I informed them waspishly. "We'll just have to make do with what we have, and be thankful that old Ma can barely drag herself around." My wholehearted admiration went out to the other party, and their extreme exhibition of courage. In my mind I wondered: "Will those fellows get through with little kayaks?"

Official letters, I must make clear again, had assured me months ago that the Peace River canoe trip was considered a reasonable undertaking for the experienced riverman. Here was a river! Rivers naturally all have their little ways. Anyone knows that. Officials might make recommendations that rivermen be physically fit, and that their craft should meet certain specifications in size and should preferably be powered; but officials did not interfere if citizens or noncitizens decided upon any kind of expedition here — even to swim. If a person believed he could tackle the river, he had the basic right to elect himself for this undertaking. It was some-what like a man challenging a bull in the ring in Mexico. But on the river he would experience a good many more nuances of cour-age and a good many more moments of truth than the bullring offers, and his dream offered beautiful scenery rather than blood. However, the individual who sets himself up to be captain of his own boat and his own life would do well to be fully aware that the authorities usually give up their search for missing persons on the river within a period of two or three days, because they never find them here.

Thinking this over, the sheltered wobbly little person who has never before faced up to such a degree of freedom wonders if he is ready for it.

"When you go out into the North," I heard many persons say both in Canada and in Alaska, "be prepared for anything. Things can happen. You never know if you're going to be out there for a day or for a year."

Quite true. Whether you travel by boat or by small airplane, in the event of power failure or some unforeseen miscalculation, you will have vanished into that wilderness, and if the northern authorities give you up for dead, you might starve to death. At one time I had become completely at home with such risks. But I now wondered how I was going to get used to them all over again.

The danger here was not just capsizing. The danger was losing your boat and dying of exposure. My big bugaboo was that somehow when we slept ashore the canoe might get away from us, and all our things in it. To overcome this fear I got rings put into each end of the canoe, and used chains with clip snaps instead of ropes. I was afraid that ropes might fray, or a beaver or porcupine might chew them — I had had that happen, once.

But the chains which arrived turned out to be cheap, flimsy things. I had asked for an eighteen-foot length of heavy-duty chain on each end. I ended up with ten-foot chains that were lightweight, and one of the nose rings was weak and wobbled during the whole trip. That's the way things go. In our civilization many people who fix things either have no imagination or don't care. I intended, therefore, always to camp in creek mouths or in eddies out of the main current. This was theoretical. Of course it did not work out that way.

Another aspect of the bugaboo was the dropping water levels. In choosing campsites, whether up some creek mouth or along the edge of the Peace, we would have to be vigilant that our heavy boat did not get so hard aground in the mud that we could never launch it again. That might be nearly as serious as losing the canoe.

And I was alert for other kinds of boat trouble. For instance, some campers have had their canoes destroyed by bears. We would therefore always take our guns ashore when we camped, and most of the spare ammunition, in an emergency pack containing a few other things to be kept right beside or even inside the sleeping bag. Bear marauders are possible but not usual. The real reason for keeping the guns right with you is for food insurance in case the canoe escapes, leaving you stranded. You should have ammunition for a half year or so. Furthermore, the big rifle might be used to signal some passing boat, in case of emergency. Since you might be camped off the main channel, it would certainly take a rifle to reach the ears of any passerby. No voice could rise above their boat's engines, even if they happened to come close to you.

From now on we were on our own and we would be practicing survival and camping techniques routinely day by day. Here in northern Alberta, all but lost and swallowed up in green forest and swamp, were Canada's furthermost farmlands, and we hoped to meet some of these pioneer farmers as we continued north.

Not so very long ago all this area used to be a part of the Northwest Territories, but in 1905 Alberta was put into Canada proper and became a Province. Gradually the NWT shrank and receded, as Canada and the United States carved out national boundaries from the far, wild countryside they shared. The population of central and northern Alberta even today is sparse.

Now the little motor purred softly in regular cadence, and the green-forested Alberta hills rolled by. At last I was feasting my eyes and spirit upon green. Here were the green and blue distances so loved and longed for by the longtime wilderness dweller; the feeling of freedom, the space, the golden sunlight, the clear, pure air like wine to drink in. The children opened their senses to the spirit of an empty land.

From across the water came a muffled pumping sound.

It wasn't man-made. "I think it's the slough pumper, God bless him." (I was quoting from our recently released guide for the benediction.) "The great northern bittern. Funny bird, he sounds like he's trying to pump the slough dry."

"He'll never make it, Mother," laughed Ann. "There's a lot of water here."

Jean was sole boss of the motor. She had proven to be the one in the group who had nerves of steel as well as an aptitude for mastering mechanical monsters, for which I had little love. Our lives were in the hands of a fourteen-year-old girl, I thought. Jean got very tired and her back ached from sitting sideways all day crouched over her motor jealously with greasy hands. I sat in the bow to plot our channel, and to watch for dangers, weather, man, and beast. Ann lazed away the hours opening cans of food or drink to pass around, or snoozing under the "bearskin."

The bearskin was really just my old skunk coat. It looked exactly like a black bear. It wouldn't do for a woman explorer to wear this in the woods — she might get shot! — but I had brought it along from the States to use as a comforter in the boat and for a bed skin in camping. Spruce tips and balsam boughs may be all right as a supplement, but they can never take the place of animal robes.

We had filled the canoe up with spruce tips, and had put our entire load on top of the springy, water-resistant boughs. For three people there were three wooden slat seats. The seats were built high up out of water and mud which would collect in the canoe: one seat in the bow, with leg room, and two seats quite close together in the stern. That's the way I ordered it from the factory. The high seats enabled you to observe the water half a mile ahead or more, so that you could choose your channel and not get drawn into what you didn't want. Our load was covered with canvas.

"This is Burnt River on the map," I called to the expedition members, as we approached a river mouth.

"We want to see it," came the cry.

I realized then that I was going to have a hard time getting us to Great Slave Lake in just one summer, with people who wanted to stop and see every creek along the way. But we turned in. This was the beginning of a summer of endless creeks and rivers. What were we looking for? I couldn't tell you what I was looking for in the twelve years I wandered the North before the children were born. Looking into creeks and rivers can simply become a way of life.

We nosed into Burnt River's stagnant red algae and found ourselves floating in sudden primordial silence; the humming clouds of mosquitoes which met us sounded very loud. A few big fat raindrops pattered down, the hoods of our parkas went up and the bug lotion was passed quickly from hand to hand. This typical maneuver would be repeated a thousand times until the countering readjustment tactic to nature's tactic became second nature in living afloat in the wilderness. We took up our paddles to make our way slowly through swaths of timber that had accumulated where the

Peace River in flood had backed up half a mile into the creek mouth.

As the canoe tunneled into the forest the high-water mark was above our heads. Six feet above even the reach of our paddles, its heavy gray line cut across tree trunks and along the willow fringe. Vegetation was dead from mud. Branches and leaves were festooned with mud as snow may festoon a forest. Log jams sagged over seas of mud.

"Mud," I told the kids. "Not many people have seen a sight like this." We marveled at the pure havoc of nature.

Up the river we found a moraine of continuous boulders jamming the creek bed. Everything in this whole country was either jagged rocks or mud. There wasn't a square inch of conventional, tame, normal ground anywhere.

"I want to make camp and sleep here," insisted Ann.

"No," I said. "And that's final."

We had spent an hour of daylight exploring and marveling. Off we motored, then, out of Burnt River, and on down those moving, broad sheets of water of the skylit Peace. Ann took along several large flat rocks she had gathered.

"You know what, Mom? These rocks are what we need to make steps the next time we come ashore." I smiled tolerantly, hardly dreaming what genius this child possessed, as I allowed her to take her rock steps along in the canoe.

Presently the Peace became completely glassy, almost hypnotic, as night's clouds gathered. I recognized danger.

As the shadows settle the only sound is the gurgling of the swirling boils of the river, and the occasional sound of a distant bank caving in. The whirls and boils are golden in the light of the setting sun, the sun which rolls like a ball around the horizon during the night, dipping just below the rim of the world to set in the north. The fifty-foot whirls and boils merge and dissolve, and merge again; you watch them, fascinated. Now, later, they are turning red, brassy, copper, and at last purple and black. Now the black coils of water squirm into a million changing mirror facets. Gradually it becomes impossible to tell which waters are moving in which direction. You search for indented coves where you might get ashore, but each cove is veiled in shadow, and getting in close for a look is courting danger. The old guide had cautioned against getting swept down small, narrow side channels. In floodtime some of them might be spanned with log jams. As for telling which was island and which was mainland — well, that was not always readily possible, even in broad daylight, until you got in very close.

"We've got to get off the river," I kept saying aloud to Ann, who lay near me apprehensively, on top of the load with the bearskin.

"Mother, I'm praying," she said. "You pray, too."

"I'll pray with my eyes open," I concurred, as I continued to probe the twilight with the binoculars. Big rivers can make you religious very fast, if you aren't already.

It was nearly dark when we found Griffin Creek. At first I thought it was an island. I couldn't be sure whether it was a boat trap with a rushing narrow channel behind the island, or a safe creek from the mainland. "Turn in, turn in," I waved to Jean, and the canoe obediently turned toward the opening. Yes, the water in the opening was quiet water. Still frozen with fear, we went right into the purple darkness.

"You see, Mom, I prayed," whispered Ann sincerely.

It was hard to believe that Ann was the same twelve-year-old who a short time ago spent her whole life studying her reflection in the mirror, worrying about keeping up with the fashions of America. Who telephoned the U.S. Weather Bureau imperiously to determine which ensemble she would wear for the day. Who used up all my nail polish, razor blades, deodorants, eye make-up, and a full can of hair spray for one week's attendance of seventh grade.

I guess it was hard to realize that I myself was the same person, too, because I was now very much without the above beauty aids, and a few dozen more. As for Ann, she had forgotten they ever existed, and I should like to contend that this is a wholesome thing for twelve-year-old girls.

Griffin Creek, like Burnt River, was full of the backed-up waters of the Peace and half-submerged logs and mud. But it was safe, and we were thankful to have it.

After Jean cut the motor we heard the sweet chirping of baby frogs in chorus. They could have been angels. Paddling up around

three bends of the creek, I still had no true idea of our whereabouts, when a beaver swam across our bow and cracked the water
cheerfully in the gloom. That beaver materialized like a river pilot,
as though he had come just to be our guide.

As the creek rapidly narrowed to nothing, a kingfisher rattled in
alarm from the weird snags overhanging our heads. He had been
sleeping. There was a pervading smell of wet raw earth and mud;
the place smelled the way you would think coffins and earth and
graveyards ought to smell, I thought; the smell of death and decay.

"Kind of a funny place, Mother," spoke up Jean, quavering.

"A rather objectionable place, dear," I agreed with trembling
voice, "but we've got to make a camp here for the night somehow."

Suddenly my gaze fastened upon an object ahead in the muddy,
stagnant creek bend, just as we were pushing forward, sounding
with the paddles, and the hairs on the back of my neck prickled
and simply stood right on end.

The object I saw ahead was the exact shape and size of a partly
buried kayak.

Poling inch by inch toward the horrid object, I was certain that
we had here before us the grisly remains of one of the American
canoeists who had preceded us down the river. Then, just as suddenly, the object clarified itself into a perfectly ordinary, kayak-
shaped white sandbar rearing out of the mists.

I groaned audibly. "Relax, Mother!" said Jean out loud. "We'll
take care of you."

I had to poke at the sandbar with my paddle to make absolutely
sure. Then, we turned the canoe around, retracing our way back
around the bend. Somewhere in this impossible place we must
make a camp tonight. We searched up and down the stagnant cutbank channel. The only way was to cut steps up the sheer sixteen-
foot raw mud walls, and choose a place that would not cave when
we did it. Then we could pitch our tent on the grassy prairie up on
top.

"We can use my rocks to make our first steps," offered Ann.

We set to work stamping out steps up a traverse crack in the soft
and oozy mud wall, and eventually carried all our junk up.

After some hours our little band of intrepid female explorers had accomplished the herculean task. Floundering through deep mud we got the thirty-pound tent package, the stove, the grub box, the rifles, the water bucket, and three bulky eighteen-pound sleeping bags high up on the wet but clean pasture above. Here we over-looked the depths where our canoe lay tied to small poplars. Once up on top, we tugged and hauled on the tottering tent poles, and at last hitched her fast to her stakes and to some limber willows, tying the tent fly with a neat bow knot.

"You will always find that the handiest things in life," I told my campers, "are bow knots and large safety pins."

Of course there were a few cracks over the head with the tent poles, which had a way of collapsing; and a few yelps of rage rent the peaceful night. But the main thing is that in all these episodes, we survived.

On top we had a surprisingly cheery camp. A crackling stove inside the tent poured out its smoke from the little stovepipe, and we drank the turgid, fishy water in a nourishing warm prepared soup mix. The prairie grass was long and filled with water. But camping right on top of such long wet herbage can give you a good camp, for if rain comes, I told my crew, it will soak right into the porous mat and there is no runoff. But you must have not only a canvas floor tarp but plenty of fur robes and eiderdown bags. Our bags had cost one hundred and twenty dollars each and were heavy duty. They were suitable for polar winter as well as summer.

It was midnight when we rolled out the three sleeping bags; but the distant sky remained pale yellow, for it was the longest day of the year.

"Listen, children, to the red-winged blackbird," I said, as the day turned. "There must be farmers nearby."

I spread the bearskin out under my own bag, adjusted a life pre-server under my head for a pillow, and crawled into my sack. All lapsed into silence.

"Thump, thump!" came mysterious sounds, close to the tent.

Jean looked out the tent flap on her hands and knees. Was it a bear? Thump, thump, thump.

"Mother, what's that noise?"

"It's only rabbits. It will be a good rabbit year next winter."

"Mother, can I go out with the gun?"

"Not tonight, dear. For mercy sake, I haven't had a night's sleep in weeks, can't you settle down?"

"Couldn't I shoot one to eat?"

"Well, you can try, if you like. I've never been able to see one in summer."

Jean took the .22 — we didn't have the flashlight up on the bluff — and went outside. You could hear the dew falling. It misted onto the tent roof and saturated the long, green prairie grass. Occasionally you could hear a breeze sigh across the tent, rattling the tin safety against the little stovepipe, a breeze that spoke of our arctic prairies up north where nothing stops the wind and there is no habitation. "If only we can do this with safety!" I thought. I wouldn't want to get them into some of the tight spots I got myself into during my early life. Someday one's luck runs out.

Out in the night Jean stood silently with the little .22 rifle, surrounded by wild primroses in full bloom — Alberta's flower — and by the lovely scattered bright field lilies which were the official flower of next-door Saskatchewan. Jean's feet were wet and cold, and she had a tendency toward bronchial pneumonia; she had been hard to raise because she was allergic. She had taken years of allergy treatments. Only modern science had kept her afflictions under control and protected her from the menace of asthma.

I worried that she might shoot through the tent, what with excitement and myopia. But she never saw a rabbit — the thumping, playful varying hare or "snowshoe rabbit" which was pounding the ground with powerful hind feet. Lepus americanus macfarlani is rarely visible until the leaves drop. Then, by winter, when its tracks can be seen in the snow, it can be caught in snares or in Number 1 or 2 traps for table.

Jean was one of those kids you see occasionally who has no visible social life — like the Lepus americanus in summertime. Living in the city most of her life, she saw the others of her species only dimly though smeared glasses; and the concrete streets she walked she saw not at all. She took refuge in some inner dream because, except for our pets and the tree she climbed, she hated where she was. She became an honor student in school but aside from that became absent mentally and emotionally. Walking across a room she stumbled into things, and frequently tables, lamps, and dishes collapsed into disaster.

She lost books and sweaters and sneakers, and you caught her reading books that were far, far beyond her age, and on every notebook cover and scrap of paper she drew beautiful pictures of idealized wilderness scenes containing animals. In her early years most of the animals were horses. She cared nothing for people her own age, or friends. Her friends were animals. Her dreams were of some beautiful place that she had never been but which some uncanny instinct in her soul informed her surely must be there, if she could but find it.

Jean remains graven for me at this moment of her development on one summer night, alone with our tent. There she is, gratefully breathing in the fresh mysterious scents, and trying, eager as a pup, to catch those elusive thumping rabbits throughout the subarctic summer night. In the Peace River summer Jean was getting the chance to be young out in nature, and it was helping her to grow into some kind of real person.

What a shame, I thought, that all the awkward, miserable adolescents in the world cannot have this little time and big setting in which to dream. We don't let them dream any more. Dreaming is so very important, during the years we must wait, the decisive years in which we must be allowed time to mature, in which the right dreams can unfold. If growth is mechanically forced, we have missed these sweet experiences, and there can be no dreams.

How good it was to be out here with stern but honest nature, at least for a while. How glad I was that the children could have these experiences. How will the individual know freedom if our earth is deluged with overwhelming numbers? What if these millions have never seen, tasted, touched, savored the various delicious flavors of freedom? How can they, then, ever know what it is?

Robert Louis Stevenson, poet, advised the civilized world, all of us, wisely long ago he said: "Seek out where joy resides, and give it a voice. For to miss joy, is to miss all."

Now I don't mean to say that I turned away from civilization altogether. I knew perfectly well that everything I ever had in my life civilization gave me. It gave me health and life and material abundance, and it even gave me the language I used.

I only thought that we were paying an awfully big price for the civilization we built. Everything was getting too big and too cumbersome to handle. I want to point out that the values of true civilization are threatened today. These are freedom, reason, and joy.

6

Of Mud and People

WE sprawled sleeping in the wobbly, brave little tent. I was dreaming. In my subconscious dream I was saying:

"I am going to take you to the secret places of nature. Yes, here in our earth home, our only home. Then, ever afterwards, for the rest of your life, you will stand aside a little bit, and realize the colossal conceit of mankind. You will be careful. For as long as there is the living memory of these places in our land, the love of nature's strange morality and a respect for her retributions will exist."

When our day began it was windy; the little stovepipe rattled and scratched against the tin safety vent of the tent. I mumbled in my half sleep that we must stay over in camp on days like this—for close vigilance always is the price of life and freedom.

We woke again near noon. The sun was high and the prairie grass bent before the wind. From our sheltered spot within hidden Griffin Creek, we could see muddy, tumultuous whitecaps rising in frothy fury to confront the passage of humans on the broad Peace out beyond. We had two years, I thought. We had plenty of time.

As the wind kept the mosquitoes down I rolled out in the sunny pasture before the tent on the bluff, on the bearskin, and Jean gave me a chiropractic treatment to take out some of the knots. "Mother has this problem, see? You have to get the knots out of her neck in the morning, and then she is pretty good for the rest of the day."

Soon the kids and I were setting out a line for fish. There among the bluebells, goldenrod, asters, and gentians we were camped on land that had once been plowed, and would be plowed again by someone; and we built a pit fire down out of the prairie wind, and ate baked sweet potatoes in foil, canned meat, canned tomato juice drunk out of the can, and hot biscuits with canned butter and honey, served on tin plates. And I girded myself to attack the river again when the wind dropped.

The girls found a spring of sweet water across the fields, and taking the .22 rifle they explored, spotting a man on a tractor on the distant skyline. In the distance there sounded two high-power rifle shots, spaced in a leisurely way, and I heard the blood beating in the thin passages of my ears as I listened. Whoever he was, the hunter sounded competent, and I guessed that he got his game. These farmers poached moose and deer, of course, out of season.

Ann raised the wobbling .22 rifle to her thin shoulder, and shot at a bird sitting in a tree. She missed. When she returned to camp I cautioned her that a .22 bullet can travel more than a mile, and kill. This is why the law reads that game birds are shotgun game, not rifle game. You can't have bullets flying all over the country. If we killed, in the wilderness later on, it would be for food only. We had plenty of canned stuff along, and obnoxious as canned food is, we did not plan to kill but mostly to look.

On the next day we went on to Peace River town. It was the last town — around four thousand — and it possessed the third and last bridge across the mighty Peace, linking Canada's new Mackenzie Highway up north. Here Mackenzie had built the first trading post and fort. The town lay on the outside bend of the river, where there was a fast current, just below the confluence of the Smoky River. An assortment of big timbered islands lay in the Smoky's delta, making the whole river a mile wide.

As we saw the town I experienced a qualm that the motor might quit. If it quit here we could miss the whole town. We could be carried off into the North with probably not a soul to know the difference, for in a town of this size the people don't look out upon the river. The river turned north here. The next settlement was little Fort Vermilion, about four hundred and ten miles away.

But the motor, with Jean monitoring the gauges, faithfully kept on beating, and soon we had crossed the wide river through the islands and were following the fast current along a cutbank twenty feet high, above which the municipal buildings lined the waterfront.

Grabbing the binoculars I read them off: the city hospital, the Forest Service, the Royal Canadian Mounted Police building. More than halfway down the waterfront the cutbank fell off to admit the Heart River, which we had been told about. Quickly we turned into its quiet, safe, stagnant waters, filled with red algae, which would harbor us.

An elderly citizen stood there with a fishing rod in his hand.

"Good morning. Would you mind watching the boat, sir," I asked the citizen, "while we walk over to the Mounties' office and report in?"

"Heh? What's that?"

"*Good morning, would you mind watching the boat while . . .*"

"Take it easy, Mom," said Ann quickly. "He's deaf."

"I'll try again. *Good Morning. Would you mind . . .*"

"CAN'T HEAR YOU. WILL YOU SPEAK A LITTLE LOUDER, PLEASE?"

"GOOD MORNING. WOULD YOU . . ."

"HOLD IT, MOTHER. You're waking the whole of Canada. Just tie the boat to the tree, and we'll go."

Thus, having to warn the Mounties that we had completed the first one-hundred-and-seventy-five-mile lap, we left the perplexed citizen still fishing beside our tethered canoe. I worried about whether the guns would be all right. Yet we could not carry them with us as the young Mackenzie had done without embarrassment.

Soon we were clumping along the sidewalk where 99th Street joined 103rd Avenue — it was an ambitious town which apparently anticipated a perfectly gigantic population in due course — and entered the building marked with a sign in regal gold letters: Royal Canadian Mounted Police.

The Mounties, in keeping with their Canadian background, expressed a very correct, restrained sort of pleasure in seeing us, but

they were a little concerned over our tardiness. They always expected us to travel faster then we did on the river.

They had got the worldly idea of the faster the better, it seemed;
and some of them even went so far as to point out that there are
easier ways to travel in their country nowadays.

"Commander A. E. Stevenson, Peace River Detachment, very
pleased to greet you. We have been expecting you for some days.
Welcome to Peace River. Did you have a good trip?" A large, well-
fed, rosy man, exuding good cigar smoke, held out a ponderous
official hand.

"Yes, delightful. The children are enjoying it a good deal," I
replied, beginning to perspire under my heavy woolens in the
steam-heated office.

"Ah, yes, I should think so indeed." Pause. "Are you Ann? Are
you Jean?" the immaculate, olive drab and blue Commander asked
them firmly in a deep voice, leaning forward, his pistol at his belt.

"Yes, we are. I mean, I am," Ann squeaked.

"Sergeant" — the commander was a sergeant — "here is some
mail for the Helmericks party," interrupted a tenor-voiced corporal, just then, and to our great delight a bundle of letters from
home was handed over.

"Where is Mr. W. L. Littleton with your party?" boomed the
Commander heartily.

"Not with us now," I said. "We set him on the road at Dunvegan."

"I see. Do you not have a large black dog named Sylvia?" asked
the Commander then.

"Yes," I squeaked, and then cleared my voice. "Not with us. In
the States. But — how did you know about Sylvia?" I felt rather
dizzy.

The Commander disdained to answer this, and it will always
remain one of those mysteries for me which pertain to the Royal
Canadian Mounted Police.

"I am given to advise you that the dog is quite well." He leaned
toward the children again. "She misses you, but she sends her very
best regards and kind wishes."

The kids were nodding in unison with wide eyes. "Thank you," piped Ann formally. "We have a grandmother, too, but she didn't come along this time."

"You have two very nice children," the Commander said aside to me.

"You Mounted Police are just unbelievably thorough," I thanked him with open-mouthed astonishment.

"Well, we try to be." He accepted the compliment with modesty. Then, "Now, would the three of you like a nice hot cup of coffee?"

When we said we would, a lady Mounted Policeman, wearing the olive drab and blue colors in a skirt and blouse, stepped with sprightly alacrity from her typewriter to the convenient office coffeepot and poured.

"So now you have coffee breaks," I observed. "I was a visitor to some of your Air Force places in the Arctic, only, let me see, that must have been fifteen years ago, and you had coffee only at mess for breakfast. The rest of the time, tea. Tea all the time, everywhere. Have you changed to coffee now?"

"Ah, we're getting to be more like you Americans all the time," confirmed the Commander. "Easy to get into the American habits," he sighed.

"Constable Abernathy!" his voice suddenly boomed.

"Yes, sir!" The Constable stiffened.

"The Constable will accompany this party when they return to their — ahem — canoe, and will look into the matter of where will be the most appropriate place for them to camp, that is, pitch their — ah — tent, while they are here with us."

"Yes, sir."

"Did you ever know Sergeant Lean?" I asked, sipping. "He was stationed at Aklavik in the Mackenzie Delta some years ago. I often wondered what happened to that fine old man."

"My cousin," replied the Commander firmly. "Deceased. Plane smash during a rescue mission, poor chap."

"I'm sorry to hear that. Real sorry. In the old days," I said, "we used to have an explorers' permit issued by the Department of Transport. They didn't let anyone into the North without it, except the missionaries. It was kind of a closed reserve. But on this present journey I wasn't sent any permit, and I wondered."

"They may have stopped issuing them," mused the Commander. "Of course, everything is changed nowadays. All our work is air patrol and highway patrol. I don't believe we have many left in the Force now who have boated or used a dogsled — other than for sport, you know. This is not to say we don't have some boat and sled patrols yet, somewhere. It escapes me now, just where they are, up north. We have a total of three hundred and fifty RCMP officers serving in administrative and patrol capacities in the Northwest Territories where you are going by river. It's a million square miles, you know. Oh, incidentally, you may expect complete cooperation from the NCO in charge of Fort Vermilion with regard to any further assistance in northern Alberta. I am forwarding your correspondence to police authorities in the NWT, and you may expect a further letter with regard to accommodation over the winter, school, possible explorers' permits, etc. as necessary, when you reach your destination, Yellowknife, in the fall."

Hardly pausing, he continued. "As to the portage facilities at Vermilion Chutes, you seemed concerned about that, naturally, in your letter. Through our Fort Vermilion Detachment the NCO suggests that you stop at that point and utilize the radio facilities of the forest ranger — unfortunately, our own service has no radio facilities in that area — and in this way contact reliable persons at Little Red River to implement the necessary arrangements so that a reliable Indian with his horses and wagon will be available at the Upper Landing when your party arrives there, that is, I believe about fifty miles beyond Fort Vermilion, and I don't think you'll have any trouble with the rapids, or the Chutes, handled in this way. ARE YOU READY, CONSTABLE?"

"Please, sir," said Ann at this point, "may I go to the rest room?"

After we came trailing out of the rest rooms, having enjoyed that ultimate frontier hospitality, the starched and rosy Constable Abernathy accompanied us with our canoe some yards on up the Heart River into the center of town. Here our tent was pitched on the green, while the canoe rode close alongside at what had been the original famous old swimming hole of the early pioneers and which was today venerated as a historical spot. It was a real honor to pitch our tent here. I recognized the old swimming hole immediately, with its red algae, deep mud, and red cliffs, from an old oil painting in Dunvegan's museum.

We took our rifles in their cases, our glasses, camera, notebooks, and mail into the tent, with the sleeping bags and bearskin and I covered up the rest of our junk inside the canoe under its snap-down canvas — an invention of mine — and prepared for a day or two in town for restocking and checking everything. We would have a washday at the last Laundromat. From our tent we could take meals at the town's best restaurant nearby, and we could use the rest rooms there.

As I started reading my mail in the tent, I noted that some young boys had appeared and that Jean and Ann were talking and laughing with them. The boys arrived wearing swimsuits. I kept on reading my mail, noting vaguely that Jean and Ann, having jumped in with their clothes on, were laughing and cavorting in the old swimming hole, where an ancient and slimy raft floated beside the cliff. Looking out later still, I saw that a friendly beaver, swimming along the river in due course, had joined the first inmates of the pool, and marveled at the convivial enthusiasm of that old swimming hole, with its assortment of dedicated sportsmen more or less frozen in with red algae.

Two housewives drove to our tent, bringing their husbands with them.

"Ha, ha, so you're Americans!" said their leader. "Look, love, they're Americans, I told you so. And look, love, they're *swimming* among the *beavers*." Brief pause.

"We are glad to have you come to visit our little town," said this spokeswoman, who was direct from England and who possibly had not seen Americans very often. "Now we hear that you are a woman and two dear little daughters, and living in a *tent*. Now, what do you think of *that*, I says to my husband. We must go and call upon them and give them some kind of welcome here. No, it's not necessary for you to live in a *tent*. Would you come and

stay at our house while you are here? Please tell us that you will."
She paused for breath, with a homely and endearing middle-class
English smile.

"I sure would like to," I responded with heartfelt appreciation,
considering it. "But we've got to sleep here and keep an eye on our
outfit."

"That's right," said the other housewife. "Never thought of
that, you know. It might not be safe, like. So many strangers coming up the road these days."

"But then, anyway," said the first lady, "come over to the house
and have yourself a hot tub! We have these marvelous government
homes, and with a bathtub in every one of them, and all of the hot
water for the taking. What do you say, now?" The two ladies
nodded. Their husbands nodded weakly.

"I like animals better than people," announced Jean at this
point, with uncalled-for frankness. I pinched her, and she turned
up her lips in a forced — and rather ghoulish — grateful smile, so I
hope that possibly her remark was not understood.

The upshot of it was that they hauled us off in separate cars to
those wonderful hot tubs and fed us in their homes on cake and
Peace River strawberries and cream.

And as we left our boots at each door, each woman said, quite in
character with womankind the world around, "Please don't pay
notice to my house today. It's in a terrible mess."

At sundown, following baths, we took leave of our hostesses and
returned to be met, by prearrangement, by a rather elegant bachelor of mature years, who drove the children and me about the area
sight-seeing far into the bluish twilight of northern summer night.
The northern people so loved the summer night that other drivers'
car headlights could be seen moving up and down the roads at all
hours. In summer the northern people turned night into day; and
the farther north you went, the more this was so, until you reached
towns that never seemed to sleep at all.

In Peace River there was a radio station and a weekly paper, a
golf course, Ford garage, municipal pool, and motion-picture theater, some cafés and motels, and the usual amenities of small, com-

plete towns. We would not see a town like this again this summer.

Later that night, when the kids and I were fast asleep in our tent, we heard loud voices and a tooting of horns in the predawn blackness. There were roars and grinding of gears, and bright headlights, as I raised my head from my sleeping bag in dismay. In northern towns which never sleep in summer, drunken gangs of men may occasionally roam at large, fighting and playing, and it seemed that a car full of them had driven along to our tent, slipping past the Mounties' all-night patrol. A neighbor telephoned in our behalf. Immediately a starched boy constable came and took off to jail the carful who were charging up and down, threatening momentarily to careen out of control through our tent walls.

"Real sorry that happened," apologized the embarassed Commander the next day. "They get a little wild, construction and oil workers from outside, you know. Were you much disturbed?"

"Oh, that's all right," piped Ann, making an on-the-spot sociological analysis, as her new friend had won her confidence. "I find it very law-abiding around here. Here they're only drunk. If a woman and two kids pitched a tent in the middle of *our* town, they wouldn't last the night. They'd be murdered," she announced with grisly precocity.

"Tsk, tsk," said the Commander, controlling a shudder.

"Insane maniacs," Ann further enlightened him, and the Commander looked faint.

Of Canada's some eighty-three hundred Mounted Police, perhaps none in the course of the last twenty years has had occasion to draw his gun and actually fire at a man in this region. It wasn't in the regulations. Of course cosmopolitan eastern Canada, now infiltrated by gangsters and rapidly breeding its own talented countrymen from a diversity of some forty-five different national types, is rougher. But even there the honor code of the Mounties remained the same. Side arms, while worn as part of the uniform, might never be unsnapped from the locked-down holster. There was no, "Halt or I'll shoot!" The only reason for which an officer might fire upon a citizen was if he were actually fired upon first. The pistol remained but a symbol, and here in this last politically stable large area left on earth, the symbol of the uniform had until now sufficed to keep order among a respectful population by a sort of mutual agreement; which in the end is the only way order can be kept in civilization.

When we had heavily restocked food and gas supplies, we left Peace River town and started on the river's long swing northward beyond the world of mankind.

Apart from the poles of the earth, there are few places, if any, that are so totally uninhabited, so completely empty, as here. Not even in the wilds of Asia and Africa can you find this space, this emptiness.

Up until this time I had not been 100 percent sure that I would go on with Jean and Ann. After all, I came from what is known as a child-centered culture. You may risk your own neck if you wish, but you are not supposed to risk your children's. In the United States children are like the sacred cows of India. Their spirits may be malnourished in many ways (some of which may be bizarre in the extreme) but to suggest that they are not sacrosanct is to violate the most basic taboos.

Yet, after all, I had spent as many years camping along northern rivers as almost anyone except Indians and Eskimos, and I felt as though this should be my children's natural heritage. They both had their beginnings north of the Arctic Circle: Ann along some river of uncertain determination; and dear Jean, surprisingly conceived in the eleventh year of our marriage, out on the polar ice pack north of Alaska during the spring sealing.

Now, after briskly loading our boat, the two youngsters and I pushed off cumbrously and ingloriously through mud, ventured out of the Heart River mouth, were seized by the mighty Peace, and suddenly knew we loved this wicked river. This was living.

There were no navigation maps of the river ahead for a few hundred miles. The two Forestry maps I had would be helpful in orienting us as to where we were generally. I asked Forestry if the ranger stations which were on the map series starting beyond Fort Vermilion were manned. But I only learned: "Sorry, can't answer that, like. You see, we are Provincial [Alberta] here in this office, and they are Dominion. You would have to find out in Edmonton where they are placing their men this year, for they jolly well don't tell us."

Today the river was dull gray and the sky was gray and misting in as we traveled. I had been keeping my eye on it closely for some time, sitting in my place in the bow, snuggled deep into my Arctic Dew Line parka, and deep in my thoughts.

On a big river, you never knew when you would meet a head wind right around the bend. The waves kicking up reminded me I was glad that we had invented our "wave splitter." It was an over-hanging canvas on a light frame which shielded my knees; but most important, since the bow rode high, you could stow the rifles and glasses and camera and those maps immediately in use under the canvas shelter, and they would stay dry there. You could carry film there in your big handbag, wrapped in cellophane, and letters from Gerald, written in a thin, spare, intelligent hand with words that were cautious, thin, and spare.

Dr. Gerald Corby, my dear friend, was a rare intellectual, a jewel of the asphalt jungles; the gray world where he lived was made less gray for his being there. But nothing he could ever do could color it green, and my color was green. Yet it is one of the nice things about our modern civilized world that we do have such a diversity, such an epicure's abundance of characters, and only this kind of world, apparently out of its chaos, produces them.

The question is, do you dare give your heart to them? Can you adjust to their habitat?

I must have looked odd with my big handbag along the river, whenever there was anyone to see. In my early arctic years I didn't carry a handbag, but I had grown into it with children. Up under the canoe's bow beside the handbag we always carried wads of birchbark for fires. Matches were carried on our persons at all times in individual waterproof containers, while the reserve supply of matches was in a wide-mouth glass bottle with a screw lid, some-place in the wooden grub box with the skillet and pots and pans and the teakettle.

As the waves rose, each wave smacked briskly when the bow caromed down upon it. I waved to Jean to go quartering across each roller, avoiding much of the chop. We started a slow, lateral traverse across the river as it turned. Soon Jean and Ann, behind me, became drenched with icy spray; but I was warm and dry in the overhung bow, although uneasy.

"*Mother*," the kids shouted, "you picked the best place for yourself in the bow. Let's get ashore. It's raining."

So it was. Gray skies closed down and turned to sheets of sudden summer rain that drummed on our nylon parkas, the rivulets running down our faces. The raindrops bombarded our eyes like pellets, blotting out the shores, making it impossible to see.

I wasn't used to these sudden squalls without warning. Beyond the Circle you don't have heavy rains or thunderstorms. The rain only mists softly. Here these treacherous heavy blasts could knock the unwary boatman or the camper off his pins. I began to realize that this summer we would probably not be able to avoid numerous complete drenchings. But the climate was relatively warm.

Miles slid by as we tried to get ashore. Finally, we chanced a landing along an endless mud flat. I gave a wild leap from the bow. I was wearing low shoes on the theory that it was better to be wet and bug-bitten about the ankles than to drown in rubber hip boots (a theory I still subscribe to). As I leaped onto the mud flat I felt myself go down, down into thick, gluey mud, with the already-rusty boat chain gripped in my chapped red hands. In a split instant I lunged for a long, limber willow and I caught hold of it and knew everything was all right, although of course muddy.

Willows are lifesaving things. They never break, not green willows. They are your guide ropes ashore. The most arctic form of vegetation known, they would possibly exist even at the North Pole were there not ocean at that spot. Often they can be friends, although farther north they get so stunted that they barely pop their faces aboveground, and are termed creeping ground willows.

With a death grip on rusty boat chain and limber willow limb, I hauled myself shoreward, and the children, hopping lightly off the boat like corks, immediately surprised themselves by sinking down like gunned battleships nearby, and like me became immobilized.

The three of us were floundering in mud, nearly helpless, on the long willow-grown mud flat. But as I reminded myself, we must be grateful for any terra firma, even though not firma.

I once wrote a review on request for the *Saturday Review* in which I had rebuked an author for doing a book about a river that he had not taken the trouble to go boating on. The author only saw his river from the air, and had flown to and from a few spots along it, asking the natives questions of course. That author had no sincerity. He simply dashed off his river book the cheapest and quickest way to his editor's desk. I stated severely that the author had no right to the river until he actually lived in a tent along its shores, lived with its moods, traveled upon its waters, and better still fell into it and tasted it.

Here on this mud flat I was suddenly eating my own words.

Extracting our feet from sucking depths was to become a major maneuver of the summer's travels. Everything we did in making camp that night was done in the slow motion of relentless adhesion. Yet we managed to roast a chicken over a wood fire on this mud flat, as the canoe sawed and heaved uncertainly at her anchorage. We ate greasy, rained-on, scorched, half-raw chicken without salt, because, it goes without saying, you never get to the salt the whole voyage long — and it was good.

"We can't stay here, Mom" Jean said. "Night will come on, and this beach is caving, and it's exposed to the wind."

"Quite true," the other two expedition members agreed.

We were forced to voyage onward, through more sheets of rain. Through the whiteness of sky and river we spied the gleam of a silver roof from afar. It seemed to grow in size. And at last it turned out to be only another little rodent-proof, tin grain storage bin, alone in a field of yellow rapeseed in flower, adjoining a field of blue vernal alfalfa, which in turn adjoined a field of lake-blue flax. Here again we hauled ashore, grabbing at long, limber willows that grew resiliently out of the receding flood. We had been guided to land here by that glimmering beacon of silver roof in the rain, and by a vision which slowly became a giant, gaunt, bleached drift log lying stark out upon the riverbank. Something solid to tie to there, we thought. You can't just tie to limber little willows, can you?

Wet, swollen shoes pulled off our feet in the sucking mud, and here it was that I lost my shoe, lost it forever. Although I reached down, down into the very spot where I extracted my foot, down into the cold, primordial ooze of creation's dawn, the depths closed over the shoe, and it was gone. I was now rendered barefooted on one foot, for the heavy rubber boots in the canoe were useless as were the beaded moosehide moccasins bought at Peace River town. You could easily run a sharp stick through a bare foot on a mud flat like this. "Four hundred miles to go to Fort Vermilion with one bare foot," I thought, "silly girl."

And the big stranded drift log was too huge to tie to, what with our skimpy chains. It was as big as a house. How could the canoe be tied? The whole thing was ridiculous. I started to laugh, standing there in the mud. How useless the day of labors at the town Laundromat had been!

When Jean asked caustically why I was laughing I sailed off into guffaws again, and twelve-year-old Ann said reprovingly, "Mother, for heaven's sake, grow up. Why do you act so young out here?"

"This country makes you act young. Or you're done for." I stopped laughing.

"Hey, Ann," guffawed Jean. "We don't have to worry about anchoring the boat tonight. We can just tie it to Mother. She's anchored."

When Jean mentioned the phrase, "anchor the boat," it came to me then how we would tie it. I would have Jean fasten the boat chains — she was the strongest — onto small logs or sticks for toggles. Then we would have to bury these toggles shoulder-deep at cross angles to the canoe's berth along the mud flat. That's the way we used to tie our boat north of the trees where there was nothing to tie to and where you had to carry your own toggles along in the boat.

Eventually we struggled up the incline to the edge of the field of yellow rape, but then of course came the problem: how could we carry the tent and supplies up here through this terrible soft goop?

To my surprise it was Ann who took charge. Jean was nearly paralyzed from hours at the motor and found herself pushed down the command scale before she knew it. Ann said in a now-hear-this voice:

"Shut up. Everybody listen to me. What we have to do is make *steps* out of this driftwood. We'll make a human chain and pass the sticks down from the bank until we have built stairs right to the canoe. Then we can just carry our junk right up the stairs."

It was mostly Ann's dynamic skinny energy which enabled us to do this; and all the time she kept whip-lashing us with her most flexible and caustic tongue.

Here was a treasury of stranded, bleached driftwood stacked in windrows all along the shore, a lot of it real collectors' items. The wood came in smooth, wonderfully convenient lengths and shapes — everything from baseball-bat size to railroad-tie size. It was relatively lightweight stuff, mostly, for it had been leached of its sap and finely turned on the lathe of the sand that ground it in the river waters.

While some sticks lay partly buried and could not be extricated, and some were soggy with water, there were untold tons lying along the tops of the drift piles that were fairly dry. I noted greedily that there were many plump, neatly turned pieces ten inches long which were exactly firebox size for the camp stove. Squaw wood.

Anything is squaw wood that you don't have to chop. It travels down the great northern rivers and lies waiting on polar beaches for the women and children to pick up in their long caribou skirts. Children in caribou dresses, resourceful, muddy, hearty, dirty children, used to feel the pleasant wood in their fingertips as they hunted and roamed with their families throughout the long history of the northern races.

Plop, smash, chuck! went the sticks, as each one thudded into its place, and we struggled to build our stairs down the riverbank, to Ann's domineering, shrill heave-ho. Railroad-tie sizes and knots and stumps, and curls of an artistry that only sand and water can carve, went to build our stairs. The long day was ending again. Our day on the river may have been twelve or more hours long. Time, in the usual sense, was meaningless. There was only us and the broad river, in the middle of an adventure that was like a dream.

It was lucky for us that we pitched a very good tent, with care. It went on raining and we were here for three days, perched on a flooring of driftwood laid over soupy mud, while rain rivulets furrowed underneath and the camp sank and sank, and the bank sloughed.

I sat at the stove in the tent, cross-legged and content, watching the muddy bubbles boil in the food bucket. I decided to make cocoa.

Jean was drawing pictures of friendly horses' heads. Ann, from a position of semiencasement in her sleeping bag with her stuffed guinea pig animal beside her, was reading a book entitled *What Every Boy Should Know.*

Occasionally at our camps I read aloud to everybody from such exciting Canadian bulletins as *Northern Welfare Problems.* Actually, the latter was a particularly good book because it included articles by qualified sociologists along with articles and stories written by individual Eskimos themselves, explaining their life and their problems. Some of these Eskimos had been taught to read and write. Reading their stories from the inside of our tent made us understand them better, perhaps, than those who lived all their lives inside snug houses, and who saw the world about them only from windows. You have only to make a tent your home to become quickly Eskimoized.

We were unaware of it at the time, but the twice-monthly *Peace River Gazette,* distributed far up the Mackenzie Highway meanwhile reported the weather, thus:

Heavy rains pounded the North Peace River District over the weekend, bringing thirsty crops the first moisture in nearly four weeks.

Agricultural officials said the rain had perked up drooping crops and made chances of a normal harvest "much more encouraging."

One district farmer summed up the precipitation with: "At least we'll have a crop now."

Officially 1.75 inches of rain fell at Peace River municipal airport during the twenty-four-hour storm. . . . Farmers in Manning and Peace River Districts were happiest to see the rain.

Field Inspector Stu McAlpine said in Manning the crop situation would be "healthy following the storm." He said there was little damage from the heavy winds which accompanied the storm. . . . "The prospects look very encouraging," he said.

Heavy rains in the Hudson Hope and Grande Prairie areas jacked up the water level in the Peace River. It rose nearly six feet Tuesday night, but since dropped back nearly to the pre-storm level. . . . Wind gusts of up to thirty-five miles an hour battered the Manning district. In other parts of the North Peace, district roads became impassible Saturday night, but no accidents were reported. Some rural telephone lines were knocked down.

While we lay encamped we saw our log steps sink and vanish under the eroding riverbank. The canoe was filling with water, but there was nothing we could do about it. We couldn't get to it to snap down its cover properly. Anyway, it held fast for the time being, anchored to its deeply buried toggles. Now our whole banked stairway of logs and sticks came pushing downhill and slowly poured into the canoe. The push was as slow as a snail's pace, to be sure, but inexorable. Straining, the canoe chains grew taut. Here was a pretty pass.

We could have lost our canoe here. But we didn't. Only much later Jean happened to discover that one rib got caved a bit.

My years as a nomad have convinced me that devious nature, who has so many tricks up her sleeves, quite often gives us warning, or at least the grace of another chance. But you must never take your eyes off her. You must accord her due respect.

Our legs were scarred from scrambling through the sharp willows of the mud banks, and Jean had a festering willow cut on the sole of one foot which had little chance to dry out and heal. I thought briefly of the French and Indian Wars of eastern Canada in 1759. We were on our way toward getting a more than merely academic understanding of North American wilderness and history.

In the woods and mud along the river we scratched perpetually at mosquito bites, although we disdained to use the stuffy headnets yet. Probably we could get by without nets and boots this first year, for as we progressed slowly north into the worsening mosquito country — and everyone knows the mosquitoes become worse and thicker in numbers with each mile north you travel — the effect of passing summer was already diminishing their ranks.

At last the sun shone and we went to bail out the boat, with many a glissade through the slime.

There, floating placidly in beautiful festoons in the still water inside the canoe, were the multitudes of the girls' big pink foam-rubber hair curlers. Perhaps for the first time in their adolescent lives, the hair curlers had been abandoned, to go down, if it so happened, with the ship.

"*Mother*," screamed Ann, enraged at the elements. "Oh, my curlers! My curlers!"

"There goes the Screamer again," remarked Jean, whose mop of sticky hair, like mine, was pulled back with an elasticized head-band. Jean commenced gathering up the curlers and bailing with one of the food buckets.

"I am *not a screamer*," screamed Ann. Then abruptly, she got hold of herself and went to work. Her habit of screaming was gone, right at that moment. I christened the spot Point Screamer.

Overhead I noted with a certain contentment that a small flock of arctic terns wheeled and screamed, and scattered, whirling and dipping gracefully, out over the river. It was the southernmost range of the arctic tern in summertime, right at this point.

7

Fergusons' Flats

FAR down the river in the dappling sunlight the binoculars picked out a little boat bucking up the current toward us in silver plunges.

Two men were in the boat. As our two craft met we waved and cut our motor, and they grabbed hold. Then they drifted along with us, circling down the current, and we exchanged information the way strangers meeting in the middle of nowhere are nearly obliged to do.

Close to, I saw that their faces were eager and their eyes seemed bright and greedy-looking, and had a reckless glint.

They were itinerant construction workers, farmhands, and drifters. They looked somehow like Bum Littleton. They could be said to be typical of the population indigenous to this country in the third generation. They looked wild and they were filthy. So were we.

It wasn't like Alaska here. In Alaska a new population having the high American educational level and technical training arrived each year to try their luck. Farming in Alaska, because of unfavorable geography, was nearly nonexistent. But after I left Alaska it had made great technological progress with the help of funds that a rich United States government had poured into it, especially the airfields and military bases, in the years following World War II.

But here — these people had never had the support of a rich government. Three generations ago the people started drifting into the Peace River country on their own, attracted by open land, and they had dug in and had stayed in an almost unchanged condition, living close to the soil indeed. Many born in the Peace River country had never been out of it. Psychologically the clock was turned back fifty years. Some aspects of this state of affairs might be good; but other aspects might be for the worse. At least we, as travelers, would have a chance to see how people behaved and thought according to the codes of fifty years ago.

The men had gained access to the river by truck on one of the few rutted side roads from the Mackenzie Highway to the west of us. They hoped rather futilely to find a clear creek for fishing.

"Quite a lot of driftwood ahead of yez," one said, pointing. "They's a couple farms along the river you'll see. The Fergusons."

"Women are scarce in the North," said the other one, looking at my daughters and me with eyes as wild as a hawk's. "Take care this river. We can't afford to lose what few women we have in this country."

"Where are yez going?" they asked, quite slack-jawed at seeing we were all women. The two boats were revolving backward down the eddies of the river, held together by the bronzed, battered hands of the men.

"The Arctic Ocean," piped Ann.

We left them astonished, watching us with their bright, greedy eyes. I was not aware of it at the time, but one of them turned to the other and said, "It will be a nice trip for them — if they make it." I later heard about that remark a few hundred miles to the north.

Down around the bend farther we came into driftwood. The men had warned us about it. The wood was sliding along pleasantly down the current, and it seemed harmless.

"Throttle back, keep your power down, Jean." To balance the load better, Ann was riding up front with me, which became, from this point on, our regular traveling procedure.

Curious, we cut close to the big floating trees. We touched them with our paddles and pushed sluggish sticks and pieces of bark and branches out of the way. We got used to the occasional thump of the propeller knocking against smaller pieces, which we couldn't easily see in time. The feeling of the prop thumping and churning against wood gives the boatman a distinct sense of uneasiness. But our motor had the new slip clutch, which disengaged upon impact, so that we broke no shear pins. Sometimes the motor would jump up in Jean's hands, but instantly it would readjust itself and go on churning away with no fuss. Occasionally the prop became entangled with chewed-up sticks and floating sides of bark, and the motor stopped. Then Jean had to lift the motor on its hinge, tilting it into the stern where it locked into place with a click. In that position the propeller was clear out of the water where Jean could reach it. Then, leaning out over the water, she pulled the wood out of the prop with her hands.

Because her life preserver was too bulky to do this work adroitly, Jean shucked it, and thereafter seldom — if ever — wore it. The indigenous population also resisted wearing their life preservers. Near forts one of the duties of the Sunday policeman was to patrol up and down the river in the RCMP boat, checking on people to see that they wore them.

As we threaded our way through the floating drift my glasses scanned each bend of the river ahead.

"The glasses don't help much. It's like pack ice. It all telescopes in the distance. It looks like solid pack, but there may be lanes in between," I mentioned to Ann. She scrambled nimbly up to take a look for herself.

"What do you think?" I handed the glasses over to her.

"Well, if those *finks* made it *upriver* through the wood, we can easily make it *down* the river through the wood," she calculated quickly.

"Watch your language," I said. "And hold onto the glasses tight. Keep the strap around your neck."

Ahead of us, the outside edge of the river's curve was solid with wood. We took the inside. We found a little water, just as we had guessed we might, opening out between the changing lanes of drift. The current was a manageable six miles an hour, no problem. Silently the wood converged, filling the whole great river with its floating mass. Small birds, and sometimes mice, rode on it. The birds would flit off at our approach, reluctantly leaving their tidbits of bark beetles.

The tens of thousands of tons of wood were fascinating to travel along with, a silent, ghostly company. But we must hurry to pass through nimbly. We must never forget that this company was a treacherously dangerous force of nature. "We'd better get out of the river at Fergusons'," I thought.

Finally we came to the little farm at the edge of the river. To be sure, we didn't see the farmhouse at first. I smelled woodsmoke, and then, I swear it, I was certain that I smelled fresh baking bread. Some eddy in the clear northern air brought the smells from far off. After that we saw a glint or movement, and the glasses came to focus upon an enormous family laundry hanging out to dry on the distant shore and all but dwarfing a small house and barn.

The glasses swung and we saw boats tied at a landing which was cut down the bluff in such a way that it slanted with the current and afforded protection for boats and a homemade barge.

We headed quickly in, so as not to be swept by in the driftwood. We hooked our canoe onto their barge chain with the other boats there and, barefooted, commenced to climb the short, steep, bull-dozed road from the river up to the farmhouse.

The little frame house was set in a clipped lawn of such a brilliant green, such a rich, burgeoning, emerald hue, highlighted by beds of brilliant flowers, that you nearly had to squint your eyes when the sun came streaming out. There was such a loveliness to the sky, such a watery green mistiness to the surrounding forest, at the very moment of the full flush of summer, that you were struck with a sudden insight and knew with all your senses what all our continent used to be like before modern farming methods came to provide us with mass-produced food, but alas, not necessarily with beauty or joy.

You breathed in the stillness and remoteness of the young continent here. You sensed the great diversity of nature all about, encompassing the small wilderness farm in a harmony that seemed to hum.

Beside the house a large vegetable garden throve, filled with rows of potato plants, young corn, cabbages, beets, onions and carrots. Ringed by the forest, a few milk cows grazed and tinkled their bells. Wild strawberries grew underfoot. Chickens roamed free in the yard, scratching for bugs.

"Liberty for chickens," Jean commented, in taciturn approval, as we stopped at the top of the climb.

As we paused and glanced back at the great river out of which we had come, then turned our heads to the small house, the grazing cows, the cackling chickens, the barns, the toolsheds — a golden shaft of sunlight fingered through the mounting thunderheads which had silently marshaled themselves above, and the tiny farm seemed consumed in a burst of glory. You get these moments of strange glory in the wilderness.

In the same golden shaft you saw the children's toys before the door, and beside the house the old gasoline washing machine, at this moment turned to gold; and in a partly tilled field yonder a small red tractor, dropped there like a child's toy because the man had gone hunting. You knew they used kerosene lamps inside. They would have linoleum on the floor, and storm windows, and they would have a flowered oilcloth on the big round kitchen table, just like a memory of your childhood if you are one of those who can remember. Or if you can't remember, you have seen it somewhere in books: our history, the place where we stood just the day before, only yesterday.

And the golden shaft of sunlight chose exactly this moment to poke through a suddenly towering thunderhead, illuminating all in the most minute detail. The birds in the forest were still now, and even the farm animals listened, and all nature was listening intently in the complete stillness, just as though we had stepped through time to some place that we have been before, for us to knock on the door.

Only the mosquitoes reminded us that this green wilderness was real. The swarms which had met us at the river margin had caught up with our strides. They could be heard tapping and spattering against the tight nylon weave of our parkas. We swatted at sweaty faces, which erupted into burning welts in thirty places.

Sally Ferguson popped from the door before we reached it, with two toddlers at her heels. She was dressed in trousers and jacket and was wearing those large pink curlers on her head with which we are apt to be met anywhere on earth these days by our surprised hostess.

"Well, hello, there!" she said. "I was just going to hang out another load . . . ." She referred to the laundry. "Are you on the river? My husband has gone hunting, and the rest of them. But they'll soon be back."

Fresh-faced, slim, active, incredibly strong: the proprietor of the sturdy vegetables looked as self-respecting as our great-aunt Abigail looked when she too bustled about her kitchen garden, her clipped lawn, and her flowerbeds. Nothing surprised her. Cautiously friendly, she didn't particularly want or need company.

"I'll tell her I am from Alaska," I thought quickly, and did so, standing on one foot and scratching my opposite itching ankle. She seemed to receive the information of my own pioneer background in a good light, and gave us permission to erect our tent on the green.

"I'll help you carry up your equipment," she said in her clear, English-sounding voice.

"Are you out of meat?" I asked at once. "You can have some from us if you like, from Peace River town."

"It's the first time we've been short this summer," she admitted. "We're not getting much out of the ground yet; too early. Well, if you have plenty. I'm sure we'll get something soon. Please don't put yourselves out."

"On the contrary. Why don't you have dinner with us in the tent?"

She was intrigued by the invitation. Their people amounted to her husband, his brother and the brother's wife, Grandfather Ferguson, and the two babies.

In tent entertaining, people often bring their own dish, spoon, and pocketknife.

"Kids," I urged, "let's get the tent pitched fast. It's going to rain. I'm going down to the boat and dig out my old sealskin boots. I wonder if they'll hold up after ten years' storage."

We unloaded on the firm ground, and buttoned up the boat. I

brought the boots up and was pleased to see that they were softening just by being in the moist northern climate. For the time being
I hung them over the tent ropes, as the Eskimos do, tied together
by their sealskin laces. When the hunters returned they found a
strange tent in their front yard, there was smoke pouring out of the
little stovepipe, and supper was ready. They crept in and were
seated packed together cross-legged on the floor, a position in
which I had not entertained the local residents for some time.

Ann liked being a tent hostess. Jean, of course, possessed all the
normal attributes of a growing boy.

"We've got to watch out all the time," explained Jean to the
company at large. "You see, some men helped us break camp at
Peace River town and nothing has been the same since. They ruined our tent poles. They bent the little metal pegs and sockets out
of position, so now we have to watch out all the time that the
whole tent doesn't fall down on us."

Everybody laughed agreeably. Of course we also had the stove
which was our legacy from Bum Littleton. It kept routinely coming
apart at the joint where the pipe was attached, because it had no
proper lip to hold it. Our camp was all right only so long as there
wasn't a strong wind, and so long as everybody watched what he
was doing carefully. But the fall winds started early in those latitudes to which we were going.

The Ferguson clan were quiet as Eskimos, or Indians. None of
them said much. Even the children were quiet. There was something about the stillness and emptiness of the country that made
people have a stillness about them. On the contrary, modern
Americans have the world's noisiest culture.

"But I too am an American," said the other young woman, in a
low musical voice. Her glowing giant of a Canadian husband, as
handsome as any matinee idol, had made a visit to Los Angeles
only the summer before, and within six weeks had made his selec-
tion of a wife from the Los Angeles population.

The farm here was practically inaccessible. The clan liked it that
way. The farm lay all by itself on the east shore, the side where the
highway wasn't. Years ago the east shore had been closed by a
wisely conservative Provincial government which held the wilder-

ness in trust for the future. But because sternly chiseled Grandfather Ferguson had homesteaded here and obtained the parcel before the Homestead Laws were repealed, the young clan of our day had their side of the river as a wilderness paradise all to themselves, with no danger of neighbors moving in. They had, roughly, three thousand square miles of little-disturbed woods and swamps, rivers and lakes of North America, stretching toward the distant Atlantic, and perhaps fifteen hundred miles of the same unfenced America stretching north to the polar shores, to give them a feeling of elbow room — as had all of the people we would meet from here on.

Most Peace River pioneers didn't think of their geography this way. But perhaps the Fergusons did, for as the grandfather told me the next day, when winter came he departed from the young people, leaving them here, and flew to a remote and exotic property in South America in which he had become interested in his later years.

It wasn't all milk and honey even for today's generation in the Peace River country, what with the long, cold winters. All the possessions of the Fergusons had to be brought across the river. Their tractor, the washing machine, their beds and furniture; in fact even the lumber with which they built, every pot and pan they cooked with, the iron stove, and the cows and the bull, had all crossed on the flimsy barge by summer, or on winter's ice and snow. Everything came through distant North Star, a bare crossroads settlement on the Mackenzie Highway, to which their swampy wilderness road connected from the river's opposite shore.

To the Fergusons the driftwood brought a welcome harvest. In the morning sunlight I saw Grandfather sitting serenely on a bench that overlooked the river, watching with binoculars by the hour. Every time something good came by, the Fergusons were ready with powered boats to dash out and get it. The treasure might be wild logs, lumber, barrels, containers, or any other useful thing that got away from civilization upriver. While we visited there, two fifty-gallon drums of gasoline were captured. And imagine our excitement when the bridge from Pouce Coupé came floating down on the current! But it was too big for us to try to hold.

"Perhaps the Gatewoods down below will get it," was the opinion.

"Who are your neighbors down the river?" I asked instantly, "and how far?"

We had just breakfasted in the house on pancakes, homemade sugar syrup, fresh milk, and slabs of rich, succulent deer meat from the night before. Now we were taking down our tent.

"Only the Gatewoods, ten miles. On the opposite shore."

"All older people like Mother?" inquired Ann. No one answered her.

"Do you know anything about the river beyond that?" I persevered.

"That's as far as we've been. You might ask the Gatewoods."

That day we had lunch with the Gatewoods, who lived amid a cluster of red-painted farm buildings and trucks and cars with broken windshields, at their own road terminus. We just neatly escaped a cloudburst during the hour we were sheltered there. Lunch was eggs, tea, fresh bread, and canned meat lightly fried.

At this point the river and the highway, which had been from eighteen to thirty miles apart, departed from each other entirely and went their separate ways, leaving the river remote and unsettled. Gray wooded soils predominated from here on; the subsoils of this region, according to our literature, were tough impervious clays. Although the black soils of the upper Peace were judged quite fertile and of good structure, even they required that grasses and legumes be rotated with cereal grains, to maintain and improve the soils and to control water erosion. The gray wooded soils of lower inherent fertility needed a permanent management program, started as soon as the ground was broken. They required forage or soil-building crops 50 percent of the time. No one would be able to undertake farming here on less than a half section; and more land would be preferable, said the manual which I perused.

I interrupted my reading in the bow to wave Jean to cut the motor. Unsnapping the locks on the attaché case behind me, I replaced the bulletin and slipped the attaché case under canvas again, while we drifted, free of mosquitoes.

Now, a bulletin from the Alberta Travel Bureau:

" . . . after passing the mouths of the Cadotte and Whitemud Rivers . . . the valley widens and there are sizeable river flats that are developed into farms. For many years these hardy settlers used river transport as the only connection to Peace River Town but they now have a motor road to North Star and Manning on the Mackenzie Highway."

I read on: "After passing Fergusons' Flats there is no settlement and only the odd trapper's headquarters cabin along the river until the old trading post of Carcajou is reached. A trading post is still in operation there and there is a trail west to the Hudson's Bay Post and Métis Colony at Keg River on the Highway, but there is very little summer travel over this, and Carcajou has lost much of its former importance as a trappers' summer headquarters and trading post . . . there are many small islands . . . with colorful herbaceous growth," the bulletin commented ". . . stocked with spruce and balm of gilead" (what we called poplar trees, I guessed) "and numerous sandbars subject to high water flooding on which red willow struggles to maintain a footing against the fluctuating water levels . . . The water channel crosses from side to side, as deflected by bends and islands, and subject to yearly change . . . And do look for the odd tiny trapper's cabin," I read. "Trapper's Cabin, usually vacant at this season but interesting to explore to show the ingenuity of the woodsman in his substitutes for the common household equipment, his vacuum washer being an inverted jam can with wooden plunger handles; wooden hinges on the cabin door; rodent-proof larder; and elevated meat cache are only a few of his many substitutes for modern appliances."

"You kids ever known any trappers?" I turned around in the canoe and asked them. They looked at me seriously.

"It says you can only see the trapper's cabin," advised Jean skeptically. "It seems to say that the trappers vanished years ago. That government bulletin was printed before I was born. Do trappers still trap?"

"It's trapping country," I explained. "I think we can not only find the cabin, but the trapper himself."

"Oh, boy!" said Jean.

"Young or old?" asked Ann.

"How should I know? But trappers are usually fine people, if you can find them. We may be dinner guests of a trapper today or tomorrow, for all you know."

It was with this anticipation that we rode the sweep of the river to a tiny boat landing, almost hidden among the trees. In fact, we had to look sharp and gun the motor fast to catch the landing when we spotted it.

The clink of our rusty boat chains resounded above the rushing sounds of the river as Jean snapped onto the chains of a larger, tethered boat. Off went our cumbersome life preservers: and, wiping rust-stained filthy hands upon our trousers, we stepped stiffly over the side into the big plank scow tied there with seventy feet of line that disappeared into the trees. The current was deep and fast under the scow. One by one, teetering, we catwalked from the high, wooden bow up over the rushing river on a very narrow plank — not more than nine inches wide. It had cross boards nailed on it for notches and it sagged beneath our steps. The long, limber plank bridge ended at the top of a thirty-foot embankment; it enabled the resident here to adjust to fluctuating water levels and avoid the flood. From the top of the embankment a narrow, hard-beaten footpath plunged into what the bulletin called the herbaceous growth. As we followed it we heard chained huskies back in the woods set up a wild commotion; and suddenly we saw the tiny log cabin and its inhabitant.

Yes, there he was, a lean, slight, aging figure, in faded blue shirt-sleeves and suspenders, with faded blue eyes and graying beard stubble, the trapper caught unposed and casual, in his natural habitat. Standing there in the middle of piles of tin cans and bottles, he looked at us.

Chopped-off tree stumps ringed his cabin all the way around, and the cabin was exactly in the middle of the stumps. In the tall rank grass of the small clearing multitudes of animal bones festered underfoot, having been tossed out of the cabin door from many a feast and skinning session.

The resident stood there, looking surprised.

"There he is, girls!"

"I don't have on my glasses," wailed Jean, in a voice filled with woe.

"Right *there*," hissed Ann. "Standing in a dump of trash."

"What's he doing there?" Jean's voice sounded shocked and confused.

"I don't know," said Ann. "There's a lot of bottles everywhere. I think he's boozing it up."

"Hello, there," I called out, walking cheerily up to the man. "I'm Connie Helmericks and these are my daughters Jean and Ann. We are making a boat trip on the river. What's your name?"

He mumbled his name, saying. "Well, I was just thinking, I was just thinking I heard some noise, some people or something, on the river. I was just thinking I might go and see. So here you are. All ladies? All alone?"

"Yes, all ladies. Going to the Arctic Ocean, a two years' voyage. We're Americans."

"Yes, well, aren't you now," he replied. "Not many people stops here."

"We're Americans," Jean rallied, "but we're almost like Canadians because my mother used to be a trapper in Alaska."

"Alaska?" the resident mumbled. "Always wanted to get over to Alaska, like."

"Like cool," added Ann helpfully.

"Do you think we talk like Americans?" pressed Jean.

"Heh, heh," chuckled the resident, "I don't talk to many people of any kind. But I would say that you have very little accent, like, for an American, you know."

"What did you say?" said Jean.

"I said, you have but very little accent for an American," he wanly complimented her. "They are said to have terrible accents. Come inside, ladies. I'll get the stove started and make dinner."

We filed with difficulty into the gloomy, cluttered little hut, stooping to enter the tiny door and stepping up over its high sill. A smell of sour, stale liquor suffused the place. There were two tiny homemade stools. Some of us could sit on the bunk bed. To make room, the trapper removed the draped filthy mosquito netting from it. He was very nervous about having company. He was shaking.

"Oh, Mom!" cried Ann spontaneously. "Did you notice that he's got grass and flowers growing on the roof?"

"The flowers just grow up," he explained. "Wild roses and fireweeds. They spring up all over where the sod is disturbed."

"It's so tiny I can stand and touch the roof," said Ann.

"I've lived in little houses much like yours," I told the resident. "In Alaska."

"Oh, yes, up in Alaska," he croaked thickly, as he fumbled, shaking, to light a fire in the old, greasy cast-iron stove. Ann and I were examining the homemade table as our eyes became accustomed to the darkness. We saw that the single tiny smudged pane of a window had been sealed in with putty after the window opening had been framed in willows cut with a pocketknife. We saw corroded tin plates set in a rickety cupboard and an old iron skillet filled with cold fish from some leftover meal. Our eyes met. Plainly, Ann was wondering what dinner would be like.

"Mother, I've been thinking. As I grow older I have been wondering what to choose for a career. Do you know what I think I would like to specialize in? I can see how people really need it."

"Tenting, or trapping?" I asked.

"No, silly. Can't you see the need for it everywhere? *Interior decoration.* Or maybe I would become a great forest ranger," she added as an afterthought.

Like Jean, she had internal struggles to form her system of values. "You don't have to choose right away," I said. "You and your sister have plenty of time yet. "Please," I halted the shaky resident in his frenzied preparations at this point. "It's good traveling weather, and we had better travel. Where did Jean go to?"

"How about coffee?" croaked the trapper.

"Thank you, but no. Jean, *Jean!* Those idiot children . . ." I was falling into my country's timeworn phrases, when a premonition of danger erupted suddenly into conscious alarm bells.

Not stopping for formalities I bolted out of the little door just as the uproar of wild huskies burst upon our eardrums. From the sounds, I wondered as I ran if my darling eldest were already chewed into mincemeat. Both girls had been warned not to walk up within reach of chained sled dogs. Every year in the northern world several people, especially children, are torn apart by these dogs.

We found Jean standing there, shocked, just at chain's length, while the objects of her affection leaped crazily at her, their fangs displayed.

Each husky was chained to its own little log house. Each was underfed, bored to distraction in the idle summer season, its fur and eyes and nose crawling with insects; and each was understandably wild with jealousy over any attention paid to any of its teammates.

At the girl's approach each dog, sleeping upon the roof of its little house to avoid the wetness of its own filth, had set up a melee of barking and insane screaming which could be heard for miles. I pulled Jean back.

"It's no use," I urged her, jarred myself by a sight I hadn't seen in a long time. "They're all crazy. They're not like the dogs you know. I've tried to tell you. These dogs go insane on those chains winter and summer, and that's the way it often is with work dogs in the North.

"When a dog gets too old to work, and a dog's life here is less than six years, the trapper probably chops it up and feeds it to the other dogs."

"They're born wild," smiled the trapper indulgently. "You can't never trust them. You have to keep back. Only the owner can handle them."

It was no use to try to tell him that the dogs were not born wild and crazy, and that it was simply circumstances that made them that way, just as men in prisons became crazed, or in great stone cities of packed humanity or on slave ships or in chain gangs, when they are denied the normal freedoms and affections.

"You see that man?" I told the girls, after we pushed off down the river. "That man, too, is in a bad predicament. He's suffering from malnutrition. He may die here alone, or have an accident alone any time."

You don't necessarily have to suffer from malnutrition in the woods, I used to say.

I lived once for a year two thousand miles north of here on just meat, even without salt. We were young explorers. It can be done, but not the way most trappers live. Few would be wise to try today, for our big game has been largely destroyed, and it takes a lot of big game.

The man we had visited was probably living largely on home brew, and had lost all interest in food. When that happens in the woods, the person is doomed.

What kind of furs did he trap? Fox, squirrel, beaver, rats — meaning muskrats — principally. Lynx in good years. A few ermine. Marten if he was real lucky. Probably his income did not exceed four hundred dollars a year, and that's extreme poverty by the standards of today. Only yesterday this scene was fairly typical and was perhaps considered to be the normal risk and hardship of life everywhere.

We had left a few cans of food for him, including some juices which would supply Vitamin C. The difficulty was always in extracting anything out of the boat and getting it ashore.

"Well," I said, as we floated moodily down the current. "So much for the resident in *that* bunch of herbaceous growth. I guess that's that."

Jean bent over her motor, her face set and stricken. Cynical, pseudo-worldly little Ann — how on earth did she pick up some of the weird bits and scraps of knowledge that she possessed? — settled herself on top of the load, where she made a little indentation or nest, with her stuffed Piggie.

I know how they feel, I thought. Disillusioned again. At least, at moments I know how they feel. All my life I have felt these swift, sickening stabs of grief about things. An unbelieving, suffocating disappointment in people. A terrible disappointment with the way the world was going, and particularly with the way my life was going, some days.

Of course, dear children, you were looking for your father, or something very good and wonderful in the forest. But you did not find him.

Here you are now, twelve and a half and overweight confused fourteen, and you teeter on the brink of adulthood, achingly. Life is always harsh, whatever age you are born in; and this is the age of the absent father. In your teens you can turn to the beaches, the ski slopes, the fast cars and fast beat, to ease your unease in the new world, and sometimes it can be a pretty good world after all. Maybe you'll be ambitionless, aimless, and unmotivated. Maybe you'll defend yourself with a loud voice against life, like Ann, or maybe you'll be taciturn like Jean, clutching your disappointment to your heart as though it were some rare treasure — as perhaps, in adolescence, it is. But at least you have a better chance than that old man over there on the shore. Think of that.

A sigh came over the water, and we felt ourselves slowly relax. Now enveloped and swallowed up by the river and sky, we drifted. Like a dot we drifted for a while, growing lean spiritually in the wonderful limbo of nothingness. I waited. Something good was going to happen after this. Some revelation in nature. It simply had to.

8

The Troubled Spring of
Hjalmur Feeshbeidt

EVENTUALLY we came around another bend, through a rising river full of driftwood, and into sight of the log cabin of Hjalmur Feeshbeidt.

Built of logs peeled of their bark, the weathered cabin sat cradled gratefully in the arms of the gentle forest. Here at this bend of the river Hjalmur Feeshbeidt had lived for thirty-three years. Spring birds sang sweetly, and the winter snows came and went; at intervals the river overran its banks, and wolverine tracks appeared about the door. And the lonely Norwegian trapper, who had come as a young man, grew old.

He had meant to go back once. Back to what? Back to where? Maybe he did go back; maybe he tried to make a go of it in civilization. Then that cooped-up feeling got him, the restlessness in a man's stomach when he has got used to a wider country and freer ways.

The years went by before he knew it. Perhaps, watching the seasons come and go, he simply forgot other things. That can happen in the North. The seasons conspire to take up a man's whole attention out here under the sky. What you can't get done this summer, you plan to do the next. There is always next year. You keep watching the enchanted damnable river — which some men call Yukon and others call the Peace — in front of your cabin door.

Few venture into this beautiful land to live; so to these few men really belong the fresh lakes, the inland waterways, mountain ranges, and game herds — this fantastic wealth of great, fragrant space.

This arctic frontier of the world, six times larger than the American West ever was, will never be tamed by the plow. Down north no plow has cut the earth since time began. Oh, to hunt and loaf in these timeless solitary latitudes, to dream the prodigal dreams of those who are not bound by other men!

"Aha!" I was saying to the girls as we drifted toward the strange, well-built log home. "Here is a place to stop. We must put in before the driftwood scours the river out of its channel, and us with it."

"We don't want to stop at any more people's houses," the crew objected.

"We're going to," I said. "The mud is so awful we're going to have to use people's landings in order to get off the river to camp. Maybe all summer."

We put in at an ancient boat landing at the lip of a steep, grassy embankment and clearing. Here someone had leveled the coarse wild grass with a scythe. Also leveled were the tall weeds and willow, large ugly heaps of which adorned the clearing around the house. The sharp stubble could pierce our bare feet. Unsnapping our life preservers as soon as the canoe docked, we slid into our rubber boots. Then we saw the man. He was standing so still he could hardly be seen, watching us, right outside his cabin door. Why didn't he come forward with northern hospitality and help us tie the boat? Why didn't he come out?

We could see a kind of red shirt, really a wine color. We could see the gaze of direct blue eyes. Only one man stood over there, all alone, silent and stooped. There was, strangely, no path down to the river. The white chips and stumps of three large, newly felled poplars glared at us. Clambering around the felled trees and the big brush piles we came up, and were met near the door.

"I am Hjalmur Feeshbeidt. I am very glad to see you, to see some people come along here," said the white-haired resident, in a gentle Norwegian accent. "I am not speak English good," he explained. "But my goodness, I am surprise to see people coming downriver, in boat. I don't see many people here, ha, ha."

"I like animals better than people, myself," said Jean flatly. The white-haired old trapper looked at her in surprise. Jean and Ann were staring at him, evaluating him with the merciless eyes of the very young. His kindly, surprised gaze seemed suddenly to sag. To my distress, I realized that tears were very near the surface.

"Come. Come into house," he said gruffly, turning, motioning to us to follow him.

The old Norwegian face with the direct blue eyes and grizzled hair was a face an artist or a sculptor would have liked. It was a face you would instinctively trust. Seamed from weather and age, the expression proud yet gentle, the anger behind the eyes honest — it was a face you would not be apt to see among the hurrying crowds of large cities. "But he looks so frail," I thought. And then we realized he was leaning heavily on a cane, panting.

We followed the limping man into the house. "Did you hurt your leg?" asked Ann.

'No, no. Not leg," he reassured us. "Only, he no walk very good. Heh, heh. I got this trouble in spring beaver trapping, much better now. Oh, my, that was bad time this spring. Bad time," he told us. "I got my left arm much trouble same time."

"When did it happen? What happened? Have any people come along to help you?"

"Please. Sit down," he said, as we found homemade stools. "I make coffee. You eat."

Whatever had happened, it began in March, we learned. We had to imagine snow deep on the ground in March. The trees were bare and wind-blasted along the banks of the ice-jammed Peace River. The cold was intense.

It was the month to leave the headquarters cabin, this big, well-built house we were sitting in, and go for beaver. It was twenty miles to the unnamed frozen little lake he tried to describe with inadequate words, where the beaver were, back inland.

"Oh, I have five cabin," he told us proudly. "Trapper need have cabin stocked with stove, with food, other places, you know." We nodded.

"Look, Ann," said Jean, "this cabin we're in is just his headquarters cabin. He goes around to his other cabins at different times of the year."

"Probably very inaccessible," Ann added thoughtfully.

"Only yourself? Haven't you got a partner?" we asked.

"No, heh, heh, I don't want no partner. Besides, who want to be partner with old man like me, heh?" he retorted. "I always trap alone."

"It's not good to be entirely alone," opined Jean, in an unexpected reversal of her usual philosophy. "Don't you even have dogs to help you?"

"No, no dog. One time I get dog. That fool dog, he got in big bear trap. He seen me bait that trap, but he go back right into it, broke the leg. I come many miles for to shoot my poor dog. I never get dog again. Dog much trouble for to feed the dog. Dogfighting, too. I never more get the dog, I take pack board on the back."

"That's a lot of stuff to carry on just your back. Traps are heavy," I said. "And I don't see how you could ever build all those cabins with just your *back!* It makes my neck ache just to think of it."

"My mother has a bad neck and back. Do you?" asked Ann, with some sympathetic insight.

"Well, you were telling us," said Jean, "you walked twenty miles to your other cabin on the beaver lake . . ."

"Oh, yes. It getting late spring, I got beaver. I living at that little cabin dere. Not so good cabin as this one. I got no supplies there that time. I was just going to bring some food, and roof start what you call, snow is water, coming down?"

"Was the roof leaking from the snow on top?"

"Yes, that it. Leaking. Water coming down from roof and I trying to sleep in my sleeping bag in that bunk bed, that place. Then I notice them beaver they make more, very *big* dam this spring in that lake. That lake is flooding near my cabin, and I think maybe in spring breakup is going to flood over my little cabin from that lake water."

He paused to pour scalding coffee into tin cups. We shivered expectantly. In my mind's eye I began to see a picture of the spring breakup and the little cabin standing in low, marshy land with water perhaps for miles all around, as the ice melted.

"Oh, yes. I sleep there, and next morning I wake up, I almost finish with beaver late spring, oh, my goodness, I try to move myself, you know, up from the sleeping bag, I try to get up, and I no can get *up!* I just lie there in sleeping bag, I cannot get *up!*"

The girls and I, listening, felt ourselves prickle with horror. "He couldn't move for some reason. He's telling us he couldn't move!"

"I think he must have had a stroke," said Jean.

"But how did you live? How did you eat? How did you ever get home here to headquarters cabin?" We pressed him, but the story came slowly.

"That was hard time." The old trapper shook his head simply. Finally he went on, with each word dragging out of him.

"Well, you see them beaver dam flooding spring water inside my house, coming higher and higher. They never done that before," he explained.

"Go on," we cried.

"That water inside cabin come up to my bunk bed. My goodness, I lying there many days in sleeping bag. I dying of thirst for water to drink. God was good to me," he said. "That was terrible time, but that water come right to my mouth. After while I able to turn little bit on my side and I *drink water.* I pray. I thank God. After while them water he start to go down again."

"Oh, heavens, you might have drowned there in your bed."

"Oh, I know *that.* Yes, I nearly frozen, too. I think many times I am going to God. But He say to me, 'Hjalmur, I am near you. Hjalmur, keep trying.' That's what He said to me, Hjalmur. I am not a religious man, but this is so, I tell you the truth.

"So, I keep trying to get up, and after while I sitting up, I get stick for cane. Water going away, I make fire in stove. I get warm again. I drink snow water. But I have nothing to eat that place. I think it April now, maybe May."

"Why do you think it was May?"

"I hear geese. But I have nothing to eat. No food, nothing. I drink the water, but I know I have no food, and I am really dying."

"Starving to death!"

"Yes," he said quietly. "I am really starving to death. I am so weak I don't care. I try to eat old head from beaver at my cabin, I try to eat beaver hide, but it no good, my life is lost."

The trapper told us how he lay paralyzed in an arm and both legs as the snow melted from all the land about and the ice shrank from the sides of the unnamed lake until it made one big pan, and finally how winds moved the pan about, shrinking it daily, until it broke at last into little pans which slowly dissolved, while he watched, starving, in the doorway of his flooded shelter.

His paralyzed arm began to come back. Once he got a shot at a coyote from the cabin door. He scored a hit, but it dragged itself away. "I am sure now I am going to starve to death," he repeated.

"What kind of guns do you use?" Jean was pleased to learn that the trapper's choice was the same as ours — his .30–06 and .22 rifle.

"I decide I make raft," he told us then. "When ice gone out of lake, I push myself on that raft. I float around in lake and try to kill ducks, rats, and beaver to eat."

"Did you do it?" Our eyes must have been popping with admiration.

"Oh, yes," he replied simply. "Finally I make raft from my bunk bed. Oh, my goodness. Them was terrible days. But God is with me all the time, I guess. I float around on raft in that lake. I get duck and take them to cabin and I eat, and I am living again!" he cried jubilantly.

I marveled, knowing from experience how nearly impossible it is to hit ducks that are riding on the water, with a rifle.

"After that? You walked back there twenty miles through the wilderness in late May?"

"Oh, yes," he replied. "I have to lay down and take a rest sometime, you know? But I make it home again. I bring ducks."

We looked about the bare cabin. Aside from flour, rice, beans, and coffee, there was nothing to eat, and no signs that the old man had eaten anything for days. He had no fresh meat. No cans of anything were to be seen, since the trapper's life rarely afforded canned food. He had no fishnets and no boat, and apparently did not use the river. God alone knew how he was alive at all.

"Oh, I don't eat much," he reassured us. I could believe it.

"Quick! We'll pitch the tent in his front yard and feed him up," Jean and Ann decided at once.

First, a dab of mosquito repellent all around and then to work. It was curious to us that the old man was not familiar with mosquito repellents. He may have been amazed at the wealth of equipment which our canoe contained. In all his years at this bend of the river, the boats which had stopped here probably numbered on the fingers of one hand.

"Driftwood pretty bad," he advised. "I think best unload your boat safe in little creek by my house."

Jean leaped into the canoe and Ann cautiously shoved the *Jeanie Ann* some two feet offshore with a paddle. Jean pulled the starter rope and commenced motoring carefully up against the sea of driftwood, keeping as close to shore as depth would permit. It was only a few yards up the current to the creek mouth, which was a tangle of vines and foliage.

"Be careful," I wailed involuntarily.

"I am always scared that river," croaked old Hjalmur, hopping about fairly nimbly with his cane along the brink, and among the chopped white tree stumps.

Hjalmur, Ann, and I assembled at the creek. We could see Jean in the canoe pushing aside the creepers and poling into the shallows of the creek mouth. She was just a canoe length out of our reach where we could not help her when a gasp arose from all of us. "Hurry, Jean, hurry!"

Looking up from her task Jean saw bearing down upon her from right around the bend an irresistible raft of wood. Then, with only inches to spare, the canoe slid nimbly into the little creek mouth, where old Hjalmur waited in agitation, leaning upon his cane. The heap of collected wood weighing several tons sheered sharply across the creek mouth where Jean had been a moment before. Carrying vines with it, it bounced off Hjalmur's steep front yard, and went careening on its way downstream.

Very relieved, we tied up the canoe in the hidden creek. That river was no place for a canoe. It looked like we might be here a while.

"I always been scared that damn river," repeated Hjalmur, shaking his fist at it.

"It's like the Los Angeles Freeway," said Ann sensibly. But Hjalmur did not know to what she referred.

During the warm days that we camped in Hjalmur's front yard

above the river, we cooked our most attractive meals for the handi-
capped man; soon his normal appetite picked up, and with the
revival of his health and spirits he told us quite a bit about himself.
We shan't forget the wonderful camp we had at that spot: the tent
pitched snugly in the stubble, the river running driftwood before
the door, and the circling sun pouring down. And one day the
realization came to me, unobtrusively stole into my whole being,
that gone were my accustomed headache and my psychosomatic
pain in the neck. Gone forever, I hoped.

I lay back upon luxurious robes in the tent to write Gerald right
away about everything that was happening.

But dinner was about ready. "Go call Hjalmur from his house,"
I asked Ann. "And ask him please to make one of his wonderful
smudge pots nearby to keep out some of these bugs."

Inside our sunny, breezy tent, living on fresh deer meat from
Fergusons', we watched the river traffic go by. What more could
anyone ask than days like these? With health, and family, and
plenty of stovewood chopped by kindly old Hjalmur? He was an
industrious, energetic type of man who had a compulsion to chop
wood continuously — more wood than even a dozen campers could
use up. It was a type of man I had always admired. But — what
would happen to Hjalmur when we went away and left him?

When Ann had fetched him into the tent and we had eaten our
dinner of deer meat, biscuits, and canned fruit, we got him to talk
more about his life, particularly as I had in mind the hope of ad-
vising him to leave the woods and seek Provincial aid. Although I
was not conversant with the terms of the Alberta aid program, it
seemed fairly certain that the Province had an interest in taking care
of old men like Hjalmur when the time came that they could no
longer take care of themselves. To whom could I report the plight
of Hjalmur? How would he get out of this place, provided I could
talk him into getting out of it? Where to go?

He would have another stroke for sure next winter, and die all
alone in the woods, perhaps a terrible death. I felt a sickening fear
for his sake and a terrible responsibility to do something about it.
But what?

"The most strange thing that happen to me," Hjalmur was telling the kids, "was them snakes come into my house this spring."

"Snakes?"

"Yes, I coming home from beaver lake, I going just to my bunk bed."

Nodding all around. I was thinking. We are hearing at firsthand anecdotes of the incredible hardship and valor which fill in the lives of the few wilderness people who are left in North America today; lives unchanged since the days of Kit Carson or Daniel Boone. You wouldn't believe that you could still find it today in North America — such a way of life. How rare it is now for children to be able to listen at the knee of such a grand old man! Such are the last of their kind. When those old men are gone, there will be no more like them, ever again on the earth.

What was he saying about the snakes? I hadn't imagined that any snakes would live this far north. But a man who spent a whole lifetime in the woods might observe unusual mysteries.

"I laying in my bunk at headquarters cabin right here," he was saying. "Then, be gory, come them snakes! Coming through the chinks of those logs, coming up from floor. I get up and I go outside, looking, and is more snakes, coming down that hill there. You see that hill back my house?"

Carefully he described to us what must have been a veritable avalanche of garter snakes coming out of hibernation from the rocks at the top of the hill and heading for the river. A migration of snakes, thousands of them this particular spring, pouring into the river, the way he described it. The serpentine exodus took a number of days. If some scientist could have been there he might have documented on film a most wonderful sight in nature. That his description was accurate and not fantasy was verified by other people who maintained later that it had been a strong year for snakes.

"I keeping busy carry out the snakes from my house," he laughed gently. "Little snake is same like all of us," he said. "A child of God, only looking for happiness."

"I hate people that kill snakes," Jean said with conviction. "A lot of people aren't fit to live on this earth, because they don't appreciate things."

"Is truth!" exploded Hjalmur, agreeing with her enthusiastically. "Them snakes is not all that happen this spring." His voice dropped almost to a whisper. "Do you know, there is some man in world more low than snake?"

"Who?" asked Jean, in the ghastly silence following the bombshell of his last sentence.

"Jacques Mileaux, that who. Jacques Mileaux and his wicked brother. One them brothers killed a man and the RCMP took him to the prison. Other brother, he was killed himself that trapline next to mine. That trapper honest man killed him when he caught stealing fur from traps of honest man. Now there is Jacques Mileaux and his other brother what has trapline next to mine, they coming, them two, all the time every year trapping my country. I tell them go back where they belong, they laugh at me. They laugh at old man!"

Old Hjalmur had become terribly excited and was trembling with righteous fury as he described Jacques Mileaux and his remaining brother.

"Jacques Mileaux," repeated Jean. "Sounds like a Frenchman. There don't seem to be any French here in this country. We never met any."

"He not French," vehemently exploded old Hjalmur. "He thief, he killer. Oh yes, he got French name, long time ago. But he really Indian. He is breed. Nodding worse than those French Indians," the old Norwegian stormed.

"Do you really think that Jacques Mileaux is robbing your traps? Is he really dangerous to you?" asked Jean. "Why don't you tell the police?"

"What has Jacques Mileaux actually done to you?" I interposed.

"They tricky," the old man told us. "They full a tricks all the time, wanting my furs. I no got much fur. For why do they want him? They kill me if they dare. But I say to them, 'You don't dare kill Hjalmur Feeshbeidt, for they watching you all the time, the police.' I say them, 'Get the hell off trapline of old Norwegian man, you breed sons-a-bitch!' "

Hjalmur had shown us his trapline registration certificate which was nailed on the wall inside his cabin. Although he could not read or write his name, he had legally acquired the rights to trap in a specified area; and this title was officially registered at what would correspond to a county seat — North Star — whence he obtained his grubstake once a year. In Alberta traplines are leased out according to how many men the country can carry on a sustained yield basis without depleting the furs. A trapline became available only when its owner died or moved out. A trapper was not supposed to infringe on his neighbor's territory.

I was wondering where I had first heard about it — perhaps in some long-ago adventure magazine — but the phenomenon of the bad half-breed stealing furs from the good guy's trapline seemed familiar to me, far away in the mysterious North, in country where I had never been before, where the warring inhabitants were always policed by vigilant Mounties wearing red coats. Now here it really was, in a way.

According to old Hjalmur, his French-Cree neighbor trappers were veritably living off him, springing his traps whenever they could, out of gleeful malice, when not actually robbing them of furs. Furthermore, the older man feared they would actually do away with him in some way, if they could contrive a means to get away with it.

As I listened to him, I began to get his point.

The Mounties were far away. Naturally they could not be every place at once. This was a lonely area. Many things can happen to a man living alone. Two of the original four brothers made open sneering threats against Hjalmur's life whenever they crossed his path. What else could an old man conclude, when you considered Hjalmur's position?

"Those brothers, they know I am missing man around here when I gone away more than two months last spring. They not come to beaver lake to look for me! They not help me!" he cried bitterly. "They not tell the police I gone. They not tell nobody come look for me. Aiyi, they hope I am dead!"

"Please," I tried to soothe him. "Please don't get so excited."

"Excited? Excited? Who is excited?" The old man was nearly sobbing. "When I am laying in my bunk bed this spring *right here,* I see many dollars' worth my tools and six hundred rounds my ammunition is gone out the cabin. Yes, stolen! Yes, I know who took them things! I laying there in bunk bed and them two brothers coming along, open the cabin door. They think I am dead in my bed. They take up my big rifle, my .30–06, from peg on wall, they start taking everything out of my house," he sobbed. "*Right when I laying in the bed.*"

"How terrible! How awful!"

"Oh, I jump up out of that bunk bed," he reassured us. "I holler at them brothers. They drop my rifle, they scared, they leave everything. They go away," he ended.

It appeared that the French-Cree Mileaux brothers had indeed robbed the vacant cabin of much of its wealth when Hjalmur had failed to come back from spring beaver camp, and they had been criminally negligent in not lending assistance to the stricken man. Surprised in the very act of their depredations when he reared from his bunk bed from seeming death to swear his vengeance at them, the young brothers had fled the premises, at least for the time being. It seemed plain enough that, like jackals, they now merely bided their time, awaiting the old man's natural demise.

I believed every word that old Hjalmur said. I could see it.

"Now, I am sick man," he told us in a faint tone of dejection. "But I am not really so old. I think I am maybe sixty-two. Something like that. Sixty-two is not so old. Why do I get sick like this? That old man downriver, Mister Nookey, he eighty-four, he not sick like me," he lamented.

"Mr. Nookey? Is he a trapper, too? Where's he?"

"Ai, he stay maybe about thirty-five mile down. He and Mrs. Johansson. They got nice little place, I hear. They tell me some time they got good place. Oh, they coming by here in boat last week going to North Star for get the groceries. They got farm, I hear. They do little trapping too in winter time. Yes, that old man eighty-four, he more strong than me!"

"Well, people are different. Some are more strong than others. You have to consider, Hjalmur, that you cut out fifty miles of trails and built five cabins all alone without a single person to help you. Maybe you worked too hard."

"Yes," he said bitterly. "I always like to work. You know, I enjoy to work hard. I like to build up a good place. I did not know I would hurt myself, heh, heh." His good-natured chuckle was forced from a broken heart, as he tried to appear pleasant.

"I don't know," he sighed. "I cannot keep this place no more. It getting too much for me. See, I get trouble in my legs." He pulled up a trouser leg to show us an arterial system knotted with the blue distended ropes of what appeared to be advanced pheblitis. Any one of those blood clots in the legs breaking loose and carried to heart or brain at any minute could cause death. "But that old man, that Mister Nookey," he wept, "he is so strong, and he is eighty-four."

The bitterness of the comparison between Hjalmur's precarious health and the superlative octogenarian downriver was perhaps even more demoralizing to Hjalmur than all his human and natural enemies. His lips trembled. He had looked death right in the eye, in its most frightful forms, only recently, and the stamp of death was on him.

"Hjalmur," I cleared my throat, "I believe you have got to get out of the woods. You know, you shouldn't be hiking around. You shouldn't even be on your feet. And as for chopping wood, well, that is something you shouldn't do either. In fact, what I'm trying to tell you is that you should leave your home here in the forest. You must get out of here before next winter comes. Do you hear me?"

"I think about that," he answered slowly, and for a moment I thought he was going to agree. Then my heart sank as I knew what he was going to say.

"I cannot leave my home," he said. He seemed paralyzed with fear. He had lived in the woods so long that he was mortally afraid of the world outside, the world which had gone ahead and left him behind during the years he was here.

"Can't you get Mr. Nookey and Mrs. Johansson to take you to North Star? You know people there. You go there to trade."

"I just go once a year," he replied. "I don't know nobody there no more. I got no money for stay in town. I got to stay here because at least I get little fur out here for make money."

"No, you haven't got to stay here. You are disabled. You can get

a disability pension from the Province. They will take care of you. You need nursing care. You may need to go into the hospital."

The old man bristled, taking grave offense, as I had feared he might. "Ya, I will not go on relief," he shouted. "Ya, I will not get into the hospital."

"Would you like Jean and me to sing you a song?" asked Ann in the silence that followed this outburst. She added comfortingly, "Mother says we have a couple of nice selections."

"I can draw pictures of animals," said Jean. "I'll draw you a horse, if you like."

So it was that despite several discussions I had with him on these subjects we failed to convince old Hjalmur that being in hospitals and going on relief are good things, no matter in what rosy lights we tried to present the idea.

One evening, Hjalmur and Jean and Ann had returned to the cabin after a hike along one of his trapline trails — a trip in which, Jean later confided, the young people were hard pressed to keep up with him. Now as the shadows of evening lengthened in that unending twilight of the northern latitudes, I could hear the gurgling sounds of the river, the soft breathing of the forest, and the sweet voices of the children. I listened painfully. They were singing songs to the old man a few yards away up the hill at his cabin door, in the haze of a mosquito smudge pot. The solitary old man and the children: they shared some inexpressible sympathy from which other ages were shut out.

While the children and old Hjalmur were enjoying the songfest at his cabin I became aware of a vague humming sound. It was not a sound exactly; only a vibration. A mechanical vibration. There is no sound like that anywhere in nature; it must be a motor. I sprang out of the tent to greet visitors on our shore as the sound stopped. It was the motorboat of Mrs. Johansson and Mr. Nookey.

I saw a fine-looking, upright old Western cowboy getting out of the boat. Eighty-four, so I had been told many times. He was lean, tanned, well groomed, and really handsome. As the old cowboy tied up the boat, Mrs. Johansson stepped ashore neatly, wearing Indian-made beaded moosehide moccasins over long wool socks, and a loose jacket and trousers.

She was a fairly large, bulky woman, perhaps weighing one hundred and sixty pounds and twenty years younger than her escort. The skin of her face was white and fair, offset by graying hair neatly tied back with a net. The thing you noticed (or should have noticed even if you didn't) was that it was interesting that such a large, cumbersome woman had such small feet in the little moccasins, and when she came ashore she was the only human being on that shore not to get her feet wet.

Of course we all greeted the landing party with enthusiasm, and immediately my girls and I had them all come into our well-ordered tent for tea, and then to eat.

"In this country," I had told my girls many times, "we must always have a well-ordered tent for the people we meet."

"I believe you must be an American, aren't you?" I asked Mr. Nookey very soon after we met.

"Oh, yes, my goodness," he said. "I just packed up and come up here a few years ago. I'm still an American," he reassured me. "I'm from Idaho."

"Do you ever miss it back there?"

"Oh, my goodness," he said. "Once in a while I do. But it's changed a lot back there."

"So it has," I said.

I liked Mrs. Johansson immediately as she sat crosslegged on the floor of the tent and looked us all over with her bright, narrow eyes set in fine fair skin over flat cheekbones. And I could see that she approved of a well-ordered tent when she saw one. She liked our pots and pans, our small cupboard, the way everything was laid out in the tent, and she even liked sitting on the floor.

"You know, I just love living in a tent," she said, making neat gestures with her small hands. "I used to live in a tent quite a lot in the summertime. We used to always put up a tent in the yard in summer. The light is better for sewing in a tent. It's so breezy and cool. A house gets hot and you have to work so hard in a house, isn't it so? I think what you and your daughters are doing is perfectly wonderful, don't you, Edward? But you don't seem to be afraid of the river at all."

Mrs. Johansson, a woman in her sixties, a bubbling, natural-born extrovert, sat in our tent sipping tea; and   looked at her lively, animated face; and as I looked, just when Ann was politely passing sugar for the tea, I seemed for a moment to hear the wonderful, minor, throbbing sound of Indian drums. Then they seemed to fade away into some dark spruce forest, like the forest that was all around us.

Mr. Nookey and Mrs. Johansson, partners for several years, invited my girls and me to visit them without fail when we proceeded onward in a day or two. They explained that their house was on an unfrequented channel of the river and not visible from the main channel.

"In fact," smiled Edward Nookey from old-time Idaho, "the channel where we live dries up and you-all wouldn't be able to get to us later in the summer. But there's plenty of water if you come to visit us right now."

"But you'll have to hurry up," urged Mrs. Johansson. "Because the water's going to drop from now on."

"The river's going down. When she starts to drop, she drops fast."

"Draw me a map, so we can find your place," I requested, and this they did.

"But I wish you could talk Hjalmur into leaving the trapline," the sensible Mrs. Johansson said. "You know, he is too old to live out here alone. It is not good to be so alone. Edward and I — Mr. Nookey — we worry about him, living here year after year alone. Do you know he nearly died last spring?"

"Yes, I know."

"You should go to North Star, Hjalmur," was the consensus, to which the stubborn Scandinavian continued to shake his head.

"Those Mileaux half-breeds cause him a lot of trouble, too," added Mrs. Johansson.

"Is it true, what he told me? Are Jacques Mileaux and his brother stealing his furs and threatening him?"

"Oh yes, we are glad that we don't live near them. They have a bad reputation around the country all right. Hjalmur, it's too hard out here for you, so many different problems. Think once again. Should you not go to North Star before winter comes?"

There was no more that anybody could say to Hjalmur. But I felt that the matter was not closed, so far as I was concerned. Somewhere, even hundreds of miles along the river perhaps, I would have to solve it. Something must be done. I would have to find the right person, a social worker for the area perhaps, who would know how to take the necessary steps to bring our brave friend Hjalmur out of the woods. Or the alternative was that he would be eaten by the animals as certain as winter came; and we were civilized after all: we could not allow that to happen to any man. No, not in civilized North America today.

When the visitors, so happy and prosperous, had hopped into their boat and gone their way downriver to prepare for our arrival, gloom settled upon us once more, while we continued to try to iron out Hjalmur's irreconcilable problem. There was always trouble between the white European trappers and the breeds, or half-Indians, he said. He said this part of his problem was not unusual.

"Why is that?" we heard him ponder aloud. "I don't want nothing from nobody. I only want what is mine own. Why they always want to make trouble for me? Here is nice big country, not many people here. Why can't everybody get along together and be good friends?"

"Jealousy, maybe. It's like the trouble between the Negroes and whites in the U.S., perhaps."

He nodded. He had heard something about that. "Just like that, eh?"

"Well, it's like that in most of the world. It's like the competition to survive between animals, I sometimes think. The strong don't let the weaker have any of the good things, mainly because there is never enough of the good things to go around. Like the real good-paying jobs. Why," I elaborated, "it's even between men and women in my country — this competition to survive. Men against men. Men against women. Women against women. It's really awful competition, and in the richest country in the world, too! Well, it all amounts to what we call population pressure on the resources, and mankind's greed, you know." He looked amazed. I wondered if he grasped the brilliance of my dissertation. At least he understood the emotion with which I spoke.

"So you see, Hjalmur, I'm surprised myself to find this competition even way out here. Yes, even here, there is not enough fur for everybody. Well, anyway, that's the way I think about it, since you ask me."

"Ya, I think so, too." He nodded good heartedly. "But why that man so young at eighty-four old, when I feel so old and am only sixty-two?" he still wept, looking for some answer to his misery.

"Do you think it is because he is American?" he finally asked. "Them Americans got everything. He got woman, too, at eighty-four. Them Americans is strong people, live to be very old."

"You've got the wrong idea," I replied. "Americans are quite strong because their riches make them strong, and their riches permit them to be kindhearted too — sometimes. They eat better. Well, Mr. Nookey lives to be old partly because he is lucky, I guess. But also because he's got that strong Indian to take care of him. I'll bet you'll find that Mrs. Johansson runs the tractor, runs the trapline, and does most of the work, if you looked into it."

"You say Mrs. Johansson is Indian?" marveled Hjalmur. "My goodness, I often wonder about that many years. Be gory, you are right."

"What you need, Hjalmur," interposed Jean, "is a wife or a strong Indian to take care of you."

"Mrs. Johansson is Indian!" he kept repeating in wonder. "Why, you seen her yourself, and so it must be so.

"But — I am bachelor. I always live alone." His voice broke on a high quavering note of alarm.

"Doesn't it get lonely?" the kids asked him.

"Sure, it get damn lonely sometime," the old trapper admitted bravely. "But," he cried, "it too late now. Long time ago I had lovely sweet girl. It back in Norway. I come here to New World. I write letter to that girl. But she forget to write more letters. I get so mad at her. I no write no letter to nobody. I come out here to the woods. I too late now to get partner. It too late for me."

"I'll tell you," Ann later told her family sagely, "I already know all about it, Mom and Jean. Listen, you guys. Don't get Hjalmur excited on the subject of women. Hjalmur's girl got married in Norway and that's why he lives out here. You see, he's mad."

So it was that Ann had learned how Hjalmur was once in love. Ann at twelve was far more astute than I about such things.

It was decided that the girls would write letters to Hjalmur since he had never received a personal letter or a post card in about the last thirty years. Of course, he didn't know how to read English. But his neighbors downriver could read a letter to him if he received one, he said.

For the time being he said he would remain here at his cabin in the woods. This was his desire, and we could not budge him. I knew I had a problem. I intended to get him out of the woods for the sake of his life, but it might take a little time. It was something I had yet to figure out.

Before we left the two children drew him some of their pictures of animals which they tacked up on his cabin wall. There, so far as I know, they still remain, the beautiful pictures of wild animals in an idealized wilderness setting, to bring a man comfort for whatever worth they might be.

9

At Mr. Nookey's Home with a Cree Outlaw

WE found Mrs. Johansson and Mr. Nookey far back on a side channel of the kind which dries up when midsummer comes. We motored to a stop alongside of two boats which were drawn up and hidden in the weeds.

So that we wouldn't miss their place, they had hung out a large orange flag. Only when we followed the trail up the bluff to the big blue sky above did we see their tractor and the wide flatland of their rapeseed farm (a crop used commercially in making oils and margarines) and the one-room log house chinked with prairie mud, to which an additional tarpapered plywood room had lately been added.

Like the Gatewood farm upstream this far northern pioneer farm was tenuously connected with the distant Mackenzie Highway by a home-dug road. In the North there are two kinds of roads: the year-around road, which is rare; and the winter road only. In summer, the Nookey road is mostly impassable through the bogs.

We saw house, chicken yard, toolsheds, and a leaning outhouse. Pans and old dishes of every kind littered the ground around. What were they doing here in this green, lush vegetation, half filled with rainwater? Certainly most had been here in their ugly repose for many a season, gathering interesting molds and rusts. A nine-foot powered toboggan stood against one side of the house. In front of the house, when we came up, three wolflike dogs gnawed at a deer's hind leg.

"Down! Down there, Wolf! Down, Fang! Down, Tracker!" Old Mr. Nookey skipped into our sight, calling off the dogs and greeting us: "Glad to see you-all. Come right up, ladies. Jacques Mileaux, he just come by and give us this little deer meat today. Didn't you meet with him on the river?"

We shook our heads, and the two girls bent to pat the friendly wolf dogs, who never had known a chain and who offered moist, blood-smeared noses and gleaming white smiling teeth, sniffing and wagging. "You must have missed him among the islands," Mr. Nookey said. "Well, well, so you made it real fine this purty day. Well, come right on in. The old woman can't hardly wait to see you."

Here was a scene that must have been common throughout much of North America fifty years ago. Certainly it was common in Mr. Nookey's youth in the West. Dear children, people have always lived much like this, with their casual ways, and their filth and their dogs — only you haven't always been around. It is only a sudden new modern world which has eliminated, or tried to eliminate, this cluttered, dirty, laborious way of life. Of course, dogs and kids weren't consulted when the new way of life was forced upon the world. And neither, perhaps, were the old men.

When the friendly frontier people led us inside, we at once found ourselves squeezed beneath a low ceiling, strung with a grid of ropes and tags of strings over which hung, even now in summer, the bulk of the family wardrobe. Two beds, in opposite corners of the room, were tidily enclosed by screens of hanging clothes. There were no visible arrangements for washing clothes or for bathing. Perhaps it was not considered terribly important. At least, not every single day. Here the people lived, in a clutter of unclean dishes and equipment thrown everywhere. Quite naturally they spent a lot of time outdoors when there were brilliant, halcyon days like this one.

The pioneer dinner they set before us was entirely home-grown: potato salad, jellied cold chicken, smoked fish from the river, and fresh little radishes as hot as fire but as sweet as apples. Then there were the ever present pitchers of hot brewed tea, chunks of fragrant homemade bread with white sourcream-butter called "winter butter," and for dessert, fresh rhubarb stewed with strawberries. Only a few basic food staples, seed, and tools, had had to be store-bought.

I think the thing my kids liked overwhelmingly was the complete absence of any hurry or nervousness in this atmosphere. All homes, whether hovel, shack or mansion, had essentially this same unhurried atmosphere all over the world fifty years ago; but in country after country leisure has strangely vanished, giving way to rush, rudeness, and anxiety. But we never heard any of the quiet wilderness people try to analyze these things. They never even thought of questions such as, "Is life worth living?" or "What is my life really all about?" or "How will I ever make the grade?" as they plowed a furrow or cleared a field or cleaned a big river jackfish over a stump, making the silver scales fly in the bright sunshine.

Perhaps there was no need here to ask these important, soul-searching questions. At least, we never heard them asked.

"You must just stay with us for a few days anyway, won't you now?" Mrs. Johansson asked. "We can soon get your guest room ready for you."

"Where's the guest room?" Ann's face lit with interest.

"I don't want to stay in a guest room," Jean said glumly.

"Oh, that's our tent we can set up right by," Mrs. Johansson reassured them. "We can set it up easy. All you need's your sleeping bag, isn't it?"

Both girls looked at the motherly woman with surprise and pleasure.

"Go run get your sleeping bags," Mrs. Johansson urged them. "Don't just stand there." They loped off, the dogs loping after them.

Mrs. Johansson turned back to the wood-burning cookstove where the potatoes, gnarled and pitted and barely scraped of their mud, were boiling away in a bubbling muddy pot. She opened the firebox and with capable, kindly hands put in two more sticks of wood. Looking into the cooking pot and its foaming mud, she said to me, "I just think you ought to take a bucket of potatoes from the field when you go, Connie. It's a long trip, all alone in these wilds. It would be terrible to run out of food, and the farther you go north down the river, you know, the less people and the less food they is. And could we give you some moosemeat in quart jars?"

"Sure, thanks so much. I'll really plan on that. . . . Do you ever get used to cooking with the muddy water?" I asked.

"People get used to it around here," she told me, fanning herself placidly in the stove's heat. "We just dip it out of the river with a bucket, and it's all right. They did that for generations of people here. Matter of fact, it keeps the bowels in good action. All that grit and sand in the intestines gives everybody one good free and easy movement every day in the Peace River country."

"That's reassuring to know," I said. I was thinking about Jacques Mileaux, the French-Cree trapper who was said to be a bad outlaw, and I thought I would seize the opportunity to ask more questions about him.

"Well, he's not white like us," Mrs. Johansson, whose face had the lines of a noble old Indian chief, confided of the wild young trapper's background. "If you should meet him, well, he's very, very dark. He leans all toward the Indian, if you know what I mean, and his brother killed a man."

"But is he all bad? He gave you fresh deer meat today."

"Yes, Jacques," she sighed, "he does a lot of good things, of course. We pay him a wage sometimes to work on the farm. But he don't like farm work. He just likes to hunt and fish and trap his life away. Sometimes we are really afraid of them brothers in the winter, though. In the winter it is not like in the summer here."

"How's that?"

"Well, we realize we are older people living all alone here in this place, and the Crees, but especially the half-breeds, they are really jealous of white people all the time in this country. That's why we give him money sometimes for helping on the farm, not very good help either. And we always ask him to set down and have a meal. He can always count on us for meals when he is traveling between his trapping cabins, winter or summer. Because we are a little afraid of him in the wintertime, you don't know what he might do."

"What could he do?" I persevered.

"He could burn the house. Maybe us in it," she said reluctantly, in a low voice. "The days are short then. Lots of darkness. Anyway, if he burned the house in winter, that's pretty serious in this country, because people freeze to death if their house burns down. It has happened sometimes. So," she ended, with methodical logic, "if he tries our patience with his ways sometimes, and even if we know he is an outlaw and he steals from our traps all the time, we always still try to keep on good terms with him."

"What do you think of your neighbor, old Hjalmur?"

"Well, Hjalmur, he is a peculiar man, you have to understand that." Mrs. Johansson turned and began thoughtfully washing her hands with a muddy bar of soap in the hand basin by the door. "Hjalmur, now he's stubborn, and he draws away from other people all to hisself these many years, and we don't get to see much of Hjalmur since he got no dogs and he got no boat. But he's a brave man, maybe a foolish man, and we know that Jacques steals from his traps for the reason that we know he steals from us. It follows like. Poor Hjalmur, he's a good man inside, very honest. You can believe exactly anything Hjalmur tells you.

"But Jacques might be dangerous under some circumstances. I guess Hjalmur told you how those brothers robbed him when he lay sick and starving in his cabin last spring. Mr. Nookey and I, we always take care, like you do with the weather and wild animals, and things like that — just take care to avoid those circumstances. You may meet Jacques yet," she told me. "As for you, you wouldn't have to worry none. It's not winter now. He wouldn't bother an outsider none, He wouldn't bother tourists. He might just be very nice to you. In the summertime."

As we sat in the kitchen I learned from Mrs. Johansson about her earlier life and how she happened to be living here.

As a young girl she had married and had five children. As fast as the children arrived she had to go to work and support herself and them, for her husband had no regular work; and when he did work, he used his money for "chasing the gals" and for drink. She worked as a scrubwoman in the tiny Mackenzie Highway village where she was born (before the highway was built, of course), perilously dodging drunken blows when at home. Her husband apparently was of Indian blood, despite the Scandinavian name, and because of him in particular, she had no use for "Indians."

At last one day when she came home from work to their shack, her husband beat her into insensibility. Many times before he had beaten her. Several times the beatings had sent her into a hospital bed for a temporary rest. On that last occasion, clubbed over the head with a chair, she fell into the searing stove in the shack, burning the hair from the side of her head and the flesh from one side of her face.

Her eldest daughter had managed to drive the drunken man out of the house, and then pleaded, "Mama, you must leave him, we have told you that. You must get rid of him this time or someday he will really kill you."

When she got out of the hospital the authorities had jailed him and she and the children continued on Alberta relief. When the last child was grown, upon meeting the wandering and aging Mr. Nookey, she went with him to live on his farm, and in this way was able to make a new life with a large degree of freedom and the assurance of regular meals. She showed me the white scars on her face over which the gray hair was drawn on one side. These had been her happiest years. Mr. Nookey was a kind and wonderful man.

She was showing me pictures of her descendants in a scrapbook when Mr. Nookey strode nervously into the house, and in his company was a slight, shadowy, furtive, and nervous Jacques Mileaux.

"Mom," Mr. Nookey addressed her, clearing his throat, "we have company. Here is Jacques come to visit us twice today. He just come in from the river. Guess you women was gabbling so you didn't hear his boat. Sit right down, Jacques. We was just going to think about having dinner. Isn't that right, Mom?"

"Yes, Edward," said Mrs. Johansson. "Jacques, we have company, you see? Have you met this lady from the United States and her two daughters who are visiting with us?"

I looked at the slim, dark handsome Indian of twenty-eight years, in ill-fitting work-worn clothes, and I said my nervous how-do-you, and he said his how-do-you; then he shifted his eyes downward, and sat down uncomfortably. And I realized that we were all very edgy as we took our places at the dinner table. Jean and Ann came in staring.

Then I thought how all up and down the river people knew we were coming. The gallant old Mr. Nookey with Mrs. Johansson had stopped at taciturn Hjalmur's place especially to meet us, because they heard about us from the Gatewoods. Now young Jacques, shifty-eyed Cree trapper who was known to his neighbors on all sides as an outlaw, had tracked us down promptly in a watery world where everyone knew the sound of everyone else's motor on the river. Curiosity was such, or his desire for human company was such, that he was drawn.

Jean wanted to ask, "Are you a real outlaw? How could you find it in your cruel heart to steal from an old man?" But, characteristically, she kept her mouth shut and waited. Here was the man who robbed other people's traps, eating right beside us, and possibly wondering to himself if everybody here knew it. He was too nervous to do more than barely fiddle with his dinner, and he looked neither to the right nor to the left. His flat coppery Cree face was set and stolid. Yet somehow I got the impression that he wanted desperately for our party to think well of him — a small matter of vanity, as it were.

Jean meanwhile altered her usually terrible posture. She was trying to hold in her stomach — a matter of a little vanity again, and one which well became her.

At once I thought of our precious rifles in their cases, lying there in our boat. The highly powered neat little outlaw boat was pulled up right against our boat in the weedy landing.

Our guns had never been registered in Canada. As it happened, they were becoming hard to get, too. The fine woods used in stocks like ours were growing scarce, and were giving way to — heaven forbid! — plastics. When I had scrounged in the secondhand stores and managed to find these used arms, I had calculated that they would probably last my lifetime.

"Jacques," I asked the dark, slim-hipped trapper directly, "do you know anything about rifles? We have a little problem with our rifles, and I wonder if you can help us?"

Taken by surprise, he raised his beautiful, long-lashed, black, glittering eyes. Their dullness gave way to a gleam of genuine interest and he looked at me straight for the first time.

"Oh, I know a little about rifles, not much," he admitted modestly. Of course, if he had intended to steal our rifles he could have lifted them right out of the boat at the landing, and not even bothered to come up to the house, I reminded myself. But he had come here to meet us.

"I was wondering," I went on, "if we could borrow a ramrod to use, and clean our rifles. They are in danger of rusting and molding. You see, we lost our ramrod, and we have the oil and the solvent, but we have no way to clean them."

"This climate sure plays hell with rifles," said Jacques with a sincerity one could not doubt on this subject. "I would be glad to look over your rifles if you wish."

"Oh, yes," I said. "Could you go with my daughters to our boat and bring the rifles up here to the house and clean and oil them? Also maybe you can give the girls a lesson in how to do it. We need a man to help us."

The young people immediately thought this was a great idea.

"They're loaded," I called to Jacques as they went. "Be sure to unload them first."

"Oh, I won't forget that, Mrs. Connie." He smiled, almost laughing.

Soon this good summertime friend was industriously cleaning and oiling our neglected rifles with the kids in the can-littered front yard. Then they pitched the tent which was to be our family's guest room. Handling the rifles and pitching the tent with young girls was a recreational occupation for any young bachelor on such an idle summer day; yellow butterflies danced, and perfumed scents wafted from thousands of miles of flowering swamps and forest. Jacques's dark sins were so easy to forgive in summer. But after the rifles were handed back to me, I put them inside the house for the duration of our stay, to avert any outlaw temptations.

"Do you remember when you wanted to stay there and live with those people?" I was asking Ann just the other day. "Tell me, now that you are a little older, did you really think you could stay?"

"I knew you wouldn't let me," she replied. "But I thought I would ask, anyway." And that, I think, indicates the way we all felt about that way of life of fifty years ago. My girls lived history, for the world will never go back.

"Think, Jean," I asked my other daughter now to refresh my memory. "Think, can you tell me exactly which direction the Nookey outhouse leaned?"

"Maybe it was to the north," said Jean.

Ann said, "No, Mother, it was definitely to the south."

"I was trying to get the description exact," I told them.

But we have not quite been able to remember, to save our lives. We visited so many. Some tilted forward, some back, some to one side or the other. The tilting was due to the heaving of the ground from winter frost.

The Nookey outhouse faced the house with a shocking lack of privacy, the girls have reminded me: it had no door. It had only one very slim board on the side which would conceal the tourist only if he could hunch back into the shadowy interior, and, listing at a fifteen-degree angle, cling to the wall like a mariner to a pitching ship.

Followed by the dancing yellow butterflies and myriad insect swarms, through buttercups and daisies the timorous tourist trod the outhouse paths into the land of fifty years ago; and having taken care not to sit down upon some clumsy, bumbling bumblebee, promptly departed without arriving at much of a philosophy at the time. Only later a philosophy emerges from the experience and attempts to stand us in good stead in a world which moves all too fast for anyone to comprehend.

"I could give you some fish from my net, I think maybe," offered Jacques at the breakfast table next day. He had slept in his boat in the clothes he lived in.

"Yes, that's right, I'm glad you thought of that, Jacques," opined the handsome Mr. Nookey over coffee. "Yes, Jacques sets a net in a little slough of dead water down about three miles on the river, and he could show you the way there with his boat, and give you a few fish to send you off."

We accepted this, like other handouts, with alacrity. Jean hastened to give Jacques a detachable handle grip which could be used on a motor, extending the length of its handle. It had been given to us upriver in British Columbia. He seized upon it at once with great pleasure, and I have no doubt, uses it to this day in his riverboat.

Then a horrid thought came to me. "Oh, we've lost some of our films," I cried to the assemblage. "All our exposed films. All the pictures we've taken of the whole trip this far. They were left on the bank in Hjalmur's front yard, upriver. Oh, how could I?" I wailed, reduced at once to a pitiable pulp.

"Don't worry about it. Jacques can go fetch your films for you, I am sure, can't you, Jacques?" said Mrs. Johansson comfortingly. "Going upriver don't mean a thing to him, with an empty boat. He could mail the films for development next time he goes to North Star. He goes to town often. He goes to see the girls."

Jacques blushed under his dark skin as all eyes turned upon him. "Yes, of course, I go to town quite often. My brother and I, we have our town place," replied our summertime friend. "I will be only too glad to take care of it for you. Please do not worry," he immediately reassured me.

"Well, here, let me give you a five-dollar bill for your trouble, and for the expenses." I held a bill out to him, awkwardly.

"No, it is a pleasure. It's no trouble," demurred the helpful outlaw. Only when I pressed him further did he finally take the bill. I was not by any means certain that we would really see our films again, but it seemed a gamble worth taking, at least.

Standing on the bluff, Mr. Nookey and Mrs. Johansson waved good-bye, as our two craft went sociably off down the river together. Young Jacques had a powerful motor and his boat was completely empty, except for his battered rifle in its case beside him, and the one can of gas he carried. He cut a debonair Frenchy figure and sent up showers of jeweled spray, showing off.

We followed his boat down to the hidden deadwater slough, where the bushes closed behind us.

"It is against the law to set a net in Alberta," Jacques explained, "but there is plenty fish in this river. Nobody bother to catch them. And the game warden, he never comes here. I need fish for to feed my dogs at my cabin."

"That's what we need, Mother," Jean informed me, not for the first time. "I wish we had a good fishnet."

Our instructor began raising the sagging wooden floats from the heavy net, and worked the net through his hands loop by loop, stooping neatly from his tilted boat. Ann, watching from our boat as we floated quietly, gave me an angry look: she felt badly about taking the fish from the hungry dogs. For word had it in all directions that Jacques treated his dogs badly and that they seldom got a good meal.

One by one through the turgid water the large gleaming white bellies appeared. Most were dead in the net. They had drowned. Because it was a gill net, through which the fish tried to pass, all the fish were of a uniform size — at least their gills were. The fish were lying there hidden under the water, hung by their gills. Selecting three fat ones that were still alive, I asked Jacques to club them over the head and toss them into our canoe, which he nobly did. They had been taken in two-inch mesh and weighed three or four pounds each; they were pike, or jackfish, and freshwater or lingcod: types which would not bite on lures with any consistency, and which were otherwise unobtainable except by net.

"I seen your tracks at my brother's landing, a few days ago," Jacques told us now. "Remember some time, you stopped upriver and looked around an old cabin, it had a sign, *Hotel Riviera*, on its door?"

We nodded. Yes, looking through that smeared cabin window we had seen poor old Hjalmur's stolen radio, without knowing it at the time. A wave of revulsion seized me as I remembered the so-called *Hotel Riviera*.

"That's my brother's place," he told us proudly. "He's a bachelor like me. But I didn't think when I seen your tracks that you would be right here at my fishnet today and that today you would enjoy to eat some fish that I was going to give to my dogs, hee, hee."

"Well, we do thank you for everything," we told him, slightly red-faced. "That's a lot of trouble going upriver to Hjalmur's place to pick up our film. It's a lot of gas for you to have to burn." (And it certainly was not going to be comfortable for poor Hjalmur to have Jacques stop.)

"Oh, I don't care about that." He waved this off lightly. "It's better than going into town and getting drunk."

"Indians can't buy liquor in Alberta," reprimanded Ann suddenly, to my complete devastation.

"How can you arrange to buy liquor?" asked Jean, intrigued. Perhaps my girls sensed that it was their last chance to get at the truth about the strange person they had known so briefly.

He looked at them levelly. "There are white laws, and then there are Indian laws here," he replied. "Unfortunately, I am a half-breed. I am half white, so this allows me to buy liquor, and that is one good thing. I am supposed to obey the white laws. But this is the country of my ancestors. This is really my country. I do as I please. Just between you and me, I got no use for to obey any laws they make, any more than I can help it.

"Look," he said, "and watch out for yourself on the river. The laws will not help you do that." He laughed bitterly. He pointed, and we looked as he did so. "Look out to miss that island right in the middle that way. You see them little willows that's sticking little bit out of the water? The island is under water today, but later it come up in fall. There is fast, dangerous current over that shallow bar. Always stay away from them places. Take the right-hand channel to be safe.

"Good-bye," we called, and Jean pulled the starter rope, and we turned back to the open river.

10

With Mrs. Finkleglimmer
in Indian Country

DOWN the wide reaches of the Peace for hundreds of miles we watched and waited in vain for the pleasant sight of Indians at their "fish camp" which I remembered from the Yukon River in central Alaska in years past.

But the country remained empty. Some whites later told us that the reason was that the Indians on dole had become too lazy to fish. But this was not the whole story. In Alberta what had happened was that the law had put all classified Indians in reserves. Yet laws prohibited non-Indians, like Jacques the half-breed, from setting a net in the open public domain. Jacques's little net was the only one we saw along the eleven hundred miles of our summer's voyage, although others may have been set furtively. The fish, such as they were, lay untapped in the mighty river.

Many people in fact believed there were not many fish because, they said, it was a "scouring river" which scoured out all plant life on its tremendous rampages. But the Yukon and the Mississippi rampaged, too, did they not?

So I continued hoping that we might see Indian fish camps later, after the Peace became the Slave and entered the Northwest Territories. The Indians at their fish camps used to be the traveler's touch with humankind in the wilderness, and they were always good for a kindly handout. From here onwards we were to find that almost all people, except for imported government personnel, were of at least part Indian blood, whether this was immediately apparent or not.

It was, in short, Indian country from central Alberta northward. Drifting on down the mighty Peace on a slow current, I had plenty of time to think about the great wilderness lying ahead and to all sides of us, and about the wilderness people. Take Jacques as a prime example. Here was a man who had to live as an Indian lived, whether he chose the life or not, for it was actually all he knew. He was uneducated and had no other way to make a living except by trapping, fishing and hunting, and by very occasional employment. There was no real employment in this whole North. Nobody's fault. Just a fact of geography. What was a man expected to do?

The settlement and industrialization of Canada have been determined entirely by the agricultural potential of the soil and by the climate. What is not commonly recognized by outsiders to Canada is that these are favorable only in the south; and there only in scattered, limited areas. Lumbering and mining have brought some settlers to the North, to be sure; but economists question how these extractive industries can ever maintain permanent settlement in many areas. Therefore, throughout the northern lands, the Indian and the métis — as the Canadians call the half-breed, using the more polite French term — and the indigenous white, all face really the same environmental problems of survival.

The nonagricultural area of Canada in which the indigenous people scratch out their precarious living is enormous. In general it comprises interior British Columbia, north of Caribou; all of the Yukon Territory; and all of the Precambrian Shield sweeping across Canada from sea to sea, aside from those parts lying south of the main line of the Canadian Pacific Railroad. In this vast forested land with its long, severe winters live one third of Canada's Indians, remote from population centers and supply lines; and so also live ever growing numbers of half-breeds or métis of various mixtures. Completely without agriculture, they depend mostly upon hunting, fishing, and trapping to live. They find casual employment limited to menial and laborious tasks (at lower pay than whites get for the same work) and even that kind of work is available only when offered by temporarily imported "outside" whites.

At worst the attitude of the transient white in the North is one of contempt for the Indian and métis. At best it is one of superior, amused tolerance. So it works out that the indigenous people of these far-flung lands cannot elevate themselves to a higher standard of living within their geographic environment; and harsh geography itself remains always the predominant factor in limiting their economic and social status, and of course their future. Only very recently has Canada begun efforts to take an official interest in these people. In the last fifteen years airfields and a few public schools have been established here and there, as a beginning; and, of course, there is the regular family dole for each child which is paid by the month to all families in Canada on the dubious supposition that eventually an increased population will solve the problem of settling the wilderness spaces.

In framing laws, however, Canada made special provisions for Indians, ignoring the other people in the area, in much the same way as the United States government made laws, agreements, and treaties with our own Indian bands as civilization pushed west. Treaties were made for peace with each Indian tribe or band separately, so there has emerged in each district such a jungle of conflicting and often impractical laws that nobody can understand them today, not even the experts.

In Canada a man's status as an Indian was defined by whether his blood line could be traced from May 26, 1874; and by whether he chose to be an Indian by joining a band. If he left the band he became a non-Indian. Indians belong to tribes speaking many different languages, and live on reserves which, however, they do not own. The reserves belong to the Crown, which closely supervises the land use, and is very much concerned that the lands not be abused, because these lands make up a great part of Canada's total dominion. After 1900 the Crown very wisely saw to it that the resources of waters, forests and furs were not seriously depleted. On lands that were not set aside as Indian band reserves, the trapping laws were enforced and limited trapline licenses were issued, as we were observing here at firsthand. Our river ran near occasional reserves but we met no reserve Indians.

The widening wave of settlement had made urgent the passage of the British North American Act, culminating in the last treaty with the Indians of the Northwest Territories in 1921. In their treaties the bands ceded "their rights, titles, and privileges" to definite prescribed areas, in return for which they retained their birthright to hunt, fish, and trap "for as long as the sun shall shine and the rivers shall flow," and with the provision that they receive cash annual payments from the Crown, and annual gifts, usually ammunition, fishing twine, and clothing. Educational facilities were promised — but were very slowly provided by the government, because of the costs and distances.

Although the treaty of the Northwest Territories was signed in 1921, the allotment of reserves for the Indians was delayed so that at this time the NWT is not actually a reservation, nor are there any Indian or Eskimo reservations in it.

People we talked to always concluded: "The life is much freer up in the Northwest Territories, you know." The conclusion was that this was true principally because the law with its many intricacies had not yet intruded very much.

Imagine our surprise miles down the river to pick up Jacques Mileaux again in the binoculars, skimming along lickety-split. Could he be following us? What for? I frowned, jerked out of my reverie. I didn't want him to see us in this completely empty country. Certainly we didn't want him hanging around our next camp.

Perhaps he had some business in this area. After all, it was a beautiful day to visit secret traps and nets and other mysteries. Although he lived in perpetual debt to the Hudson's Bay Company, as did most of his countrymen, he loved nothing better than to speed up and down the river in summer burning expensive gas. No doubt it gave a feeling of release to his wild young spirits. Now he was going right on by us, apparently not seeing the *Jeanie Ann*. We had cut our motor and were adrift at the time; and the sun, striking as it did, was in his eyes. Soon he passed behind a distant island and was gone. Yet I felt ill-at-ease. He had left his proper domain far behind. He should have been some seventy miles up-stream by now.

The girls and I settled down to solitary sunbathing, drifting, and bathing. Because of the insects we had not been able to expose our bodies for days. But bathing could be done drifting along the river on this day of ninety-six-degree temperatures in a safe, slow cur-rent. I ceased worrying about the roving trapper somewhere around. That tiny, lone figure in a speeding boat was a part of this great landscape, a tolerable and even valuable addition to nature so long as there was but one of his predatory species spaced at fifty-mile or hundred-mile intervals.

This is what I loved, this is what I had waited for: the absolute calm of a great and placid river. Drifting to nowhere through a sun-drenched day. Such days are jewels when they come. Under the brassy sun on the brown, brassy river, the boat circled somnolently, tugged by the current, and the heat waves danced. Past four-hundred-foot chalk cliffs the river wound in big loops, picking up its current to a lively pace at the cliff's base, and then spilling you out upon the outside turn of some forested flat to doze, to bask in the golden heat hour after hour, moving at a snail's pace. You force yourself to pick up a paddle and move the boat out into the current again. Or you wake to find yourself going aground in mud the con-sistency of peanut butter and about the same color.

Almost asleep, you sit hunched for hours with the binoculars propped, elbows on knees, and scan the twinkling white stems of the close-packed poplars of a big island, looking for game. There should be a moose in this forest somewhere, if you just keep look-ing.

The birds are asleep in the heat of the day. Only an occasional melodious note escapes from the forest. As for ducks and water-birds, they aren't to be seen on the river at all in summer, for they are on the inland lakes, rearing their young.

The complete silence that hung over the river was broken by a sound ahead of us along an island shore. It sounded to our strain-ing ears as though some human being were chopping wood; a crashing kind of sound, with breaking branches. By the time we had drifted abreast we saw clearly that the sounds were coming

from a cow moose browsing upon a willow flat. She was tearing off
and eating willow limbs so noisily that a keen ear could have heard
her a mile away.

At the tail of another island a second cow moose was interrupted
at her meal by the humming motor of Jacques Mileaux who passed
on the opposite side of the island. His motor drove this moose into
the river; she crossed before our bow. Fortunately, I thought, the
keen-eyed trapper never saw the moose. But did he see us? Was he
waiting for us to make camp?

As evening slowly descended, we made a number of tries for a
campsite, but, as before, upon each occasion were rebuffed by the
conditions we found. Whenever we approached an inviting-look-
ing shoreline, the mirage faded into the harsh reality of fifteen-foot
cutbanks or giant debris of upended logs and timbers. We could
have climbed over the logs, perhaps, but to no avail: for behind
each ridge of debris along the shores the receding water had left
quagmires and ponds of mud from the spring overflow. Where we
hoped to camp, there was always water behind the ridge of wilderness refuse. Everywhere were brambles, overflow waters, and deep
mud. Perhaps the nimble trapper had no difficulty finding a place
to sleep on the ground of his native land — and without insect
repellent or nets! — but as for me, I found I was a fairly heavy
woman with feet like stilettos, and all level-seeming spots were pure
mud soup.

So we motored on, praying for heavenly guidance to get ashore.
The map indicated we should be nearing Carcajou. I thought that
this name must mean caribou in French. (It doesn't. It means wolverine.) I now placed my trust in this mere place name on the map
of the river. If people of any kind lived there they should have
some kind of a boat landing. I visualized us tossing the boat chain
to friendly helping hands. Then, the cup of coffee in the log cabin,
supper very likely, help with pitching the tent. Most of all, we
would be secure from the worry of being all alone in the country
with Jacques Mileaux, who was called an outlaw.

I was searching each shoreline ahead in a kind of stupor when
the girls spotted a boat landing and people directly opposite, in a
small niche in the forest already withdrawn into nighttime shadow.

What followed was one of the weirdest experiences I have ever had. The glasses picked out a matronly woman standing there at the water's edge, in what seemed to be a pale blue house dress. "You said 'people' " I mumbled to myself. "There are no people, only one woman, alone. Well, perhaps her menfolk are nearby, hidden in the trees." A surge of gratitude swept over me. Everything was going to work out all right. Jean of course had already headed the boat in.

That the woman was real and no mirage became more clear at every moment of our anxious approach. Her skin was of that milk-white pink-cheeked coloring which is so common in Canadian woman of Germanic stock, and she had mild, vague blue eyes set wide apart. Her plump arms were bare, and on her head she wore a black brimless hat with a veil pushed back, of the kind a woman might wear in church; and on top of the hat were a pink rose and a spray of daisies. She wore cotton stockings and black country walking shoes that laced.

There wasn't really any boat landing — just a footpath leading to a plank boat chained there. The woman's black and white dog was taking a cool bath in the river, and skittered up the bank as we came crashing clumsily in. How often had I heard that horrid splintering of wood as we charged another fellow's boat! It is an embarrassing sound, I can tell you, especially when you are just about to meet the other fellow for the first time. Ah, well. Apparently the lady never noticed.

Awakened from prayerful stupor I stiffly clambered ashore, and we tied the boat fast with only minimum damage done. As we introduced ourselves and asked the primly attired and pleasant woman if we might camp for the night here, I got the strange feeling that I had met her before in some woman's club somewhere. To our surprise, she was quite alone.

Strangely, the mosquitoes which at once set to work to drive us nearly mad swarmed around her person but didn't seem to bother her.

She did not seem surprised to see us. "Good evening," she said. "Oh, this is very pleasant to meet you here. Have you been voyaging on the river? It is beautiful in the evening, isn't it? Do you know, I'll have to tell you something, I've been expecting you. It came to me just now, I have been expecting you all the time. Now you see, I was just speaking with Aurora — she's the dear little Indian girl who helps in my house — and I said to Aurora, I'm going to go down and look at the river in the evening. Yes, something told me to go down to the edge of the water and look out. You know, I rarely do. I rarely come to the river. But the evening is so lovely, isn't it? I felt I had to come here, like. I felt that some people were coming from the river, somehow. And so, of course, here you are. Isn't it marvelous?"

"Marvelous!" was all I could gasp, listening to the pleasant, rippling voice, the little bursts of laughter with which Madam Chairman would naturally welcome visiting ladies into the club. I didn't know whether I could live up to the gaiety expected of me at the moment, but I intended to try.

"I have already saved four souls, you know!" She wagged her finger at us prettily.

"How long have you lived here?" Ann asked, while our party wondered privately where "here" was.

"Oh, seven or eight years, I think it may be," she tinkled. "But what does God care for time? What does He in His infinite wisdom care for time, I ask you?"

"My daughters and I must set up our camp and rest and eat as soon as possible," I lamely explained. "Can you advise us?"

"But of course!" she agreed ecstatically. "But of course, you have just come from the river, from your voyage, and you are tired, and hungry, too, I should imagine. You can come to my little house, if you don't mind. You can put your sleeping bags out on my living room floor, and at least have roof overhead. We shall have a lovely dinner. Oh, we shall have Christian fellowship together. Wouldn't it be wonderful if we could have some prayers? Yes, we could sing hymns together." She beamed. "I've been waiting for someone to come and sing hymns with me."

"Yes," spoke up Jean, seizing the initiative, "after dinner."

"But of course. After dinner," cried the enthusiastic lady.

"After dinner," our party echoed, one and all.

We had plenty of food in the boat, but it was in an unprepared state and we were fairly exhausted. The problem of preparing our own food tonight was further complicated by the fact that no fuel was to be seen. As we groped between the trees we saw that only a sparse fringe of trees here actually separated the river from fields and meadows, from which all natural debris had been neatly cleared. As we depended entirely upon wood for fuel this complication seemed almost too much to cope with. We were worn out, physically and mentally, from too long hours on the water and too much sun.

Just then, from the little path leading into the firm, parklike grounds, a troop of young Indian girls came up, and it was plain then that the matronly blue lady was their teacher.

"Mrs. Finkleglimmer, Mrs. Finkleglimmer," giggled the girls.

"Yes, dear," Mrs. Finkleglimmer said, turning. "Oh, here's Aurora!" she announced to us ecstatically.

The Indian girls, some in summer frocks, some in jeans, somewhat unwashed and greasy, all wore large pink plastic curlers in their hair.

Ann tugged at me, outraged, freezing when she saw this sight.

"Mother, they're looking at us. They're laughing. They're laughing at *you*, Mother, and at Jean and me because they think we're idiots and look so terrible."

"How do you know so much? What makes you think we look like idiots?" I hissed, more than a little irritated at this trivial turn.

"Mother, they're laughing because we're in filthy trousers and boots, not dresses. And we haven't got our hair fixed."

Unfortunately, Ann's uncanny intuition was usually right. "Oh, Mother." Ann was rigid with hostility as she viewed the opposing group. "You never understand anything!" I could feel every muscle in her lean body go taut as she grabbed my hand. "They think you are a *freak*. They think they're better than we are. They just bug me!" she hissed.

As I staggered under this social crisis, the girls were introduced, in an atmosphere of arching cats' backs. "These are some of the dear girls I was telling you about," Mrs. Finkelglimmer enthused. "This is Esther. This is Evangeline. This is Rose. This is Mary. This is Aurora."

"This is Ann and this is Jean," I said. "And I'm Mrs. Helmericks, the mother of *these* dear girls."

Ann sneered a feline smile, and the Indian girls glared back. Only Jean had her mind on other things. Very likely she was calculating gas capacity and mileage to the next refill, and worrying about how well the boat was tied up.

"Oh, for goodness sake, I almost forgot," said Mrs. Finkleglimmer. "These dear girls are waiting for me to get the milking done. They have brought their milk jars, haven't you, girls?" She wagged her finger playfully at the glaring group. "You know, I promised Aurora and her friends some milk to take to their homes, and here it is, long past milking time. My, how time flies."

"I think it's about ten o'clock. Or ten-thirty," said Jean. "We have a clock in the canoe, but it stopped because it's growing mushrooms inside."

"Yes, it's long past milking time," purred Mrs. Finkleglimmer. Then, suddenly: "Do you know how to milk, dear?" she asked Ann.

"I do!" yelled Jean, with bright enthusiasm, before anyone could stop her.

"Oh, no," I thought, nearly dead on my feet. "Sing hymns, milk cows. Oh, oh, I wonder how many cows?"

Of course, I thought, northern people prowl all night in summer and sleep means nothing to them. It was a curious insight into Mrs. Finkleglimmer's mind and world that she took it quite for granted that any twelve- or fourteen-year-old American girl would naturally know how to milk cows.

Fortunately, the girls had learned well from old Hjalmur how to make smudge pots, for the small, hilly barnyard with its mooing, bloated occupants, was literally roaring with insect hordes. So terrible were the tormentors that the cattle and pigs groaned rhythmically with each breath they drew. Looking into the pigpen I saw that the porkers had buried themselves in the soft earth as far as they could get, in an effort to protect their bellies and they groaned awfully as the mosquito swarms settled upon naked flapping ears and anguished twitching snouts.

"Mom," called Jean, from the portable stump that served as milking stool, her free hand brushing across her face like a windshield wiper as the milk began squirting noisily into the pail. "Just come over here and look at this poor cow's teats. The flies have eaten two of them almost off. She's only got two good ones you can use at all. She seems nervous and badtempered too." To my consternation, I saw that these cows had long horns.

After a quick look through swarming insects: "I'll go get our flashlight," I said, "and bring up the sleeping bags."

"Bring up our precious rifles to the cows, Mom," Ann reminded me, quite earnestly.

In the meantime Mrs. Finkleglimmer had got on a tractor and gone across a field to see a neighbor — some necessary social obligation, she said. I have no idea who the neighbors were, and have sometimes wondered if there really *were* any neighbors. At about 1 A.M. she came back, abruptly stopping the little tractor and crawling under a fence. Her clubwoman's hat with the rose and the spray of daisies on top remained pinned firmly in place and still she had no noticeable insect bites.

Ann and I had tried to prepare Jacques's gift of fish in the dark. The ugly old pike and cod had stiffened into bent corkscrews during the long traveling day, their scales turned to dried-out armor. We scraped them at length at the riverbank, where ever more insects joined the festivities. Then we returned to the cow pen with our stinking booty, smeared with fish scales and slime, itching from mosquito bites, to join the roaring swarms through which Jean persevered among calves which crowded her, wanting their mothers.

We hadn't eaten or slept in eighteen hours. Jean milked three cows, but in turn they kicked over the bucket, and she went skidding down the hill through wet cow manure. We had not yet been invited into the teacher's little house, but we still had flashlight-dim hopes when she returned.

"Well, my dears," she said brightly, "I was gone longer than I meant to be. Did you get the milking done, Jean?"

When Jean, nearly tearful, exhibited the quart or so of milk she had gleaned from hours of labor, Mrs. Finkleglimmer was disappointed, but, accepting the outcome in good grace, sat herself upon the stool, and as the miserable cow turned her neck and looked at her mistress with rolling eyeballs, she quickly finished the milking.

"You couldn't help it," Mrs. Finkleglimmer said to us kindly. "The cows don't know you as a friend, so they hated to give up their milk, dear."

"Oh, they gave up their milk for me pretty good," said Jean. "Only thing is, I had to rope their hind legs and their tail down, and then they got restless and kicked over the bucket each time anyway, and you know I had to run when they charged with those long horns."

The country teacher brushed this off lightly. Ann remarked that it was a shame something couldn't be done to alleviate the animals' misery from insects. She brushed this off lightly, too. "Yes, they twitch a lot," she admitted. "But that's normal for cows and pigs."

The active little lady in blue, her hat upon her head and a light shawl now about her shoulders in a land where most explorers would do well to dress in armor, then took us about as she fed her stock by flashlight. We followed numbly, stumbling among holes in the dirt floor of her barn.

"But you are all alone here? Have you no man to help?"

"I am not alone," she said. "It is always a joy, living one's life in the Lord."

At long last we were invited to enter the little cottage under the trees where she had hours earlier asked us to spend the night. The cottage might have come out of the pages of *The Wizard of Oz*, or *Alice in Wonderland*, or *The Wind in the Willows*, although it is doubtful if the builders, whoever they were, knew these stories.

We members of the Canadian Rivers Expedition felt almost unreal in our extreme fatigue, when we entered the cottage; sinking upon chairs we watched in a daze as our hostess scratched a large match and lit a gasoline pressure lamp.

We saw a bare living room with bare wood floor, a water barrel and dipper, a sink and drain. We saw a cast-iron woodstove and a modern butane cookstove. A hinged trapdoor in the floor provided an entrance to a large food cellar beneath the house. Soiled milk bottles stood everywhere. There was a luxurious overstuffed sofa and a heavy oak table and matching straight chairs. Adjoining was the teacher's chaste single bedroom with its bed draped with mosquito bars.

The dear little Indian girls who had waited in vain for milk had gone hours ago, presumably to their homes, wherever they were.

In the world of this little house Mrs. Finkleglimmer at once seemed more of a mystery than even before. We offered, of course, to help at once with the supper, but in this endeavor nobody seemed to make headway. It was like one of those dreams we have all had where we try to do something, such as run or fly, and it just doesn't come off. I felt caught in a dream here, as though hypnotized.

Mrs. Finkleglimmer, pleasant and chatty as ever, and apparently tireless, seemed to me then as though she were living behind a pane of transparent glass and really untouchable by anyone around her. She was polishing the big oval hardwood table with a cloth. We waited expectantly for food. She just kept on polishing and polishing, and I pinched myself to keep from dozing off.

It occurred to me that she had not asked us a single question about our voyage down the river, or about where we came from or who we were. She accepted the fact that we were here, but she did not ask the questions other people asked. She mingled with us the way dream figures mingle with one in a dream.

She said that there really wasn't anything we could do to help in getting supper. The clock on the wall said two-fifteen, the darkest part of the night. The gasoline pressure lamp hissed pleasantly, with a white glow, and I sank back in my chair and the children sat sleepily in their chairs, our red-rimmed eyes fixed hopefully on Mrs. Finkleglimmer, who continued to polish the table. Presently I fell asleep and when I awoke fifteen minutes later she was still polishing!

"Can I help you get the knives and forks, or something?" Jean spoke in dry gasps still trying to be polite.

The blue lady then set about placing silverware precisely, with agonizing slowness. There was no food in sight, except cream and milk from yesterday, left souring in jars.

"We need some cups," said the lady. Jean looked at Ann with

deep fatigue, and Ann sat quietly in a deep trance staring into space. Mrs. Finkleglimmer placed cups upon the table. Then she picked them up again and put them away in the cupboard.

"Let's put the cups on the table," I offered experimentally.

"Oh, yes," said she brightly, and put them back on the table again. We were making slow progress toward food, indeed.

"Perhaps we should have something from the garden," Mrs. Finkleglimmer said suddenly with a delighted laugh, and dashed out with me at her heels, to the dark garden a hundred yards away. She plucked at something with sure hands, as my eyes tried to probe the darkness, fascinated.

When we returned to the lighted house she thrust the result of our errand into my hand. I counted seven radishes. Only when I saw the radishes did I begin to get a prickling sensation as I struggled to escape my own daze of fatigue.

"We need some cups," laughed Mrs. Finkleglimmer. It seemed to me we had been through this before.

"Annie," I spoke across the room to where our youngest member lay in her chair. "How would you like to eat some wonderful radishes?"

"Not now," she replied crossly.

"Look here," I said, "these are wonderful radishes. All seven of them. I suppose you are getting hungry. It's nearly three in the morning now, and you didn't eat yesterday, remember? Of course, you will find a little farm dirt on them. I don't know how to wash them. There seems to be no water here because the water barrel is low. Aurora's father neglected to fill it for the teacher. But we don't mind that, do we? Now, how about some radishes?"

"Mother," said Ann, with more spirit than I thought she had left, "what's the matter with you anyway? You must be out of your mind."

"Oh, not I," I said softly. The blue lady had skipped into her bedroom to put away her shawl.

Jean who was slumped across her chair woke up and looked at me sharply, with her eyes in focus. "What did you say, Mother?" she asked.

Deliberately I popped radishes into my mouth, dirt and all, and started chewing and their bite seemed to bring quick moral and physical strength. My young daughters watched me with fascinated attention. The blue lady flitted, humming a tune between bedroom and dining table.

"More cups. More cups. Move down. More cups," said Jean.

"That's from *Alice in Wonderland*," said Ann. "I just hate that book."

"More cups, more cups," sang Jean. "You always liked that book."

"You act like you're crazy," Ann told Jean in disgust. "Say," she said suddenly, "Mother, what are you and Jean up to, anyway?"

"Listen to Mother," said Jean. "Just listen to Mother once in your life, and shut up."

Ann listened, for once. "This is extremely interesting," I said. "You see, you have just gone through the looking glass. We have all gone right through it, and my goodness, who would imagine that would ever happen? I mean, *really* happen?"

"I don't get it. How's that?" asked Ann irritably.

"Well, we went through the looking glass, is all," Jean tried to enlighten her, at this dismal hour before dawn. "We're on the other side now."

"But I don't want to play. I told you I don't like that book!" raged Ann. "Can't you shut up about that junk?"

"We're on the other side now," repeated Jean, meaningfully.

"But, Mother, there's nothing to *eat!*" Ann hissed *sotto voce* at me, with mounting resentment.

"That's just it, dear. There is nothing to eat on the other side of the looking glass. You should have read the book better. You only make believe you're eating."

"*I don't like it.*"

"Then, shall we try to do something about it?"

"How?" queried Jean, abruptly, in the deep silence.

"Politely," I whispered. "You always have to be very very polite, just as Alice was a polite little girl, when she was the guest."

"Let me help you," said Jean cheerfully as the blue hostess flitted by. "Let me pour the milk into the cups. Isn't that milk there in those jars?"

"The cream, too?" suggested Ann, from the low ebb of her starvation.

We seated ourselves at table and the children politely but firmly served; and although Mrs. Finkleglimmer suggested that people don't usually drink straight cream, Ann had a pint of it, in company with some excellent homemade bread and raspberry jam the lady was persuaded to set before us.

There was only one more problem of survival. To get to the outhouse in the dark before bed required a journey made perilous by the lady's enraged little dog, whose habitual beat was the outhouse path, where he lay restrained by a chain whose length just enabled him to grab a nice hold on the wayfarer's ankle. Also, there was an open cesspool, obviously unrepaired for years, across the top of which the walker must teeter on dubious planks to get into the doorless little house itself.

Next morning — that is, after three hours abed — the little lady was dressed and awakening us from our sacks on her floor.

"There is an Indian here who says he knows you," explained Mrs. Finkleglimmer. "He has been waiting since dawn, hoping you will wake up. He says he has some films for you. He also says you lost a little kit that he has, containing your toothbrushes."

"Oh," I groaned. "The outlaw strikes again," and got up. Jacques Mileaux had succeeded in tracking us down. He had gone two hundred miles out of his way on the river to find us, that kind soul.

Safely ensconced under the teacher's roof, we welcomed him in daylight like a lost friend.

"He is a very dear boy," reported Mrs. Finkleglimmer who had already become well acquainted with him at the cowshed.

"If you don't mind," she said, "I have invited your nice friend to have breakfast with us. Wouldn't that be nice, after his long trip?"

She added that in fact Jacques was out doing the morning milking at this very moment. We shuddered for his sake.

"Shall we cook the fish for breakfast? The ones you brought with you?" asked our hostess, who by this time showed evidences of hunger herself.

"Oh, yes!" replied Ann. "As a matter of fact, those really are

Jacques's fish, you know. They're the ones he gave us up the river two days ago."

Jacques trudged wearily in, accompanied by an insect cloud, upon which the door was closed quickly. "Hello, Jacques. I guess you never dreamed you'd be enjoying breakfast with us here with Mrs. Finkleglimmer," said Jean, "and helping us eat up your own fish that you caught for your dogs."

His black eyes glittered in an Indian smile. "Well, I like to travel," he explained then. "I thought, I will just travel down the river and see that place called Carcajou. It was a very good day to travel, you know." We nodded agreement. "Well, you were going that way, too. They say up the river there is a new family moved there, and I will take this opportunity to meet them."

"Hmmm," I said. "Opportunity to meet them? Girls in that family, by any chance?" I suggested.

Jacques turned red under his tan, for I had hit a tender spot. The rumor had it that the new Indian family at Carcajou had many young daughters.

I knew I would have to buy Jacques an extra five-gallon can of gas at the next trading post to enable him to get back home up the river, but that was all right. He had merely capitalized on opportunity when he glimpsed a tourist's wallet.

"Now we can all have a few hymns together," exclaimed the lilting, lyrical voice of Mrs. Finkleglimmer after our fine breakfast. Our outlaw friend's face blanched under its tan, but there was nothing he could do to escape this turn of events. At the same moment Jean poured salt into her Ovaltine. It seemed that Mrs. Finkleglimmer, we learned too late, always kept her salt in the sugar bowl.

At any rate, all was worthwhile, when we saw her smile radiantly and approvingly at us. Our effervescent hostess, who sang like a lark on the wing, was not slow to capitalize upon events when they turned her way. She gathered up the travelers there firmly beneath her benevolent roof, and did with her captives sweetly as she willed, with song and prayer.

11

The Mosquito-Fanned Tent Fire

THE canoe was passing the mouth of the Battle River.

"Yep," I was saying. "The Crees and the Beaver Indians had a big battle here — let me see — in 1790, I guess."

"The Crees massacred the Beavers, didn't they?"

"Well, yes, dear. Right over in those bushes, maybe. New growth covered the battlegrounds long ago. Thank goodness for new growth."

"That's the way in the United States, too, only in the United States, Mother, creeping asphalt is the new growth."

"There's too much history and too many wars to learn," Jean stated categorically in the silence of a wilderness day, drifting on an eddy at a strange river's mouth.

And Battle River slipped behind us, having called up a dim memory of horrid war whoops and painted Homo sapiens there engrossed in his age-old pursuits.

For a long time the Crees held all this country, all of North America's subarctic heartland. They slaughtered their rivals over hunting grounds, or possibly just on general principles. The result was that Homo sapiens was kept in balance with the other species, and all the kingdoms of nature flourished securely, each in its sphere, not so very long ago. Some students of prehistory believe that our whole continent supported in this way not more than three million warring and quarrelsome but essentially ineffectual aborigines. They were ineffectual, that is, so far as permanently damaging the earth is concerned.

The Crees around here were keen traders. They liked to travel, it seems, and they traveled between the tribes of lesser enterprise than themselves, and even north beyond the tree line to do business with the Eskimos.

When European men appeared two centuries ago, the Crees continued in their natural role of traders, guides, and traveling interpreters. Writers always call them "the wily Crees," for when the white explorers asked what lay yet farther north, the Crees described their brown brethren as worthless idiots and monsters; and in fact they claimed them as their own slaves, as they wished to keep the corner on all the business for themselves.

Today we have the Slave Indians so named by the Crees. That is why we have the place names on our maps of Lesser Slave Lake, the Slave River, and Great Slave Lake. I showed the girls on the map where the enormous Great Slave Lake lay ahead of the *Jeanie Ann*'s resolute bow.

About the only Cree I ever knew was Jacques Mileaux who followed us two hundred miles on the river, making us feel quite ill-at-ease by his presence. But in the end he sold our lost toothbrushes back to us, as well as the films we had laid down on the riverbank —and these actions, I'm confident historians will agree, were wily indeed.

Modern man, alas, is hard-pressed to understand the Indians and the way they think. People who deal closely with Indians in both Alaska and Canada year after year have told me they always find them inscrutable, mysterious, and secretive. It takes simply years to know Indians, and they have plenty of time and we don't — so they can afford to outwait us.

The general impression I get of the wily Crees in northern Alberta is that they are angry. It seems that on June 21, 1899, according to history, the Crown signed Treaty No. 8 with the Crees, the remaining smallpox-decimated Beavers, Chipewyans, and others. The treaty did away with their ownership of the region we passed through: a part of B.C., all of northern Alberta, and the Northwest

Territories extending to the south shores of Great Slave Lake. In return for treaty presents and yearly annuities, the ancestors of Jacques Mileaux gave away forever to the advancing white civilization 324,900 square miles.

On top of that, people like Jacques who had white blood in their veins did not even get the presents and annuities. They got nothing. They were disinherited. They had a special grudge.

But people like Jacques couldn't put their mixed feelings into words in front of someone of an alien race and culture. So they just held their facial muscles rigid. Or they just turned their backs and walked stolidly away. In dealing with the whites on occasions when necessity absolutely called for it, they frequently deceived them or tried to get the better of them in some underhanded way.

Here in the Indian country, unseen by the children and me as we traveled, some six million acres or more of arable land had been marked out for farming. The great, broad, hundred-mile-wide river valley extending into the Arctic had been "opened" by the government more than fifty years ago, since it was thought that its alluvial soils and long days of summer sunlight waited only to attract sufficient numbers of sincere farmers to make it yield. In those years lumber mills also sprang up to glean the estimated three hundred million board-feet of marketable timber.

To the broad north Peace Valley were drawn rugged Italians, Poles, and Ukrainians. A colony of around three thousand people from Holland were enticed from Europe to join Canada's farthest northern agricultural experiment. Crops were wheat, barley, oats, the alfalfas, flax, and rape. Rapeseed turned the fields to solid sheets of yellow flowers, and paid better than wheat. Fields of flax were blue in July. Grain elevators rose from the New Great Slave Railway Line, at the siding at High Level.

Before the Mackenzie Highway was put in, farmers had paid fifty cents a bushel to ship their grains to outside markets; now they paid only thirteen cents. This lowered cost was a great inducement to new settlers.

As our boat wound through the turns of the Peace River we had in our minds the anticipation of Fort Vermilion ahead. It was the very nexus of the far northern farmlands and the only town built right on the river. It connected by government ferry across the river with a fifty-mile piece of gravel road to the Highway. Past the old Fort lay the rapids and cascades — called "Chutes" by the Canadians — and the portage problem. After surmounting this problem we looked forward to voyaging the long, empty, totally uninhabited lower Peace River through wilderness into the Slave River northward. Our total voyage on the Peace to the Chutes was six hundred miles.

Down the river we saw a white house with green trim ahead of us on the distant shore. But when we tried to approach it, it moved off swiftly. It was a boat, of a queer shape and pretty fancy, too. Madly we pursued it, and we finally caught it.

As it swung endwards to our view and sidled into the massive current, we realized suddenly that what we were chasing all over the river was a government ferry.

Maneuvering in to shore just below a river curve, we beached near a little row of green and white government houses that sat upon a steep hill. A dirt road was cut from the bluff here, connecting with La Crete and new lands across the river which were being opened. The government ferry in summer operated free of charge twenty-four hours a day, encouraging pioneers to cross the river and expand their fields and build their towns.

As the men operating the ferry watched us with blank and guarded eyes we tied the canoe to a log, crawled through mud, and looked wistfully up the steep hill overhanging us. We could see women with children watching us from up there at the doors of their tidy government houses; they were blond mostly, with blue eyes. We would go and call, I thought. To get me up the fifty-five degree, five-hundred foot bluff, the girls got behind and pushed.

We had all but achieved the hill's inviting crest and its fair-skinned female inhabitants, when to our dismay they turned as one woman and walked into their homes deliberately, all closing their doors.

"Mother," hissed Ann, "I've never been so insulted in all my life. Mother, do you realize that we have just been *insulted?*"

"Oh, dear," I puffed, and sat down in the grass.

"Darn them," said Jean. "Here we have come hundreds of miles on this river. I didn't want to see any people anyway. But since people are here already, they could have at least closed their doors when they saw us start at the bottom of the hill and not waited until we made it almost to the top."

"Mother, aren't you going to do something about it?" Ann bristled.

"Mother, it's better to poach a moose for your meals," Jean reminded us stringently, "than wait for the government people to feed you."

"Well," said Ann turning, thumb to nose, up the hill. "Spit and spiders to *them.*"

"Do you know what?" I said. "Those people are Dutch Mennonites. You see it's quite an exclusive group that has colonies in Canada and Mexico and the remote places they can still find in South America, and they don't care for the way the modern world is going. So they think we're modern, I guess."

As we climbed down from the bluff we could almost feel the imprint of burning eyes upon our trousers and unladylike apparel, glaring in outraged community disapproval. We could sense slight stirrings of curtains at sightless windows — those windows which were furnished to European aliens by a hospitable North American government.

"Love not the world," was the Mennonites' belief. "Neither the things that are in the world . . . If any man love the world, the love of the Father is not in him . . . Swear not [allegiance to any country], neither by heaven, neither by the earth, neither by any other oath . . . lest ye fall into condemnation . . . And all that believed were together and had things in common. . . ."

The Mennonites and the Hutterites in Canada have been slow during their fifty years' residence to become integrated. Thinking about it carefully, I decided I was a little suspicious of the word "integration": it was just a little too facile on the tongue. The trouble with the word and its philosophy, I decided, is the implied assumption that everybody on earth must become as alike as dull stones shaken up in a sack. In a way you had to admire these Mennonites and Hutterites, even if you disagreed with them, because they were *not* integrated with the rest of the mob. They could still get away with being different out here.

That evening down the river a few miles we tried to find a place to make camp. We had been on the water again, exposed to the elements, for at least a twelve-hour stretch and we were beat.

The river was dropping fast, dropping about one and a half feet a night.

Finally Jean said, "There's a grassy bluff over across the river there, do you see it? See that big white log? We could tie to it. Then we could climb right up the log over the mud and get to firm rocks that way."

As we approached the spot we noticed that the trees on top of the bluff looked smaller and smaller. It was a pretty big bluff, bigger than we thought. In fact everything in this country was bigger than we thought.

Our little mooring chains seemed small and feeble and the twenty-foot freight canoe itself seemed a toy as Jean snapped around some snag limbs on the monster log at the cliff base. If the chains grew taut due to falling water levels and we couldn't unsnap them the next day, I had a distasteful vision of myself feebly trying to saw through a log as big as a house to get free again. Was this anchorage a trap? — this was a recurring question when we camped, about which we usually conferred anxiously.

"I've chosen the camp tonight and I'll take care of my family," announced Jean. She began with great labor to haul the tent and its poles up the cliff hand over hand, having found a semilevel spot part way up. A small avalanche of rocks and boulders cascaded down in her wake. "Maybe there won't be any mosquitoes up there so high."

"We'll take care of Mother because she's getting middle-aged," added Ann helpfully.

"Listen, you," I replied, teetering over the river on the big log with my arms full, "that's not fair, and it isn't accurate."

"Mother is an elderly eccentric," added Jean to Ann aside, with a shocking lack of respect. "All she ever knew was old people."

As I tried to hand up the eighteen-pound sleeping bags, craning my neck upward, clawing at hardy shrubs on hands and knees and dragging my rather bulky gear behind me, I began to see that the innocent bluff which had enticed us from afar was in truth a malignant killer. Jean's campsite was at least ninety or a hundred feet straight up the cliff.

"I'll bring up our precious rifles," said Jean.

Crawling obediently up to the campsite, I just lay down and left the rest to the children. "It's so dry and clear, why don't we try to sleep outdoors without the tent tonight?" I suggested.

"Not a chance, you guys," Jean sternly told us. "It's a mistake in the North if you ever imagine you can get out of pitching the tent. A big mistake. I intend to pitch it even if you're too lazy to help."

Ann and I toppled and stretched out in the wild grass completely clothed, our headnets quickly pulled down from hat brims. But headnets do not work out for sleeping. They are useful only when you are upright. When you lay your head down an amazing activity begins. An unseen diva of the plants and of green growing things waves her wand. She sets the wings of innumerable nectar-sipping creatures in motion and accelerates their pulsations of life. Or, as Ann put it, "They rev their motors."

As you lie on earth's bosom thinking of peaceful sleep, strange whirrings and buzzes arise around you, magnified horribly, close to the ear and eye. The net from the stiff brim of your hat will insidiously droop, touching cheek or chin or neck, enabling the dreadful winged attackers to drill right into you, using a long probing proboscis attached directly to wicked eyes.

To the mosquito the pores of the skin are convenient large drilling holes; and plainly, the human sweat welling out of those pores is to be preferred over all sweet forest nectars. Besieged, the human victim, covered in poplin and woolens, veiled in nets, inserts himself now into a heavy, eighty-degree-below-zero sleeping bag. Surely inside this arctic bag he will find security from the beaks. Not so! Within a matter of minutes the insect howls reach such a crescendo that the victim rushes pell-mell into Jean's wobbling tent, pursued by swarms and dragging his sleeping bag with him. The walls of the tent are become as a city under siege. The enemy roars in wild rage, the battle lines are tightened. The elderly eccentric parent who is unfortunate enough to be here on a cliff yells out, "Daughter, pitch the tent low. Bury the bottom walls of the tent with something all around quick!"

Sweat-drenched Jean is throwing sods and stones and loose dirt with the camp shovel which she has brought from the canoe, burying the tent the way we used to do in the old days in the true Arctic. Not a moment may be lost in this battle for survival; we are discovering that the descendants of the many insects I used to know are the true daughters of the mothers who bore them.

"The tent's a little wobbly," Jean puffed. "You know when those Bay men tried to help us unpitch the tent they twisted the metal fixture so we can't use the tent uprights any more. So I chopped uprights out of young poplars on the cliff. I've roped the uprights together with the ridgepole, and don't you worry — can you hear me inside there?"

"What do you mean, don't worry?" screeched Ann. "Jean, you have already knocked me out twice with that ridgepole falling down right on my head."

"Just stick your dumb head inside the bag and shut up!" commanded our strongest member, outside. "Excuse me, Mother, but you too."

I had no way of knowing it there in our niche on the cliff, but something was about to happen which was to be one of the most frightening experiences of my life. There was all the potential for terrible danger.

As the kids slept I lay through the dim hours, in a sweating, sweltering daze. The Ladies of Alberta wanted our blood, all of it.

The female mosquitoes must drink warm animal blood to implement the progenitive processes of their species. Only wilderness travelers who have lived with these diaphanous rubescent ladies can understand that they will not take "no" for an answer. Only we in this wilderness possessed warm blood. We were the life goal of an absolutely fanatical mob of mainliners. Their demand for blood could bring on panic if you didn't keep hold of yourself. The demand in their voices and in their wings could cause accidents in camp.

The trouble was, the insect spray can had got lost somewhere in the canoe duffle, way down there at the foot of the bluff. It was our last can. The supply was to be refilled at Fort Vermilion ahead.

There I lay, thoughtfully, as large black insect silhouettes blundered against my headnet, momentarily blocking out the light of the world. I listened to their motors and whine. Beside my head many hundreds crawled, probing restlessly up the canvas tent walls. New ranks were filtering through underneath the tent corners from outside, whining in the primordial silence.

We had had no supper — impossible. Again we had had nothing to eat all day and all night. Bugs and mud made it impossible to get ashore and cook. We were dehydrated because we shrank from drinking the muddy water. We should have hauled water up this cliff and boiled up a lot of soup or tea or something, somehow.

Back in the woods a bird called monotonously. Tonight it got on my nerves. The lonely, remote bird's signal kept on repeating the same notes. A shiver coursed through me unexpectedly, my sweat was suddenly clammy, and I was afraid.

As I listened, all nature, which had always been my friend, became a threat to my life and my children's lives. Some danger was intoned in the monotonous birdcall and in the rustlings and hummings about us.

I recalled a certain expression in the eyes of old Hjalmur Feeshbeidt the trapper, when he told us how Death came to call on him. Fear comes at last one day to each animal in the forest. Always you are young and beautiful and strong in the forest, until one day it comes to you, the realization. It comes to you in a musical sigh from the heartless, impersonal cliff breeze, catching you up suddenly from what you are doing; or you learn of the waiting Presence in a strange bird's song. It is the song of Death.

Of course I knew my restlessness and morbidity were merely the results of getting too tired, and of lack of food: the primary dangers inherent in wilderness travel. Such conditions quickly affect the mind and judgment. I promised myself to control my mind and in the future to take meticulous care of our creature wants.

I got up and went outside. I looked around at our green jungle world from behind my veils. The sun hung about fifteen degrees above the horizon, muffled by a sullen purple early-morning cloud bank. Below the cliff, the great river churned its mud, glinting wickedly with purple and gold. Where was the canoe? It was parked at the foot of the cliff and I couldn't see it from up here. I didn't like the canoe being out of sight, not for one minute.

Perhaps I had better go down and check? Should I make the grand attempt, and haul food and water up, and build a fire? How about some action right now?

Looking off the cliff, I thought of Gerald. I thought of Grandmother back home, all worried about us. How was she? Was she all right? I thought of my menopausal girlfriends at their desks and in their offices. I immediately decided I was the luckiest of them all here, even on Jean's crazy cliff.

I peeled silvery bark from the little birches on the cliff and broke slivers of twigs, lacy and delicate, from underneath the little spruces near the tent for tinder. Then I grubbed up handfuls of grass and leaves, all damp. "I'll blast these accursed mosquitoes out of the tent first of all," I thought. Now I sat before the camp stove inside the tent and let the acrid smudge pour out of the stove comfortingly, suffusing the tent and the sleeping children. The many Ladies of Alberta wilted on their long legs. The flying wings with their thin beaks took nose-dives. An imbecilic smile spread over my face even while I choked in smoke.

I left the tiniest, most puny fire going in the stove. The wonderful healing smudge was puffing out a crack in the stove door, and the tent walls were squirming with our disabled tormentors. I would hasten back from the canoe in just a minute.

Looking back now I can only excuse myself by thinking that somehow my judgment must have been a little distorted and the normal sense of caution dulled because the mosquitoes had almost driven me mad. I find it otherwise difficult, in fact impossible, to explain my leaving the tent while in the process of "smudging."

I was at the canoe when I heard yells and screams from the cliff above. "Help! Help! The tent's on fire!" from Ann. Then from Jean a shrill shout, "Ann, hurry. Get out."

The kids, drugged with exhaustion, awoke to find our shelter filled with flames. Ann saw the flames first, flames which blocked their exit. The kids could not get out of the sides or back of the tent because the tent walls were solidly buried under toggles and earth. Ann ducked her head into her bag just as the tent wall collapsed at the point where her head had been.

Jean leaped out the tent door through a sheet of fire. From outside, seeing the tent wall collapse, apparently upon Ann, she was frantic, and shouted, "Ann, hurry. Get out," the words I heard.

At this Ann emerged from her bag into scorching heat. She had tied the cord of her sleeping bag around her neck to keep out the mosquitoes — unknown to me. Nobody knows to this day by what miracle she escaped — by agility and thinness, perhaps.

I tried to leap up the cliff when I heard the screams but was so weak with terror that, missing my leap, I fell crashing off the big log stairway we had used, nearly caving my ribs. Emerging from the edge of the river six feet below, I tried the cliff again, losing precious time. I scaled it crazily, grabbing at roots and stones which gave way.

By the time I reached the top the children had saved themselves. They were standing there in a state of shock, while a pillar of flame shot skyward. The tent was gone. It was too late to save it. The children's blackened faces were runneled with tears and the ends of their blond hair were singed. They smelled scorched.

I snatched out two sleeping bags from the circle of flames, plus socks, bras, boots, the smoking-hot camera. Jean saved the rifles but her glasses were cremated with the oily tent-floor tarp.

Only a blackened tent frame and a few pegs in the ground remained.

Fortunately there was no time to feel sick in the pit of the stomach. In civilization it is possible that a shock of this sort would injure the psyche of a family for years. Here we simply hastened to put on our clothes and adjust to the fact that we were suddenly homeless and houseless and had to survive.

The strange bird which had been calling went on its way and even the mosquitoes which had caused the havoc retreated from the neighborhood, repelled by the great smoke, as though to say in all innocence, "Just what was the commotion all about anyway?"

The five o'clock sun broke through the cloud bank and a new day was here. A new lease on life from narrowly averted tragedy. A fresh shot of adrenaline for Mother, at least.

"Tent fires are one of the greatest dangers in the North," I told the kids shakily and probably unnecessarily as I worked. "Eskimos and Indians are always burning up tents. Let that be a lesson to us all."

"Did you and Father ever burn a tent?"

"Well, let me see. I guess it did happen one time. Only time in twelve years, though. We partly burned one of our tents. There was a light fall of snow on the ground in July, and it was on the polar plains. I recall that that fire was put out by dousing it with our breakfast, a five-gallon gas can full of caribou stew."

"I wish we had some caribou," piped Ann, who lay shocked and chilled in one of the bags as Jean and I worked.

"I wish we had a new tent," said Jean. "Can we get a new one at Fort Vermilion? How about a different kind, more lightweight?"

"Sure I guess so," I said. "Those light tents are really too light to last in country like this. But it would be a whole lot quicker to pitch each night, and with a sealed floor, completely bug-proof. Make life easier, wouldn't it? We'll have to get rid of our wood-stove. Just cook outside from now on by campfire. Maybe get a folding gasoline stove and carry fuel for it. Won't be any way to dry socks. Miserable life on bad days. Miserable to eat outside with the bugs. But what do you think, Ann? What kind of new tent do you think we ought to get?"

"The lightweight kind," voted Ann from the sleeping bag, and got up.

We loaded the canoe and shoved off toward Fort Vermilion, about a ninety-mile run. Jean myopically grabbed hold of a triple-threat fishhook as we shoved off. Gingerly, she unhooked her hand. We stared at each other with round eyes, no words spoken.

We ate in the boat as we traveled, free of bugs, out on the water. Ate big hard pilot crackers and jam, and chunks of butter spread on top of chunks of peanut butter on a knife blade; and cold canned peas slurped from uptilted, ragged-edged cans.

Sleep would not be possible again until we reached shelter, except by catnaps in turn as we traveled. We had learned that the Ladies would not let you sleep without a tight, fumigated shelter.

Hours later a sawmill operation appeared along the shore. "Would you like to make another call on the friendly Mennonites?" I asked Ann.

It was a temptation to get out of the boat for a stretch, since the pebble beach here was firm. Ann didn't think much of my idea, but she came out of the boat with me. Jean lay asleep. It was a Sunday morning and the lumber camp seemed totally deserted.

We walked through stacks of lumber and reached a little dirt street with houses. One wife was at home, peeping out through her screen door, with four little ones hanging on her skirts.

"What you want?"

"Ahem, I am Mrs. Helmericks and we are Americans." (An introduction which so far this trip had failed to impress anyone.) "Our tent caught fire and burned down. My two daughters and I are traveling in a boat down the river."

The woman scanned Ann and me with dour suspicion. "Where you from? Where you go?"

My answer apparently did not convince her that we were not darkly sinister characters, possibly from the nether regions, what with our fire-singed hair.

"My man, he gone to church," said the woman. "He come back pretty soon. Then you come in and I make dinner. You can wait out there." She indicated the great outdoors.

"Some Christianity!" I thought. "And on a Sunday too!"

"No thank you!" I said.

"Thank you," piped Ann forlornly, and we walked to our canoe.

Anyway, Fort Vermilion would eventually heave into view if we kept going. Many Mennonites, we were to learn, till the soil in the area around Fort Vermilion where there are also around five hundred and fifty stoical, shabby Crees, mostly on the dole, who do not till.

Swept through many channels we followed the river hopefully toward that jewel in the heart of the lotus, Fort Vermilion.

"First we'll check in with the Mounties," I encouraged my scorched, sooty crew. "Then, we'll go get a real restaurant meal, I hope. Then we'll head for the Bay Store and restock supplies."

Fort Vermilion was established in 1846 when Father Joseph Vourassa opened a mission there, followed two years later by the alert Hudson's Bay Company.

Fortunately for the traveler as well as for the northern resident, the Bay has increased its services and diversified fantastically in the North since the old days of mere fur trading. Since the 1930's it has quadrupled its original assets to take care of the total needs of families everywhere in Canada. The Bay has brought factory-made snowshoes, outboard motors, fresh meats, and frozen vegetables. It has brought curling rink equipment — a necessity of social life in every northern town — baby diapers, fox traps, oil-burning stoves, butane gas stoves, girdles and hoisery, and even the "Bay bra," the company's very own answer to figure control, into the far, far North. Beyond the Arctic Circle, beyond the tree line. Beyond the continent, even, to those remote islands of the arctic archipelago which stretch out nearly to the North Pole.

But before we reached Fort Vermilion through the glasses we saw ahead two boats ashore and a floating dock.

When I climbed out onto the dock my girls were in a state of such total apathy that they could not be induced to come ashore and had no interest in my investigations. But something told me to look around. True, this wasn't Fort Vermilion. But sometimes the suburbs are better than downtown. Walking a few steps up the path, I found a dirt road and presently a large cabin trailer set high up off the earth on tremendous wheels, just parked there, surrounded by large cultivated fields.

Pulling myself up Paul Bunyan-sized steps, I peered inside the trailer for signs of people. Although a radio blared from its interior, no one was at home. Sunday. The two bunks were empty. Dirty dishes lay beside a two-plate burner. But this was a big farm operation. This trailer was the semipermanent base for men to live in while working in the enormous fields. Later I learned the fields totaled eight thousand acres. It was a far bigger operation than even the Canadian government's northern experimental farms, and privately owned.

"It's a big modern farm operation!" I reported to the kids with enthusiasm. "It's a real going thing. I've never seen anything like it in northern Alberta. Somebody working this place knows what he's doing. A lot of money invested here. I'm sure we would be welcome to sleep in the bunks inside the trailer, out of the bugs. We're going to stay right here until the men come back, whoever they are."

But the girls had been inculcated with a respect for private property, and to my consternation they rejected my idea. Nor would I leave the spot. To compromise, we fell upon the warm dry grass in the sun, and with headnets pulled down fell dead asleep in the field.

About three o'clock the farm manager returned. He was an American, hired by American interests.

"I'm Mrs. Helmericks and we are Americans . . ." I began my song.

"I know who you are. I know all about you," he smiled. "We're Americans, too, and from your part of the States, I believe. Why didn't you go inside and lie down on the bunks instead of lying on the ground?"

"They," I pointed, "wouldn't go in. Respect for private property."

"You got a lot of bug bites. Looks like some of them may be getting infected," he said.

"My foot's infected from a sharp willow stick I stepped on. I can hardly walk," admitted Jean to the kindly, practical farmer.

"I've got bites all over. And they're infected," added Ann. "Our tent burned down, too. Mother set it on fire by accident." I winced.

"Now your mother shouldn't have done that," he said. "Are you hungry? I'll bet you are."

"A little, our stomachs are shrunk."

"Well, I just came down to haul some water for the flowers

around the house. Soon as I fill these cans," he said, "we'll drive on up to the house, and the wife's got chicken dinner about ready by now, I suppose. We was just waiting dinner. Now isn't it lucky I decided to water the flowers today?"

As we bumped along in the pickup toward the farmhouse, it soon appeared that he knew quite a few people we knew back in the western part of the United States. First I was pleased to discover he knew just one person I knew. Then, working ever closer to home, I asked if he knew another and another, and the answer was so frequently yes that it was amazing. Finally, with some hesitancy, I asked, "I wonder if you could have ever met my sister and her husband when you were farming back in that region?"

"Well," since you mention it," the pioneer American replied, as amazed as I, "the wives used to play bridge every week. Well, we used to square dance with them a few years ago back there. Guess they moved away then. We moved too. That was your sister, you say, your own sister?"

"Sure," I said. "Well, I guess you knew my sister and brother-in-law very well then?"

"Well," he said, "as a matter of fact, they were our best friends when we were living there. Now, what do you know about that? Small world, isn't it?"

"Well, I just can't get over it," I exclaimed.

"Well, as a matter of fact," he ended, as we went on expressing our astonishment at the mutuality of our background, "I knew who you and those kids were the moment I saw you because we have quite an active moccasin telegraph in the North, you know. As well as other kinds of telegraph, of course. But what I never would have guessed is that you are their sister. And they were some of our best friends! We were guests in their home many, many times. It's good to hear about them and to get in touch with them again."

Bumping along the dirt road we explored the coincidence further. And that is how it happened that upon climbing out of the Peace River and falling asleep in a field, we were found by the American family, the Able Hardworkers, year-around residents nowadays of Fort Vermilion, and their fifteen-year-old daughter Effervescent. Jean and Effie soon became close friends.

12

The Emergency Appendix

ONE of the many terribly attractive things about the Americans
— to other Americans — was their indoor plumbing.

They had a town house in Fort Vermilion twenty-six miles away
by dirt road, with a tile bathroom with tub and matching companion fixtures.

They had bought the house and remodeled it out of a century-
old Hudson's Bay barracks, developing their own water system
from a sand-filtered well over which the house had originally been
constructed. Other people in Vermilion for the most part purchased their water horse-hauled by an Indian at fifty cents a barrel,
untreated, directly out of the Peace River below town.

The Hardworkers, let's call them Able and Mabel Hardworker,
finding the water system less than ideal for their appetite and having acquired their own independent water supply, installed a pump
in their basement and shipped in forthwith the only bathtub and
flush toilet, other than those in the hospital and mission, in literally thousands of square miles. There were two motels in town, with
cafés, used by traveling businessmen. But they were served by outhouses. The motel rooms were supplied with a tin basin for bathing, a large tin pitcher of cold water, and a slop bucket; and in
summer a mosquito spray bomb awaited each businessman hospit-
ably on his private bedside stand.

The Hardworker home could be recognized from a distance by
its gleaming picture window and from an even greater distance by

an enormous silver butane gas tank nearly as large as the house itself. By contrast, the ancient mission boarding school stood flanked by hundreds of cords of stacked wood.

After we had spent a night at the farm, it was suggested that we proceed into town as the Hardworkers' guests. We could not continue to use the bunkhouse, for the labor gang came back to work on Monday and the farm lacked other accommodations.

"You may have noticed the condition of our bunkhouse," lamented Mr. Able Hardworker. "Would you believe it? Only a year ago I had it all freshly painted and fixed up for our field hands." He shook his head. "You wouldn't believe possible the destruction these men can wreak in a place in one year. Break the backs right off chairs. Twist the plumbing so hard the handles come off. Kick out the windows. Even pull the door off the hinges. Fact is," he told us, "some of them, men coming to us maybe even thirty-five years old, men with families, have never seen a shower before, you know. They never had a bath in their lives. Well, they just don't know how to live in a house, and they don't care. They break everything faster than you can keep it in repair."

"Like in our own West fifty years ago," I suggested. "Just wild."

"They left your radio going out in the trailer and were wearing out the battery when we came along," Ann put in.

"Oh, they don't give a damn," said Able.

"Your bunkhouse table right this minute is covered with spoiling food that they didn't put into the fridge when they left for the weekend. Wouldn't you think, with as little as they have, they would be more thrifty?"

"Sometimes I don't know where their brains are," commented Able, in sad Americanese. "Anyway, the company does the best we can for them, and that's our labor here."

"But I read they made tremendous soldiers during the war, that type of man," I recalled. "Anyway, even if they have their shortcomings they gave a lot of blood."

"That kind is used to hardship," Able admitted. "They've got real steady nerves, that's one thing you have to give'm credit for."

"Canada is not what you usually think it is," said Mrs. Hardworker. "It's really a very loose collection of a lot of people from

Europe, combined with Indians; and out from the cities you'll find the educational level is very low, compared to what I expected before I came here, anyway.* But it's wonderful how all these people get along, as a whole. They have freedom, and they have respect for law and order, and, my goodness, Canada, you know, didn't even have a *flag* of her own until nearly the first hundred years she was a nation. They just borrowed the English flag, and got along that way, in this big country. Effie, you can start washing the breakfast dishes now, while Jean and Ann can get busy and dry."

The Hardworker girl Effervescent had been reared for several years in rural Alberta without knowing any American girls. She and the usually taciturn Jean became immediate friends. They had things in common: horses.

Effie did not particularly subscribe to a philosophy of hard work as her parents did — that is, unless pressed into it, as was frequently the case — but at the age of fifteen rode horses like the wind. Horses are fairly cheap in the North Peace River Country, if you don't mind medicating the poor beasts with salves and disinfectants to cure their many untreated sores, and if your father can manage the problems of winter barns and winter hay. It's about the northernmost latitude at which horses were practical. Also, the horse latitudes end at the end of cultivation, you might say. As Effie Mae told Jean, "Horses are some of my best friends."

"Sometimes you can see bears in our fields in the summer," Effie said to Jean, glowing. "Sometimes we can chase the bears out of the alfalfa on horseback. She explained that her dad, having been granted permission by the Forestry Department to clear his fields of bears, had shot fifty-two during the last three summers. Her father had almost as much difficulty keeping Effie Mae on horseback out of his fields as he did the bears, but she forgot to mention this.

It was arranged that Ann and I would canoe on down the river to town, and Jean would eventually follow by road with the Hardworkers the next time they came to town with their grocery list.

"Can I run the motor?" Ann asked, as we adjusted empty gas cans.

* Only eleven percent of Canada's population today is actually rural.

"Of course. I'd be absolutely unable, alone, dear."

"Just get yourselves all rested up in our town house," said Mrs. Hardworker. "Plan to stay a few days. We'll keep Jean busy on the farm and I'll see that her infected foot has care. You'll have to wait awhile probably to get your orders from the south. Call us on the house radio telephone and let us know you arrived."

Ann and I, alone together, looked out thoughtfully on the grand slow-moving river. A capable pull on the starter rope by a lean, childish arm. Her one hand controlled the motor deftly, with absolute nonchalance and a complete lack of fear of the river, while the other hand balanced a large pilot biscuit dripping with blueberry jam.

A couple of hours later Ann made our landing at Fort Vermilion quite capably. The distant town basked in somnolence, reminiscent of days of fifty or a hundred years ago, its frame buildings of all sizes and shapes scattered along the waterfront. Scattered always because of the danger of fire.

Little bright boats were pulled up at intervals on the shoreline.

"Picturesque, isn't it, Ann?"

"Looks like a real swinging place, Mom."

"Dearest, it looks almost like the old days that I remember so well. The old days on the Yukon River in Alaska, twenty years ago."

"But I can't say it turns me on," said Ann sensibly.

Unfortunately, because of the steep riverbanks, I was not able to see the village above when we motored in close to it. It was because of this that I mistakenly guided Ann to a landing at the base of the Mounted Police refuse pile which tilted into the river. I didn't realize it until we found ourselves walking knee deep in ashes and clinkers, and Ann pointed out the many tin cans. However, up the trash pile we waded gamely.

Above, unseen by us, seated in the RCMP building across the waterfront road, a young man, smartly uniformed, booted and spurred, not more than twenty-three, answered a strident ring on his telephone.

"Royal Canadian Mounted Police, Constable A. J. Freddie Pilkington speaking," we might have heard. Regulations required that the full title be given each time the telephone rang, although in this instance it was quite a mouthful.

Then if we listened we might have heard, "Ah, yes." Pause. . . . "Yes, yes, I'll be right along. I'll be right along and attend to it."

Young Pilkington was fresh from England. He had been selected from among thousands of applicants in two countries, who must have an eleventh grade minimum education qualification, in addition to which good character is particularly stressed, for a Royal Canadian Mounted Police career.

At the same moment that we were struggling up the trash pile toward this good officer to report in, a Cree laborer emptied another trash barrel cunningly down the bank, barely missing our heads. And, still unknown to us, Constable Pilkington — everyone for hundreds of miles familiarly called him "Freddie" — came out of headquarters, got into his patrol car, and drove briskly off.

Our timing was so often wrong in the North. Dirty and weary, Ann and I rang the bell at the official door a minute later. A sign had been turned to the front. "Gone out," it said simply.

Constable Freddie Pilkington had been sent for by a distressed parent, a Dutch Mennonite, as it happened, a Mr. Hans Krunchknuckle. This gentleman's daughter was at this very moment dancing to the lively tunes of a jukebox which had recently been installed in a café. Her dancing partner, an indigenous citizen of the country, was a Cree Indian, and both were drunk.

"My daughter is white girl," cried Mr. Krunchknuckle, his voice breaking with all a parent's enraged and helpless pathos. "When is white girl to run with that black Indian, I tell you. . . ."

"Mr. Krunchknuckle, will you tell us clearly. . . ."

"I got seventeen children, all Christians children, all is behave themselves but this one. My family been white for thousands of year, I tell you."

As Constable Pilkington pointed out to the irate Mr. Krunchknuckle, the law was not empowered to keep young people apart for racial reasons. Nor was the law empowered to remove the offending coin box and its sulfurous musical records from a licensed public café. However, if a girl were a juvenile, something could be done about the drinking. Not so much on account of the girl as on account of the Indian. It is against the law, for their own good, for Indians to buy or possess or consume liquor in Alberta, and the law-enforcement officers are very much concerned about this. Raiding Indian liquor stills back in the woods may be one of the major duties of RCMP officers in the rural areas of some provinces. But still nothing prohibits the Indians and Eskimos across the border in the Northwest Territories from alcoholic indulgence.

While these little community upheavals were taking place, Ann and I had floated on down the village shoreline, tied our canoe, and entered the Hardworker town house, removing our boots outside the door.

Soon long underwear and dirty socks were dancing to Tchaikovsky's *Nutcracker Suite* on the record player as the wonderful Hardworker washing machine ground through its rhythms. Suddenly the telephone rang and there came Gerald's civilized voice through the miles of forests, saying, "Are you all right? You know, I've been just terribly worried. Yes, really. I had to call you. For heaven's sake, haven't you got into the Northwest Territories yet? I've been trying all over there. I've been having these terrible dreams. Nightmares. Can you hear me? Have you been in some kind of danger? I say . . ."

I told him the tent burned down, and we were waiting for a new one now. "We're with Americans. Yes, American friends. Yes, just wonderful. Everything is fine now. They fed us when we were nearly starved, and I'm so happy to hear from you, and we're staying a few days in their town house here. . . ."

"I know it," he interrupted. "They have a bath. The operator at Peace River town told me where to get you. I'm certainly glad I caught you. I wonder when we'll meet again. . . . Don't you think you should consider returning south when winter comes up there?"

"I don't know. Right now the long underwear has been washed and it's dancing in the electric dryer like mad," I added inanely, trying to think of something to say in my surprise that Gerald would call all that distance.

"I could dance like mad, too, with you," he said fiercely.

"Oh, Gerald, that's the maddest thing you've ever said," I cried.

"Well," his tone changed, "your mother is here at my elbow. She wants a few words with you and the kids." He handed the telephone over, and I heard my mother's eighty-one-year-old voice, so loving, so patient, as ever the mother.

"Oh, my dear child," she was weeping. "How could you ever attempt such a trip? Are you still alive?"

"Still alive, and very old," I shouted vigorously. "And, oh, my dear, how about you?"

"Mother," interrupted Ann at this point, "I don't feel good. I feel like I am going to throw up."

"Bosh!" I said. "Speak to your grandmother."

Presently the Hardworker group came from their farm and took their baths. They shopped at the Bay, and leaving Jean off with me returned to the farm. Effervescent had made good her promise: the girls had indeed chased bears on horseback. Jean's horse had reared on its hind legs and had thrown Jean fairly hard.

"There goes a real good kid," sighed Jean.

"There she goes indeed," I said. "She's going to go away to a girls' boarding school in the States. I believe that's what her mother has in mind for this fall."

"Now why should they want to do that to Effervescent?" Jean heaved a long sigh of melancholic perplexity. A pause. Then, "But what will become of all her horses?"

"How should I know?" I said unfeelingly.

"Can we have them? Oh, Mom, can Jean and I have the horses, if nobody cares for them?" shrilled Ann straightaway.

I saw that she had entered the normal American girl horse stage.

"Sure," I said. "All of them the canoe will carry."

The farm family cast but a hasty backward glance as they left us there in their town house, and at the time we did not expect to linger for long. The Americans were particularly busy because their shipment of bees from the south had arrived that week, and the bees had to be organized. To perpetuate alfalfa seed you have to have bees. You have to import them into the North, since nature never supplies them there. Furthermore, the trick is to organize things so the bees arrive very late in timing with the blooms for far northern alfalfa. Otherwise, they are apt to starve to death before your alfalfa can be pollinated. Now rain began to fall coldly day after day. The order did not come from the south. We had no tent. Jean had no glasses.

All the things I half remembered about my Alaska days came back sourly, the things I hadn't liked to remember. The endless cold and gray overcast. Once it sets in, a whole season can literally be doomed. The intractable, stubborn misery which is the North, a world of dark evil waters and dark rainy endless spruce forest. Closed in, you sit and wait. What *is* the North? The North is harshness and meanness. The North is elemental, untamed and untamable. The North is *waiting*.

The North has all the time in the world. But you don't.

Still, I loved it. And to my great pleasure I saw that my children were taking to a canoe like ducks to water and were beginning to get a clear idea of the things they saw around them.

We were playing records as rain drizzled by the window and Jean sat soaking her bad foot in the Hardworker dishpan. Here, at least, was the respite of shelter and a chance to heal up our hundreds of bug bites before going on.

Then that night Ann became sick. I cared for her as she vomited, thankful for bedsheets, shelter, and modern plumbing. So goes a mother's predestined routine, and a child's penalty for childhood. But Ann got worse and worse. A small pain started in her tummy, and grew.

At five in the morning I anxiously staggered for the telephone and called the small hospital run by the nuns. They told me the doctor's phone number. I had not known there was a doctor around here. He was the only surgeon in possibly fifty thousand square miles, the only one in northern Alberta and the entire Peace River country north of Edmonton. As a matter of fact, he lived in one of the shacks we saw on the waterfront, only about four blocks away.

The town's taxicab, supplied by a housewife who used her own car, bumped over the dirt waterfront road in the pale morning light carrying a pale, exhausted, and miserable Ann, in night-clothes.

In a dark shabby office the wide-awake, booming voice of the surgeon welcomed us. With confident hands he quickly probed the patient's small body on his table.

"Ah, I believe we may have an appendix here," he boomed heartily, with a British accent, his mustache bristling with enthusiasm. "We can take it out for you right away, if you like. Wonderful canoe trip you've been having. A trip I would like to make myself, if I could get away. Did you experience many rapids? Now I like a large motor myself. What kind of motor are you using? What do you think of this country? How do you protect yourselves from the mosquitoes?"

"Oh, we like the country very much," said Ann feebly. "Shouldn't we get a blood test to confirm the diagnosis?"

"Ah, yes. Sister Evangeline is our biologist at the hospital. Just a moment. I'll give her a jingle. Is your cab waiting? Good. Now you just run along to the hospital, and I imagine we'll plan to operate within the hour" — he glanced at his watch — "that is, about 6 A.M. I say, what horsepower would you seriously advise for a long river trip? Could you give an idea of your gasoline consumption on the trip thus far?"

Ann sat up. "About forty gallons so far," she advised. "You must always carry your extra tank filled and ready to hook right onto the motor, and be sure there are no air bubbles in the fuel line. . . ."

"Aha, well I say."

"You have to strain all your gas from the cans when you funnel it into the tanks and make sure there's no dirt or water in the gas," Ann continued helpfully.

"Very good, very good," he boomed, helping us into the waiting cab. "See you quite soon, I think. We can talk more later about the river trip," he added.

Meanwhile I was wondering if an appendectomy actually was to take place. Gradually I was growing terribly upset on many counts. Would this stop our river voyage?

Before I could think clearly Ann's appendix was out, after a neat, quick spinal anesthetic, and she was resting in a narrow white bed in the Fort Vermilion Hospital.

The surgeon sent the appendix to the pathological lab in Edmonton, thus complying with Provincial law, he explained.

I sat by Ann's bed, holding her bug-bitten little hand, now so limp. It was three days later. "You are such a fine girl. I am very proud of you. Do you remember the time you were five and you almost jumped into the Grand Canyon? You always were so impulsive. Goodness, you often made me nervous. But the doctor says we'll have you out of this hospital in a week, my love."

"We've got to get on with the expedition," Ann agreed.

"I'm going to run along, for this time. I've got to try to get more information about the river ahead, and I haven't had much luck so far. Nobody here ever goes below the Chutes. You know, of course, that we have two portages yet ahead this summer?"

There were no communications between the officials here and those in the Northwest Territories because of differences in organization and departmentalization.

"Go to the Indians, Mother. They are the ones who will know. Go to the Indians," advised Ann from her bed.

Finally, I did. The Indian shack I approached through a field of oats beside the river was so tiny that any reasonably large woman explorer could reach out and touch its roof. Near the doorway two smudge fires fumed. Dirty, bug-bitten small children were visible near the house, which stood in a welter of castoff boots and cans, worn-out brooms and old tires.

The people of the little house saw the white explorer arriving, armed with large maps, puffing and slapping at bugs. They turned their heads and looked away, stoically. I knocked on the tiny, unpainted wooden door and stooped to enter, stepping over the high northern sill.

There was the old father or grandfather. I smiled into a seamed and kindly face, bronzed, with narrow, slitted eyes and a dark thatch of hair salted with gray. The old face is more often than not a good face. He wore bangs. Bangs protect the sinuses against winter wind, and also, to an extent, against summer bug bites. He wore denim work clothes. He spoke a little English but to him my maps were an incomprehensible rendering of the land he knew in his mind's eye.

"They tell me there is a wise man living here who knows about travel with a boat upon the river," I said in Hollywood script style.

"Ya, ha." The man nodded pleasantly.

The lady of the house, in a black dress with bare arms and cotton stockings above mocassins encased in rubbers, spoke no English. She had a sagging muscle in one side of her face, causing it to droop.

A teen-age daughter with soft creamy olive skin interpreted. She wore a short-sleeved blue print frock and her head was encased in large pink plastic curlers. Very possibly the tots outside were this girl's children. A couple of iron bedsteads with rags nearly filled the tiny room. There were the usual bare wooden table and unpainted straight chairs and stools, and a wood-burning cooking range in addition to a small wood-burning heater not larger than the one we had used in our former tent.

On the walls were large color pictures of the late Pope John and the Beatles. There was the smell of sour mildew and the smell of poverty — which may indeed be mildew, I decided.

The old man described two different sets of rapids on the Peace below the Chutes and portage. I was concerned about rocks sticking up out of the rapids, for some X's indicating rocks were marked on my official navigation map series starting below the Chutes.

As I checked and double-checked my information, it seemed unfair in a way that the Alberta Travel Bureau were so free with their encouragement of a tourist voyaging down the Peace northward through Alberta. For then they suddenly dropped all interest in such a tourist, just as the Peace entered the turbulent Slave River to career madly into the Northwest Territories, where absolutely nothing in the way of human habitation or assistance could arrest his mad ride, *in case he should change his mind.*

The fine old Indian told me truthfully that the Slave River as far as Fort Fitzgerald (where navigation ended abruptly at a second portage) was "fast water, rapids all the way, and many rocks."

In days following, other Indians came to the house to give what

information they could, and also to offer their condolences over Ann's appendix. They stepped hesitatingly in out of the rain; and I must say I felt uneasy about allowing them in, since the house was not my own and the Hardworkers made it a rule not to let Indians into the house. I hustled them out smartly, feeling hypocritical and guilty, because our house was rich and theirs were poor.

One of the Indian women took me to meet Quinby Rapp. Back in the forest this man lived in a well-pitched canvas wall tent with a stove. An outdoors table under an overhanging tent fly accommodated my maps while Mr. Rapp instructed me minutely. The smudge fires fumed and rain-spattered leaves gleamed wetly. Mr. Rapp was a man of about forty with blond hair and pale blue eyes.

"I came here with three boats," he said. "My cabin is up the river about thirty-five miles above Carcajou. I have my mother living here in town."

"Why do you have three boats?"

He grinned amiably. "All my dogs."

"Oh, yes, I see. You have to take them wherever you go, of course. They have to eat."

"Yes. I am a trapper."

"Do you have children?"

"No, we have no children."

"Then you don't have to worry about school in the winter?"

"No."

"What do you do for meat right now?"

"Oh, I am thinking to go back up the river soon. We need a moose. Just about out of meat. Where the ranger don't catch me," he laughed gently.

"The RCMP — Freddie — he said you might be going down to the Chutes and that we could follow you with our boat to the portage, perhaps?"

"Well, I don't think so now," he replied. "I was to take a fellow down that needed a ride, but he changed his mind."

I swallowed my disappointment, feeling forlorn. "Do you speak Cree?"

"Sure," he said. "I am Cree. My mother is Cree. My wife here,

Emma, as you can see, she is Cree. My father was American. I am therefore métis." As we pored over the maps he tried to reassure me that there was really nothing to fear in the forest. "You won't have trouble. I don't see why you would," he insisted reasonably. "I used to live down there at Fifth Meridian. All nice country, you won't see many people. I worked for the Forestry Department for five years at the buffalo kill, farther down. You'll be going through buffalo country nearly all the way. Around seventeen thousand buffalo in that country."

"Buffalo! What? Well, who kills them and how are they killed?"

"Oh, just the government," he said. "Nobody else supposed to. The government kill the herd surplus, the selected animals. The government sell them for the meat, you know? We shoot them each fall for that."

He used a .357 Magnum, the former official killer told me. "They round them up in the fall and get them into corrals."

"How do they round them up, by truck?" Somehow I couldn't see a truck used in the swamps I had so far seen.

"No, buffalo will charge a truck and tip it over," he explained. "They just won't drive. Some of them are the big black forest buffalo, bigger than the plains buffalo, too. They're always in a bad mood. So the rangers use helicopters now and drive them that way."

"Is it easy to kill a buffalo in a corral?"

"Well, no. You have to be very careful to shoot each one alone, just behind the ear. And they won't stand still, you know. They are excited and they are charging all the time around the corral. Takes a strong corral to hold them."

"How many does the government kill each year?"

"Oh, I would say anything up to four hundred. We can take care of about ten a day at the abattoir, a three-hundred-thousand-dollar plant."

I nodded. "Have an airfield in that country?"

"Oh, yes. But they don't fly the meat out. They truck it out after freeze-up, on the Winter Road to Fort Smith."

This was how I learned about Wood Buffalo National Park, the largest park in the world, 17,300 square miles in area. We would get to pass right down the side of it when we rode the Slave River into the North.

"Go to the Indians, Mother," Ann had advised. But when I got back to the house, I found the Indians had come to us. That is, the younger generation had.

I heard the sound of male voices when I opened the door. Above the loud music of the record player. "You seen Effie Mae lately?" a teen-age Cree boy asked me as I stepped in.

"No," I replied, taken by surprise. There was an uneasy shuffling of bodies standing dimly by the kitchen door. Suddenly I saw Jean, and close beside her a dark Cree youth, who to my dismay was standing very close to my daughter in a familiar attitude and who appeared to have his arm around her.

"You'll have to go now," gasped Jean in an unnatural voice. "My mother's home."

"Jean is only fourteen years old!" I told the wild young Indians, and clicked off the record. But realized, as soon as I said it, that my words meant absolutely nothing to them.

The sons of the forest slipped slyly out the door. That door which they knew the Hardworkers had a rule they could not enter. They scampered, sniggering, with the insolent, cigarette-puffing, cocky sneers of resentful youth, to their hopeless, poverty-ridden shacks in the rain.

What does the parent do now?

There was nothing good or interesting these poor boys could do with their lives. They were the kind that our people termed "no good." They looked only for amusement or mischief to fill their time. The sparse employment which existed certainly bored them. They were permanently on government dole.

My first words to Jean were contrary to all the democratic principles we believed in. But I saw now that it would be very hard to be democratic in Fort Vermilion. It wasn't practical to be democratic in the face of such a wide "culture gap" between the rich and the poor, the educated and the ignorant, as existed here — especially when you had a son or daughter nearing the age at which sexual attraction becomes an incipient danger.

As I tried to tell Jean, no fourteen-year-old girl can solve this problem, and I don't think a fourteen-year-old girl should be placed in the position where she has to try to.

"Mother," argued Jean, "I didn't know how to get them out of the house. You don't understand. They are so awfully lonely. They only wanted to hear a little music, and come in out of the rain. Ma, they couldn't even finish second grade. Well, they probably may not even have the brains for it," she admitted, facing it herself. "Mom, they don't know anything about the outside world. They only know they want to have some of the good things. . . ."

"Yes, that is true," I said. "But, my dear, even back in our own city we have people like this. The helpless, ignorant poor. So, please, listen! I am not just an old fuddy-duddy as you think, but I am trying to make you see the world. Perhaps later on you can choose a profession and be trained, and help the world. But right now, you are a fourteen-year-old, inexperienced girl, and these aimless, mindless young men are completely parasitic and just see you as someone to prey upon."

She didn't like to see that at all, not one bit. But I think she finally saw it after we talked. "Oh, why, why, is everything so awful and horrid? Why is everything so mixed up and cruel in the world?" wept Jean. Minds far wiser and older than hers have wept at almost these very same thoughts. Only Jean felt it all overwhelmingly at this moment, with the poignancy of idealistic youth. She wanted to change things right now and make the world a better place, somehow.

"Let's clean out the canoe. Get our outfit ready to go," I suggested. Jean looked up from her stormy tears.

It is almost useless to argue with a young girl. Perhaps it is best just to get busy doing things for a few years. Things of youth and joy. The world's problems can only be coped with if the young have the opportunity to cultivate their own gardens first, and to grow in the sunshine for a little while.

13

Edmonton Revisited

THE wildest, and therefore the most interesting, half of the summer voyage still lay ahead. Beyond Fort Vermilion we would have to travel at least five hundred miles by water, through wilderness, if we were to reach our goal of Yellowknife this year.

That town lay, we knew, in Yellowknife Bay of North Arm, a frigid inlet which is the northernmost extension of Great Slave Lake, a body of water slightly larger than Lake Ontario. And there was this little problem of getting across Great Slave Lake to those remote beacons of civilization perched upon the grim Precambrian rock Shield to welcome the venturesome arctic *voyageur.*

You can't cross Great Slave Lake in a canoe. It is ninety miles straight across. Yet going around the lake seemed out of the question since that distance was hundreds of miles, with a surf that did not permit many days of travel for small craft. Too, there was no gasoline in that part of the world to fill the tanks. Yet I had some plans.

Beyond Fort Vermilion the Peace River joined the Athabasca River, both then becoming the Slave. Then the Slave River carrying all these waters made its way into Great Slave Lake's south shores by a mighty and treacherous delta.

Months ago I had been in correspondence with the owner of one of the Yellowknife hotels up there on the north shore of the lake, and this chivalrous entrepreneur had promised to let us have a hotel apartment for the winter at very nominal rates for those regions, if we accomplished our historic trip.

He was a member of the Chamber of Commerce in Yellowknife. He was a member of the City Council. He was a patron of the Caribou Festival which takes place annually in March. He served devotedly on the Moose Kicks Committee — said by some to be a drinking group — for Better Dogsled Racing and Cultural Enrichment. He was a booster, not a knocker.

Stout old Joshua Cluck, known as "the only Jew in the North," was described to me everywhere we went. It was said he had bought and continued to buy many a poor bum a meal there at the inn he owned, and a drink at the wide-open Gold Brick Bar — everything is refreshingly wide open in the Territories — and that he had grubstaked many a gold-seeking and uranium-seeking prospector around the Great Slave Lake area.

"Jolly Josh the Jew," they called the plump little innkeeper with a lion's heart and a British-Jewish accent that somehow was strangely appropriate on the frontier. When a man has a nickname in the North, it means he is loved by many, if not by all. Of course I had never met Jolly Josh, but his few terse letters held out hope that the beacons on those rocks at Yellowknife Bay would keep flashing as long as he was there, at least.

If we could make it to Yellowknife by canoe, we could stay there all winter. The kids had to go to school somewhere along the way, and at Yellowknife they could get enrolled in School District No. 1 at one of the world's friendliest and most interesting gold camps, which did not charge newcomers a tax. It was a friendly, lively town, it was said, with a population of over four thousand. Yellowknife was the only northern stopover on our way which had a high school, and Jean was ready to start her first high school year. Also, Yellowknife sat just about on the halfway mark to the Arctic Ocean by water, and was the dividing point of our projected two-summer voyage.

Jean and I awaited Ann's recovery and our departure from Fort Vermilion with impatience. We hadn't started out to make an exploration of hospital accommodations in Canada; but explorers have to take events as they come, just as do other people.

Meanwhile, large groups of Mennonite females poured into Ann's hospital room each Visitor's Hour, each woman in her black kerchief and apron, and the men anonymous-looking in their work clothes. At Visitor's Hour large numbers of mosquitoes came in also, every time the hospital door swung open.

Over Ann's bed, to her acute anxiety at first, but presently to her amazement and pleasure, now bent friendly Mennonites with words of sympathy for the little one — for they truly loved children, and in the bed next to Ann lay their own little daughter, sixteen, who had undergone an intestinal operation.

"Mother, this is my friend Millicent, and she is a Mennonite."

Millicent favored me with a wan smile. But Millicent was very busy. Each day this young girl's betrothed came to visit, accompanied by his or her relatives. The patient, one of a family of seventeen children, looked out upon an old-fashioned world with serene blue eyes from her place in the very center of a closeknit in-group. Her gaze was sure and complacent, perhaps very much as our own grandmothers used to look, and her interests, like our grandmothers', were entirely domestic and reproductive. Ann was fussed and nonplussed to find that Millicent, in fact, felt superior to as well as a little sorry for her, regarding the American child of the modern world as a kind of curiosity.

"I can hardly wait to get well and then we'll be married," Millicent told Ann grandly, "and then I'll have a home and children of my own."

"Mother, her only ambition is to *get married*," whispered Ann to me. "They think I'm educated and queer," she explained. "They all come to me and ask a lot of questions because I'm the only one around here who has finished the seventh grade."

"What those farmers haven't figured out," analyzed Jean, making doodles on a pad, "is that if each couple has seventeen kids, within twenty years from now they'll bring to a stop the kind of life they believe in: that is, they won't be able to go on living on farms in the country, because there won't be any country left. They'll fill it all up solid with people."

In one of the conversations with the engaged girl it was brought out that she had never heard of New York City. So Ann decided she should tell her about it.

"Well, Jean and Mom, I was telling them how I rode the air-

lines back west from New York that summer, remember? Then her
father spoke up. They speak English. I told him how I flew right
over the Great Lakes.

"And her father said, 'Ya, ya, them lakes is in Mexico. I know
dem. I tell you.'

"Jean and Mom. He is so *stubborn*. He doesn't know Mexico
from the United States, isn't that something? And the most surprising thing is, he doesn't *care*," she said, dismayed.

The patients surrounding Ann were low Dutch Mennonites and
Crees; and so also, she presently realized, were most of the hospital
staff. The village boasted only two qualified nurses, so they hewed
their aides out of local timber as best they could.

In the hospital there were just two toilets shared by perhaps
twenty-eight beds, accessible by a nice walk down the hall as soon
as you became conscious. No screens were placed around beds.
There was no concern for coddling or privacy. Nobody brushed
their teeth or washed their faces or had a bed bath there to our
knowledge. Because the jerry-trained local aides came out of shacks
to which running water was but a dream, they looked at times less
than pristine. Their uniforms, worn many days without a change,
were sometimes spotted with blood and other indications of their
profession.

To while away the convalescent hours Ann caught mosquitoes
and put them into a glass jar under a screw lid, making a collection.
She asked for bug spray but none seemed to be available at the
time.

It was interesting, if you were twelve and had an alert mind, to
hold your jar full of captives, while lying on your back in the half-
cranked-up hospital bed, put the jar next to your ear, and listen to
the tonal variance of the hums there, for the mosquitoes seemed to
increase their screams to a crescendo when they discovered themselves confined in the jar.

Why did they howl like that? Were they getting very angry?
Was it possible for such a tiny, simple, frail thing as a mosquito to
experience the emotion of anger? Ann hopped in and out of bed,
catching more subjects.

"These are my controlled experiments," she told the indifferent Millicent.

"I conclude from this," she told Millicent another day, "that in school they should teach us that anger is one of the basic instincts."

"What's a basic instinct?" asked Millicent.

"Well, I don't know how to explain it," said Ann, "anyway in school they never knew about the mosquitoes around Fort Vermilion, I tell you."

Two days after the stitches were out and Ann was discharged and I had paid the surgeon his fee and he had left on annual holidays, Ann's temperature shot mysteriously to 101 degrees on the thermometer I carried. It happened just as we were beginning to pull ourselves together to resume the voyage.

The relief doctor who had come in, and who did not anticipate practicing surgery while he was here, suggested that Ann could be catching a chest cold. Or perhaps a deep internal abscess was developing.

To bed went Ann again, in the Hardworker sheets. She was put on round-the-clock antibiotics rationed out to me at the hospital dispensary at the below-cost government rates of the frontier.

A dull continuous ache developed in Ann's innards and waves of black dizziness followed, and she experienced sharp stabbing pains when she moved which made her cry out. She began to swell before our eyes.

I showed her to the relief doctor with a sickening lurch of terrible fear.

Something had to be done at once. The words "Emergency flight to Edmonton" began to form in my mind, even as the new doctor confirmed my thoughts. "I'm not keen to operate on her myself here," he said. "She's not my patient. I don't feel I want the responsibility."

On that point I heartily agreed, and we passed it by tactfully. It was in the next point of procedure that difficulty arose.

Within a few hours the relief doctor talked with Provincial authorities in Edmonton, discussing with them whether the hospital airplane should come for Ann. Fort Vermilion had no scheduled flight service. It did have a six-thousand-foot grass field, the largest voluntary airfield in Alberta, kept in repair the year round by the local citizens. The Alberta government quite routinely furnished free emergency flights south for the northern population as needed.

But when I interviewed the relief doctor a second time he had been informed by the Provincial authorities that their rules prevented them from sending the hospital flight unless I paid its charter fee of five hundred dollars, because I was an American. Alas, Ann did not qualify for the Alberta rescue plan! She clearly needed surgery soon but the rescue aspect itself was a matter of legal definition!

At this news I simply staggered. I could raise the five hundred dollars to be sure — but I was on borrowed money already, I was in a foreign country far from my own home, and with children. The debacle would amount to little less than absolute financial ruin for the expedition at this point, what with the first appendectomy emergency we had just come through.

"I think your daughter might get a ride out to Edmonton by auto," suggested the relief doctor who was new in his role here. "It's only a matter of about fourteen hours.* Some people go straight through."

"On that rutted, gravel road?" I asked, feeling a spasm of shock and fear followed by a slow burn of indignation. A lot of other factors at the same time crowded into mind.

"Ah, yes, well, I believe so. I've never driven it myself. Your daughter could go straight to the Royal Alexandra Hospital in Edmonton, where they will expect you," he said. "I have another patient, little Millicent — I'm not quite satisfied that she is, ah, healing well. It seems she has had this type of surgery several times. I'm sending her out. Her father will be driving and taking several mem-

---

* Mileage (by gravel road in part):

Fort Vermilion to High Level	50
High Level to Peace River	190
Peace River to Edmonton	308
TOTAL MILES	548

bers of his family, I believe. They might have room for just one more."

"But my daughter's case is acute. Isn't it?" I eyed the doctor, realizing even as I did so that all the doctors I had previously known didn't like arguing with patients. "What kind of condition do you suppose their car is in?" I went on, in considerable alarm. "What if the car should break down on the way? Have you thought of that?"

"Well," replied the relief doctor, showing impatience with my attitude, "I was only suggesting. Of course, you can do as you like. Now, if you'll excuse me, I have an office filled with patients, waiting. . . ."

"I will not subject my girl to that automobile drive," I said firmly, and walked briskly out.

It all seemed like a terrible nightmare. We were caught in government red tape. No *man* at the head of the family, no husband, no one to help! Somehow the woman raising children alone always reaches that point of distress where she imagines that a *man*, the right man, could help somehow. Probably a fallacy, but this is what one thought when the chips were down. And sometimes it seemed they were always down.

I walked down the river road, thinking. "Ann's little life is in my hands," I said aloud. "In mine, alone. Nobody cares, really. *Nobody cares.*"

I dried my tears and reached automatically into my trousers pocket for the mosquito rub-on, and thought some more as I walked. In the United States that I used to know, that I thought I knew (but did I?) a private doctor under the system of private medicine would take the responsibility for all the arrangements that were necessary, *somehow*. That was his medical oath. He would see that the things were done that must be done when a human life is at stake. The life of a little child.

Perhaps the harassed government doctor was as helpless as I before the "rules." He seemed to be. And so, not knowing himself what to do, he shrugged us off testily!

However, private enterprise was to come to the rescue and solve the hideous dilemma in its own ingenious way. Somehow there always seems to be a way to get around the strangulating "rules," so long as even a little part of our world remains sane.

There was a local bush pilot. Very busy all the time, he was hard to catch on the ground, but if you caught him it was worthwhile. He was one of the dwindling tribe of individual pilots whom the big airlines have not yet driven off — simply because in this instance there was no airlines service. This pilot always had a full load of businessmen and others. He had business stacked up and waiting weeks ahead. But he made room. He managed. In his spare time, he did his own mechanical work.

I could share the charter flight costs, and taking Ann with me get her south for just forty-eight dollars, and do so immediately. Consequently, this pilot took me and my little patient, heavily sedated before her embarkation by means of a tremendous horse syringe, speeding across river and forest to Peace River town, very quickly. There we were able to buy two airline tickets, just barely catching the regular flight — last flight into Edmonton before the dead weekend.

In Edmonton a cab whirled my numb and sleepy girl and me through the city, and within minutes we sat before the chief of staff of the Royal Alexandra Hospital. He was a kindly man, a brilliant man, a surgeon of personal dignity and an austerity of bearing that one could only describe as "European." He diagnosed the tummy promptly in a most kindly voice: "Aaaaaahhhhhh."

Then, as I hung on his words: "Interesting incision we have. A little larger than we are used to here. It's rather like the ones we used to see in World War One." He fingered it fondly. "But," he added helpfully, "we'll open her up again for you and see what we have here.

"Your name is Ann, isn't it?"

"Yes, sir," said Ann dizzily. Somehow she must have known that he was the kind of man who might expect to be addressed as "sir."

"I say, what are those curious little bumps you have all over your arms and legs, and on your little tummy, too?"

"Oh, they're mosquito bites, sir. From Fort Vermilion Hospital,"

said Ann, honored that the great man asked. That he was no fron-
tiersman was obvious.

When I hastened to query the chief of surgeons about his fee he
demurred that it would be modest. When pushed for a frank answer, he surprised me by giving the amount of just twenty-five dollars.

"But you have your insurance?" he suggested politely — for
everyone in Alberta, since 1958, has his entire hospital care given
him for not more than two dollars a day, with no premiums to pay,
either, and needs only to pay his doctor and his ambulance.

"Oh, no," I said, not knowing the Canadian system at that time.
"We have never had any insurance. A mother and two children
can hardly afford it in the States. Everything's so high there."

"Yes, I suppose so," he said. "I've heard that."

"I don't even have life insurance for this canoe trip," I added.
"That is, in order to make the trip you see our lives are made out to
the people who lent the money, naturally."

"Amazing," he said. "Well," he concluded, "in this case I really
don't think we shall ask for a fee for our work. It's a simple operation, really nothing to it, just draining her out, you know. We
shan't charge you a fee this time. We wish you well on your canoe
voyage, which I am sure will be a benefit to all Canada, perhaps
even bringing many other eager canoe tourists from your country
— although perhaps not everyone has the good sense to see it at
this time. Well," he ended, "very good. Let's get on with it."

And abruptly our little patient was wheeled away by attendants.

Ann was waving her hand feebly to me as she was carted off, still
in her frontier clothes but soon to be scrubbed and gowned in
white. "Mother, I love you so much. Don't worry, Mommie. The
operation doesn't worry me in the least. You will see that I am not
a little brat any more the way I used to be when I was a child. I'll
be a big help to Mother, just you wait and see."

"You never were a brat, my dear, you are a wonderful person." I
turned, tears running rivers. But they were tears of sheer relief.
Everything was going to be all right with Ann.

The hospital in Edmonton was enormous, palatial, and teeming with British-sounding accents. Its entire establishment was starched and immaculate to the last degree. There I sat during Ann's operation, having called my mother in the States — Gerald was in England. I felt punch-drunk, a prisoner to piped-in music in every gleaming hall, a viewer of potted geranium plants. I watched nationalistic-type television programs on such timely events as the changing of the Scottish guard in Ottawa, and I received some natural history instruction on the life of the tree. King-sized jigsaw puzzles partially assembled on long tables fairly begged the enthusiast to sit down and play. But as Ann would have put it, these treats did not "turn me on" today.

One of the surprising things about this hospital was that more patients appeared to be walking up and down the halls in their dressing gowns than actually in their hospital beds. They had movies in a theater. They had social events and cultural lectures. They had several chapels. When they tired of taking their meals on trays they got up and paraded to dining rooms where they could fraternize with other patients, in tastefully decorated surroundings.

There were no lab fees, no X-ray fees, no operating room rentals, no drug or dressing charges, no fees at all. For just the flat two dollars a day, including wonderful meals, the patient got everything he needed at this country club of hospitals. My own costs for Ann were a flat twenty dollars a day for the four days she was there because unfortunately I had not thought to live in Alberta for eighteen months ahead of time and therefore was not eligible for the plan.

Meanwhile, on a lower floor, Ann's old friend Millicent wandered around in a new dressing gown, enjoying, we suppose, the sociability of the pleasant scene. Her betrothed was with her, a humbled and suitably impressed young man ready to fall upon one knee at any moment, the slave to his love's obvious fragility. I was glad to observe that they had made it safely into Edmonton. Their car, for all my anxiety, had not broken down. At least, not this trip.

Out of the Royal Alexandra came Ann with her insides repaired, to be helped into a waiting cab. She had a great hole in her side which was draining into a thick gauze bandage pack. It could not be closed surgically. When I saw the hole and the surgeon explained, I was quite dismayed, weighing our prospects for canoeing on into the North. The hole had to fill itself in very slowly by granulation and it would take the rest of the summer.

How could I take her on in such shape? What would become of our expedition now?

As Ann convalesced in our hotel room in the city, I was thinking hard. I hoped we would come up with some kind of answer to cope with our awful predicament.

Jean meanwhile was with the Hardworkers at the farm twenty-six miles out of Fort Vermilion. She had been set to hand-weeding those burgeoning north Alberta fields with Effie Mae, their backs bent in honest labor, while the birds and bees worked about them.

One evening Ann heard the phone ring in our hotel room.

"Are you there? Are you there?" came a thick British voice. "This is Joshua Mumsford Cluck. Calling from Yellowknife."

"Mother's in the dining room," cried Ann excitedly. "The mayor of some city in the East is feeding her a dinner and champagne."

"Well, I should think so. By the way, I intend to run for mayor of Yellowknife on the next ticket myself, young lady, tell your mother that. Your mother has red hair, hasn't she? Are you the little girl who had the appendix, I say?"

"Oh, yes, Mr. Cluck, I just had my second operation here in Edmondton by the Chief of Staff himself a few days ago. Mother and I are living at the hotel now. Mr. Cluck, how did you know that we are here?"

"A little bird told me, flying up here all the way to Yellowknife," came the long distance voice. "Also, I read about you in the Edmonton *Journal*. We arc calling to ask about your health, brave little Annie."

The voice blurred. There seemed to be some kind of a party going on in the background.

"My health is pretty good," replied Ann thoughtfully. "Except I have this enormous hole in my side."

"Oh, dear. What are we going to do about this canoe trip now, I wonder?" mused Mr. Cluck. "It would be a great shame not to complete it. Quite a lot of people, ah, men, of course — have made the trip with small craft from year to year. But your party is the first ladies to do so. How old are you now? And where is your sister?"

There was a pause while Mr. Cluck had some kind of a mild seizure and regained control.

"She is waiting for us with friends near Fort Vermilion. I am twelve."

"I suppose it doesn't seem wise, does it, under the ah — circumstances, that you should continue the voyage this particular summer?"

"We don't think so, Mr. Cluck."

"Hmmmmmm. That's what I thought," resumed the voice. "Now, some of the boys sitting around here were thinking that perhaps we should put you in the airplane and *fly* you to Yellowknife. Do you think you would like that, little Annie? We have doctors and a clinic and a hospital here, too, by the way. How would you like to just come on up here on the airline, and then your sister and your mother can join you later with the canoe? You can stay with my wife and me at my hotel. Let me say, dearest Annie, the town of Yellowknife is *waiting for you*."

"Oh, Mr. Cluck," cried Ann ecstatically, her every dramatic instinct aroused to the occasion — for she was born to be a dramatic woman. "Oh, Mr. Cluck, that would be perfectly wonderful."

"You wouldn't miss your mummie at all?"

"Not at all," said Ann, becoming practical. "At least, not much."

"Do you think we should ask Mother, then?" came the benevolent voice. "You ask her, my dear, and have her call me collect." He cleared his throat heavily. Mr. Cluck seemed to have an extraordinary amount of phlegm.

"I'll run right down to the dining room and tell Mother right now," cried Ann with enthusiasm.

"No, my dear, I wouldn't do that," cautioned Mr. Cluck, exerting the tact which would serve him in good stead when it came to fighting the future battles of his mayoralty. And with a final strangled cough and choke he instructed Ann, "Just ask her to call me back collect tomorrow. In the late afternoon, my dear," he ended, and hung up.

Subsequent calls to Yellowknife confirmed the marvelous fact that a number of mining persons, led by Mr. Cluck, had become interested in watching the progress of our small expedition — even while we had believed that we were most alone. These persons had kept in touch with our progress stop by stop along the lonely Peace River, and now the bets were on as to how we would navigate the Slave and cross the border into the Northwest Territories and proceed into their domain.

When I myself spoke with Mr. Cluck I could nearly visualize a forest of binoculars held by trembling hands and trained eagerly upon Yellowknife Bay, scanning even now those treacherous and remote glacial waters, awaiting our canoe's victorious arrival.

Thus the clouds of despondency and indecision lifted once again, as though by some magic decree. Only two days later I said good-bye to the brave and most resourceful Ann for the rest of the summer. I saw her little figure, wearing a new pair of city stretch pants and moccasins and parka, go aboard a shuddering DC-3 at Edmonton Industrial Airport, accompanied by a kindly traveling man in a business suit who shouldered her sleeping bag for her; and I saw her safely handed to the airlines hostess. The DC-3, battered workhorse of the North, swallowed its miscellaneous load of humanity in matter-of-fact course: business men, Indians, and uncouth laborers. Thus it happened that Ann was the first member of our family to see Yellowknife, all by herself.

What was Mrs. Cluck like, I wondered. The moccasin telegraph, which had a direct line out of the North, right into the large Macdonald Hotel, had it that Mrs. Cluck wore bedroom slippers due to large bunions on the joints of her big toes. And on the very day that Ann left, the alarming news came through to me that the seams of her stockings were always twisted.

Furthermore, Mr. Cluck, kindhearted and good though he was — so clicked out the alert moccasin telegraph — ate garlic sandwiches. He had his own recipe for the filling. Everybody shuddered who had heard the recipe. It consisted of about four whole chopped raw garlics for each sandwich filling, minced with anchovy paste and strong cheese. He ate them constantly. And Mr. Cluck was reported to be alcoholic and to have white or bluish rims around the irises of his eyes showing a progressive hardening of the arteries in conjunction with cirrhosis of the liver; and consequently, due to these afflictions and the aberrations in his diet, he was apt to forget what he had said only five minutes after he said it.

The moccasin telegraph of course worked both ways. It relayed news out of the North and it relayed news back into the North with equal vigor. This obvious fact of its operation made you wonder just what it relayed back the other way about you.

You, too, have your little peculiarities, your little foibles. Some of them could prove mighty embarrassing when repeated over one million square miles of wilderness to become a delectable, mouth-watering conversational meal for many a hungry neighbor whom you may never even meet.

But the North has this consolation: it differs from the rest of the staid, solid, everyday world in a really wonderful way. For up here the people *expect you to be peculiar*. They consider you have the right to be if you want to be, and they usually forgive you for it.

14

Hitchhiking the Mackenzie Highway

NO sooner had I seen Ann aboard the weathered DC-3 with its mixed assortment of passengers and watched the plane swing away toward the Northwest Territories, than I caught the next plane myself, bound westward for Peace River town. This would save time by putting me right on the Mackenzie Highway heading north. But money was short.

"I'm going to try to hitchhike up the Highway," I thought. After all, no air service existed along the Highway except charter flights.

Let me say quickly that I do not hitchhike in the United States nor do I pick up hitchhikers in my car. However, I'm old enough to remember happier and more casual days in our country when Americans, at least in fancy, often turned to our open roads. Like many of my countrymen I harbored still in my heart a special sentiment for vagabonding through a land of quiet friendly towns and country roads in the summertime.

I was waiting there at Edmonton Industrial Airport when I thought I saw a familiar face. She was a trained nurse at the Manning Hospital up the Highway. For goodness sake! We had met a few nights ago at the hotel when, like me, she was temporarily in the city.

I said to myself, "No, it isn't, it can't be that same big girl. Got a big shape to her, though. Certainly is large. Sure looks like her. Very distinctive type. But she was going off to Montreal, wasn't she?"

But she turned out to be one and the same — only today here she was, wearing a different dress and carrying a large open-top satchel from which a bottle of Scotch unabashedly gleamed.

She was Irish, she had told me. She came from three generations of pure Irish, but they lived in Glasgow, Scotland. So that made them almost Scottish in a way. She was kind of a commuter to Canada. A lot of the people in Canada are not Canadians. The Commonwealth nations exchange their citizens about with an ease and informality that might well make us Americans rather discontented with our own provinciality.

The big girl had bright blue eyes, a lively sense of humor, and the rosiest cheeks you ever saw. Now it is necessary for us to think up names for all the people we met and enjoyed so much in our travels. Since we must call her something, it comes to me that we might name her Nellie Cement. The reason I think of this is that she happened to mention the fact that everything she ate unfortunately turned to cement — an affliction from which I myself have suffered quite horribly. It is the affliction wherein every calorie is deposited in the wrong places and stays there, no matter what you do: just like cement.

It seems that Nellie Cement had already been to Montreal and back. She applied for and got a job in Montreal where she would become superintendent of some seventy nurses in a large institution in a very few weeks. But today, right now, large, world-traveled, intellectual, witty Nellie Cement was here.

Miss Cement had picked up American phrases readily from her travels and reading, yet I almost jumped when she addressed me suddenly, "Where 'ya goin', kid?"

"Well, it *is* Nellie!" I cried, tremendously pleased to see her in this strange place, just when I was feeling particularly lonely and let down.

"Yes, now, and you know me," she assured me. "Don't you remember, we met at 'The Mac'? What are you planning to do now? Are you here to catch a plane? Would you care to have a nibble of the national food today?" (Offering the bottle.)

"I'm not very used to it," I replied. "Well, yes, if you are having one, I would be glad to have a wee nip."

"Oh, come on now," she said generously, "and it will help to make you relax, after all you've been through this summer." As she passed the bottle over, I looked around surreptitiously and was reassured that nobody I knew was sitting there at the strange airport; then, with a guilty and daring gesture, I poured a little into a paper cup, adding water from the fountain.

"Oh, I was just reading about your adventures, in Montreal," she told me, "where I would be wise had I stayed, and taken my holiday back home to Glasgow. Dear God," she sighed, and unfolded her sad tale. "It took thirty-seven hours to get to Montreal, from the time I left Manning, Alberta, would you believe it? Yet, when I live in Montreal, where everyone in his right mind and a civilized human being ought to live — for looking at these English around here, as you know well, is like coming face to face every day with a jolly frozen mackerel — well, I can get to Glasgow in seven hours. I really think I must have been a little bit out of my mind to leave my lovely apartment waiting there in Montreal, and all my arty educated friends in that gay wicked city, to have come out here on this wild-goose chase, where it is so wild and lonely and out of the way. But I won't be around here much longer, I can tell you that."

So listening to this and much more I boarded the plane with Nellie Cement; but it happened that on this day of the week the plane went all the way to Dawson Creek, British Columbia; so of course we went with it, in order to get back around to Peace River town, Alberta, where it seems we both were going.

At Dawson Creek, in the rest room, I banged into a paper towel dispenser which in truth was perched in a most awkward place on the wall and which had a sharp metal corner. It cut an inch-long scalp wound right over my forehead at the hairline. I emerged staggering as the plane, held by stout Nellie, patiently waited for me with its two propellers idling; and I damning the world softly, with blood running down my face. It was perhaps the most ungraceful exit a lady ever made from a rest room at an air terminal. But it was not a serious wound. The airlines hostess requisitioned paper towels and aspirin and Nellie patted my hand, while I thought mournfully of my children.

Soon the good nurse and I were set down at Peace River, where we pondered what to do next to expedite our travels north.

"The miserable bus only runs once a day," said my stout friend as we walked into the Peace River airport. "Dear God, I'm late getting back to duty. This is terrible. I don't know what you have in mind to do, but as for me, I haven't time to wait for the bus. We would have to wait over a full extra day, you see, to catch that bus tomorrow, for today it has already left. I think our best chance would be to catch a ride on the road with someone going north, if we can do it."

"Sure, and we could, like," I agreed giddily. "In the United States," I told her, "we call it hitchhiking."

"I know that, luv," she said.

It was not long before Nellie halted a Polish farmer who came right to the airport with his truck. He knew at once that Nellie was the regional nurse, and was glad to help us out. Some hours later, hours of traveling through that land of cracked windshields and cracked hub caps and cracked heads, we rolled into Manning, the dusty village where Nellie worked. There I was a guest in the nurses' quarters of this fine hospital superintendent, and again, through some perversity of fate, became an explorer of hospitals. There was no resident doctor here — just the hospital and Nellie and a few other nurses, although there appeared to be an adequate small operating room.

The next day I awoke to the lonely sound of a distant train whistle. It was the solitary diesel engine pulling four cars of materials up the single track of the Great Slave Railway through swamp and forest. This summer most of Manning's men, as well as other farmers and trappers throughout northern Alberta, were building the railroad, whose cost was given as just sixty-six million dollars, and whose length, when completed, would be four hundred and fifty miles to the south shore of Great Slave Lake. Its purpose: to export iron and lead ores. It seemed like a little toy railroad in this wilderness. It was almost a railroad you could *love*, I thought, as I rose from bed to the wail of its whistle. It would never have a passenger car. It was said that along this same railway route in early years oxen went mad from mosquitoes and bolted from the trail as they pulled their loads. Those times weren't so long ago.

I couldn't know it when I had breakfast in the nurses' cheery dining room that morning, but there must have been a reason all along for my being here. I was being given the opportunity to see the Peace farm country by highway, which is a totally different experience from seeing the Peace River by canoe, and I was certainly getting the feeling of the land. But there was some other factor I couldn't quite catch which was curiously being woven into my odd meanderings.

As my friend had gone to work early, I waited in the nurses' parlor for bus time. Mrs. McCrumble, the aging Scottish matron, bustled about me polishing, cooking, and cleaning the nurses' home.

This lady's accent was hard to understand, but presently I caught on that she was a widow of less than a year. Soon she got out her album of snapshots and sat down to describe her life.

"My husband and I, we never had no children," she said. "But we was very happy. Jock had such a hard time to get started in Canada."

"You came from Scotland? What year did you come over here?"

"Well, Jock, he come first. It was in 1927. But I dinno' come till 1953," she said.

"You were engaged to be married all those years?" I sat upright in sudden amazement at the statement which implied a psychological hardiness of romance that I had not often seen.

"Well, we were, and we weren't," Mrs. McCrumble told me.

"You see, m'dear, he wanted to send for me, but he couldn't afford it. His crop failed every year for the first five years. Then, he come over into Alberta here, and there was some years we dinno' write a letter to each other."

"What was his crop?"

"Oh, it was grains," she said. "In Manitoba."

"In the meantime, what were you doing in Scotland those years?"

"Me mother was getting old and sick. I could not leave her, you see."

Finally, following the deaths of both her parents, the Scottish girl whose profession was nursing came to the New World and became the wife of Jock. They had less than ten years together in their later years.

"Well, it was a hard life here in the New World," she admitted. "I was used to indoors plumbing all me life, and I guess *that* was part and parcel of the problem. I dreaded that cold little house out back. But I'm glad now that I finally made the decision. Now, it's lonely without Jock."

"I've heard that Scots marry late and aren't very prolific," I suggested with sociological helpfulness. "Why do so many marry late?"

"Most people don't understand it," she explained. "But I'll tell you. It's quite severe in Scotland. There's never enough jobs to go around, you see, never enough employment in the Old Country. So a lot of the young men leave Scotland. They can't really afford a family, you know?"

In the light of her sparse, succinct Scottish remarks suddenly the bleak austerity of a whole country was revealed — at least as it was in her day and as it had affected her life — and you could understand why it came about that it was the Scots, of all peoples in the world, who historically had proved to be the most fit for exploring and settling northern Canada.

"But now it's the Italians, and the Poles, and the Dutch, and the Ukrainians, that is filling up Canada's lands," she added. "And today now, the government has big programs to help 'em. We did not have government programs then. They are successful farmers, too," she added fairly, giving the ounce of credit that was due, painful though this was to her.

I chewed on that. "Why do you think they are more successful now?"

"Well, of course the government," she said. "But another thing, they do have mixed farming. Livestock. Not just one crop. I think that helps to carry them over, and people altogether has learned much about farming in this country since the early days."

"If only you had come over here to the New World earlier you would have had many choices for a husband," I speculated. "You were a pretty young girl. Women were scarce here.

"For instance, this very summer I can tell you about an example. My kids and I were going down the Peace River in our canoe and we met a trapper who had never married. He is Norwegian. He is a very fine man. He must be about your age, by the way. He's sixty-two. He told us that he never had the chance to marry."

"Does he live around here? What is his name?" she asked.

A rush of emotion suffused me, as I remembered suddenly the man in the forest, the man that somebody had to help. "Hjalmur Feeshbeidt," I said, and waited.

She didn't say anything for a while. Slowly I went on and told her how we had first seen the fine old man leaning on his cane at the doorway of the little log cabin on that bend of the river where he had lived alone for thirty-three years. I told her how he had had a stroke. How he nearly died of starvation the previous spring, of how he lived all alone in the woods, and wouldn't leave.

"Oh, that poor man," she said. "What bend o' the river do you think it was, now?"

"Well, it's awfully hard to describe. I might be able to show you on my map." I hastened for my briefcase. "He goes in to North Star once a year for groceries."

"North Star? Why, that's only up the road a piece," she calculated.

"The postmaster or the store would know him there. Strange, in me years here I have never heard that name."

"Few know the name of Hjalmur Fecshbeidt," I said.

"Oh, that poor, poor man," she said warmly, her fine Scottish features melting into a soft tenderness.

"He needs help immediately," I went on. "He should go into the hospital for a complete check-up. The worst of it is, he's planning to go right on into this next winter, trapping, the same way, all alone!"

"Oh, that's very foolish, he should be eligible for some disability pension," said Mrs. McCrumble, with quick practical insight.

"Well, he is a very proud and very stubborn man."

"Yes, yes?" she echoed hastily. "But we should not be as proud and stubborn as that!"

"Someone should stop him from going on alone into winter at that lonely place," I reiterated. "He wouldn't listen to me, of course."

"What does this man look like that you are describing?"

"Oh, he has white hair," I said, feeling my way carefully. "He is tall and thin, I mean slim, and a little stooped, of course. He has great personal dignity," I said in a burst of inspiration, "even though of course you understand he is not an educated man."

"Yes, I understand that," she said. "My Jock, as a matter of fact, was not an educated man. "Well, it seems someone ought to take a boat perhaps, and go out there on the river and find his cabin and him in it. But would he come out to town, would it do any good? But of course, this is a part of the work we do here sometimes. The hospital could get a truck and a motorboat, and an Indian to operate it."

"Dear Mrs. McCrumble," I urged strongly now, "if someone doesn't go out there and bring that sweet man" — I was careful not to say old man — "back to town in the boat, and get him hospital care, and then find him shelter where he can use his pension, he is virtually certain to die alone in the wilderness!"

"Well, we shall certainly see about that," she said severely, her ire aroused. "We canno' let a man die alone like that. I am very glad that you happened to mention this, my dear. It is my duty to requisition the hospital boat and go after him. After all, I am the traveling public health nurse for this district."

"You are?" I nearly collapsed. And I thought: "At your age?" but I didn't say it.

"It's a curious thing," I told her. "I have been looking for the person who will assume responsibility for Hjalmur Feeshbeidt. And now I find that you are she." Bright elation filled me. It was almost like a shining light, it was so bright.

"Here is my map. Now, to get to the Peace River you find a dirt road that goes down to the river, about thirty miles, I think. I do know there is such a road, I don't know just where . . ."

"Don't worry about that. Some people around here know. . . ."

"Now, Hjalmur lives up the river about thirty miles from Mrs. Johansson and Mr. Nookey, and Hjalmur's cabin is on the opposite side of the river. . . ."

"I'll inquire. I'll go out and find him and bring him back," she told me with a firmness that was positively astounding. "That poor, brave man. Does he speak well? And quite nice looking, you say?"

I nodded, wondering how with his accent and hers they would manage to communicate but believing they would manage somehow.

Heaving a little sigh of relief, I accepted the cup of tea and the homemade cookies the aging, intrepid Scottish hand offered. Hjalmur Feeshbeidt had never really been off my mind. It seemed as though unseen forces had been at work to bring me along this dusty road and through the little dusty communities to exactly the one person who would rescue old Hjalmur, and do so firmly, and in just the right way.

A few minutes later, Nellie Cement handed me aboard the battle-scarred bus, and I went rattling along up the gravel Mackenzie Highway northward, watching field and forest flash by, entirely content with this day.

The sun poured down its beneficent warmth upon the Peace River country: Rough Break, Battle Prairie, High Level, Rocky Lane. We jolted past rows of thistles and milkweeds in bloom, and a million black-eyed Susans lined our course. Occasional billboards or frame shacks instructed, "Drink Kik." At one post office stop I saw a peeled log cabin that was painted pink with a baby-blue door and baby-blue window trimming.

My companions aboard the bus were some seventh and eighth grade boys wearing the red shirts and caps of junior forest rangers. They had earned their insignia through the Provincial forest program. At sixteen they would be eligible to fight forest fires, a career to which most eagerly aspired. The boys wrestled, squealed and squabbled like boys anywhere, as the bus swung onward. One of them with a particularly loud and offensive mouth periodically sent his companions into paroxysms of laughter by making retching sounds, possibly for my special benefit.

When we reached the Peace River crossing, the ferry took the big clumsy passenger bus across to Fort Vermilion. It did this every day — only today I was on the bus, and I worried when we took to water. It seemed to me that the driver hadn't any concern about where he placed the bus wheels. But we made it beautifully, a mile across.

The post office closed at the exact moment of the bus's arrival each day at Fort Vermilion. However, the postmaster met me in the dirt path and handed me my mail, which included Jean's glasses and a notice that our new tent waited at the Bay Store.

Inside the Lard and Fry Café the native waitresses were busy frying foods over a double electric burner and a four-burner propane stove, and serving them over the counter to dust-laden customers. The music box was jumping at full blast so that as you gazed at the several moose painted on the wall, they seemed to get up all together on their hind legs and dance around the walls in unison, somewhat like a well-trained chorus, while the painted wild geese seemed to fly.

Near the end of the counter of the Lard and Fry three snaggled-toothed old men were discussing something that caught my ear.

"Them crazy women," one was saying. "What do they want to go down the Peace River for anyhow? What do you think they got in their minds? No roads down there, nothing. How they going to get their canoe around the Chutes and not get drowned, eh?"

"And that poor old Indian who works the portage," said another. "They hired him, you say? Imagine that poor Indian making a fifty-mile trip for just twenty dollars. I wouldn't do it for that. He has to come from Little Red River and return there with his horse and wagon, besides lifting that canoe and all that stuff they got into the wagon and unload it again."

The gossips, who perhaps had never been near the Chutes portage road in their lives but who had only heard about it, neglected to say that this same Indian customarily made his living each summer transporting loads of several tons around the Chutes for the same fees — for Little Red River got its food and materials only in this laborious way, aside from the small plane owned by Fort Vermilion's local bush pilot. And the distance the Indian had to come to meet us above the Chutes and return home was said to total twenty-eight miles, not fifty.

In the café the gossips argued and agreed that "them women" — they did not think of my little girls as children — "should stay at home with their pots and pans where they belong, and not cause trouble for people."

A voice greeted me and I turned on my counter stool, and looked into a face I had seen before — dark, saturnine, and half Cree. There stood the young man my daughter Jean had spoken with near the kitchen door.

"Oh, hello, Johnny, how are you? How's it going?"

"Got troubles," he said.

"What's the matter?"

"You remember you littlest girl got the appendix cut out?"

"Sure, how could I forget?"

"Maybe, you didn't know, I had mine out too. It was about — well, almost the same day, I think."

"Well, for goodness sake. I didn't know that."

"Well, I known for long time I gotta have it out. But I been in hospital all this damn summer since you gone away," he informed me. "My operation, it got trouble. So he cut it open again, that new doctor. I sure don't like that," he elaborated. "I didn't know I gonna have so much trouble this summer. Then they put the tube into my side and I been in Fort Vermilion Hospital all the time since you gone away. What a summer," he ended his complaint.

"What a summer," I agreed. "Well, I'm glad you're okay now."

"Yes," he said, cheerlessly, "I'm gonna be okay."

I bought him a big double vanilla ice-cream cone and a cup of coffee to match my own, and he took the adjoining stool and we sat there and solemnly munched.

"He thinks I'm a rich American," I thought. Everywhere you go they think you're a rich American.

"Well, what of it?" I thought. "Maybe I am."

15

Beyond Fort Vermilion

I determined to push on beyond Fort Vermilion at once. A whole month had been cut from our canoeing summer with these unfortunate multiple appendectomies. Now there were complicated maneuvers to extract Jean from the Hardworker Farm twenty-six miles out from the Fort for the resumption of our voyage.

Meanwhile Ann arrived in Yellowknife, Northwest Territories, and was recuperating well. She phoned to say that she was busy making flights in small aircraft operating on floats about Great Slave Lake, hosted by the prospectors and developers of the region, and was even considering investing up there.

I could tell she was the pet of the hotel and I had a giddy vision of my bright twelve-year-old tap-dancing for the miners on the bar in the Gold Brick Saloon, cheered on by the rude and hearty guffaws of those golden hearts of the frontier. Ann would have liked it that way. Unfortunately for the vision, she had not had tap-dancing lessons.

It was wonderful to see my larger and more stalwart daughter again: good-hearted, wholesome, handsome Jean, with her round cheeks and a cleft in her chin. Jean had always been the less troublesome and the more pleasant and accommodating of my daughters. Yet I sensed that I had rather lost contact with her in the last three weeks or so. It was one of those unexplainable situations when a parent wakes up one day to find that somehow the old gay comradeship is fading. This can happen so suddenly at fourteen, or indeed at any point along the way. Naturally the alert parent tries to regain the old footing that was so pleasant throughout most of the dependent life of the child.

"My, how you've grown in just three weeks," I cried, embracing her. She made absolutely no response to this remark, or my hug. In fact, she gave me an annoyed push. I thought awkwardly that I had said the wrong thing, and began again.

"Well, we have lots of work to do," I said with enthusiasm. This too, seemed the wrong approach so I added desperately, "You're looking just wonderful, Jean. You always were such a nice, *big* girl. You look, dear, like a green giant somehow."

"Mother," she said witheringly, "are you crazy?" That was about all she said for weeks afterward, as I recall.

Jean and I pushed off from Fort Vermilion on a lovely day. The river had dropped in its banks and at last offered some firm pebble beaches. We started off, at least, with a clean canoe, freshly hosed and scrubbed of its mud, and with some new foods added to the old grubstake. All our socks were fluffy and the suits of long underwear were immaculate from being freshly dried in the tumbler. The rifles were oiled, and the sediment bowl of the motor was cleaned out, and the motor had new spark plugs. Jean called her motor Skipper. It became evident that my taciturn companion intended to speak as little as possible and that she and Skipper were teamed up in a sort of two-against-one arrangement.

"I wish Skipper was a horse," she growled once.

Even if she didn't have a horse, she had the comfort of horsepower, I told her. It was true. The little motor had a secret life and personality of its own which only Jean began to know. And after a while horses went out of her life. The magnificent dream horses faded away to be replaced with other dreams more in keeping with Jean's immediate habitat, until one day she was out of the horse stage — probably forever — and I breathed a sigh of relief.

In the meantime the forty-mile voyage down to the formidable portage we faced was broken by lunch on a clean gravel bar.

"Here, Mom, catch! Here's your coffee!" Before I knew what was coming the bottle sailed from boat to shore. I failed to catch. Crash! It shattered on a rock. Good-bye coffee.

they are in our area and also assist them, if necessary." That was the end of the letter.

"Well, come on, Mom. Let's get on with it."

We put off in the canoe again. I recalled dimly as I thought about it that my eldest had made it clear, when Ann dropped out of the expedition, that she would have preferred to make the exploratory voyage from Fort Vermilion five hundred miles to Yellowknife on the north shore of Great Slave Lake alone. In fact, she had recommended strongly that I go by airplane. "Have you noticed," she said, "that all the fellas in this country travel these rivers, with not a one of them having their *mothers* along to tell them how to navigate?"

Actually, at the time I had only noticed it subconsciously. I remained unconvinced, despite Jean's arguments, that their navigation was any the better for their *not* having their mothers along.

As we approached the portage area described in the letter, I warned Jean how careful we must be. There was one place where all the "fellas" came ashore and to miss the spot meant being drawn inextricably into the rapids.

"Drifting and dreaming." Jean laughed at me. "And then, whoosh! No more me, no more canoe, no more Skipper, and no more you, Mom!" With these words the girl at the helm cut out from shore recklessly to get away from the shallows and weeds, showing off her maneuvering skill.

"Have a little faith in the motor, Mom. It isn't going to quit."

I was never sure of that. As the current picked up to about twelve miles, I begged, "Get into shore. Please, Jean. Stop ashore. I want you to listen."

"You what?"

"Listen, you idiot. Just *listen*," I yelled.

"Stop screaming at me, Mother. You make me nervous," yelled Jean.

From far ahead came the merest murmur, an unnatural tiny vibration. We were ten miles above the Chutes when my antennae caught their sound. After that, each time I made Jean stop to listen, the mighty roar of wild waters came ever louder.

Now, directly ahead hung a penetrating, rainbow-spanned mist which hung over the Chutes, indicating that they must be very near indeed, while the earth-shaking thunder of the waters below nearly paralyzed me.

Jean sang out:

> What makes this valley so beautiful?
> I asked the man with the hoe.
> Thirty-six inches of rainfall
> And the other eight months of snow.

I broke into urgent entreaties to put ashore — for there, about to whiz by, was the locked and empty ranger cabin, our signal to get off the river.

We put ashore neatly at just the right spot above the rapids which led into the mile-broad maelstrom. With a one-two-three heave, we breached the canoe half ashore and chained her with everything we had there in the thundering mists. I hoped this effort would become easier each time we made it. An exhilarating bond united Jean and me at that moment, following the thrilling ride, while our cooperation boded well for our future exploration of the Lower Peace.

We got the new tent pitched, with Jean doing most of the work of constructing it, and myself totteringly assisting. As soon as supper was over I crawled in and stretched out on the old "bearskin," my black skunk coat which a Vermilion Indian lady had stitched up with sinew thread following the tent fire. The snug little peaked tent, with outside aluminum jointed frame, zipped up tightly and was ventilated by a charming mesh window, the flap of which could be closed down when rain came.

But only weekend campers should use such a light flimsy model, I thought. It would wear holes from hard travel, and when a little cold weather came in the fall in these latitudes those metal joints would weld themselves solid.

Jean stayed up late, listening to the cataract's roar, dreaming beside the campfire and watching an untimely display of Northern Lights. The nights were now dark for several hours, for summer was passing.

Early the next morning we heard an unfamiliar jingling sound of harness. Here was the Indian we awaited, coming out of the narrow, rutted forest road, with his wagon and team of horses.

With a barely perceptible greeting he unhitched his horses to graze, as I set food before him from the coals. Then when he had eaten we three backed the wagon down the bank, bracing the rear wheels with a log, lest it plunge in and down the cascades.

First we loaded most of our duffle. When the wagon overflowed, the Indian indicated we should put the canoe over it upside down, though it seemed precarious and almost dragging.

I had been dismayed when I first saw the wagon. Homemade of unpainted planks, it was just thirty-six inches across and only half as long as the canoe. However, its width was exactly compatible with that of the wilderness road around the portage. I think most of us today have no idea what the roads of our pioneer forebears were like. This one was just a tunnel through the forest, with branches slapping horses and passengers from either side, and often meeting over the top to close out the sky.

Two portage trips would be necessary along the four-and-a-half-mile road from the Upper to the Lower Landing, where we could again take to water.

"My girl can help you," I informed our freighter. "My girl is strong. You will need help to unload at the other end. She can walk," I added, as there obviously was no room for a rider.

Taciturn Jean and the taciturn Indian companionably hitched the horses, Jean doing most of the work; then the two went ambling off into the forest.

In the meantime up the road appeared two French monks with a cargo of household furniture in a tractor-tread vehicle. Dumping the furniture, they returned over the route Jean and the Indian had taken. Speaking little English, the cheerful monks managed to get across the fact that the forest ranger stationed down at Little Red River was going "outside," and his furniture must go this way, to be met by Vermilion boats the following day.

I made the last trip with Jean and the Indian, covering myself in the wagon bed with canvas against the angry insects blown back from the horses' backs, and bathing my hooded face with repellent.

Nothing was visible but forest although the river's fierce roar could be heard nearby.

Jean rode up front on the buckboard seat. Only later, when it seemed to me that she was acting rather odd and stupid, she said cheerily, "Hey, Mom. You know I had my glasses in my back pocket?"

"Your *new glasses!*" I set up a parental dirge. "We just got them!"

Pause. "Well, Mom, they're broken."

"*Not again?*"

"Now, it's all right, Mom. Don't excite yourself. It's just that I had them in my back pocket in the wagon, and . . ."

"You won't be able to *see anything* for the rest of the summer! You won't be able to see Alberta or the Northwest Territories."

"Don't worry, Mom. I'm not awful interested, as you are. Skipper and I will pilot us through," she replied with the greatest unconcern.

By the time we neared the Lower Landing a crashing thunderstorm had moved in. First came a light patter; then, boom! The sky opened. "Just ignore it," Jean advised. Ignoring it, we unloaded and hauled our posessions downhill through streams of running mud and wet crushed greenery, and ran the canoe out on a rock ledge over log rollers. Receiving his money, the Indian wagoner left at once.

In fading daylight a gray, windy river faced Jean and me. Behind us, a quarter of a mile upriver, we could see the white wall of water of the Chutes we had bypassed.

"Hot dog!" said Jean. "It's real nice out here, you know it?" The thunder rolled. We were drenched. "We can camp on firm rocks tonight. You just tell me where, Mom. Sleeping bags may be a little wet, but I'll make you a real good camp tonight."

There was low visibility and a mean upstream wind. It would soon be night. "I'll tell you where we're going to camp tonight." I used that firm tone which parents have to assume at times. "Just four miles down this river, right on the floor of the ranger's dry boathouse, or some sensible shelter of that sort at the village."

I had my way and we went on. Then suddenly: "How would you

like to shoot a black bear, Jean?" We were moving quietly down the oily current through the mists.

"Where? I can't see it."

Getting the rifle out of its case I looked quickly through the 'scope. Jean adroitly put us in closer on the current toward shore.

My black bear was revealed as a small Cree hunter in a black shirt, paddling in a pale canoe along the shoreline. I had seen only the figure and failed to spot the canoe in the fading light.

"Well, it was a poor idea anyway." I put the rifle away.

"Gee, Mom, I was scared, when I got to thinking," Jean later admitted. "How could I ever face people the rest of my life if my mother shot an Indian when we were the guests of Canada?"

That Indian had looked like a bear for several minutes while we made our approach, but fortunately there was never any danger of an accident because I had not yet put a shell into the chamber. With bears and other big game I told my girls that you must not fire until the target is clear and broadside, and within seventy-five feet.

It is an interesting commentary that in the North, just as it was in our West years ago, the hunting accident is all but unknown. Also unknown is that civilized phenomenon known as "getting lost in the woods." My defense for this, so far as I was concerned, was not to leave the canoe.

A couple of days later, loaded with several dozen cartons of eggs and with fresh vegetables and raspberries from the abandoned gardens of the ranger, Jean and I continued from the post of Little Red River on down to Fifth Meridian: a community of one hundred and fifty or so Indians and one white man, the handsome twenty-two-year-old Bay trader.

The young trader was of Ukrainian descent and hailed from Saskatchewan. We could see him on the skyline, standing at the top of a chocolate-colored cutbank, when we came motoring softly down the current. From his high place he let down red-painted wooden laddersteps in sections, somewhat like a fire escape, to his floating dock. With him was a large blue-eyed white husky and above him the Union Jack danced from its tall pole in the breeze.

Jean introduced us. "I know it seems ridiculous to have your

mother along, but she wanted to come along and she's quite nice."

"How do you do?" I said meekly, overwhelmed.

Where were all the Indian villagers? Out hunting. Scattered for miles. The trader put us in the two extra beds in his lonely sagging frame house. The river was eating toward the house with ravenous appetite. Later, by odd coincidences, we would meet people who had lived at Fifth Meridian; and they would always ask, "How close is the river to the house now?"

The young trader fried slabs of fresh bear meat for supper.

"How many of the Hudson's Bay posts are there, anyway?" I wanted to know.

"About two hundred in the Arctic Division," he told us — meaning posts up north of the trees. "And three hundred or so here in the Northern Branch, where I am. No hardship pay here, still too civilized. So they think, anyway."

For servicing their more remote posts the Bay Company maintains its own little fleets of powerboats and aircraft on floats or skis. For nearly two hundred years this organization has explored and studied the North. All authors and travelers have remarked upon the curious quality of loyalty which the Bay Company, like the fabled Mounties, seems to extract from its men who serve under the most trying conditions for meager pay. Nothing is done to coddle these men, except that they are given wide discretionary powers: therein lies the secret of success, perhaps. Yet Canada's newer, much pampered government servants in other classifications, such as teaching, are beset by psychological problems which make it impossible for some individuals to stay longer than a short season in the northern solitudes without risking profound depression.

When we left Fifth Meridian the sun was shining but we found that the river had risen again and was teeming with drift. We looked in vain for a place to get ashore and eat but everything was flooded. Trees stood in the water; there was literally no shoreline. Then the glasses revealed the beached Indian canoes.

"We'll lunch there," I pointed. "Where they did."

Within twenty-five minutes we had our lunch cooked using both our portable gasoline stove and a campfire. Dark faces looked out from the tall bushes on the bank above.

"Keep a watch on the Crees, Jean." I flopped down in the two-foot margin of land above waterline, and, taking my tin cup of tea in hand and letting my knees hang over the thwart of an Indian canoe, closed my eyes for a few moments in sun-dappled bliss.

Then out of the bushes lightly moved the silent Crees in their worn jackets of fringed moose skin, carrying their rifles in fringed and beaded moosehide cases: a hunting party of young men. They responded briefly to our greeting, and taking their canoes away they went, paddling easily up the side of the great river.

"We visiting," one of them had explained, smiling politely.

We pushed back into the bushes where they had been visiting, expecting to find their hosts. It was an empty place, kind of an Indian lunch stop. Under the tall white poplars were ax-hewn picnic tables and some tepee poles were propped against the tree trunks, awaiting the next traveler. There was not a scrap of paper, not a tin can. Nothing but the coarse fragrant grass and the clean wind. A rude bench, facing the river invited the visitor to rest and contemplate the view.

All along the rivers under the tall trees the silent Crees have many secret resting places. They are carefully not marked but the Crees know where they are and you, the outsider, stumble upon them only by accident.

Now our canoe slid down the center of the river, a speck embraced by water and sky. Under scudding clouds we followed a current that was almost like a lighted boulevard. The water felt soapy, for it was made of bubbles and foam. When you dipped your paddle into these fast suds they seemed lighted from within as star sapphires are lighted. On either hand the slower water was black and roiling. We took the fast channel.

Late in the day we searched for the vacant ranger's cabin indicated on the map, but failed to find a trace of it. On the rivers the abandoned cabins would have many stories to tell if they could speak. There was a cabin where a young adventurer bled to death alone after chopping his leg with an ax. There was a cabin, at the junction of the Jackfish River, where a four-year-old child wandered away and was never found. Perhaps, after all, it is best that those cabins in the wilderness can't speak.

The current became extremely fast again from flooding. Great loops and bends of the river cut into the banks, lopping off trees which hung by their roots helter-skelter: there was no place to get ashore for miles and miles, with the wind freshening and whole woodyards of drift jamming up in the bends before our eyes. Under a lowering sky the weird warped spruce trees stood like ghosts guarding a world's end. Each river bend ahead showed the grin of death and we were borne on, out of control.

Just then Jean, who had been unavoidably bumping driftwood off and on all day got the prop clogged with wood, and our power went out. She pulled the kicker back vigorously with muscular arms and leaned far out over the wild water to untangle it, her tangled wild blond hair blowing across her face.

As she worked the ferocity of the waves increased, and we were being carried down upon the dreaded woodyard. Just ahead, one log was upended vertically as though stuck in the river bottom.

"Hurry, hurry, Jean!" — as I saw the thrashing monster ahead.

"I am, Mom."

"Hurry, faster! We'll be wrapped around that thing in a minute."

"Don't *nag me*, I am hurrying."

At last she got the motor operating once more, then cut figure eights around and through the driftwood and out away from the worst of it. No more valiant Viking of a girl ever lived, I thought proudly, with clenched stomach muscles and clenched fists.

16

Wood Buffalo Park

LUCKILY for us, after another hour more of travel the glasses picked out a safe little cove set back out of the current in the cutbank, and we landed and clawed our way shakily up on shore.

Here we rested our nerves for two nights under the spruce cover, subsisting on fresh eggs and roasted potatoes, coffee, powdered milk, biscuits and canned butter, and all the sweet wild raspberries we could stuff down. As we went berrying we always carried the big rifle slung upon the back of one of us. There were no grizzlies in this lower country, but even black bears among the berry bushes can make you a bit jumpy. The blacks keep to themselves in the valleys, I told Jean, because the grizzlies kill them and drive them out of the high grizzly range. Cow moose with calves are also something to keep your eye open for. We picked along, and the air was filled with the musky, swampy good smells of highbush cranberries in varying stages of ripeness and rottenness. We boiled these down with sugar, since they are an exceptionally sour, seedy, swampy berry indeed, although an epicure's deight. Geologists call this whole area the Alberta Plateau.

Beyond Fifth Meridian the river had entered the 17,300 square miles of Wood Buffalo National Park. The park straddles the northern boundary of Alberta and extends into the Northwest Territories. It is the world's largest national park. I have since learned that there are persons who would like to cut this park up and even diminish its dimensions to half or less. I deplore such a move. History shows that when a wilderness area is put into another land category for use by man, the demise of such wilderness is inevitable and irreversible. It will never be wilderness again. If I had a vote in the matter, I would keep the world's largest national park, or wilderness area, as it is, for posterity. The wood buffalo are North America's largest animal, weighing from three thousand pounds to an occasional two tons. Yet they may be curiously hard to see under the heavy cover, black as they are, dwellers of swamps and jungles.

As far back as 1903 buffalo killing was prohibited throughout Canada, with the result that the small original herd of wood buffalo which inhabited this area near the junction of the Peace with the Slave River had increased from five hundred to around fifteen hundred animals when the park was created in 1922. Then, some sixty-six hundred plains buffalo were moved here by rail and barge from Wainwright, Alberta, and deposited in these swamps. Perhaps the area had seemed to the government a convenient dumping ground for Canada's extra buffalo. Naturalists and biologists still deplore the mixing of the two strains, since the wood buffalo were nearly eliminated altogether by cross-breeding when the plains buffalo overwhelmed them, but it seems almost too late now for anybody to separate them again.

These lucky buffalo have rarely if ever seen a human being except for their friendly park ranger, who pursues them with inoculations, ear tags and such, using helicopters at roundup time — for these animals will not consent to being driven by land vehicles, but will turn and charge a truck if pursued. Their great preserve is of course unfenced. The shaggy beasts may be found scattered at various distances about the Subarctic; corrals for them have been strategically located along the natural buffalo trails.

Jean and I, peering through the nearly impenetrable thickets along the river, kept a wary lookout before and behind. As we went, sometimes reaching a hand through some slanted shaft of sunlight to clutch at a festoon of bright red berries dangling in the solitude, we spoke briefly and cautiously.

Using the field glasses and the rifle telescope constantly, we kept our wilderness surveillance nearly night and day. Binocular equipment, for the explorer, is far more than an extension of the human eye: it has the peculiar ability to capture and condense light, and thus penetrate through darkened forest as well as clarify those distant specks which often puzzle the explorer.

We had counted on spotting game on the river bars but this river all summer long had had no shores for game to stand on. One day we did photograph at close range a sullen swimming lynx caught among the driftwood. As the lynx reached shore with heaving sides and sprang up the bluff, I raised the rifle and fixed her in the 'scope. She paused in silhouette just one jump from the forest. Jean had turned the canoe so that we were drifting backwards.

"Shoot! Mom, shoot!" she cried, and waited for me.

I lowered the rifle, and signaled for Jean to steer us on our way. Why should anyone shoot a migrating, starving lynx who hopes for a rabbit on the other side of the river?

"Storm coming, Mom. Shall I try to outrun it?" Jean started up the motor and our hearts leaped with the power we had waiting at our command. Quite a few times this summer Jean had outrun those prowling storms.

Not this time. Having successfully dodged it all day, we got caught in a cloudburst near night. The storm swept in from behind us with sudden fury as we ran toward the nearest shore. Blinding white it came over the mile-wide river, veiling the low islands.

Up went the little yellow, sealed umbrella-tent on its jointed metal frame, set on a thick carpet of spongy sphagnum moss under the dark spruce trees that were beginning to seem like home.

"Jean, baby, we're getting to be experts!" I yelled cheerily. But we could not unload the canoe fast enough. Down came the rain, with hailstones. We were drenched. To keep the sleeping bags dry we kicked them into the tent pell-mell.

Jean wanted to start a fire in this downpour. It was insane, utterly impossible: I wouldn't have tried. I would have just retreated into the tent. But she must deal with this exhilarating challenge of the elements which spoke to her with many voices. Match after long wooden match she struck on the sides of her soggy match container. The abrasive quality seemed gone in the rain. Finally, she struck one using the metal zipper on her jeans. I, the assistant cook, furnished a wet candle stub held under my dripping field jacket. But the wick wouldn't burn. Out went each wax-dipped match in turn. We contemplated a supperless night.

At last Jean took up the primus-stove tank and sprayed gasoline onto her pile of soggy wood, and was able to light the side of the pyramid. Bad business, I admonished, although we had seen a licensed guide do this trick back in British Columbia. In fact, it was the secret of some guides' wonderful, magic-seeming fires.

But the flickering flame licked up only as long as Jean stood there hosing a fine spray of gas continuously upon it. I hovered by, terribly nervous. After minutes of this dangerous game the dauntless, stubborn girl gave up her campfire idea. But she denied that it was dangerous. "It can't explode, Mom, really. You see, if you were only able to understand some of the simple, elementary laws of physics: no air can get sucked back into the tank to cause an explosion because the gas is squirting out of the end of the tube all the time, see?"

I'll leave it to the reader to decide whether Jean understood the laws of physics. I believed that God protected us. We tried to get some hot water for the soup by using the small primus stove, but even its burner wouldn't work in the heavy rain and then to our dismay caught fire. So we crawled storm-beaten into our bedrolls in a tent that was threatening to float away momentarily.

Deep in the black night I awoke to the smell of wet canvas and wet vegetation, and listened keenly. My boots were safe under my head, and all my clothing, dry matches, some wads of birchbark and sticks of dry wood, as well as the emergency backpack containing extra socks and quick foods, were all inside my big ninety-by-ninety-inch sleeping bag with me. Inside the tent and also close by was a white enamel chamber pot with a carrying handle and lid. This convenient utensil was an embarrassment to my daughters when people came to see the loaded canoe. But the pot never fulfilled its intended purpose; for it was, with its tight lid, the only dry place where the expedition could preserve a year's supply of ammunition.

We had camped here on pretty low ground — no other choice. If the river rose slightly our camp could be inundated. But the river was quiet. Unzipping the tent door, I leaned out into the night and with one arm threw back the outer flap for fresh air.

Instantly dozens of greedy mosquitoes hit my arm. I withdrew the arm and zipped up again in a hurry. Soon now, though, those whining wings would wilt as the annual late summer fungus infection would spread among their ranks.

"Mom," said Jean in the darkness. "I have to go."

"Sure," I said. "There's the outdoors. Here's the bug spray. And good luck."

My daughters were both always good sports. They knew I would never consent to taking the ammunition out of the pot.

In the darkness I reassured myself that the big flashlight and rifle were close at hand. It was good to touch them in the dark. They were my courage at such times. As for Jean, she was courageous by nature.

After the rain Jean's morning campfire was an absolute glowing masterpiece. "Come on, Mom, time to get up," I can hear her call now, as I think back upon those times. One of the finer moments in canoe life is changing into all dry wool things by the side of a blistering fire, even while the bugs are getting in their last few autumnal belts. But how would our wet clothes get dried out from here on? The peaked tent accommodated no stove inside, and no clothesline could be hung. Whoever designed this tent never thought that some people like to get dried out occasionally.

Jean invariably would be the first out each morning to build our late summer and fall fires. Perhaps it was my age and experience, but I always felt that I really hated to get up more than she did. I hated to put on wet clothes, and I abhorred cold. Indeed her nature was such that she didn't feel the cold; or so she claimed.

Her indifference to the elements of wind and storm profoundly shocked me, yet I had to remember that at one time I had been very much like her. I had furnished the expedition with proper apparel as I saw it, but my efforts to protect this new, inexperienced generation from natural perils went unappreciated. Clinging stubbornly to the same eternally wet, low leather shoes, now falling apart with rot, Jean refused to wear the lightweight rubber half boots which I had bought for us at Fort Vermilion. Possibly she didn't care for them because they were called "ladies boots" in the local Indian trade. According to Jean, they were too clumsy and too hot and they made her feet sweat. But of course every riverman has his own ideas about boots. She may well have been right. It was her plan to be prepared at any moment to swim. As for me, I determined to meet my end, if necessary, with warm feet and with long underwear on.

Jean survived in glorious health, I must add. She never caught a cold. She gradually became habituated to exposure. The person who is allergic to air pollution or pollens simply does not have these to contend with in the North; nor are there viruses to be caught in its pure environment, unless you meet the humans with whom they live.

On the matter of life preservers we also disagreed. Jean had concluded that our life preservers were practically worthless and might even drown a swimmer in the event of a sudden capsizing. And again, considering the inadequacies of life preservers in general, and the sodden state ours were in much of the time, Jean may have been right. At any rate, I always wore mine and she never wore hers.

Our camps slipped by — Wet Camp and Windy Camp, and Buffalo Wallows. They were marked in our passing by perhaps the occasional black lace undergarment hung upon a tree, or the discarded broken water dipper, or other worn-out things which we unloaded going north: for in the beginning I had taken almost everything we owned. Much of our equipment went for house gifts. For instance, the Americans at Fort Vermilion got my pressure cooker; and Mrs. Finkleglimmer got a lovely set of household spices, only slightly muddied and molded. Here our camps might not be seen by Cree or Chipewyan for another fifty years, even as we sometimes recognized the barely perceptible traces of camps many years old, not visited by any human being since.

We went on down through some miles of fast water, including Boyer Rapids. The young trader at Fifth Meridian had shot these rapids a number of times, and he told us how to cut them easily, winding through the gypsum cliffs.

The chop increased to four-foot waves, over which the heavy

freight canoe smashed briskly. I had tucked myself into the bow with the extra snap-on canvas over my lap, but the quartering rollers caught Jean in her thin cottons in the stern. She couldn't take her hand from the throttle to put on her seaman's rubber coat.

"Want to take the motor for a while, Mom? You know you always can, any time you want. I mean, do you think you can get along with Skipper?"

"Not on your life," I shouted back pleasantly. I recognized that Jean was indeed a good deal more skilled than I was.

Daring to cross the mile-wide expanse of rough water with an upstream wind and a ten-mile current took some thinking over. But this craft of ours could take a lot of sea and roll with the punches. We had to make a crossing somehow. There was no place to stop along miles of cliff base on either side, and the map said the ranger station was on the opposite shore below.

Eventually we reached the station at Peace Point. And living here was the brother of blond Quinby Rapp. Selby Rapp, with his little family of mixed Cree blood, was one of the keepers of the buffalo. Wood Buffalo Park has year-round quarters for four rangers and their families, so the ranger's wife told us, and they make their permanent homes here. A hundred sled dogs summering at the Sweetgrass post farther downriver supplied the rangers for their winter patrols.

"You can put your canoe on a truck right here and go by road to Fort Smith, if you like, instead of by river," Selby Rapp informed us helpfully. But we said we would take the river.

Peace Point lay at the extreme end of a narrow gravel road, we now saw. The road led past the other ranger stations and seventy miles northward into Fort Smith, the administrative center or capital of the Northwest Territories. No other roads connected the isolated little capital with the villages and far-flung hinterlands it administered over a thousand miles, past Great Slave Lake and on down the Mackenzie River to the polar shore.

In the Selby Rapp sitting room over a hospitable lunch we met two Federal Forestry men who had trucked from Fort Smith,

NWT, this very day. They came to do the yearly check of the park radio equipment. We had left Alberta when we entered Wood Buffalo Park and were on federal lands.

The taller of the two men had been born of a ranger family in the Northwest Territories and had spent all his life in the Federal Forestry and Fisheries Services. I am going to call him Slim Joy.

Slim was quick to encourage Jean and me in our plans for voyaging into the Northwest Territories. I had the impression, in fact, that few if any doubts had ever assailed him about anything in his outdoors life. "Why, you would be missing the best part of your trip if you should pass up the lake," he advised, from his eighteen years of patrolling Great Slave Lake's fisheries and lands. "There is no more wonderful or beautiful place in all the world than Great Slave Lake. Hasn't anybody told you that?"

"Well, no," said Jean. "We haven't met anybody except you who has seen it."

"I have been considering shipping our canoe from Fort Smith onwards," I added. "And we might have to take the airline across the lake ourselves."

I explained to him and to the ranger that on my visit to Edmonton I had gone to the shipping companies' offices and their officials had emphatically discouraged a canoe voyage of the lake. Yet neither of the two companies would take us across the lake, paid or otherwise, for they were strictly cargo carriers, and taking passengers was against company rules.

Slim Joy declared that we should just stop worrying about what people sitting in city offices said, for the most part.

"It will all work out for you one way or another," he said, his good face alight with the joy of his memories. "Why, I've been all over the lake with every kind of little boat and canoe you can think of. Matter of fact, a lot of them that runs the lake aren't as seaworthy as that vessel you've got. People use what they got, and have to make do. Maybe them down south that told you doesn't know much about lakein'. I'll tell you one thing, I like the lake myself because it seems to me to be a far safer place than them spooky, muddy rivers full of driftwood and rapids. Oh yes, I would say the lake is the safest of the two. Well, if you've got this far, it shows you are fairly competent boatmen, and after this, the lake will be downright easy for you."

"Doesn't it get forty-foot waves, like the ocean?" asked Jean.

"Well, sometimes, Jeanie," said Slim Joy, "but I've seen the lake summer nights when it is sometimes like a great pink millpond. Not a ripple on her. Like a mirror. For miles and miles, just still and pink to the horizon. And all kinds of ducks and waterfowl filling the water and flying about the sky, and the islands hanging there in the sky, over the horizon of the world. Yes, I sure like that lake," he sighed.

"How come you're not on the lake now?" asked Jean.

"Well, couple of years ago, I slipped a disc in my back," he explained wryly. "You ever heard of a disc? So the Service, they give me a light job. I have to work inside now. I'm not sure I like town life very well. But the wife always did want to live in town. And the boy has to go to school. So that is the way it sometimes goes. Now I used a smaller boat than yours mostly," he told us, "all over that lake for years . . .

"Little more power, not much more than you have. You just go right on down the Slave River, starting below Fort Smith, and right on out through the delta, weaving through the delta islands. Plenty of shelter, plenty of firewood. What more does a person need? Plenty of places to run for if a wind springs up. Then — I can see it now — to get across the lake, you go eastward, to Grant Point, and then start to cut northwestwards through Les Iles Terribles and Petitot Islands. Then — let's see — the Simpson Islands, they're big ones and lots of them. Don't get lost in the islands. They're all forested, real nice ones. Next, you sight right onto the Wilson group. All right, then." He enumerated the island groups on his fingers.

"Head right for the Caribou Islands, you hit Gros Cap east of Campbell Bay on the north mainland, and there you are. You can't miss it. You're in sight of some kind of islands all the way if you follow the sightings I just give you. Of course, there are some rocks and reefs, especially girdling along the north shore. Like in Dry-bone Bay — you won't get that far east — and the Beniah Islands and the Middle Rocks and Jackfish Islands and the East Mirage Group. But you just follow along the north mainland shore north northwestward then, less than a hundred miles, and it takes you naturally right into Yellowknife Bay and the Gold Brick Bar and all the Gold Brickers . . .

"You can even sometimes rig a sail. Do you have some canvas? Oh, you'll love the lake. Once you lay eyes on that clear water you'll never like the muddy rivers again."

"Brother," commented Jean, "you make it sound real easy! But how are my mother and I to keep from getting those islands all mixed up?"

"Yes," I backed her up, "we can see on the map here how we would be within sight of islands all the time if we cross the lake the clever way you say. But what would happen if we got mixed up in the islands? What if we couldn't find our way through them and ran out of gas? Or had motor trouble? What would happen if we sighted too far east . . . why, the eastern fingers of Great Slave Lake just run off my map every which way into the Barrens. It's unknown. . . ."

"Oh, well, you mustn't do *that*," he remonstrated reasonably. "Nobody does *that*. Nobody goes there. It's off the shipping lanes. Of course," he considered, "I wouldn't want to encourage you to do something that you think you are not up to. There is the factor that it is getting late in the season. Winds are from the north-northeast, mostly," he advised. "Do you have a compass? Do you know how to use it? There's about a thirty-four degree magnetic variation, east. That's just in *some* places on the lake. Other places on the lake the compass returns to normal. . . . But really," he sighed, "I wish I had the time to show you the way myself, because I've made that crossing so many times, from the south shore to the north shore, that there's really not much to it. And it will be a shame if you miss the experience of navigating the lake."

The trouble was, Slim Joy meant well, but he was one of those advisers of whom the amateur should beware. For Slim Joy, modest though he was, was one of the world's most expert woodsmen and boatmen. His talents exceeded ours; but he happily assumed that everyone was as skilled as himself, or at least could pick up quickly what it had taken him a whole lifetime to learn.

Selby Rapp spoke up at this moment. "Of course, to begin with, you know you have to come ashore at Fort Fitzgerald on the Slave River, and portage in order to get into Smith?" he asked, bringing our navigation problem closer to home.

"Sure we know that," said Jean. "There isn't a single person hasn't kept talking about that since we started in British Columbia."

"Well, be careful when you see the first edge of Fitzgerald. Watch for a sawmill on the left shore. Big piles of sawdust there by the river. That means you've got to get ashore fast, on the upper side of town. Nobody ever tries to run them rapids. You'll see all the big vessels docked up. Go right in there. Someone there will load you on one of the trucks and take you eighteen miles around the rapids and right into Fort Smith by road."

"They won't have no trouble," Slim Joy turned to the ranger. "You know we lost that one boy couple of weeks ago."

"What happened?"

"Well, people tried to tell them not to run the rapids between Fitzgerald and Smith. But boys will be boys. They had to see for theirself. They got dumped, lost canoe and everything. Nobody ever saw any of it again. The one boy got ashore, somehow. He come walking into Smith. Then we got planes an' searched all the rapids for three-four days. But I think we all knew it was no use. We been through that job too many summers before. That Rapids of the Drowned never gives up a body, or a boat, nor nuthin'."

"Maybe the body got caught agin one of them rocks in the current and will always stay there," suggested the ranger.

"Well, of course the water's muddy, too," added Slim. "If it floated on down a hundred miles to the lake, well, you know below Smith there's no people to see it anyways. They always search a day or two with these cases, but even the RCMP and Forestry together, we got little chance to find a body. . . ."

"What body? Who are you talking about?" cried Jean suddenly.

"The German boys. Two of 'em come down the river ahead of you. They told people they were deserters from the German Army. They're Germans," explained Selby Rapp.

"Oh," cried Jean, shocked. "I *know them*. I met them at Vermilion when my Mom was in Edmonton. They were Germans. They were blond. One of them has such pretty hair. They were expert canoeists. Oh, gee, they were nice guys," she protested.

"Well, one of 'em's a dead guy now," said Slim. "I don't know which one you think had pretty hair. So be sure you and your Mom don't run the Rapids of the Drowned. Nobody's done it successfully in the hundred years or so they've been trying. There's no channel through there, it can't be done."

"Oh, we won't try *that*," protested Jean, still shocked. "We'll portage around that place. We're not foolish boys."

It was the first time I had heard her boast the superiority of her gender or admit any complicity with it. Yet her tomboyishness had never worried me a whit. Usually you will find that the high-spirited tomboy girl of today turns out to be the finest woman of tomorrow. More of a woman, in fact, than that old approved stereotype of the demure, "feminine" little girl, who withdraws behind the screen of supposed femininity because her upbringing has encouraged withdrawal rather than full participation in life. Jean, all along, had been a real, lusty tomboy type, and her sister Ann, too, had this summer developed fortitude.

When we entered the Slave River we would have the benefit of commercial navigation markers from there on to the Arctic Ocean. We would have to learn how to read them together. We were aware that commercial vessels on neighboring Athabasca River, starting at Waterways, ran one hundred and eighty miles into the muddy west end of Lake Athabasca, and then down into the Slave to Fort Smith, three hundred and four navigation miles in all above the Slave rapids we had discussed. But the vessels below the Fort Smith rapids, on the other hand, worked the waterways northwards; they were different vessels. We would soon be seeing these commercial tugs and barges when we joined the Athabasca-Slave system of waters.

"I'm thinking you can get a ride across the lake on one of them tugs if you can find one before you get out of the Slave River," Slim said. "Or maybe even out on the lake itself. I'll be real interested to learn how you cross the lake, anyway. I happen to know the tug captains have been looking out for you already. Why, they knew about your plans before you left the Edmonton office. The moccasin telegraph, you know. They know there's going to be *ladies* voyaging them waters. Watch out for old Captain Klinker and the *Radium Royal*," he advised sagely.

Slim Joy and Selby Rapp and Selby's wife and little ones were all on the riverbank to see us off. We asked to buy gas. Selby could not sell gas — all those hundreds of red drums were government property — but he could give gas away, when in his judgment a traveler was in need. Meeting the emergency need is always the basic rule of the North. Forty minutes quickly passed in measuring and pouring with a funnel, and mixing oil, until our empties were filled.

Meanwhile the practical ranger had cleaned our rifles and handed them back loaded. For although the rules specified that visitors passing through the park could not carry loaded arms, any person of good sense out here realized that in a wilderness such as this the matter of arms could be one of life and death, should an emergency arise. The guns should be loaded all the time, possibly for signaling or even to get food if starvation threatened. We had been advised by Forestry people before now to build a great big *fire* should emergency arise. I doubted that I would ever do that. In that country it would have required a fire some fifteen stories tall to attract attention.

Well, no emergency was going to confront us. It was our responsibility to see that it didn't happen, when the calm Canadians trusted us so implicitly with their natural resources.

"I sure would like just to see the end of Lake Athabasca along our way," I mentioned as we were — for the second time — about to depart. "Selby, your brother Quinby, at Fort Vermilion, said he knows three ways through the swamps by which a small boat can get into Lake Athabasca. Well, we are almost in the Peace-Athabasca delta right here, aren't we? What do you think? Could my girl and I just detour a little and go into Lake Athabasca along our way?"

"You would like to go over to Fort Chip, eh?" he mused. "Do the RCMP know it's on your schedule?"

"No bother about that," Slim Joy put in. "I'll tell 'em where you went. I'm back into Smith right today. You could go up the Catfish Channel. There's about a four-mile current upstream, but you wouldn't mind that."

"No," said Selby, "right now I think they may find the Catfish has the current going the other way."

The two men stood, debating which way the current flowed, while I tried in vain to find Catfish Channel on the map. Finally it was clarified by identifying the river Chenal des Quatre Fourches, meaning the River of Four Forks, but the local people who used it called it Catfish. Once a week a boat went through it back and forth to Lake Athabasca, carrying timber workers from the Peace for weekends at home. Their families lived at Fort Chipewyan on Lake Athabasca.

If you could find the right channel out of the Peace River, the distance to Lake Athabasca by boat was only about forty-eight miles. The way the current flowed depended upon the fluctuation in water levels between Lake Athabasca and the Peace. When the Peace was low the current was against you as you voyaged toward the big lake. But the Peace had been flooding, as was entirely usual in its late summer cycle, so right now we would probably find the Catfish current flowing just the way we wanted it to go, toward Lake Athabasca, the men thought.

"You just watch for Moose Island as you go on," said Selby. "That's the big one. And then there's Sawmill Island, a long skinny one that is. And then comes Fire Island right after, and the channel's right behind Fire Island."

"I'm sure it will be easy for us to miss," I told the men, "but anyway, I guess Jean and I will try for it. How about it, Jean?"

Only a hundred miles out of the way — and does a person get to see Lake Athabasca every day?

"By the way," we were asked at the last, "have you ladies noticed any dead buffalo as you traveled?"

I guess Jean and I both looked our surprise. "Mom wanted to ask about buffalo," said Jean. "We wanted to know, how are the plains buffalo getting along in these wet swamps?"

Selby Rapp stroked the short blond whiskers on his chin thoughtfully and his face looked strange. "Not so good right now," he admitted. "We got troubles."

"What's the trouble?"

"Anthrax outbreak," he told us. He paused, his face working, and one sensed a strong anguish. "I thought I had better bring it up and tell you, because if you should happen to find any dead carcasses along the river, I should warn you not to go near them because you could possibly catch it."

He went on to reveal that down below, after the Peace joined the Slave River, at the farther ranger station where the corrals were, men were engaged in burying carcasses found in that area; and for this work every man wore a mask and special clothes.

"We have no idea where they got it," Selby Rapp said. "But they got it now. Government biologists confirmed it last week. More scientists going to fly in this week. Everybody in the park feels pretty bad about it. Anthrax, well, it means the loss of a big part of our herds."

In the beginning the herds had done very well. But since 1922, Selby testified, the character of the country had grown ever more wet, changing from arctic prairies with lakes to swamps with lakes. A portion of the herds began to get hoof rot from being always wet. Then, from being wet and cold so much of the time in the swamps, a sizable percentage contracted tuberculosis, and were destroyed by the government men when testing was done at the corrals at each fall butchering time.

The park had tried hard to run a clean herd, and had been successful in marketing the meat locally, especially to the government boarding schools for arctic children. But the terrible anthrax, characterized by malignant, highly contagious pustules, was invariably fatal to domestic cattle; and now the prognosis for the buffalo herds looked tragic.

However, a famous biologist had been called on consultation from the United States; and he held out one hope. No disease, he said, no matter how virulent, would wipe out every single animal. His opinion was that rather than shooting all infected beasts, it might be better to let plague run its course, to trust to nature's built-in controls to save a few resistant survivors. Besides — how could every single diseased animal be tracked down here, one wondered.

Now learning about the anthrax scare made me feel a little squeamish about drinking the Peace and Slave River waters ahead. As I considered our little chlorination pills, I wondered if they could be altogether trusted in the face of such overwhelming chances of infection: a hundred miles of river and over seventeen thousand buffalo were involved. The circumstances strengthened my resolution to leave our Peace River forever and head as fast as possible for Lake Athabasca, which lies in Alberta and Saskatchewan.

"When a high density of population occurs you can almost always expect some kind of disease to strike," said the ranger. "In the wilds, a lot of our species seem to just disappear for periods of sometimes several years, you know. Then all of a sudden you see them again. The species come back from the small number that survived. It's a law of nature," he told us. "But we sure hate to see it happen to our herds here in the Park."

We were pushing off. "Watch for the *Radium Royal*," called Slim Joy at the last. "Watch for old Captain Klinker when you hit the Slave." We waved.

Jean and I voyaged on down to Swanson's Mills. We spent the night there, drinking their water and eating their food, then canoed onward. Jean would have much preferred to camp out.

Swanson's Mills was one of a trans-Canada chain of lumber camps owned, it was said, by a man named Swanson. About one hundred and fifty men worked here, and the place had an airfield, all still within Wood Buffalo Park. We were guests of the foreman, his wife, and their six mannerly children.

The Mills had been here for many years. It harvested some of the limited patches of tall black spruce of commercial quality in the lower Peace and Slave valleys, mostly from the big river islands, as marked and permitted by the Forest Service. Here was the source of lumber for building the Territories' Capitol at Fort

Smith; also the towns of Yellowknife, Hay River and Fort Resolution on Great Slave Lake were laboriously served with this barge-transported lumber from the Slave River.

Although it took some cagey map-reading and a kind of feminine. intuition besides — Jean had not yet developed her feminine intuitions very far — I somehow managed to locate the remote and wandering Catfish Channel behind a long run of vaguely defined river islands, and we made our way into the eastward swamps, in the direction of enormous Lake Athabasca. The delta between the Peace River and Lake Athabasca contains probably around fifteen thousand lakes and water holes. During the fall it is famed for its tens of thousands of ducks and geese, although we saw none now.

It was farewell to the mighty Peace River, our summer's enchantress. We were probably never to see it again, except possibly from the air. When you leave a river like this one, having wrestled with it and wrung from it some of the best moments that anyone could ever have, you are almost sad to leave it. You just turn a corner and it is gone. If you returned another summer, the river would not be quite the same.

But your sadness in leaving your past is mitigated, when you realize that opening up before you is a new river to explore.

17

The River That Flows Both Ways

THE incredible diversity of infinity itself is well demonstrated when you follow a river. You meet endless new arrangements of the age-old materials, endless possibilities for learning and delighting the soul. Along a river minor miracles happen every day. Yet the river is quicksilver: it can't be held in your hands. You can only borrow a river a little while from eternity.

"Kapáckta, páckta," sang the staccato motor as we left the Peace River — the Peace which drains an area of 119,000 square miles — and started following the muddy Catfish Channel away into the eastward swamps.

The channel was about a hundred yards wide, throwing the barking echo back, and it seemed like dead water. After a while I said we should stop to examine some branches drooping into the water from shore. Each branch end made a little silver trail on the water's dark surface. When we cut off the motor we drifted turgidly forward.

"This is it!" I cried jubilantly. "This has got to be the Catfish. Look at the water levels, very stable, no silt on the trees. Yes, we are heading for Lake Athabasca."

Jean was feeling the water with her hand. She commented that there are so many sloughs of dead water in this country that are not marked on any map that it would be downright easy to get lost far out in the swamps and get yourself into a lot of trouble if you didn't watch out.

After a couple of hours we saw High Rock Ranger Tower around a bend. The summer fire warden and his pregnant young wife — all the women of the frontier were always pregnant — with their small child were living here in a tiny cabin. The duties of the ranger were to climb a path up High Rock and go hand over hand up a slippery vertical ladder four times a day to make his fire "scheds." His wife in the cabin below could not have climbed the ladder to call out had an accident occurred. However, if the ranger missed a few of his schedules someone would fly in to see what was the matter.

We pitched our tent beside them for the night. We brought with us fresh meat and potatoes from the Mills, and candy bars and canned juices. We always traded goods with people like that. They had only two cans of milk left for the child. Their fishnet in the slough caught only muddy, whiskery suckers called "catfish." And the snap beans from their tiny garden plot were few. Ten days from now they would be evacuated by boat and floatship, as the fire season was nearing its end.

In the morning although adjacent Lake Berril was nearly heaving itself out of its banks in a high wind, I decided that we could push onward. We followed the sheltered swamp channel as it wound through scattered, dwindling spruce stands.

"My feminine intuition tells me," I said to Jean, "that these spruce stands may give out and leave us in the swamps with no dry ground to sit on, and no fuel. I guess in this drizzly weather we might be wise to call it a day and pick a camp pretty soon."

"You and your feminine intuition!" huffed Jean. "Mother, you just don't like any hardship, I know that."

The motor wouldn't start now for an hour or so, and we were just sitting in the boat, drifting and thinking, and watching one good spruce stand and then another go around the bend.

Then a curious little adventure befell us: we heard a very small plaintive sound in the silence — like the mewing of a cat.

Like silent flotsam the canoe drifted close along the shore and there stood a remarkably pretty young gray and white house cat meowing her head off. She stood out on the end of a log jutting into the river as far as she could get, when we came floating by a vacated cabin. What odd luck that our motor had stopped! Had it been running we would never have heard the pathetic animal's calls for attention.

We came ashore. "It will be too wild for you to catch," I warned Jean.

But when Jean went toward the cat in the grass, it ran to her with hysterical delight and was immediately cradled in human arms. From Jean's arms it then leaped to me and never had I been so completely caressed in all my life. It was a most overwhelming cat.

Are cats stupid, or do they usually remain indifferent to humans because of their own design? We have all heard the arguments pro and con. Now we had a true answer: Cats are smart enough to make themselves entirely accommodating if they wish to do so. Of course this charming animal, with her exceptionally long sharp claws and most ingratiating ways, had been abandoned by her former owner and was about to starve. She could live on mice for another month perhaps, so the northern people told us, but by late September's snows she was doomed to starve or be eaten by lynx, wolf or wolverine. And I believe she sensed this — young and innocent though she was. The Great Spirit of the animals, which gives certain instructions to each species — that intelligence which the white man calls instinct — was working hard for her salvation all the time, and, as everyone knows, the Great Spirit seems to have an especial interest in the cat family.

It happened that we had a big fish with us that very day, the only time in the whole summer that we had one. A sucker from the ranger's net, it was an item one would be loath to eat oneself, but some impulse had made us accept the gift at the moment of departure, just to have it along for extra provision. For unexpected guests, perhaps.

"Oh, Mom, gee, Mom, can we have it? We need a pet. We need a mascot for our canoe. Mom, I'll take care of the cat myself, she won't cause you a bit of trouble.

Although I heard those last words with dire foreboding, there was in fact nothing to do but take the starving, abandoned animal along.

Presented the fish, the cat set to work competently and tucked away the whole thing which was nearly the size of herself. First she ate the head as a mink does. This was the fatty part she craved. Then gnawing through the belly she ate the intestinal fat. Next the meat and bones, working backward to the big tail fin, while we watched in sympathetic gastronomical satisfaction.

After the cat had her dinner the motor mysteriously started with one pull on the starter rope and away we went, suddenly in possession of a cat picked up on the river that flows both ways.

When we first started life-with-cat I was certain that her enthusiasm for our company would soon wane, and that she would stray from one of our camps and be lost; but Lady Louise — she was named from the sound of her voice which seemed to be saying "Louise" — followed our footsteps closely when we went ashore, and incredible as it seems came quickly at a call. The first night she sprang up a tree like a squirrel. In trees she had wisely been accustomed to spend her nights. But when she saw the tent pitched she ran down the tree headfirst, again like a squirrel, and was overjoyed to come inside and there comfortably settle herself in the best place on the fur rug. Jean lost no time getting all her chores done so she could attend to the cat's proper meals.

Near dusk we were picking a berry here and there for our pans in the soft drizzle when we heard the sound of a motor coming along the channel. Around the bend, then, at a high speed suddenly appeared a turquoise-blue Flying Scot speedboat driven by an eighty-horse motor. Never had we seen such a sight. In the enclosed fiberglass launch, sitting on matching turquoise upholstered seats, were two of the tallest and handsomest Mounted Police officers you ever imagined in Canada!

They were out looking for us from Fort Chipewyan. After introductions ashore we handed them cups of hot tea — "Here's mud in your eye!" said one to the other — and slabs of fresh homemade bread dripping with highbush cranberry conserve. Their boyish faces blooming with a healthy outdoors color, they downed four or five slices ravenously.

"What on earth are you staying out here for?" was one of the first things the officers asked us. "Why didn't you come on up to the lake?"

They didn't seem to realize that for one thing our motor just didn't make the time an eighty-horse motor does.

"We thought the spruce cover might give out," Jean tried to explain. "We think there might be high waves on your lake today."

They shrugged. "Well, you are more or less right on both counts," the junior officer admitted. It was clear that during their patrols they managed not to sleep out on the ground very often.

Of course, we did not want an eighty-horse motor. We could not begin to carry fuel for that size on a long journey. Our slow progress was also safer for us. We operated usually at less than half throttle with the 9.5 horsepower we had. Speed has proved fatal for many an enthusiast in unknown and obstacle-filled waters. But our traveling method was not elegant; by contrast with our visitors our craft and our persons were inelegantly plastered with mud.

"We've been looking all over the place for you for three hours," they told us. "We used up too much fuel, too. We don't want you to get lost. Are you aware that the Channel branches into four forks up here a ways?"

"Sure," we said. "There's some Chipewyans fishing there at the junction. We figured they will set us straight."

"Don't count on it," said the senior officer of the two, whom we'll call Corporal Swinger. "We'll meet you at the Forks tomorrow at noon, and guide you on in to Fort Chip. Well, ta-ta. It's getting almost dark. Have to get on home for supper. The wife will wonder what's happened."

My stomach lurched anxiously as I heard our canoe seat and thwart crackle and bend under heavy Mounties as they climbed over our muddy craft and into their launch. Away they sped abruptly with an impressive roar.

Next morning Jean and I rolled the tent, bailed out our boat, and cleaned some of the mud out of it, hastening to get going. The day was cold, rainy, and fogged in, but we were fluffy and warm in our parkas.

Reaching the Chipewyan camp consisting of a few tents and one permanent frame cabin at the treeless forks, we learned that fortunately, without a timepiece, we had calculated our rendezvous right on the dot. In the cabin whose bare table was littered with battered tin dishes and the scraps from a fish meal, we warmed ourselves beside a crackling sheet-iron stove with the Indians as we awaited the young Mounties to whom all the world seemed a great lark.

The silent natives of the country watched us appraisingly and were kind. They didn't like these particular Mounties, but they didn't say so.

"It is good t'ing to get inside, out of this rain," our polite motherly hostess said to me. "You might catch cold. I make for you some hot coffee." I demurred. I was afraid of hepatitis and .tuberculosis and a dozen other unknowns. She was a Chipewyan, the mother of these silent, lovely children, all very poor. She had married a Cree husband, and she said their languages were different. There were not many of her people, the Chipewyans, left in the world, she told me.

The Cree husband came in. His face was darkly sullen. He took one look at the cat which Jean cradled while we dried out, and spoke out strongly.

"You sure got yourself one terrible animal, if it's a pet you want," he informed Jean sternly in good English. "Now you take a cat. It's worthless. Cats will kill little children by sitting on their chests when the children are asleep."

"Well, here's a switch," I thought. "He has learned one of the white man's superstitions, and he believes the stuff."

"Did you ever really *know* a case like that? Ever see it?" I bristled. "I very much doubt it."

"Thousands of children have cats where we come from, in the United States," Jean added, trying to make him see reason.

"I don't care about that," retorted the man rudely. "There's plenty case what I can tell you in Canada. You hear of it a lot." He had picked up the ignorant white man's crude, harsh, know-it-all manner. "Lots of children have lost their eye," he went on, "because they got a cat's hair in their eye."

Again I denied ever knowing of such a case, but he was beyond anything I could say. He was simply mean and antagonistic. "Do you know what I do whenever I see a cat?" he asked.

And before I could stop him he said, "I just take a cat in both hands, like this, see? And then, I *pull*."

The shudder I felt in my innards was at that moment transferred to a feeling of militant protection of the homeless, starved little creature we held, while Jean's eyes popped in horror and she quickly pulled Lady Louise inside her coat. Even the cat shrank.

Roaring out of the fog came the Mounties and we left the shack, Jean carrying the cat close to her body hidden from sight. She picked her way step by perilous step through the packs of half-starved hounds, whose noses told them truly that a cat was passing near.

Only the winter before a fifteen-year-old boy had fallen under his sled and been torn to death by his own dogs at Fort Chip. I had withstood the children's entreaties to bring our own big black gentle dog along on this trip because of the many perils involved. Having a pet along increases the normal difficulties tenfold.

In making the trip from here to the Fort somehow I had assumed that the slower *Jeanie Ann* would be towed. But if we had hoped to be invited to share the plush indoors seats in the launch with our escorts, we had been wrong. It may be that the RCMP had some ruling against taking passengers in the police launch; possibly they even had special rulings against women.

While we doggedly held the course they indicated, the turquoise launch with its far greater power playfully cavorted around us circling before and behind. Lake Athabasca opened up to view, showing a short cut across the open bay studded with reefs like gray elephant backs: a different geology here, as we crossed over the Shield. Straight across the windy bay our blithe escorts led us, while our little canoe smashed into the waves and at each carom our faces were drenched with ice water. Jean, holding to the throttle, became blue.

I had often drenched Jean myself. But it annoyed me a little when someone else led us into it. Left to our own devices, we would have taken a more conservative course. You could see the situation right away: this bay opened directly upon the nearly three-hundred-mile length of the lake which could blow up a real smasher when the east wind turned. I had somehow felt it when we met him: Corporal Swinger was a bit of a bully. He was making his white male supremacy felt in his territory. Some residents later told us that the young men were foolhardy at times. Once this summer they had been caught out on the big lake in the Flying Scot when they carelessly ran out of gas on an outing. Our glimpse of them seemed to reveal that they traveled about with little or no emergency equipment in their leaps through a country where the unexpected frequently occurs. But their Cree interpreter cared for them as best he could.

Perched upon the Precambrian rocks on the north side of the bay sat the Indian shacks and the few government houses of Fort Chipewyan, Alberta. Samuel Hearne, exploring for the Northwest Company in 1771, was the first European to see this cove, which lies just five miles across the bay from where the sprawling Athabasca River delta comes in from the south. And on December 24, 1771, Hearne also saw Great Slave Lake.

In 1788 Peter Pond was sent out by the Northwest Company to winter on the Athabasca River. He built a post forty miles above Lake Athabasca partly to trade for furs, but also to get information about this great water system; he got the Crees and the Chipewyans to inform and guide him. These Indians traded him twice the amount of furs his canoes could carry when he made his way back south to Isle à la Croix Lake.

At the same time, Alexander Mackenzie was appointed factor in charge of the Athabasca region. At first he based his operations at Pond's House; then he moved to Lake Athabasca, and built Old Fort Chipewyan near the Athabasca delta. But the Fort was moved to firmer ground at his instigation in 1804. There it still stands today, and its inhabitants still trap muskrats in what may be the world's greatest muskrat swamps.

It was from this base that Mackenzie sent McLeod and Boyer to the Peace River to contact the Beaver Indians. They were to buy meat and trade with them, and persuade them to bring in their furs. In 1788 Mackenzie sent Boyer to build a post farther up the Peace near the present Fort Vermilion. The Boyer rapids we had passed through bear his name.

In 1789 the ambitious Mackenzie, learning of the source of an enormous river in Great Slave Lake, followed northwestward the river which bears his name. He hoped to be led by it to the Pacific. If it had flowed out to the Pacific the course of all history in North America would be different. To his disappointment the Mackenzie River took him to the Arctic Ocean instead — for it could not cross the western mountains. But that is another story, and another summer for us.

We were very fortunate to have come over here from the Peace, though this was a little out of our way to be sure — for here was the very base of operations of many of the great explorers. Since the days of the explorers the Athabasca River, coming from the south and flowing through the west end of Lake Athabasca past Fort Chip and down into the Slave and Great Slave Lake, has become well established as a trade route. But Fort Chip is still "out of the way," remote from road and rail. Few and plucky are the *voyageurs* who have seen this route.

Putting in at the police docks in official style, our drenched party were led to the police home, were introduced to the wife, and were invited to be their guests while we were at the Fort.

An air of bygone neat colonialism pervaded the police establishment. The white wooden two-story house sat back upon green-cropped lawns, typical of the RCMP barracks one sees everywhere. Built of imported soils tenderly laid over the rock pile upon which the Fort perched, the lawn had graveled walks and neat gay flower-beds. Much work had been done to achieve this modest show of officialdom. The air of military authority got to you when you observed a multitude of newly whitewashed rocks and boulders — who whitewashed the boulders? — which lined the driveway. The driveway led to the garage, and connected with perhaps three miles of road.

Inside the office section of the barracks our cat was settled in comfortable lodgings by the good-humored officers. A small arsenal of light arms was locked up here and coiled upon a hook on the wall was a long braided leather whip.

The Canadian Mountie, idol of every boyhood dream all over the world, the Mountie of scarlet tunic and wide-brimmed hat, has been immortalized in books and film as a fearless lawman who always gets his man. Created under the name Northwest Mounted Police by Parliament in 1873, their original aim was to stamp out lawlessness in the West and calm the growing unrest among the Indians. Mounties will tell you that one reason there were no bloody uprisings and massacres in Canadian history such as were rampant throughout the American West, was the valor, tact and dedication of their little group; but three hundred men in those early days.

Of course, other reasons were the lack of horses among far northern Indians, hence lack of communications and lack of Indian armies in the far North. There was never at any time any great wave of pioneers to alarm and antagonize the forest Indians as their lands weren't coveted — and still aren't. People were separated from each other in the great silence of the trackless forest. There were only a few little Indian groups camping along the waterways, and they seemed glad, for the most part, when a few outside traders came to deal with them. The poverty of the forest and isolation permeated their lives. Starvation in winter was common. The whole geography of the far Northwest with its swamps and forests was different from the plains of the open West. One had only to visit it for oneself to realize why history had written different chapters.

And yet I have sometimes wondered if the Americans might not have avoided much of the terrible bloodshed between Indians and whites in our West if we could have had an English-type task force like the Mounties. Like those task forces used by the English in much of Africa and Asia during the same period, they would have regulated the traffic of covered wagons, made terms with the natives, and kept the peace as they did throughout the incredible vastness of Canada. Possibly there would have been no range wars, no outlaw bands, no fabled individual gunslingers: for such phenomena never existed in orderly Canada.

Perhaps the old-time Mounties rendered their greatest service during the Gold Rush of 1898. They were needed to protect white men from each other as they traveled toward the Klondike, many of these ruffians being Americans.

The Mounties have been involved in no major scandal in the nearly one hundred years of their existence, and their watchword was always HONOR, so men of even the slightest honor looked up to them. Today there are about eight thousand Royal Canadian Mounted Police and since 1920 they have served all over Canada. Their activities range from traffic direction and border inspections to international crime work. They are one of the toughest, best trained, best equipped police forces in the world, and they now make over two million investigations a year.

My young daughters and I had made two other calls upon Mounties this summer and had been treated with every cordiality. So we were welcomed into the living quarters of Corporal Swinger and his wife.

Inside the little home all was soft lighting, carpeting, and highly polished hardwood floors. Indian handicraft and art objects were collected from the region by the Swingers. Modern electrical conveniences were in operation, since community power had rather recently been acquired at the old Fort. Even for a home having no children, everything was enormously shipshape compared to most other posts. The meals set by our hostess were exquisite.

When a small group of flying politicians dropped in from the south, doing a little campaigning for the next Alberta elections, our hostess served up a cocktail or two. She was like a general's wife as she presided — not just a corporal's wife. Her home was the social center for thousands of square miles. She had married the corporal in a formal RCMP wedding, and they had walked under an arch of crossed sabers in Ottawa. The role of the Mountie's wife after marriage is a little more taxing. She has been thoroughly investigated and passed on by the Service before the officer may marry her, but now comes the test: for the rest of her life she must keep smiling and say nothing. Just that. That is her sole reason for being, in any community. It isn't easy.

So while the young master of the house briefed the politicians about the community whose votes were wanted, the cocktails went around. There were only a few voters here, actually. The Indians could not vote. The half-breeds were permitted to, but were an indifferent surly lot. Most bordered on being relief cases, or hoped for relief checks. Since there was no social welfare worker for this village of eighteen hundred souls, one of the duties of the Mountie here was to administer welfare himself.

In some very isolated posts the Mountie serves all positions. He may be policeman and catch his man. He may be judge and pass out the sentence. He may be jailer, and he may decide whether to sign relief checks, or apply for relief checks, or not.

Holding all these positions may not be constitutional, but the practice is based upon necessity of circumstance and lingers on from historical precedent. It is too much power to be invested in just one man. For even if the Mounties have an untarnished reputation for honor, sooner or later their glory could be diminished by the misfit man.

"Oh, you don't have any *crimes* here." Our host hastened to draw a picture of the community for the campaigning visitors. "Just little infractions of the law like liquor violations and drunkenness. Then — I put the Indians to work. Law says I can't work the half-breeds, though, except if they make or sell home brew — we call it 'bean juice' around here."

We had learned this summer that it is impossible to tell a pure Treaty Indian from the other inhabitants unless one knows each individual. Treaty Indians get government-supplied food orders each month in addition to having their year-round hunting and fishing rights. But other mixed members of the population trapping in the same area don't. Therefore, it has become common practice for Treaty Indians to sell some of their free food for cash, at half price, to those half-breeds who are hungry and who need food; and the half-breeds get out and sign orders for whiskey and beer for the Indians. Sometimes half-brothers and half-sisters of mixed white blood who legally can buy liquor are in the same family with full Indians who cannot. Nobody can make home brew legally, but many people do. Liquor, not being carried by the Hudson's Bay Company, has to be flown in from accredited state liquor stores, with every bottle signed and accounted for.

Reluctantly we departed, having had the motor checked out by the amiable younger Mountie and having accepted ten gallons of gas (which was all our tanks would hold) from Corporal Swinger. Our now somewhat reluctant cat went with us, every claw braced. She had seen a comfortable permanent home with the police who delighted in her, but Jean refused to give her up. We gave a glance over the shoulder at the great open sea of Lake Athabasca, all set with whitefish nets stretching across Saskatchewan eastward just below the continental tree line. Then our canoe slipped around Doghead Rock, which was painted with a thirty-foot slab of bright orange paint to mark the way. We left by way of one of three mouths of the Rivière des Rochers (Rock River); it flows slowly out of the lake carrying the Athabasca River waters and is therefore referred to as the Athabasca River where it joins the Peace forty miles below, both being thereafter termed the Slave. The Slave then, containing the Peace and Athabasca, is said to have a drainage area of 232,000 square miles.

The River of Rocks was well named. Although it sprawled out into a maze of channels through an enormous swamp, that was the only swamp I ever knew that was full of rocks, any one of which would disable us if we hit it. These rocks were of all sizes and lay at varying depths. Even in fair weather the swamp was a deceptive mirage of a place; it held a frightening, barely concealed threat of something elemental and unknown. But we must push our luck while fair weather held.

Delighted to be free of mud, we camped on a clean rock humpback. Since we could not drive pegs, we squared the tent with poles and tied ropes to them, using just one or two pegs sunk into a tiny patch of soil developed in a crevice, and anchored fast in this way.

There was something special about the swamp that teased the edges of the mind. But only later when you had a chance to look it up on the geological time chart was your strange feeling confirmed. Definitely Precambrian, dating to a minimum of five hundred and fifty million years ago, this place may have contained some of the very oldest rocks of earth dating from the Proterozoic or Archeozoic eras, one billion to two billion years ago!

Plenty of fuel was to be had from driftwood carried by the wind and the current and caught on the dim gray hogbacks. That the rocks of the swamp were used by sled travelers in winter as well was evident from the many campsites, at one of which we stuck up some ancient molded caribou antlers before the blaze for drying racks for our socks. However, the caribou which had roamed here during some winter years ago, or been hauled from the east on a sled, had long since been eaten out from under their antlers by the proliferating population which decimated them in the area.

Now we had the red and black shore markers to follow, as we camped along the regular commercial navigation route: red on your left hand and black on your right, when you are going downstream. To avoid hitting invisible rock devils you hold a strict course between the red and the black. Actually, a small boat can go anywhere, with caution. It was amazing to realize that the big stuff — the tugs up to one hundred and eighty feet long pushing strings of barges totaling a thousand feet and more — navigated neatly through all these turns. If they could do it, so could we.

The canoeist faces a drawback in the very low visibility close to the surface of the water. To the canoeist the friendly channel markers seem dreadfully far-spaced, being anything from a mile to three miles apart. Often he seems to lose them altogether. Sometimes the markers have been moved recently, even though the river charts may be nearly up to date. If he camps to one side the canoeist can be thrown off course; unless, as we did through the swamp, he camps right on the signs in full view of any passersby.

On a dreamy four-mile current we followed the foot-high banks (or often, no shoreline at all) upon limpid, glassy waters, while dinosaurian objects to each side lengthened and shortened their aspect or floated in the sky. On and on went the gently curving water over the rim of the earth. The unreality of the swamp was broken only by the occasional ten- to forty-foot gray Precambrian rock hogbacks with their little trees rooted shallowly in a fold. Once we heard a motorboat running fast somewhere out in the greater swamp off our track; we surmised more than glimpsed its dark-skinned native occupant swiftly disappearing behind a low headland among swamp grass and cattails. The sound of his motor hung for a long time in the stillness.

For a moment one thought: "Well, I'm not so alone out here. This route has been traveled for one hundred and fifty years. Here are other voyagers about me, perhaps the very descendants of the explorers."

We were told that we were the last of five expeditions to "come down the river" this season, as residents along the way counted them.

First had come the two Americans in separate small kayaks. They traveled so fast that, having reached the Mackenzie Delta they had gone up the Rat, over the portage there, and down the Porcupine into the Yukon River, and had terminated their trip in Alaska, from which, some said, they were already on American television.

During the Gold Rush of 1898 men using heavy wooden boats carrying all their possessions made this trip in great numbers. It was called the "back door into Alaska." At best, it took two summers in those old days — and easily could today — with the *voyageurs* wintering somewhere in the Mackenzie watershed. Many drowned or froze, or met other disasters.

Along with us, the other Americans were perhaps the only truly successful of this season's five. The second expedition, the two German youths, quit at Fort Smith when one of them was drowned. The third expedition, including three youths from Germany, also gave up at Smith for one reason or another. The fourth came down the much-traveled one hundred and eighty miles of the Athabasca River into Lake Athabasca. Two men had started out: one of them was said to be a Navy survival expert and the other a *National Geographic* Magazine writer. Their sixteen-foot canoe proved to be dangerously overloaded. They had only around three inches freeboard, observers noted. The Navy man left the party and the other man continued on alone, but capsized in the Slave, and lost practically all his camera equipment and other things. But he himself escaped and declared that he would return another

summer to complete his Mackenzie voyage. He was described as a
"nervous type" of man. Would we meet him somewhere in the
Mackenzie next year? Not likely. In this big country one seldom
meets anybody.

Of the five expeditions traversing either the Peace or Athabasca
into the Slave — a typical summer's crop on these rivers — two
had capsized. We were the slowest of all and so stayed the longest.
Seasonal expeditions seem to dash through the country on a quick
trip, because they have to get back to work, or in general because
most people do not think of voyaging as a way of life but only as a
lark or a feat of some kind. Such fast expeditions learn little about
the country they pass through.

When the Rocher River brought us into the Slave, it became a
couple of miles broad, with islands larger than a hundred city
blocks so numerous that you couldn't tell one from another.

"Hey, Mom, why isn't it very large?" Jean broke her long silence.

"Because we are just getting used to big waters, I guess."

No big river is so big after all, when many islands divide the
water into channels. The experienced small boatman can therefore
cope with them with caution.

But when the rocky nature of the terrain was combined with a
twelve-mile current, navigation down the Slave at once became a
critical and very precise matter, necessitating the closest concentration for me with charts and binoculars, while our engineer was kept
busy with the problem of maintaining and controlling power, and
steering according to instructions.

"Look, rapids, Jean. Turn left. Turn right. Cross over. Turn
right, turn left again."

"Where? Where? I don't see any rapids."

The engineer's mood became surly and out of sorts, as I yelled
and pointed alternately, changing channels down the surging torrent. She jerked the boat roughly this way and that, annoyed that I
panicked and changed course so often. Our cat arched her back.
Her soft voice no longer said "Louise," but turned to a hideous,
"Yow!"

I would not advise a canoe trip down the Slave River above Fort
Fitzgerald except for the foolhardy and thick-skinned. The Slave

was grinning with rapids from one end to the other. The fine old Indian at Fort Vermilion had spoken correctly when he said it "is rapids all the way."

We traversed so many as we whirled down the giant sprawling, rocky, erratic river that I did not know where we were on the charts, since some of the rapids were named and charted but most seemed not to be charted at all — long ones that ran from one into another. This is usual in charting, I later learned: only the *course* is charted. Thus in one acutely anxious day we traversed about fifty miles from our camp of the night before; for tomorrow's weather, and the days following, might be prohibitive of all travel. How can a stranger navigate such a river after the fall winds rise?

So long as fair weather held I could see the white curl of water from half-submerged rocks, and take heed. We would cross over a half mile above them and get out of their way. So far so good — so long as the motor held. Our lives were wrapped up in that little motor. To hit a rock and turn over would mean death. Many were the boat traps and snarls of wreckage caught up in mid-river on the reefs. You could see the piles of trees and logs far ahead, then must quickly select a channel to one side or the other, without hesitation.

At Demecharge rapids, our instructions were to watch out for a flag set at the head of an island, and then cut quickly across and go down around the far outside channel — for here the whole river went over a veritable falls. By an excitingly narrow margin this was achieved, and the river's sweep cheated of its prey. Safely below the island, we had still to run for half a mile with brawling white water on either side, where the currents met below the island.

Day's end on the Slave found us looking for a place to camp, any place to get ashore. All was either swamp or brambles, or vicious rock promontories with bases ravaged by whirlpools — sheer rock and nothing to tie to. As the shadows of deceptive night came on Jean found a small slanting, corrugated rock ledge we could perch upon.

To camp on this ledge Jean cut a number of sprucelings and made a framework which we filled in with tips of spruce, making a platform. Here we laid our two sleeping bags on a giant double-spring mattress, barely above the water, crowded into this space between river and forest. In case it might rain, our canvas was snapped snugly over the boat to cover its contents where it was moored to a log. Another large canvas was draped over the top of our big double bed. Then we pulled our clothing, rifle, flashlight, camera, binoculars and such things inside the canvas. Orange life jackets supplied pillows.

Far away on the horizon to the south lightning flared and a thunderstorm rumbled, but the storm never reached us. To the west the low moon sank in cloudy splendor. After midnight the sky cleared to reveal frosty twinkling stars; and for the third time this summer the Northern Lights streamed across the heavens. Each time we opened our eyes during the night we were rewarded with some new mysterious configuration. Once I woke Jean so that she could also have the experience of hearing the wonderful music of a wolf's long-drawn howl.

Fall winds rose and marooned us at Rock Ledge Camp. Although the wind kept us shorebound, sighing around the point in a mighty sea of tossing tree limbs, our rock nook became hot as an Arabian desert, so we peeled. Jean was in pink nylon pajamas and I in long underwear with the grimy sleeves pushed up, and both of us barefooted: we must keep one eye and ear open, for we could suddenly get caught by a passing tug-and-barge outfit. Such an outfit, big as it is, with all its gawking, pop-eyed men on board, can come slipping down the current behind you very fast, and so silently that you won't know they're coming on a windy day. We were camped right on target on this rock: right on the direct route of all the cargo bound for the Arctic.

The cat meanwhile had become a problem. When the wind dropped, could we catch her promptly, without wasting hours of time? She prowled nights now, since as Jean put it, "She hasn't been doing any work lately." She spent the night robbing our foods, dragging and licking our last piece of meat, and under the Northern Lights she brought one field mouse (of the lemming family, actually) and two shrews, and laid the bodies at the head of our bed.

"Well, the North has its good and its poor seasons, you know,

Mom, dear," said Jean. "Some are good for berries and bears. Ours is a good one for mice and cats."

"We're back in Wood Buffalo Park again," I said, and flipped over to the next page on my charts. "I believe we're sunbathing just about three and a half miles above Hay Camp Station."

Jean doubled up laughing. "Good old Mom," she said. "You aren't a very good explorer. You see, I didn't want to be with *people*. I wanted to camp. So when I told you how we could sleep here last night, I didn't tell you that I saw Hay Camp, and it's right around the corner from us now!"

"Oh, dear," I said. "I thought we were in the wilds."

"Well, it's wild enough, I guess," answered Jean. "I had a real good time here, and so did Lady Louise."

It was wild enough. If I had misread my river charts and the navigation targets by three and a half miles, we could have capsized over millions of submerged rocks in that twelve-mile current and been drowned easily before now. I was quite frightened, as I considered the course yet ahead. The Peace River was one thing, and bad enough with its mud. But we had got used to its ways; the Slave full of rocks was a different thing again.

We stopped at Hay Camp when the wind went down and stayed there two or three nights, while it rained softly, a cold drizzle. Having learned that only about one or two days in a row offered traveling weather, we played our luck and watched our chances to venture forth again.

At Hay Camp we ate with the buffalo crews, inspected the corrals and abattoir or butchering plant, and the ranger took us cruising in a tractor vehicle around the dryer areas of the prairie to view wild buffalo.

The last twenty-five miles of the Slave River, to Fort Fitzgerald and the portage road above Fort Smith, was as beset with rocks and rapids as ever; but right within sight of the town was the worst: a stony ridge appeared to obstruct the whole river. It was actually the first sign of the famed rapids where the Slave crosses over a spur of the Canadian Shield. We saw the ridge for the first time as we came around a turn next to the left-hand bank; it was only a hundred yards or so away, and we were coming down on it fast.

From what I could see the big vessels just skirted wide around this place, and followed the opposite shore, then heeled smartly in just above the falls. But to follow their course we would have had to have more than one hundred yards' warning and more than nine and a half horses.

Here was the stop-off place for the portage, for right below Fitzgerald's driftwood-choked indented shoreline, now crowded solid with commercial transport tugs, frothed the deadly cascades. A long wooded island in the midst of the cascades harbored a colony of white pelicans which had wisely made their summer home here, protected from man, since time immemorial.

Hugging close to the shore, we skidded over the very edge of the Shield, just barely bumping bottom, and headed into the cove used as loading and landing place. The current ran swiftly under the curving ends of the barges as we plowed and pushed our way stubbornly through nearly solid driftwood, determined to find a place. A canoe could be pulled under these barges by the current, should you have power failure. We didn't know that then, as we hastily tied to a barge guy rope. The big hawsers smacked of the open sea. The tugs were black and white and had red smokestacks, and two decks. They were chunky and rugged-looking. They served the Athabasca River southward to rail's head. They could go no farther north from here, where the Shield stopped them at the border to the Northwest Territories.

I longed to go aboard one and, as nautical people say, "make a tour of her appointments." We were hungry as always, too, to sit down to a real table and have a real meal. We had heard that they "fed real good on board." They said that practically everybody in the North came on board and ate when the boat docked.

Jean felt shy of the men and I felt shyer. She at least wore no bulky woolens with the long underwear which gives any woman's figure the exact configuration of the Barren Grounds grizzly bear.

Looking then at the steel commercial vessels, we felt the utter remoteness and self-complacency of men. Men, secure and apparently quite content in their man's world. It crossed my mind that a Navy survey of the motivations of men who volunteer to go to the Antarctic has shown that the great majority of them do so "to get away from women." Conceivably, no females from the outside world had ever seen these docks, where every item of freight that goes into the Arctic is landed, stevedored, and portaged to the lower Slave's waterways. Possibly, no females from the outside world had ever been aboard any of these boats. Well, perhaps it was about time. They were going to be seeing a bit of us from now on, the boatmen of the far North.

Good odors of a roast beef dinner came from the ship's little galley. I took a big breath and went into the shack which served as office of the shipping line's agent. I asked to use the telephone to report to the RCMP in Smith that we had safely arrived; I suspected that they might helpfully send an escort car.

Over my shoulder I could see three crewmen on board the vessel at the dock leaning over the rail to talk to Jean, and she was saying, "I know it seems ridiculous to bring your *mother* along in a canoe but . . ." Words I had heard before. Presently I saw her step shyly aboard at the men's invitation.

"Oh, Mom, Mom!" called Jean in gay excitement from aboard a few minutes later. "What do you think happened? Well, I was holding the cat, see. But she jumped. And well, before we could catch her, she escaped on the boat, and now we can't get her back. We think she is some place in the *engine room* . . .

"By the way," she called, "you can come aboard if you want to. We're going to have roast beef today."

After dinner there was a mad scramble in the engine room to catch the cat, and the goodhearted men of the boat laughed until tears ran down their cheeks. Our cat Lady Louise had at last done a good day's work and she was rewarded with a saucer of milk.

Thus we entered the Northwest Territories.

18

By Tug and Barge

WHEN Jean and I awoke and peeped from our tent on the Slave River below Fort Smith, the river rolled freely past our door. Neither rocks nor rapids existed from here down one hundred and fifty miles to Great Slave Lake.

After pulling on soggy clothes (they had been drenched in the surf the day before) and wringing out my socks and insoles, I crawled stiffly out into the feeble rays of a sun that had all the warming power of a forty-watt bulb. At once I pulled on my heaviest parka of padded nylon, and tied the hood tightly under my chin.

The canoe lay broadside to the sandbar, waves sloshing into its seaward side. It had worked loose from its proper mooring during the night. In the coldest hip boots in the world I waded ashore carrying the two-burner Coleman gas stove and set it up on the sand, bolstered from the wind between roots. Breakfast was cold steak scraps, cookies, and hot coffee: all Fort Smith gifts.

"Hey, Ma, don't you dare eat that! That steak's from people's plates in Smith. That's for our *cat!*" Jean objected.

"Well, the cat can have a small share, I guess."

We had some fresh meat, half frozen, but who wants to try to cook it in a twenty-mile wind blast? Hoping for more energy I helped myself to one of Jean's thyroid pills. In my imagination it seemed to supply instant energy. Our water in the bucket had been treated two ways the night before: with powdered alum, followed by soda ash sprinkled lightly on top to sift slowly down and settle the mud. Now carefully pouring some clear water off the top of the bucket into our blackened teakettle I treated the water a third way, with precious chlorine pills. From the ranger in the river-that-flows-both-ways we had learned late in the game how to clear muddy water. He had given us supplies which could be used next year. We had learned much.

Our camp here was pitched upon such uneven ground that, like so many of our camps, it might have qualified for a Marine survival course. Large moldering, marshy sods five feet in depth, which oozed water continuously, were the only ground. Tilted at angles by frost action, they posed a challenge which was solved the night before when we chopped limbs by flashlight and made a complete platform of brush upon which the tent was pitched, elevated above the mud. When you can't find any tent grounds you make your own.

How could we know that this was our last camp?

I had debated all summer long about what to do from this point on. When I had applied to the company offices in Fort Smith for transport down the river and across Great Slave Lake I had been rejected again, of course, because of rules laid down in the government in Ottawa, many miles away. The prospect of hurrying on down the Slave and then getting across Great Slave Lake filled me with dire foreboding: the fall winds had come and could be expected to be prevalent until freeze-up. It was too late in the season already to make the attempt. Yet, here we were, heading into it.

While I bailed the boat, Jean rolled the tent and bags. I waded out, slowly, pushed the stern around, and once I got her ended into the wind, chained her to a protruding log. There was firm sandy footing. I sat on the rim of the canoe, tipping it a bit, and bailed with my booted legs hanging down into icy heaving seas. "Clump, clump!" sounded the metal cooking pot against the wood as I scooped. Up and down sawed the canoe, up and down, dizzily, the water in the bottom sloshing back and forth.

Finally the camp was dismantled, the canoe loaded and its

hatches battened down for a rough day. A moment after we pushed off nothing distinguished that little spot in the shoreline but the mattress of brush we left.

We intended to keep close to shore this day; but as on all days, we found it necessary to cross and crisscross the river through the whitecaps, searching for shelter from the wind and favorable currents. But the mighty open Slave was perfectly straight for miles on end as it plunged for the lake, and there was in fact no shelter.

My thoughts returned in reverie back to Fort Smith where I had had coffee with a brusque little captain who issued directives and information for D.O.T. — the Department of Transport — to five vessels whose mission each summer was to put up those navigation targets and channel buoys along the riverbanks.

We were sitting in the radio room, amid the clamor and howl of long-distance static coming in over the arctic miles. In the sound of the static you felt that you could hear the arctic winds whistling and screeching like banshees. And you could visualize the radio man at the other end; very likely he, too, had a coffee cup sitting beside him. As he talked from ship to ship he would suddenly come in clearly, then dim out: "We need a couple of yardarms and cliffhangers, also two dozen gross skyhooks . . ." came the largely indistinct monotone. Mumble, mumble. Something about equipment.

The vessels to which we listened and at which Captain Spume screamed from his office were deployed along some *eight thousand miles* of arctic and subarctic waterways.

Only in the last ten years had the regular cargo routes stretched themselves into the islands of the archipelago which lies north of Canada toward the Pole, to serve the little Eskimo communities which, for hundreds of years perhaps, have been clinging there.* Another route extended along the Beaufort Sea west of the Mackenzie delta into Alaskan waters clear to Point Barrow, which buys and uses Canadian foods and products since the Point is almost always ice-locked and cut off from the American side.

* However, from 1884 onward the government had ships sailing in and out of Hudson Bay and to the arctic islands, exploring and administering. Richard Finnie, *Canada Moves North* (New York, Macmillan, 1948).

Many summers ago, long before the children were born, their father and I had voyaged along every mile of the polar coast between Point Barrow and Canada's Mackenzie. About half this distance we had covered in a homemade canoe, made in Alaska from Canadian driftwood, and that craft was somewhat smaller than the one the girls and I used now. The presence of floating ice kept down the waves, but we had runners on the bottom of the canoe to pull it over ice when that occasionally blocked the way.

Naturally I wanted to learn all I could about the development of the new routes through what I had come to think of as my own dearly beloved Arctic. How had this come about? What was the reason for all this expansion of North American polar water routes?

One factor was the building of schools, Hudson's Bay posts, and missions in the Eskimo villages. Many had no airfields due to the rocky terrain; floats and skis being used on the aircraft that served them. But these planes are necessarily quite small. Heavy equipment such as lumber and fuel oil must be brought in by tug and barge, dodging ice all the way. Civilian installations, apart from the rare bases established by the RCAF and the U.S. Air Force jointly, had to depend for maintenance upon water routes during the brief polar summers.

The need for charting water routes had grown also with intensified oil exploration and mineral development since all the big oil rigs and mining equipment, even that used on Alaska's polar plains, must reach the North by the Athabasca and Slave rivers. At the Slave portage all this heavy material was hoisted by winches and cables onto trucks and taken piece by piece down the road past Fort Smith and nine miles farther to Bell Rock's loading docks, where it was again loaded aboard other boats which ply Great Slave Lake and the Mackenzie River. Finally, the arctic station named Tuktoyaktuk on the east side of Mackenzie Bay, the freight bound for various places was sorted and rerouted. Consequently it was necessary to mark about eight thousand miles of routes and, furthermore, to keep marking them every summer, since they are subject to change.

Finally through mountainous seas appeared Bell Rock, the last outpost. At its huge ramps dozens of ships and barges were pulled from the water when winter came, ships were assembled and engines repaired. On Captain Spume's marked channel we gratefully read the navigation markers into Bell Rock.

It was a nasty landing, muddy. We tied to driftwood and waded hastily to firm ground. There we found wooden boardwalks which connected to a veritable little city of utility buildings, machine shops, Imperial Oil tanks, and administration buildings, with an occasional outhouse on the side. A multimillion-dollar operation, with kitchens and hot-water tanks, telephone lines and radio — yet they still clung steadfastly to the old outhouse.

The first man who saw us, in great kindness, took us to the mess hall, where a number of roasted stuffed turkeys were just being pulled out of the ovens by a dozen chefs wearing white smocks and tall white starched chef's hats, a charming regional sight. We removed our mud-caked boots at the door, stocking-footed it to the sinks, washed our hands, and, with hair uncombed and river-wet, took seats on a bench at one of the long board tables, our trousers still carrying their souvenirs of plastered mud.

"That vessel lying yonder, that's the *Radium Royal*," the young dispatcher told us. "She leaves for Great Slave Lake within the hour."

"Oh, my goodness! Would she be going into the town of Yellowknife, on the north shore?" I asked, breathless.

"Yes, she goes there. Last trip to Yellowknife for the season. Let's see . . ." He shuffled some papers. "We have just the one barge for Yellowknife, that's all. But if it's a ride you're thinking of, we turn them down all the time. Company won't let us take passengers, like. But have you talked with Old Klinker? It's the Captain of the ship that has the final word, you know. That's him standing right over there."

My hopes rose as my eyes searched for the ship's captain. He held our destiny in his hands, perhaps our lives if he only knew it. Would he, could he somehow take us and our canoe on board?

We were surprised to find the weather-beaten Captain wearing an olive sweatshirt with hood thrust back from a brindled mane of hair — a kind of parka, really — and faded work pants, not an officer's uniform. On his feet he wore soft moccasins. He was Icelandic, was Klinker. You could hardly call him salty, however. For all his seventeen years' sailing had been in fresh water. Klinker's green eyes were flecked with brown, and back of them in his brain lurked the knowledge of northern rivers and green shorelines, islands, and sandbars, and the big red and black shore targets sliding by.

"Do you like boys, Jean?" was the first thing he said. Apparently he thought this was the best way to start a conversation with a girl her age.

"No. Boys are creeps," replied Jean grumpily. She added, "My mother and my sister, though, they're boy crazy. You ought to see *them!*"

"You mean to say you aren't interested in *boys at all?*" drawled the Captain, marveling. "Now a person finds that downright hard to believe, a real pretty girl about eighteen, like you."

Suddenly Jean gave him a Mona Lisa smile. The remark about age had pleased her.

"She's just fourteen," I explained quickly.

Jean still flushed from the Captain's compliments. "Well, I would sure like to look your vessel over, sir," she spoke up. "I'm interested in ships. And as I am the engineer on our own vessel, I would like very much to take a look at your engines and well — will that be all right if Mother doesn't mind?"

"Sure thing. I'll have you speak with our engineer and oiler right away," replied kindly Klinker with interest. "You can have the full run of the ship." I shuddered. "Come on. We'll go aboard. Mother, want to come too?"

"What my daughter and I need very much," I interrupted, "is a ride to Yellowknife. The waves in the fall. You know. The waves, they're *awful big.* Well . . ." I felt my knees might collapse suddenly. "I'm scared!"

"Shucks, now!" said Klinker, laying a fatherly rough hand on my shoulder. "I'll tell you something. I'm scared myself, only nobody don't know it! I been scared for seventeen years. Only a fool would not be scared, I guess. I never stay more than one night ashore," he confided. "For if I did, I'd never go back on the water again, pushing cargo . . .

". . . But I was just giving some thought to your problem while we were standing here talking, as a matter of fact. I think I understand pretty well what your problem is. We in the North are not about to let ladies go out and drown themselves, I can tell you one thing. My boys wouldn't have that. None of us would have it. So, we will put your canoe on board. Can you bring it right around to Barge 209, and the boys will help you, right away?"

Jean and I set off at once to follow this instruction. But we found that our hastily tied canoe had meanwhile blown far up on the mud bar and could not be moved. I got bogged down myself in the mud in my high hip boots; I was completely immobilized!

As everyone knows, the unwritten law of the sea is that persons in ships in distress must be rescued at all costs. The question is, *how* — when the person with his vessel is bogged down in thick, gluey mud? The rescue poses a problem even when the goodwill of the rescuers and their enthusiasm know no bounds.

This rescue was effected when part of the crew of the *Radium Royal* made a human chain from shore to pull me out. Machinists left their wheels, cooks rushed from cookhouses. All the resources of Bell Rock were pressed into action. Hearing the commotion on shore, people came from everywhere to cheer the rescuers. Winches and cables were hastened into service to extract the canoe from the unbelievable sucking grip it had fallen prey to in its last adventure of the season.

Eventually the canoe was hauled aboard Barge 209 and I was hauled aboard the tug, to the delight of my daughter, by a number of strong, resourceful seamen. Then away we went down the mile-broad Slave River one hundred and fifty miles to Great Slave Lake, pushing eighteen hundred tons of barges grandly before us on a four-mile current.

Of the two lads who pulled in our anchor one was Lars Spindridft. He was tall, golden-skinned and golden-haired, and hailed from the shores of Lesser Slave Lake southward, where there are roads and farms. At eighteen, Lars, who had never been south of Lesser Slave Lake, or for that matter anywhere beyond his simple farm home, was the most gloriously handsome young man — wear-

ing rough seaman's clothes and life jacket, nimble-footed and daring — that we had ever seen.

"I believe you are the only ladies ever to be aboard this ship,"
the first officer was saying to me, while Klinker had the wheel.
"Even Klinker's wife and daughters, they never been aboard."

I gazed out upon the loaded barges ahead of us, lashed together
end to end and some side by side, and entirely closed up against
the weather. They looked like great big train boxcars. Our string.

I felt a thrill of excitement. The idea of being a cargo riverman
enchanted me at that moment, a feeling of romance from which
I'm sure I will never recover, nor want to. Was the old Mississippi
with its steamboats once something like this? Perhaps more similar
is our present Great Lakes system. Certainly we "ladies," as the
frontiersmen called females in general, have missed most of the fun
(as well as the hard work) of the world, when you think that
throughout all history it has been men who have seen raw rivers
and continents like this!

I felt a surge of renewed gladness that I had grabbed the world
boldly while I was young, as youth should do. And now, grabbing it
boldly again, I felt young again. I reckoned I had dropped about
twenty years physiologically and psychologically on this river trip.
And Jean and Ann had gained about twenty years and perhaps to
the good.

Jean and I were given the first officer's cabin where we dumped
our duffle, and I changed to my alternate trousers. The cabin contained a washbowl with hot and cold taps, a warm air radiator, and
a desk and chair. On the desk lay a spool of black coarse thread
with a large needle stuck in it; an unsheathed sheath knife; an
ashtray; a comb; a lighter; pencils; a partly eaten pack of hard can-
dies; and a scattering of pocket change discarded hastily when the
former resident changed pants. A cheap cardboard picture stood
upright on the desk. It showed a plain, broad-jawed and tight-
lipped female with a corsage of flowers over a lace frock, and under
the picture was a signature, "with love."

There were no pictures of nudes or pin-up girls on board, no
rough talk. Never a crude word was said. The young crew from the

south, thirteen in number, would be different individuals each year, serving a captain who seemed more like their father than a boss. The duties of the crew were but minor while the ship was under way, since it could be navigated by three or four men only.

On this homelike vessel we were soon put at our ease by one and all.

Down the broad Slave and through the buffalo country we went with our barge train, and I could see it was a good thing that we had not tried to canoe this piece in the fall — for the fluted yellow buttes on either side most often rose straight up from the water, allowing no camping shelter from the northeast winds. High on the buttes above the river stood the typical northern coniferous forest: black and white spruce; jack pine and tamarack; aspen stands on upland sites or burned-over areas; and, interspersed with the forests, the peat bogs known throughout the North as "muskegs." Narrow prairies between the bogs were dominated by grasses with such showy flowering species as shooting star, bluebell, goldenrod, aster, and gentians.

Much of the Alberta Plateau is underlain by limestone, with a prominent limestone escarpment to the east. Between this escarpment and the Slave River flood plains lies a narrow prairie called the Salt Plains, whose soils have a high salt content originating in a number of springs from the escarpment. A carpet of specialized vegetation thrives there. Such famous early travelers as Mackenzie, 1798, and Lieutenant George Back, 1833, made use of these mounds of salt as they made their ways to the Arctic Ocean along the rivers which now bear their names.

The eastern portion of the Alberta Plateau is dimpled with sinkholes formed by dissolution of the underlying limestone by subsurface drainage. Thus there were lakes and rivers near the edge of the area we traveled, but we did not see them: all is the domain of moose, wolves and bears and all the other species natural to the North.

Looking for Jean all over the boat, I climbed hand by hand up the black steel ladder to the pilot house. There Klinker stood before the huge polished mahogany wheel, while the shores slid by.

"Where's Jean?"

"Oh, she's been helping steer during the last hour," the Captain said.

"Oh, no! She doesn't have her glasses."

"Doing very nicely, too," said Klinker. "She just run off some place when you came in.

"One of our crew might be has a crush on your daughter," continued the laconic Captain. "Name of Lars Spindridft. Nice boy. An Icelander. Very nice lad. Looks like Jean might have a little crush on him, too. They seeing each other around the ship."

Sure enough every once in a while I glimpsed Jean with Lars talking on deck. They stood on one foot and then on the other, awkwardly. They talked and talked, all day and half the night.

Jean, who claimed she didn't like boys, of course got along exceptionally well with them. Her pose of indifference had enabled her to gain the special interest of the handsomest one on board. What a teen-girl heaven, such a boat as this!

"Oh, dear!" I thought to myself. "I had just begun to get used to them being *children*. But I suppose it was bound to happen sometime."

We traveled the black night using radar and a long-range beam of light to spot the distant shore targets. Nights were dark now.

When I awoke early the next morning Jean was already up and gone. I came out on deck to see Fort Resolution under the purple cloud banks of dawn; we were on Great Slave Lake.

A sliver of lemon moon hung over the open water. A solitary housewife in slacks, holding two small children by the hand, seemed to be almost the only soul awake in Resolution, as our crew hastily hoisted cargo ashore into a warehouse. Had she come for a walk at this hour? More likely she came to the docks hoping to claim some piece of long-awaited cargo dear to her heart. The dampness and sea-cold pervaded everything. Our steel decks were covered with rime. Beside a bleak unpainted clapboard house hung a long string of colored laundry — almost as long as our string of barges in full train. It began to flap in the wind. We hurried.

This coast was fully exposed to the lake. You had to sneak in and out of here craftily, and Klinker knew just how to do that. Our barge unloaded, we started up again with a rumble and clank of the two nine-hundred-horse engines and returned to sea, skirting around the treacherous shallow delta of the Slave. Then we went upriver into the head of the delta. By ten o'clock we were in the largest east channel where Klinker was accustomed to "hanging up" the extra barges in his string while he shuttled around the lake. Each captain finds his own sites along northern shores for this purpose. Warm golden sunlight broke through and birds sang in the almost tropical-seeming delta. As we inched ponderously into shore, we heard and felt the crackling of twigs and branches, and a shower of leaves scattered over the barge train.

When Jean in the pilot house had "helped" back and turn and the quick-footed deckhands had hooked the extra barges to shore with snub ropes, we left the extras there safe in the delta, and with Number 209 headed back out to sea. We had her on a tow cable, for while cargo is *pushed* on the rivers — anything up to three thousands tons can be pushed downstream — it is *pulled* out on the open lake when it's rough. Now at last Number 209 was bound for Yellowknife.

19

Great Slave Lake and Yellowknife

THE barometer looked good, Captain Klinker said. But fall winds, the Polar Easterlies, were to be expected.

By the time we had returned to the lake the wind was blowing at eighteen knots out of the open sea; there was nothing to do but tie up behind Round Island in front of Fort Resolution and ride it out. Here the muddy waves rolled and the tug heaved for twenty hours on her line, as though trying to pull the little island out of the lake. Jean was glad. I was patient. The Captain went to sleep. The cook was sick.

Twenty hours later when the wind dropped a bit, Captain Klinker decided to cross, and, pulling Number 209 on a thousand-yard tow line, we started the ninety-mile crossing of open Great Slave Lake. At a good brave clip of ten miles an hour, the trip would take about nine hours. The cook got sicker.

Every time I wanted to communicate with Jean, she disappeared around corners. The way I got messages to her on the tug was by asking crew members to deliver them. I never got any replies. It was a game of hide and seek — friendly in part, but deadly serious, too: the child decides that the parent is the enemy after all, the real enemy to growth and independence. The parent must somehow be dispensed with, or at least avoided. Jean's smile disappearing around corners was that of a coy and grinning gamin.

Rough weather pounded us from the start, steadily worsening as we reached the middle of the lake. The cook thought he was going to die. The hearty young crew enjoyed it all.

When things got rough I went to my cabin. The decks were awash. Inside I felt cut off, but I wouldn't risk the decks. It seemed to me safest and most sensible to stay in bed. Doors slammed, the port window banged, the desk and chair slid back and forth across the room, all the pocket change and open knife blades went sailing. To dodge these objects I stayed in the bunk.

Once Jean came flying by, peeked into our door, shoving back the pile of furniture, and called in tipsily, "Gosh, Mom, get up and *look*. Big huge waves. It's *clear water* all around us now. The water, it's beautiful clear green, with white crests on top, and it's not muddy any more, and you'll just love it!"

She was gone before I could stop her. She felt one with the green waves that washed the deck, with the wind that sang. All of us have wildness far nearer the surface than we think. She had exhibited the same qualities when navigating rapids, I had to recall. Youth loves danger!

But if a person had been washed from this deck he would have been lost in a moment. He could never have been picked up, for it takes several miles even to turn the boat around.

Now in the very middle of the lake the seamen in their life jackets and sneakers dove to and from bunkroom, galley, and bridge along the pitching decks, clutching the insubstantial handrails. And Jean was jumping all over the boat with them, or so it seemed to me, hand in hand with Lars Spindridft and his fleet comrades.

"Captain Klinker!" I cried from my bunk when he haplessly stuck his kindly, grizzled face through the door to ask "how Mother was coming along." "Please, please give a command to one of your seamen to *catch* my daughter. You see, she has myopia. She's nearsighted, and she doesn't have her glasses. Order her — for me — to this room and her bunk until the crossing is over!"

It was a long time before she forgave me for that. She who was so elated at the very intoxicating thought that here and now she was going to cut the parental apron strings with a stroke. But she stayed in her bunk for the remainder of the crossing, on Captain's orders.

Once, about seven years ago, one of the tugs went down with all hands in the middle of Great Slave Lake. Some believed it was because the tug had got wound up in its steel tow cables and been pulled down by the barges in rough seas. Later, another old captain I talked with far down the Mackenzie, who knew the vessel, questioned that theory. But there are some varied objects, you may be sure, lying along the bottom of that lake. During World War II, for instance, the lake claimed some heavy American equipment including tractors and pipeline. Since 1945 it has taken its fair share of lives each season.

Great Slave Lake totals 12,500 square miles. Its average depth is estimated at around five hundred feet. But Canadian Fisheries people will tell you that some deep holes go down to twenty-nine hundred feet, making it one of the world's deepest lakes.

As late as 1955 there were but *two* astronomical fixations in the entire Canadian North, so little were its features known: one north of Great Slave Lake, and one on the south shore of Great Bear Lake.

We came chugging along the north shore at nine in the evening, out of the east. The sun dropped into the southwestern sea. Foreshortening its arc by about eight minutes daily, the sun permitted winter to come on with giant strides at earth's high latitudes. The clear sky was cobalt blue. In it the yellow new moon sailed, swelling her nightly girth. Klinker was at the wheel. The cook was weakly trying to cook. Two of the crew were tidying and scrubbing the galley.

Along the moonscape shore of the inland arctic sea lay reefs and boulders (unmarked) that would put any normal rock pile to shame. Klinker knew them all by heart. He made our way craftily between them yet kept far from shore, even as the blue wrinkled sea crawled about their hazardous sides. Now in the velvet night the moon soared high and silver, streaming radiance. A sound from civilization drifted to us from far away: a soft, cheerful tinkle of radio music coming across the miles into the pilot house where I stood, as the First Mate monitored the radar. Jean was on deck saying good-bye to Lars Spindridft. Good-bye forever to a brief but poignant dream of wonderful youth.

The north shore and in fact much of Great Slave Lake lies across the Shield. Consequently as we turned north into remote Yellow-knife Bay, we found ourselves in the low moonscape of a kind of world which goes back to the beginning of time on our planet. This world is harsh and stark. No mollusks or small snails are imprinted in its rocks; they existed before life on this earth. The exposed ancient bedrock almost completely lacks any kind of soil. Only ancient primitive lichens and dwarfed plants make their precarious living there. Dwarf spruce and poplars grow out of soil pockets in the tops and sides of boulders. They make up an extensive but thinly scattered north shore forest, which dwindles out eastward into the Barrens. The tiny forest is only ten feet tall and sometimes less.

Named for the Yellowknife Indians whose knives, according to early explorers, were made of yellow copper, the town of Yellow-knife is visible far out to sea because of its oil tanks, and at night the inviting beam of its flashing beacons as they rotate and pulsate steadily beneath clear skies. Its modern colored frame houses are anchored up and down rock domes at varying levels.

I'll never forget sailing into Yellowknife on a cold late summer night, on the farthermost northern inlet of Great Slave Lake, called North Arm, under a soaring moon and with the Northern Lights hanging like colored curtains over the little gold town.

Nor the nimble-footed deckhands bringing in 209; cranking up the windlass, coiling up the long steel cable even as we inched into port. They brought her up alongside the dock and snubbed her fast among a crowd of every imaginable kind of small boat. As Klinker said, "Jean did a real good job of it." I only wish I knew today one fourth as much seamanship as Klinker and Jean demonstrated on that one trip. Somehow I had a hopeful feeling that it would not be by any means our last encounter with the friendly river tugs and barges. But for us the summer was at an end.

I could see Ann waiting there in the black night with Mr. and Mrs. Cluck, standing under the glare of the dock lights. They had been summoned by the ship's radio. Helped by the seamen, I climbed over the side, from slippery tug to slippery barge to strange frozen shore, lugging assorted duffle. In the excitement I had come

off the boat carrying two left boots, a matter which would be recti-
fied another summer.

I grabbed Ann, who was wildly excited and dancing up and
down like some tall hysterical bird on the docks.

"Good old Mom!" she shrilled. "I heard you got stuck in the
mud, and I said to them, 'That's my Mom.' " She would be thirteen in the fall.

"Jeanie," I heard Ann greet her sister tactlessly: "You must have
been *eating* again. You look *fat*, dear. *Awfully fat.*"

"Keep your big fat mouth shut," Jean greeted Ann, and failed
to introduce her little sister to any of the crew, to the latter's
disappointment.

The friendly Clucks whirled us off by taxi to their hotel. The
three-story Gold Brick Hotel stood on a main street which had
been blasted by dynamite out of bedrock to make it level. The
main section downtown was called Old Town (established in
1937) while New Town, a mile inland and a hundred feet higher,
was on a sandy plateau.

Yellowknife boasted a forty-bed hospital, two doctors, a radio
station linked to CBC, a weekly newspaper called *News of the
North*, and a small golf course. The main clubs were the Elks, the
Royal Legion, and the Masons. Canadian Coachways came three
times a week up the Mackenzie Highway to its terminus here; the
distance from Edmonton was nearly nine hundred miles, more than
half of it unpaved. Daily air service operated to Edmonton, except
Sundays. Yellowknife lay two hundred and fifty miles south of the
Arctic Circle, its forbidding terrain accounted for by geology rather
than latitude.

Dozens of gold properties lay in the country back from the lake.
Four principal mines produce fourteen million dollars in gold a
year. The gold is smelted down into bricks, and the bricks taken
out in regular flights south.

"I've got some of our clothes unboxed and hung up on the wall
in our room," Ann told us. "There are no closets. You know, those
dresses and things we shipped for our arctic winter in Yellowknife?
We each have four outfits to start school."

She told us there were two beauty shops in town which were

always booked three weeks in advance. She suggested that Jean and I get our appointments at once. As soon as we got to our room, Ann explained that the northern white women were very clothes conscious, and club and organization and culture conscious. She also said she had been looking at hair dryers in the store window, and that we could buy one for thirty-two dollars, and that in the North one of the things women learned was that their hair wouldn't dry in a thousand years without a dryer.

"Look, Jean," she said, "frankly, your ends are very frizzled, you know." This of course was an enormous understatement.

"Mother, also you have one large freckle, probably from when we were on the Peace River in our canoe, and somebody ought to tell you that unless you take steps promptly you might get a great many more."

"Oh, dear!" I cried, automatically raising a finger to my face. While this small talk was going on Jean looked more and more dazed. The switch apparently was just too much for an explorer. Here we had suddenly arrived in town after such a wild summer that we were lucky to have survived it, and Jean had adapted admirably to that life and its necessities. This girl had held all our lives in her hands many times, and had done the work of a man with a man's cool courage. She of all three of us had taken most naturally to this life. She had an inborn aptitude for it. She had reveled in the wildness of nature. Was this town, this narrow way of thinking, the goal of all our endeavors?

Jean simply went into a mild state of shock. She wouldn't speak to us. She went to bed and refused to get up. Her sister's chatter about hair dryers revolted her. She shuddered at the idea of staying under any dreary permanent roof and being deprived of a new view of the river each day. She would have liked to join the crew on a cargo boat up north: that would have suited her well.

"But, Jean. Summer is over. We have to stay in a house now. It's going to freeze up."

"Jean, look at it this way," added Ann. "You would smell better if you got into the bathtub down the hall, and got out of those horrid man's clothes."

Jean said, "*Stop nagging me*, both of you!" and, setting her jaw, slid miserably under the covers.

Fortunately we had on hand in the room, it appeared, three hundred comic books at that very moment. Jean reached out feebly for the first one, and started reading. And there she stayed for three days, with meals brought up on our charge.

"We will be kind to Jean," I suggested. "She has simply got civilization shock, that's all."

Jean lay there, obviously suffering, but she heard us. Ann gathered our dirty laundry and took it to the Laundromat, bringing it back clean, by installments. Ann always liked to stick coins in slots. She liked the clink and rustle of money in her hand, and she was very good in her management of family things.

"Jean will be all right in a little while," I kept saying, as Ann enjoyed nursing Jean, and Jean languished in the luxury of her temporary decline. It was a game they had played all their lives. "Jean will get back into liking civilization because in the end we all have to, you know. I've been through it many times. You go back and forth from the North, and it's a terrible transition to make."

"Jean," pleaded Ann meanwhile, "you just don't know how lonesome I've been all summer while you and Mom were having such fun. So please get over your civilization shock. If you will get up I will draw your bath and fix your hair for you."

Tears came into my eyes then as I sat looking at my girls and thought of all we had come through. Grumpily, Jean rose from bed and allowed the tough, practical, resilient Ann to prepare her.

"Now you look real nice," said Ann, as Jean's substantial biceps strained the seams. Jean would be a slim beauty one day — but that day was not yet. I put my arm around Ann. "I'm very glad for your moral support at this time, dear Ann," I said.

At almost thirteen, for the moment Ann was the strongest and most resourceful of us all as we faced civilization.

I think the three of us recognized right then that the town of Yellowknife would be lonely beyond description for three in our position. In this northern village, when winter closed in, the spirit was far more shackled than in those large southern cities that we had come from.

And it was clear from the first hour that the Gold Brick Hotel was not going to be a suitable place to spend the winter. Rocked by drunken outbursts, loud voices, and the thump of heavy booted feet at all hours, and by roaring fights on occasion, the bleak, battered hotel served the men of the North as best it could. No carpeting, no upholstery, no softening effects of interior decoration could have been profitable as an investment, for the Gold Brickers quickly destroyed all such accoutrements simply because they were unconscious of them. The hotel had been built of clapboards, haphazardly, section by section. It had an asbestos covering but that had been roasted by a neighboring fire even during the month Ann lived here. A careless move by one of the men could burn down the whole building at any time.

We couldn't stay here long. The girls and I lived at the hotel five days while I tried to solve our problem. A real estate office helped me to search for a house or cabin to rent; but no furnished living quarters were available.

I looked into the Sir John Franklin Hostel to see if the kids might perhaps attend school and live there. It was an exemplary steam-heated boarding school in a group of buildings like a small campus; but it was not set up to admit southerners, not even Canadian ones. It was exclusively for the arctic children, mostly Eskimos.

Finally I realized I would have to admit defeat. When I announced to the girls my reluctant decision to go south, they were upset. It took them a day to readjust; then we packed our boxes of clothes all over again. We flew to Edmonton; there I learned that Grandmother had gone into a decline in her eighty-second year and had taken to her bed. When her family left she had evidently lost all interest in life. There she lay alone, and nobody knew. Possibly she had had a small stroke. It was a very great blessing, the way it turned out, that something brought us back south for the winter.

(That fall, Jean volunteered to live with her grandmother, and took care of her while going to high school. Ann helped in the nursing too; but she had another stratagem of her own.

"Don't worry about a thing, Mother. Everything will be all right," she promised me truly. "Grandmother won't stay in bed very long, you'll see. I have done this before and it has been quite successful in keeping her young. You just tell her that her house is full of cockroaches. And she gets right up!"

Grandmother did get up, for a time at least; and she went on to become eighty-two, and much more.)

Unfortunately our big black gentle dog Sylvia had died during our summer in the North. We no longer tried to keep pets. No longer were there wiggly, surly guinea pigs for Gerald to catch when they went wild in the yard. No longer was there a Henrietta Hen to ride in the bicycle basket or be carried into the house out of the rain.

Jean, cutting off celery tops at the sink, was sometimes apt to say wistfully, "It's a shame to waste these when you realize that there are hungry rabbits in the world." But the pets were gone. Childhood was left behind somehow that summer on the river, lost somewhere along the way, and we never quite found it again. However, there was the consolation that there was yet one more river to explore, the great Mackenzie; and also, the terrible teens began.

That winter, Gerald and I sat on the sofa and the kids did homework just as always. Then, spring came again.

PART II

The Mackenzie

20

Birds of Another Spring

SPRING came early. The little scaled Inca doves and turtledoves came straggling back north from Mexico, and their excited cooing filled the mornings. One day a song sparrow arrived, and I heard its sudden gay cascade of notes through our window. The song sparrow said perfectly clearly to anyone who could hear, "Follow me. Follow me. Come away up north to the far places."

One afternoon I was thinking about spring and the birds and other glorious realities of earth when Jean came banging into the house with a load of high school textbooks under her arm.

"Hi, Mom!" I heard her footsteps clomp into the back bedroom and there was a thump as the books went down. She was now fifteen, stalwart and sometimes rather ferocious. And here came Ann, padding down the hall in her bare feet, wearing shorts and a man's shirt. Her wiry frame had filled out a bit during the winter, and now she wore her blond hair long, with bangs. She also had one long, carefully cherished fingernail. ("Would you mind washing the dishes tonight, Ann?" "Sorry, Mom, my fingernail, you know.") Now Ann flopped down on the rug near me in the living room.

"Is Gerald coming tonight? I need help on my algebra."

In between helping Jean and Ann with their algebra almost every night and sometimes coming around to drive them to school in the morning, the handsome professor of Elizabethan literature had taught the girls algebra all winter again. He didn't teach it well, really, because it was not his field. But we had what we called an Algebra and Mutual Admiration Society. Algebra for the children. The girls would have liked to have steady boyfriends themselves but they found, at the ages of thirteen and fifteen, that boys of comparable age unfortunately were rather undependable and horrid. So they waited impatiently. And studied their algebra, poor dears.

As for Gerald, he confided to us that the Elizabethan Department had of late years become very frustrating. He found himself asking, perhaps in common with modern man almost everywhere, "Is this really fun?" And the answer came back on bad days, a thundering "No!" Yet there seemed no way out of it.

"What you need is to come with us in our canoe, Gerald," Ann suggested to him more than once that winter.

"Best little outfit in the North," said Jean.

A deep sigh from Gerald. "Oh, thanks awfully for your suggestion, Ann," he would say. "But there is some curriculum confusion afoot. I have to teach summer school."

And besides, as Jean reminded Gerald, although it was a big freight canoe twenty feet long, it would hold only two or possibly three persons with their baggage. You can't take the whole world with you in your canoe: you must go alone. That's the whole point to it.

"Oh, we'll write each other," I said. "Our exploratory party will pass about eight forts this next summer. After we reach the Arctic Ocean, we'll return to civilization for a winter. Algebra. . . ." He nodded, comprehending. "After all, Gerald, we've been going together, you and I, for six years. You can't expect a forty-seven-year-old girl to wait around doing nothing forever, can you?"

"Oh, dear me, I suppose not, my dear," he said disconsolately, passing over the five pound box of chocolates which was on the coffee stand. "I say, did someone bring you this?"

I passed off the question with studied carelessness at the time.

Our canoe was at the halfway mark to the Arctic Ocean, and waited only for the second summer to complete the goal we had set for the expedition. The time of two years to reach the Arctic was well gauged to our strengths, although there may be those who could have reached it faster. I remembered what Robert Louis Stevenson had said — the journey is more important than the arrival.

As rapidly as possible, therefore, we prepared to leave dear Gerald to his summer school, and to say good-bye to Grandmother too. And there was a new friend, who came to play a part in the expedition of the second summer which perhaps I should relate. He had appeared during the winter.

It all started with a few casual dinners out. Then, the chocolates started coming. All too late I found I had fallen into a plot. "Aren't you getting heavier?" asked Gerald suspiciously. The new man, seemingly so harmless, had actually contrived this devilish scheme to fatten me on purpose. In this way, he nearly disposed of dear sensitive Gerald quite neatly. The dinners and chocolates were too delicious, the flowers he brought were too irresistible. The girls welcomed him only halfheartedly. "Welcome to Ancient Hag Caverns," Jean said, each day.

Sir Peter Bumbleton Pip (which I will call him for lack of another name) hailed originally from Canada; his father was a Prussian, his mother a descendant of Queen Victoria. But today in the U.S.A. Sir Peter Bumbleton Pip was called simply Bumbles, and he was a simple man, as he always made clear. He did a typical, honest American kind of work. He worked with teams of men who were busy designing, testing, and manufacturing various objects to be put on the moon.

Bumbles had come into the United States with his mother when he was a boy. His mother's death had left him quite alone at the age of fifty-two.

"Don't you call me fifty-two years old," he would say to the girls, wagging his finger at them. "When you speak of me, dear young ladies, say that your friend Bumbles is fifty-two years *young*." That kind of drollery would be met by nearly audible groans from the girls; but we were all very fond of him really. There never was a kinder man. He had inched his way into our habits and affections and we would have missed him badly if he had disappeared now. I thought of how readily he turned a hand to mend things that had been broken for years, or to take charge of the constant accumulation of errands and mundane chores that beset an urban American family. Bumbles in fact derived a marvelous satisfaction from crossing things off lists; all we had to do was provide a list of things to be done, and a pencil.

But I had not suspected how greatly Bumbles was interested in our second summer's canoe trip until one afternoon when he and the girls and I were sitting around the kitchen table. I casually threw out the suggestion that Bumbles might drive us to Yellowknife to collect our canoe; and to my astonishment he seized upon the idea with joyous alacrity. He was absolutely thrilled.

"Yes, you know what my answer will be, don't you? Yes, yes, yes!"

The girls stared from Bumbles to me, flabbergasted; in fact they glared.

"*Mother!*" cried Ann, shocked. "Are you out of your mind? What will Gerald say?"

"Rats! What's come over you, Mother?" said Jean.

"Well, I've been thinking. If you'll give me a chance to explain . . ."

"Now, everybody, let's just all try to be calm," Bumbles advised.

"Well, the problem is basically this," I said. "We need to drive the car to Canada straight through to where the canoe is this year. The canoe is at the very end of the last road up into the Subarctic. But we've got to store the car in Edmonton this summer, and the canoe is nine hundred miles north of Edmonton. So don't you see, this summer does present a kind of parking problem. . . ."

"I suppose Mom's got a point there," Ann said finally. "We really do need someone to take the car back south nine hundred miles to Edmonton and store it."

"Exactly," Bumbles agreed in tones of rising confidence. "I don't mind parking the car for you, no problem at all."

"By the way, Bumbles, I ought to tell you that the Mackenzie Highway is unpaved," I put in. "Sure you don't mind?"

"No, of course not. Why should I? You must remember that Canada is my former homeland, and we Canadians are accustomed to thinking in terms of vast wildernesses. And you do need an alert, resourceful, healthy, vigorous man along on such a trip; I don't know how you planned to do it without me."

The girls were growing alarmed at Bumbles's eagerness. They had never forgotten our unhappy experience with Bum Littleton.

"No man in the canoe. Remember you promised, Mother. You're breaking your promise," said Ann.

"You may drive us up there, but you can't go along in the canoe, Bumbles," added Jean.

"What? Tut, tut. The canoe? Don't be alarmed, dear girls," he promised. "I will merely place you all tenderly in your canoe there and then I will turn around and drive quietly back south, without a protest."

"Can you get home south from Edmonton, then? It's about three thousand miles each way," I warned him. "Better allow a month for it."

"Ladies," he said, "really, I have nothing better to do with a month. If I did not have you, I would spend the month moving my many cactus plants from one side of my house to the other, and perhaps a man should have better things to do than that."

"Bumbles, no canoe," the children repeated their ultimatum. "Mother took a man in the canoe once for a day or two, and never again will we try that. When we get to the canoe, will you go right home?"

"Absolutely, old dears. No Arctic Ocean for me," he readily agreed. And that was that.

It was sad to say good-bye for the summer to dear, grumpy Gerald. I tried to coax him into a better frame of mind. "It's just a matter of transporting the expedition personnel to the canoe," I tried to explain to him. Please, Gerald, try to understand."

"You do expect an awful lot of understanding. Well, just don't ever let me meet the cad face to face," was Gerald's final comment.

It was also difficult, besieged as we were by the attentions of the jubilant Bumbles, to say good-bye to Grandmother.

Of the several people in our world, it was Grandmother, Grandmother of the olden days and social stability and proper rules for things, who stood at the very nexus of our typical little American family. Since she had passed her eighty-second birthday she had taken to her bed and would not get up. She said she saw nothing in particular to get up for. And alas, she could no longer go on living alone in her own house what with her growing physical weakness and her absentmindedness. She had gone to a nursing home during this last winter.

When Grandmother moved out there to Green Pastures Rest Home I felt terrible. It seemed callous for me to go on exploring the Arctic as usual. Yet Grandmother's burdensome age reminded me that if I was going to explore I had better hurry about it. Some days I thought that I could glimpse in my mother those very same geriatric disabilities that were descending upon me. When I visited Green Pastures and saw all those aged people, I could practically picture in my mind's eye my own bed patiently waiting — a rather disturbing fantasy.

"Don't worry about me, darlings," said Grandmother bravely, "I have had a wonderful, busy, interesting life, you know. I've seen it all. From the horse and buggy and the spinning wheel, I've seen America grow. To electric lights, and everything else you can imagine. It was a good time to live in, my dears. A good time. But it goes fast. Why do I feel so tired now? I think this place is quite lovely, really. For people who stay abed, of course. Not for the young."

"Certainly not for the young," said Ann.

"Sometimes I do wish you'd call this whole thing off and just come here and stay with me," she kept suggesting, right to the last.

"We'll be back before you know it." I tried to ease the parting with Grandmother. "We'll go out to lunch together, and we'll have Manhattans and shrimp cocktails. . . ."

"Yum, yum," said Grandmother. "I'll get up for that."

"You'll get your hair fixed, with lots of bluing," added Ann.

"Don't like to get my hair fixed. I get so tired now. Lot of people here don't bother with it."

"But you know how I do like you blued, dear," coaxed Ann. "And we'll all go out to lunch. . . ."

"Did someone say lunch? I'd like to go out to lunch," said Grandmother eagerly.

"Yes, later, dear," Ann and Jean promised her, and tiptoed softly away.

Grandmother nestled down in bed to snooze when we left. She was wearing her diamonds and sapphires upon her long and still elegant fingers; in her day, girls always slept with their rings on. As I tiptoed away it seemed to me that this was indeed a very sensible olden-day custom.

I left satisfied that everything there was peaceful, harmonious, and shipshape. The personnel were kind and soft-spoken. The guests as they waited had no problems, no dangers, no labors of any kind. They had outlived their loves and their hates, even their dearest old arch enemies. For them, there was nothing further to be battled, discovered, or done. They had even outlived the terrible griefs of life, and felt them no more.

Yet I was bowed by grief and guilt at leaving. Seeing one's own mother in an institution in old age makes one ill with guilt, for it is against all the experience of the world up until now. But all of us are going to live to be so old from now on, that the thought is appalling. Due to the excellence of science people may go on living, not merely to eighty-two, but to a hundred and twenty, to be cared for year after year in institutions.

For us who are young, then, the choice is hard: either we must risk allowing old people to consume our whole lives, or we must send the old away to professional care. Should youth be shackled to old-age ills and old-age thoughts? Old age has a way of rubbing off on you when you live with it all the time. Already the United States, the great land that was young only yesterday, seems to be getting to be a sad, gray old place, with too many thoughts of constraint and sadness.

And so we turn to hear the birds sing. We pay up all our bills for the last time. No more rent to pay. We shall live in a tent. No more telephone. No more bathtub to wash. There won't be a bathtub! Best of all, no doctors. We are through with all of you forever.

We are heading for a land where there is but one human being for each four hundred square miles. What is more, beyond the sixtieth parallel, the people are not evenly distributed, where they do exist. In the North, Homo sapiens has an inborn tendency to concentrate in pure homogeneous stands of government clerks, scattered only sparsely throughout the vast, lovely forest.

You therefore have the wonderful situation that, in the North, there are tens of thousands of square miles where there is virtually no Homo sapiens at all; and that, too, is very nice, very refreshing.

21

Back to Yellowknife

IT was about three thousand miles' drive to the canoe. You can imagine us: Bumbles at the wheel and me sitting girlishly beside him and the impatient Jean and Ann fooling or bickering in the back seat, as we tootled along toward friends in Calgary, the Canadian Rocky Mountain Parks system, and finally the North.

"The new man can read road maps pretty keen, anyway," Jean commented to her sister, early in the trip.

"I heard that! Stop calling me the new man!" roared Bumbles, turning a severe face back to the girls for a moment. There was no more disrespectfulness.

Bumbles loved the open road. He spent the trip in interesting speculations and meditations about the kinds of road-building materials which had been used on the highways we traveled. "The base of a road," Bumbles discoursed, "is usually ten inches or more below the finished surface. It has a mixture of sand and two-by-four-inch rocks with sharp corners called aggregate. . . . This is necessary, you see, to hold the mixture in place. Then the base is rolled and leveled several times and we establish the base grade. . . ."

"Yes?"

"Well, above the base comes the subgrade fill; the subgrade fill is added, leveled, and rolled or compacted in layers until the subgrade is established, and after the subgrade is reached and leveled so that it simulates the final grade of the roadbed, but several inches below, the final fill or surface fill is made. . . ."

"Ah."

"This may be concrete, as in our major highways, or it can be any number of other kinds of surfacing. As a matter of interest, in our Southwest a type is used that is mixed on the job, contrary to what we shall find as we proceed northward. Namely, road oil or asphalt is mixed with a gravel and sand surface fill, and the surface fill is then spread to equal the final grade and then we spray it with asphalt and turn it over and over with a grader, spraying each turn-over, until the mixture is saturated with asphalt. Then the mixture is leveled and hot-rolled for compactness. Some contractors cold-roll it. Others are not too thorough in their mixing and adding of hot asphalt. This, you often see, results in chuck holes the first time you have a heavy rain. But major roads in North America are generally hot mix, as are most city streets. Some are done properly, but if not, some spots do not get enough road oil of asphalt. . . ."

It really is true, I decided, that travel with a down-to-earth man presents an entirely different view of the world; a view which a woman misses if she travels alone or in purely female company. I determined to pay attention and absorb as much as I could about this practical world of concrete and asphalt; the world that our men have built themselves out of raw nature.

And so we drove along, companionably, until on June 21 we arrived at Peace River, Alberta. Just a few miles beyond here the Mackenzie Highway begins. You have to cross the wide Peace River over a big high bridge and head north on gravel. Bumbles was fascinated.

Peace River town again! Dirt streets, and no parking meters! Even in the town there was such stillness that you could hear the native warblers in the woods beyond. As I listened I felt sure that same little song sparrow who had called me from beyond my Venetian blinds back home was here in some nearby field. The sky was a deep, gorgeous blue, and the colors of the flowering green countryside unbelievably intense. There was no industry within several hundred miles: an environmental condition which it is not possible to experience today in the United States.

There was no car traffic to speak of. There were no jet aircraft to take the blue out of the sky with their gray haze of ice contrails.

There were no big bases or fields where jets could land or be accommodated from here on northward. We were out of the jet age! Is this possible? Well, almost.

The air was extremely light and easy to breathe. It was nearly lacking in those suspended chemical particles which today infest the air of the United States and southern Canada and even Mexico from coast to coast. A slow but certain kill of citizens across our North America can be predicted with each passing year. The density of the pollutants has increased 30 percent during the past ten years alone, while the humidity has increased steadily toward the dreaded "greenhouse effect": and each year civilization seems to strive harder for all-time record-breaking kills, especially in summer. But still the busy citizens scurry about their lives and for the most part disregard the few thousands of victims in their midst who have thus far succumbed from lack of air and ventilation. The majority have proved tougher to kill than might have been supposed: tougher to kill than beetles. Homo sapiens is adapting to the exotic chemical environment in this unique way: they are ingeniously developing an indoors culture which produces its own artificially controlled environment, insulating much of the population from nature, from the changing of the seasons, and from the earth habitat which man has polluted.

Therefore, I suppose, compared with the technological wonders which people in the United States are accustomed to, the sights of the Peace River country might seem ordinary — but the girls and I were delighted to be here again, just for the luxurious breathing, if for nothing else.

The folk on the streets of the town were mostly genuine indigenous frontier people and pioneer farmers, formed by three generations in this land. The dust and sand worked into the seams of their chapped faces. They hobbled and limped.

The girls and I would soon look as beat up as they did, I thought. But I didn't mind the idea, in fact, I liked it. That rough life is the known experience of mankind, from which we all emerged only yesterday. There is little to fear in the known. It is the unknown that I fear.

The cars and trucks in the streets of Peace River town had

cracked windshields. They had extra fine mesh screens over the radiators to filter out the bugs. Without the screen the radiator would start to boil for lack of ventilation, because of excessive bug-clogging. The cars had air filters on their carburetors too, because the mosquitoes would clog the fuel intake with their bodies.

Faces you saw on the street showed a wide strain of dark Indian blood, blended nicely, as often as not, with Scotch-English ancestry, or compatible with Italian or Ukrainian strains. There was a sprinkling of Orientals. Many smiles showed ragged teeth, for dentists are in short supply on the frontier. The people were shorter on the average than the new American breeds, and lighter in weight by an average of perhaps fifty pounds per man. They looked almost incredibly slender. They reminded me that we ourselves are fast breeding a race of giants. Beefy, clumsy, well-marbled giants who may prove in the end too expensive for the world to maintain — frightening thought! These people consume not one quarter of what an American of the middle classes consumes in a year in goods, and virtually *no services*. Here life is a simple struggle with mother earth; but at least the struggle goes on under a more or less natural sky.

The two girls and Bumbles and I looked upon the mighty Peace River surging in its real, muddy, ugly, dangerous, untamed splendor. The river turns north right here. It is four hundred and ten miles by river to the next village, out-of-the-way old Fort Vermilion. We recalled the ferocious flood at last season's maiden voyage which took the girls and me to Peace River town on the crest of 240,000 cubic feet of water per second.

I have said that the Peace is in a class with the Missouri in size. What the Missouri and Ohio are to the Mississippi, the Peace and the Athabasca are to the Mackenzie River, clearly. Only, when you compare this system of northern waters to the Mississippi, you should remember that the whole system flows through Lake Athabasca and through Great Slave Lake (out of which the giant Mackenzie is born), and is fed also by twelve thousand square-mile Great Bear Lake on northward yet. In other words, you might say that a Great Lakes system is tied in with this north-flowing Mississippi. It all flows down north to the Arctic Ocean from here. We have to get used to thinking backward, since all of our lives we have been accustomed to thinking of the southern rather than the northern watershed of the continent.

There are no dams to harness the water on the northern watershed. It is all just as at the beginning of time. Americans today have never seen anything like this. Suddenly when a person sees the river running north past little Peace River town he realizes that here he can cast off and voyage out upon a great, unexploited, unchanged system of natural rivers and lakes; and that here is a privilege which future generations on our earth may not have. The experience suddenly becomes inexplicably precious when you realize that mankind is determined that soon all this sort of thing must go, because everything on earth must be utilized to support man's increasing numbers.

At Peace River I went to call upon the Royal Canadian Mounted Police. It is routine procedure from here northward to report in upon your arrival at posts, and out upon your departure, since the police in a large country like to keep an eye on travelers for their protection.

I found my old friend Sergeant Stevenson in good spirits, for he was expecting a transfer to a more populous area. "Can't keep back promotions of good men, you know," he quipped, setting aside his pipe for a moment and offering the same broad, reassuring official palm which I had shaken last year.

"And how are the little girls? I suppose they've grown . . . ?"

"Oh, yes, Sergeant, and they bring fond regards to you."

I returned to my party. "We should aim to reach Great Slave Lake," I told them, "on the exact day when all the big ice pans have moved off the north shore, because I don't want to stay in that hotel up there just waiting for the ice."

"How are we going to do that, Mom?"

"I don't know. I can't get any news about the ice. It's in the Northwest Territories, so the Mounties here in Alberta don't have anything to do with it. The airport doesn't know. The railroad doesn't know. It only goes to the south shore of Great Slave Lake, and it isn't finished yet. But we don't want to arrive north so early that big ice cakes block navigation, do we? Let's give the Mackenzie River time to stabilize herself for summer travel, shall we?" I suggested.

"We want to go now. Please, Mom!" The crew was impatient, and getting hard to hold. So we pushed on the next day, north on the Mackenzie Highway.

As we drove the Mackenzie Highway there were great, three-toed sandhill crane tracks in the ditches; and once, briefly, we saw a lean, gleaming giant of a crane flap up and vanish over the forest.

A shining, glossy black bear a mile ahead along the road made haste to disappear nimbly at the sound of the lone car. There was something about the way he moved that was entirely different from zoo or park bears. He was so fit, so incredibly active. He wore seven-league boots.

The telephone line along the road was set upon tripods made from groups of three small spruce poles each, and was strung not more than eight feet above the ground. Occasional giant micro-wave towers marched across the wilderness northward, bridging the gaps in telecommunications to distant villages on the rim of no-where. And about every sixty miles throughout northern Alberta the Forestry Department had fire towers manned in summer; pilots were stationed at field strips at posts such as High Level, to fly fire reconnaissance each day.

As we drove, Bumbles explained that a gravel road like this, held together by moist soil and properly rolled, makes a serviceable all-year road and is more practical in the North than either concrete or asphalt. The latter heave and crack with frost action.

The gravel road, however, has to be graded continually. The top layer of fill has to be replaced because the soil and gravel separate under the pounding traffic. The soil gets blown away as dust which leaves nothing to hold the gravel; then passing cars and trucks scatter the gravel along the sides of the road. We met road graders at their perpetual task, and straddled their furrows adroitly.

We are leaving the Peace River country now. That country where you see men on tractors just on the skyline. Where no one questions the odd presence of a little girl with long, stringy, blond hair, barefooted, bug-bitten, and wearing a pair of very dirty pajamas, carrying a .22 rifle as she prowls the wheat fields along the river. That was Ann in the Peace River country last year. That was our tipsy, dirty little tent pitched over there in the driftwood beside the glassy river.

Up north these stolid men never question anything they see: we found that out. The men just look dully ahead as they run their tractor or road grader or ferry barge or harbor dredge or steam pump: they are the workingmen of rural Canada, who are probably not Canadians but something else, welcomed here by the vast hospitality of Canada.

Many such men can be found, grimy with dirt, with broken fingernails as coarse as bear claws, sleeping in the cab of a softly panting diesel locomotive or waiting on a siding of the new Great Slave Railway which now pushes its way through the dense forests and sags cautiously through swamps, with the pile driver going out ahead, thawing the frozen subsoil as she goes. The railroad's purpose is to bring out ore from the lead mines on the south shore of Great Slave Lake. It will end there. No camera-toting tourist, no eager sightseeing passenger, will ever ride this single-track railroad.

The tired grimy frontier faces of the men exhibit a complete lack of expression when they see us. The kids want to say, "Hello. I am Jean. I am Ann. Who are you?" But for once in their lives they don't dare say a word to those men.

For some reason or other, all the Provinces stop at the sixtieth parallel. Then, without any fanfare you cross over north into the Northwest Territories.

What is the North? We speak of it all the time, or sometimes loosely call it the Arctic; yet the fascinating thing about it is that nobody has yet entirely agreed as to just what it is.

Some writers and newspaper people, speaking from the standpoint of plant growth and geography, call the North everything which lies north of fifty-five degrees in that it is forested — with largely unmarketable scrub timber — unfenced, and unfarmed. Others define the North as everything lying beyond the sixtieth parallel which we are crossing now, that is, everything that is held under federal administration, not Provincial. If you use the political definition, the North is one and a half million square miles or 40 percent of Canada. It is large enough to swallow up half the United States.

Yet there might well be also a geological definition of the North. A nearly soilless area of two million square miles of Canada lies in the Precambrian Shield, out of Canada's total 3,852,000 square-mile area! This means that, for all practical purposes, actually more than half of Canada is nonarable, nonproductive, and non-habitable. This nonarable big half, we call the North, or even the Arctic. It is an arctic that dips south far into the Temperate Zone, and remains untamed, not conforming to meridian lines drawn on the globe at all. It has an arctic climate. It is treeless. It has few resources but the white fox, trapped by around eighty-five hundred wandering Eskimos with their dogsleds.

Although this Arctic has been said to be brought into the age of air, and we are told it occupies a strategic place on the great circle air routes from country to country over the top of the world, these long-distance air routes actually go over it at high altitudes, and do not develop it. The North — the Arctic — remains aloof and un-conquerable. It remains itself. It has a peculiar resistance to all forms of civilization.

There is Alexandra Falls to see in the Hay River as you follow that river toward Great Slave Lake's south shore. And there is lovely Louise Falls, a study in cubism, which the traveler reaches by a short path through squishy mosses. Then, as the Highway touches the south shore of Great Slave Lake, you enter a land where the mirages let you get right up to within a hundred yards of them. Then, of course, they escape. The mirages, like those we used to see in our open West, will escape permanently, never to be seen by anyone again, when the occasional miserable gas station-café spots along the Highway grow into settlements. Already, as the road spots get names, the mirages are leaving.

The town of Hay River, over two thousand population and growing, is no mirage. Because it is situated on very low land on the Hay River estuary, it floods in the breakup. Some springs, the floods call forth rescue operations from the south. Fifteen years ago I took a color slide of the village from the air. It was kind of a pretty place before the Highway came in. It was a neat little jewel, compact and simple, set at the edge of a vast blue sea. But now, despite all the money which is being spent by government and by private industry as well, the poverty and chaos of the Hay River is increasing.

It is perhaps because of the great fecundity of the untidy poor. Their tottering, sour little shacks grow up like mushrooms every-where, spreading out. The government now provides funds for a city water and sewage system at Hay River; but the poor have a proclivity for collecting detached parts of boats, motors, and old cars and pile them up ever higher beside each house. Today's pov-erty could be defined as life in the midst of an ever increasing junk-yard of metallic scrap.

After making its way around the west end of Great Slave Lake, the Highway crossed the Mackenzie a number of miles downriver from the lake. The connection was a two ended government ferry.

All the ice had long since broken out. The Mackenzie breaks a month before the lake does. I almost wished we could have begun our voyage three weeks earlier while the ice pans were still in the lake. Indians have assured me it is their happiest canoeing season, traveling the opalescent open leads of water where the ice shrinks from contact with the shore. At this season the birds sing the most sweetly and the big spotted trout (as big as sixty pounds) lie near the surface in schools. But after a large lake opens up, winds and storms constantly endanger and delay the small boatman, as we shall see.

"Darn it, Mother," Ann rebuked me. "You made us miss the ice!" I told her to be thankful we had summer yet, though privately I did feel apologetic. "If you had any other mother but me," I pointed out, "you wouldn't be allowed to explore Great Slave Lake at all."

I had had to make an important expeditionary decision. I had decided to voyage two hundred and fifty miles down the far north shore of Great Slave Lake to Fort Providence, the first town on the Mackenzie itself. Most parties going down the Mackenzie do not at-tempt this. They truck their boats to the ferry crossing near Fort Providence on the river, and dispense with the remote, difficult lake, since the lake offers no refueling stations for their motors. Further, when you try to include Great Slave Lake along with the entire Mackenzie River in one summer, the season may prove to be too short to accomplish all these goals. If the season should be a poor one — if the ice moves late, if the winds were high — you might wait out the whole summer sitting on the lakeshore, not able to move. But I decided to risk these factors. Voyaging direct from Yellowknife, we would find the source of the Mackenzie River ourselves. How could anyone pass up a chance to see the birth of a great river?

Great Slave Lake is a treacherous piece of water, with an area possibly as large as 12,500 square miles. Varying figures have been given. We can safely say at any rate that it is larger than some whole states in the East, larger than Lake Ontario.

Lying astride the Precambrian Shield, it is sprinkled with thousands of tiny islands, atolls, and unmarked reefs of typical Precambrian formation; largely granite, gneiss, marble, and other igneous and metamorphic rocks. Its long arms stretch eastward into the little-known Barrens, where Samuel Hearne, in 1770, made the first track across lands where some areas still await the foot of another white man.

To the east, the lake has red cliffs rising four hundred feet from the water. It has deep holes going down to more than twenty-five hundred feet; and an average depth of five hundred feet is usually given (Lake Erie has an average depth of sixty-eight feet at this time), which makes Great Slave Lake one of the deepest as well as largest bodies of fresh water in the world. There are practically no safe coves or harbors. Because of its geology it is the weirdest and bleakest imaginable body of water to navigate.

Add to its wicked geology the fact that capsizal in such icy waters is tantamount to a death sentence even if one is as little as a quarter mile offshore; and the fact that its shores are uninhabited wilderness, the home of fox and wolf and bear; and you have a deadly siren call for the adventurous small boat explorer — and a world of incredible beauty.

Predominant winds on the lake are from the northeast. They may be the Polar Easterlies caused by the rotation of the earth, but geographers and meteorologists cautiously refuse to make a statement. Whatever the cause, you find northeast winds prevailing for thousands of miles across all the North American polar slope and of course on the polar shore itself. By winter the northeast winds are so faithful that travelers use them as their compass when they steer their dogsleds or snowmobiles over the ridged snowdrifts. All the drifts across northern Canada and Alaska lie at the same angle.

Commercial navigation on the Mackenzie system is limited to less than four months because of winds on the lake. Spring breakup is a drastic event and goes on from April to mid-June. By mid-September winds are violent and ice begins to form. The lake ice gradually freezes five or six feet thick. But it is not safe for tractor traffic until January because wind action keeps open water right down the middle of the lake. Pressure ridges form, ten feet high and thirty miles long, and obstruct convoys and tractor trains which need to cross the lake.

Not long after our Highway crossed the Mackenzie to the northeast side we began to see signs that we had entered an arctic region. The Highway began to dodge around great boulders and bluffs of bleak gray rock. The country became alive with hogbacks, changed to a rock quarry. Right on top of the rocks the tiny, eight-foot Boreal forest grew — the arctic spruce, larch, and white birch — holding on with gnarled claws.

Here were some of the oldest rocks on earth, the bedrock of earth. This rock went back to the beginning of time on our planet, as long ago as two billion and perhaps three billion years. There was a barely concealed elemental threat implicit in the Precambrian Shield. What would happen to a person lost afoot, or in some kind of trouble alone, in thousands of empty miles of terrain like this? Well, we would make sure that this never happened.

Why did this Precambrian world look so grim, even in summer? It was grim and stark, but it was so beautiful. I had pondered it in fascination since I saw it by tug-and-barge train chugging into Yellowknife on the water last fall. I decided the answer lies in the presence of the bedrock of the planet, which compels an awareness of how fragile our accustomed life habitat is. The northern wasteland points a finger of accusation and exhortation at careless modern man, like a skeleton's finger. The wasteland demonstrates how readily the whole earth might again return to lifeless bedrock if something went wrong in the atmospheric cycles to which we owe our existence. And Man is seriously disturbing these cycles now.

Eventually, after many a hairpin turn, our narrow gravel road brought us to our destination, the last town: Yellowknife.

We tramped into the Gold Brick Hotel where we had stayed before. The lobby was hot and filled with arctic sunbeams. The adjoining bar was filled as usual with layer upon layer of loafing disheveled, partially inebriated men.

When we came up to the Gold Brick registry desk, the girl who was helping there asked, "Do you have reservations?" just as desk clerks always do. And of course we didn't.

"Well, we'll squeeze you in somehow," she decided. The Gold Brick always managed to squeeze in extra guests in some mysterious manner; there was always room for just one more. The hospitality of the North must be experienced to be appreciated.

"By the way," the desk girl added, "there have been telephone calls for you, Mrs. Helmericks, every day. A Dr. Gerald Corby?"

I jumped. My blood pressure rocketed.

"Here are your room keys," the girl was murmuring. "You'll find your rooms right on up the stairs. There is a telephone in each room."

"Thank you," I gulped, feeling unnerved and unmasked. "Good night," I said quickly, and fled with Jean and Ann and our mountainous baggage, leaving Bumbles fuming.

"Did you hear that, kids? Gerald has been calling!"

"But Bumbles is a determined man," said Jean. "The trouble is, Gerald is not so determined."

"By the way, Jean and I would like you to marry sometime," Ann informed me as we puffed up two flights.

"Must I decide now?" I wailed. "While hauling baggage up?"

"It would be nice for you to marry for your old age, Mother. Jean and I will not be with you forever, you know."

"I just don't want to make any hasty decisions while toting baggage," I puffed forlornly. "We three girls have been together for so long. Do you think you would really want to leave your dear old mother?"

"Don't be dramatic, Mother. Hurry with the baggage."

"We will miss you, Mom, at times. But we intend to have our own husbands and our own careers, you know."

"I think we're going to get the same room we had before. If we can only find it," I said. Now we were climbing to the third floor. "You are no longer a young girl, Mother," Ann persisted bluntly. "You can't just go on living wild in a tent forever."

"Even the poor Eskimos," said Jean, "can't live like Eskimos any more." The girls unlocked the door to our room. "You said so yourself," Ann reminded me. The plight of the poor Eskimos, the earth's last free people, was so lugubrious that I dismissed it from mind, and determined to forget everything but the joys of arctic summertime, the last summer of this sort I would probably have.

It took a half day to bathe for the last time and get into our wilderness clothes, while dear Bumbles lugged all our female apparel in suitcases back into the car.

I have often observed in myself that a change of personality comes with the change to rugged frontier clothing. The different clothes, the fresh free air of the North, and the great empty distances, arouse a feeling of spiritual wholeness and well-being that no words can define. Naturalists and outdoors people know this feeling. But they are quite unable to convey it to those who have never felt it — those who do not relish outdoors hardships, and whose ears seem deaf to the siren call of the wilderness.

The expedition members rummaged with great delight in the old Hudson's Bay warehouse beside the sea. Yes, here was our old long heavy freight canoe, with its one rib dented. There were our paddles and life preservers, wooden slat seats, our dependable 9.5-horse outboard motor with the new slip clutch and the two hook-on gas tanks; and the numbers of empty gas cans to enable us to haul up to forty gallons of fuel. We had an extra propeller, a tool kit, extra spark plugs, and an extra water pump. Muddy water is hard on water pumps, and this little motor had seen over eleven hundred miles of muddy water last year. Before embarkation we would get a mechanic to overhaul the motor completely at the Yellowknife Garage.

"And look, girls!" I enthused happily. "There is our old white chamber pot with the fitted lid, in which we always carry our ammunition." The girls shuddered. Unfortunately I had to take entire responsibility for that precious pot, especially around the Forts. Juveniles are such sensitive people. They would have nothing to do with the ammunition because of the stigma associated in their minds with its container. Of course, in this way I remained sole proprietor of the ammunition and arms, and the danger of gun accidents was minimized.

It was Dominion Day — Canada's ninety-eighth birthday — when we left Yellowknife to sail the moonscape of an enchanted inland sea.

Jean had inconveniently disappeared near the moment of embarkation. We found her aboard the one-hundred-and-eighty-foot *Radium Royal* barge which lay over at the commercial docks. As we walked toward the barge, I saw Captain Klinker coming down the docks toward me. I almost dissolved in joy and amazement when I saw his kindly face and recognized what he had for me in his hands.

"Connie, I saved something for you over the winter," the veteran riverman greeted me. "You said you'd be back north, so I figured I just couldn't throw them away, although I was tempted to a few times, I can tell you."

He then handed over to me two right boots. With that magic gesture of kindness, our outfitting was at last really completed. By a habit of thinking which may be intrinsically northern in character, he had actually saved the two right boots left by mischance on the *Radium Royal* last fall, and I had still hopefully hung onto the left boots that matched them. It was remarkable that the vessel was docked here at the moment we were. It remains remarkable how northern people read each other's minds.

"Jean's in the galley," he said, taking up where we had left off our last year's discourse. "Good to see you. How you been, eh?"

"Dear Klinker! You have never met my younger daughter. This is Ann. And this is Peter B. Pip."

"Come on in the galley and let's set down," he said.

"Well, Klinker, how often we have spoken of you! What's new in the North?"

"Got me a all-new crew," he replied shortly. A new cook poured our coffee; not the fat one I knew before, but a skinny one. She smiled and we were introduced. Jean came in.

"Hey, Mom, they don't have any of the fellows we sailed with last year," Jean said, disappointed. She was surrounded with several crew members in their late teens and early twenties. "Hey, you guys. This is my little sister."

"My name is Ann," said Ann brightly.

"Nope," the Icelandic Captain went on to Bumbles and me. "Don't have none of the crew we had last season. But they are all real nice fellows. All from the union, down south. I just taken what they give me. Can't you ship with us this year, Jean?" he asked, passing me a fatherly wink.

"They're going on down the Mackenzie, you know," said Bumbles.

"That's what Jean tells me. She don't want to ship with the *Royal* no more. Be careful. It's a big river."

"I suppose here at Yellowknife is the farthest you run north?" I asked.

"That's a funny thing, now you speak of it," replied Klinker. "First time in quite a few years the company changed my schedule. This year we go clear on down the river, as a matter of fact. I made three runs down already this year. Your boots went along, too."

"Down the Mackenzie?" (We had originally met him on the Slave, of course.) "Oh, Klinker, that's simply too wonderful to be true!"

"Maybe we'll see you some place along the river." Klinker was wearing the same sweatshirt and beaded moccasins, I noticed. "Not too much white people on down the river," he informed us. "You may want to come aboard sometime and have yourselves a steak. Take a shower. You want a bath now?" he offered.

"Maybe they don't need it yet," Bumbles put in, "but I guess they will need it later, won't they? I'm glad to know they have a friend in that country; makes me feel a little better about it."

The bath and steak referred to was constantly on the move, however, day and night; and we all knew that if we caught up with it, it would be absolute magic, a miracle.

"All the tug captains will be watching out for you. We know your tent. Everybody knows you."

"We brought a new tent this year," Ann said.

"Don't you worry none, Ann, if we see a tent along the bank we'll spot you, and pass the word along where you're at," Klinker said. "Won't be a whole lot of tents in that country."

"Well, that's very thoughtful of you," I said, with sincere emotion.

Klinker told us that on his present run he had over two thousand tons of loaded barges to push downriver from navigation head on the Athabasca. He told us how the government-owned line had bought out the other remaining company, the Y.T. Company (Yellowknife Transportation Company) over the winter, thus completely eliminating private competition in shipping throughout the North. The government had got the entire competing company for a little over two million dollars. "All them Y.T. boats and barges, you seen 'em, sometimes?" We had.

"Boy, I would sure like to have all them boats," said a crewman's voice nearby.

"Me, too!" Everybody sighed.

We discussed the various vessels. The government had got the *Marjorie* now. She was 85.7 registered tons. The government had got the *Richard*, the *Expediter*, the *Husky*, the *Saline*, the *Scamp* (just forty-nine registered tons, used in smaller tributary rivers) and the *Thunder River*.

The government had got Barges 101 through 110, and the A.S. (Arctic Shipping) line. The A.S. Company had pioneered the routes that went farthest north beyond the continent; and their vessels were specially fitted for ice and their captains were ice masters. In the A.S. Line were Barge Numbers 1,2,3, and 4. Less than ten years before, the government had made a similar move when it scooped up the Hudson's Bay Company vessels: the *Pelican Rapids*, the *Watson Lake*, the *Hearne Lake*, and the *Banks Island*.

"They sure got them a bargain."

"Sure did," we said.

Thus the expansion of the Radium Line had increased the tonnage carried into the North by perhaps 80 percent in the last ten years, and from now on all cargo would move in government vessels. There were marked navigation routes, extending westward through the Beaufort Sea as well as to the Arctic Islands northeastward, amounting to eight thousand miles. They brought fuel oil even to north Alaska for oil drilling exploration.

"I was crew on an Arctic Shipping vessel last year. I went to Alaska," a crew member was telling the girls. I pricked up my ears.

"Some old geezer over there in the delta of a river has built himself a real nice house that would surprise you. About three hundred miles north of tree line there, too," the voice continued. "Just that one house in all north Alaska on an island in the river delta that empties into the Arctic Ocean, what a place to live!" he described it. "Big family of them, big tribe of them there. The old geezer fishes with nets in the Arctic Ocean, catches about thirty-six tons, and he market-hunts for caribou, legally too. Seems like they got more caribou in Alaska right now than a dog got fleas. And this fellow, he's a couple little planes on floats and skis, you know? He's servicing the Dew Line, and all kinda things like that. Living all alone in north Alaska, the only house. I been to Alaska, we was clear over to Alaska last summer to bring them Mackenzie River oil."

"I know that river," I said then. "I explored it. I lived there for years. That old geezer is not as old as you think, young man," I told the tale-bearer. "That's Jean's and Ann's father!"

"Oh, excuse me, m'am," said the twenty-year-old crewman, embarrassed. "I had no idea. I guess he wasn't so old after all, if you say so."

"Daddy!" the girls spoke up. "Mother, we want to see our *daddy!*"

"I knew we were getting closer to his country, even last summer," Jean said. "If we just keep going, we can get to Alaska along the edge of the Arctic Ocean through the ice. Wouldn't he be surprised, Mom?"

"Let's do it!" cried Ann, ready to go.

"They think it's going to be a real bad ice year over on the ocean toward Alaska," remarked a crewman. "This summer's a bad one, they predict."

"Klinker would take us to Alaska on the *Radium Royal*, wouldn't you, Klinker?" Jean asked him, slipping her arm affectionately into his.

"Wal, Jean and Ann, the *Royal* don't have orders to go through the Beaufort Sea and Alaska," he replied with his patient, grizzled smile. "I wouldn't mind taking you girls, but we would have to get Canadian government orders. . . ."

"Whatever became of the plan the Y.T. Company had last year, to build a million-dollar passenger vessel and run it down the Mackenzie?" I asked.

"Them plans all scrapped now," Klinker said. "The government runs this country themself, and they don't care a whole lot about tourists. We got new engines in the *Royal*," he went on to topics of more interest to him. "We can push a real fine train of barges now, lots more power. . . . Better stay and eat. Almost time to eat now." He consulted his watch. "It's Dominion Day, you know, nothing to do but eat. It's the only day we don't work. Better have a last meal, and then I'll walk over with you and help you cast off. Take care on this lake," he said. "Barometer looks good right now, but the barometer's always good in the North, and don't mean a thing. That lake's a bad one."

"I worry about them," remarked Bumbles gravely.

"Oh, they'll be all right," the grizzled Icelander comforted us all. "They shown last season they got pretty good sense. They're northern people. She's lived in Alaska for years, you know. They got all the navigation charts. They got a good seaworthy little craft, don't you think so?"

"Well, yes, I think so, I do hope so," said Bumbles. "It's all ready to go, all loaded, at the city dock."

So after lunch dear Klinker and dear Bumbles and a few of the crew from the south, and numbers of kind people from Yellowknife, and many, many children came to the town docks and helped us cast off. Many hands held the canoe while we got aboard. Klinker advised, "Shift your cargo forward. You got too much weight aft. Now shift the cargo to port."

This matter was adjusted quickly. "Annie, come sit up front with me and stop leaning." That did it.

"Good-bye, dears," called Peter Bumbleton Pip, good friend to the last.

"Good-bye, Bumbles, we love you very much, and we do thank you for driving us north and parking the car!" called Ann as an oar pushed us from the dock.

Jean was wrestling with the motor she knew so well. Having primed it carefully, she gave one glorious pull of the starter rope. The motor caught.

"Pip, pip, old boy!" she called to Bumbles, in her moment of triumph.

"Good-bye, Klinker. See you down the river. Good-bye, and thanks for everything, everybody!"

The town quickly dimmed in the distance, and just like that, we were out in the northern wilds again. We were heading for a journey which I suspect no women and children had made before this time; we would encounter the same perils met by the early explorers who also had braved this world in frail canoes. It was still an explorer's world here.

22

Voyaging Great Slave Lake

YELLOWKNIFE Bay, actually an extension of the Yellowknife River curved out toward the open lake under a lowering sky. As soon as the two children and I put to sea, we were met by gusty winds, rain sprinkles, and waves. Our friends of civilization, standing on a sunny dock in another world, retreated abruptly into memory. The lake lay empty, glittering in darkness.

"Head into that niche in the shore," I called to Jean. The water was too rough for the canoe to handle; so although the kids didn't like it, we waited for six hours in a cleft in the gray boulders inside the bay. We ate dry flat pilot biscuits with canned jam, and waited. Time lost its usual meaning right then.

"Man proposes, God disposes," I told my crew. "Just always remember that around here."

Why had we come here? We were faced with elemental problems of survival. Everything sharpened down to that. We were drawn not so much by a "love of adventure" as by a yearning for the great innocence of Canada. We are like the birds and animals who are migrating, or trying to, in response to unnatural things which are happening. Many North American species that were unknown in Canada twenty years ago are in the process of moving north, while the species already in Canada are in some instances pushing northward still.

Oh, to have a wilderness all to oneself with plenty of room —

what a gift, what a wealth of the healing stuff of nature. Canada contains *one fourth of all the fresh water on earth.*

Great Slave Lake lies between the Canadian Shield and the Mackenzie section of the Rockies. Its elevation is never constant, but varies from day to day from the influence of winds, barometric and lunar influences, precipitation and evaporation. It reaches it lowest level in April before the thaw; now, in June, it is at its highest: about five hundred and sixteen feet above sea level. The lake drains an area of 370,000 square miles in which there are no roads, railroads, industries, or cities. The peasants here do not till the soil; they are hunters of the wilderness. Their government is a highly civilized one: it is beneficent to them, and is four thousand miles away.

Thoughtful studies have been made of the lake by the Canadian Fisheries which permitted commercial fishing to start about twenty years ago. Two fish-packing plants are permanent installations on Great Slave Lake. The one eastward at Gros Cap is off our course entirely. The one at Hay River we saw by auto coming up. It's far south.

"It's the lack of gasoline supplies on the lake that keeps us all close to home," a businesswoman in Yellowknife had told me. "How will you manage when your gas runs out? And it will."

"The Fisheries men at Hay River showed me a bay on my map and marked it," I told her, "and many, many thanks to them for that. They showed me where I can get hold of a few gallons. It's quite a ways off. I think we can make it, just barely, on our fuel capacity."

"But can you find the bay?"

"Oh, sure," Ann told her. "Mom just reads the maps. Jean is the engineer, I'm helper, and we just go where Mom says."

"Well, it's a big lake. Another thing," said the woman, "practically everybody at Yellowknife has their little boat, you know. But everybody always has broken motors all summer long. Especially the propeller blades. What will you do when you break your prop? And you will."

Quite naturally the rocks in Great Slave Lake, like their kind anywhere, waited craftily to rear their hard backs under each passing propeller blade. It was even hinted around town that whole reefs swam around and zeroed in whenever a lonely, churning propeller could be heard underwater, even from a considerable distance. All that people did for recreation at Yellowknife, it was said, was continually to file away on chewed-up propellers with rusty files, or place orders from the Bay for new ones, and new pins, and new shafts. You wouldn't get five miles in this rock pile without a maiming.

The citizenry expected that my girls and I would end up disabled on some remote shore. In the end, they speculated, we would have to be rescued; and as they sat morosely filing away on their own propeller blades, they hated to think about rescue jobs.

"Far as I'm concerned, I won't break the prop," said Jean. "And nobody's going to be allowed to touch this motor but me."

"We have a spare prop," I told the woman, eyeing Jean.

"I just told you," said Jean doggedly, "I *won't break the prop.*"

"Not a nick on the prop, clear from British Columbia," Ann backed Jean up this time.

"Our family has been wanting to make a cruise like yours with our bigger boat," the woman I talked with began to wax enthusiastic. "Only what with the rocks and the lack of gasoline . . ." But she began to make hopeful plans and stir her husband up for a trip right then.

"We have this method," I told her. "We don't have the American craze for speed and power. I guess we're real funny Americans. . . ."

"Yer odd ones, all right."

"So we don't try to operate a forty- or fifty-horse motor. The big motors are dangerous because you move along too fast for strange water. Also, big motors, you see, burn too much gas for a long haul. We have nine and a half horses and we keep our little motor at less than half throttle. Another thing you'll have a laugh at, I can imagine, but when going into bays and across points I will stand up in the bow so I can look right down in the water, and I'll take sounding with a paddle. I always just keep yelling at Jean whenever I think I see a rock or something, and Jean cuts the motor instantly."

"Can Mother ever *yell!*" Jean took the opportunity to point out.
"And Jean hoists the whole motor out on the hinge. Then we all
three lean heavily on the paddles for a while — one of the reasons
we took this trip was to exercise the girls — and after a while we
see our way clear to start the motor again. That's the way we plan
to sneak along the north shore. I hope."

This was the way we proceeded carefully inching into the unsafe
world. Hostile rock shore glared under sun shafts and light-edged
clouds, and the lake was our own uninhabited beautiful rock
quarry, all our own. Its aura was arctic, its shorelines a moonscape.
It was a lake whose low shores, instead of being proper and definite
the way an honest lake should be, were vague and mysterious because deeply indented with coves and capricious meanderings.

Thousands of sea-washed reefs had no vegetation except lichens
splashed with birdlime. But hundreds of atolls and islets contained
small stands of spruce, larch, and birch, and a heath covering
which was no simple floral association but a complex mosaic of
charming colonies of plant life of that arctic kind frequently compared by naturalists to the miniature pristine beauty of Japanese
gardens. The varieties included grasses, sedges, arctic poppy, anem-
one, dandelion, ground birch, Labrador tea, white heather, bil-
berry, alpine, cranberry, cotton grass, locoweed, rhododendron.
Also to be found were tiny arctic ferns, red and orange rusts, saxi-
frages, crowberry, the creeping form of common juniper, dwarf willow, and the common vetch or wild pea, with its dangling, purple-
white blooms. There were even some wild primroses and wild
strawberry plants.

Most plant life here was not totally dependent upon seed production but had overwintering buds. Most had no scent or fra-
grance. The breezes of a summer day north of sixty degrees north
latitude carry no smells. Only the arctic primrose has a very faint
perfume when sniffed extremely deeply at the tip of your nose. Far
northern species do not use bees for pollination, hence do not take
any pains to attract them. As the bees seem to know that they can
find no employment, they sensibly remain south, except for the
occasional bumblebee which is found in the primroses.

Plant life is characterized by the fantastic speed with which the majority go through an annual cycle of growth in just one glorious summer month. For the rest of the year, immobilized upon their stems (the lichens and moss flowers are stemless), they cherish the precious kernel of life against the winds and snow.

Our first night out the girls pitched our tent in the sparse, pristine plant populations between rock snaggles, beside an uneasily chained canoe. There was a light rain; we were getting north of the heavy rains. We slept twelve hours, seven to seven. The few mosquitoes were easily routed from our bugproof tent by the blast can. Our sleeping bags, freshly dry-cleaned, were fluffy and nice. We saw that Precambrian rocks have much to offer to campers. They were clean, nice rocks, furnishing lovely tables upon which to lounge, to build our fires of dead sticks, and prepare our food. Our beds of course were a little hard.

"Mom, what are you soaking our pilot biscuits in the lake for?" Ann asked at breakfast time.

"Well, you see, dear," my voice broke the Precambrian stillness, "I stumbled upon the rocks, and the package of biscuits fell in. As you see, they float just beautifully. Now I am occupied with reaching for each one with an oar."

"Okay, real groovy. Spare me the details. I'll roast the remains over the coals in our hand grill. We can't afford to waste food so early in the expedition."

Unfortunately, several of the giant hard wafers could not be rescued and went floating away, and some big strange fish grabbed them at once.

"Jean, get out of the lake. Get out, you'll be fish bait!"

Jean had risen early, bathed on the icy shore, and washed her gold hair. Ann was pulling a label off a package to cast it into the campfire. A new product on the market, it urged boldly: "Hold him with longer, stronger nails."

Sun shafts cast their light tracery along the corrugated rocks as the sun climbed; the lake turned turquoise blue. "Stop wasting time, and hurry up and strike the tent!"

We struck the tent hard, and proceeded north by northwest around the turn which admitted Yellowknife Bay into giant North Arm. The inlet went north and inland sixty miles out of our way.

We had no choice but to follow up it until we could at least see across it. There was a place I had plotted on the map where we might try to cross. (This great inlet blocked our westward course along the lake's north shore.)

The thirty-five miles we went up North Arm was a maze of bird rocks, atolls, and minor inlets. We got out the pocket compass, using it with the wristwatch to clock our mileage. All landmarks looked exactly the same.

The compass wouldn't behave — at least not for me. Bearings taken on the lake as recorded on the map showed a variation of as much as thirty-four degrees east. As our voyage went on, the variations were not constant from day to day but were capricious. This compass variation was caused by the North Magnetic Pole, over to the east a few hundred miles. Soon I was not quite sure where shore lay as many islands enveloped us.

"Poor Mother," said Ann. "What a case. Give me the compass. I want to try."

"Don't drop it overboard, then. Here, be careful."

"What do you think I am, an idiot?"

Finally we just put the compass away, and the islands were all around us. But we were making progress somehow up the inlet, zigzagging. I had a feeling that we should push the good weather while it held. The sea was glassy calm. I wondered where we would run to if the sea came up.

"Your trouble, Mother, is that you are a worrier. Just stop worrying. We've got all the shelter any person would need on any of these perfectly darling islands. Plenty food, plenty fuel, plenty water. It's a natural paradise," Jean decided.

"You're right, Jean. I might as well get used to paradise again. Home out here is every place for us."

The air was filled with birdsong.

Passing farther out to sea among the islands, we could see the horizon of water and sky, and each island was a little gem. Atop each atoll's lone dead tree sat a big, fierce female eagle, symbolically guarding (though little did she know it) the glory and freedom of all North America. It was the northern bald eagle.

Instantly I thought of NORAD — the interservice North American Air Defense Command. If it weren't for NORAD Jean and Ann and I wouldn't be here. For the past fifteen years the men of Canada and the United States had joined together in NORAD in what has been called "the long polar watch" to guard this continent from missile attack coming over the top of the world. There are two supreme commanders who would jointly give the command for our own interceptors to be launched in case of continental attack — one commander American, the other Canadian. Canada without wanting it has been involved in United States actions abroad which might precipitate attack, and attack, if it came, was long believed to be most likely to come first over Canada. Canadian feeling has often run high over this point: that Canada and Canadian soil were involved in American tactical military problems. At any rate, it was often a strange feeling to be all alone in this wilderness and yet to realize that, electronically, the American and Canadian men of NORAD, were watching over every inch of it, over us all the time, day and night, the years through. It is a watch which, unfortunately, cannot be dropped, but must be maintained constantly and faithfully into the indefinite chancy future.

We watched the big eagle as she sat with hunched shoulder blades near a big, horrid, untidy nest, and she was fierce and wonderful and brave. We saw the white head turn in our direction. No gaze on earth matches an eagle's stare. Commanding and indignant, the stare burned into us. It almost made us feel guilty. The bird's thick yellow claws tightened their grasp in natural apprehension as our intruding boat nosed closer. She saw the flash of my binoculars.

The eagle flew heavily off on a five-mile-wide swing over the wide expanses of water, from her dead tree on her tiny island. We were left to worry over whether there were eggs or eaglets, or if the waiting coward gulls would harm them. After the first eagle, we spotted from afar those islets having bald eagles atop them; and out of consideration for their feelings we gave them a wide berth thereafter.

"There aren't many eagle nurseries left, Jeanie." Ann turned to her sister at the quiet throttle.

Around our canoe the squaw ducks squabbled and the loons howled and dove and howled again; whooping, mournful cries. "The Arctic Ocean has them by the thousands in summer along the shore. I've always loved it there," I said. "This makes me think of the Arctic Ocean."

How wonderful the flocks of pelicans and cormorants, the herons, grebes, coots, rails, terns, swallows, blackbirds, goldeneyes, bluebills, buffleheads, canvasbacks, shovelers, teal, baldpates, scaups, and scoters — a delightful, nonhuman company. How rare the upland plover, the Wilson snipe, the little horned lark in the North. How busy these permanent, year-around arctic residents — the arctic three-toed woodpecker, the crossbill and redpoll, inhabiting the little spruce forest near continental tree line. We heard again the organ-pipe tones of the shy hermit thrush, which flitted like a shadow among islands crowding one another under sun and shadow.

Camping upon the smooth table rocks of an island, we caught a half-dozen spotted pike with red fins. They rose to our clumsy casting as one amateur to another in pleasant greeting. The pike lay in the weeds like handfuls of jeweled daggers. Unlike other fish they cared nothing about maintaining a proper keel; they loafed in the green water beside the island table rocks, some with long snouts upthrust, and others with their tail up and head down on a fifteen-degree angle. You wanted to straighten them out level. Oh, spotted, loafing crocodiles, with bony heads and greedy, sharp-toothed snouts, how we love you!

Our ecstatic cries rang among the rocks. How quickly the shouts died out in stillness. How small was the human voice, the human presence here.

We ate several pike, after laborious and fishy scaling. The tough, slimy old luggers had heads full of tapeworms which crawled out of little holes when the fish were hauled out of water. We didn't care. We roasted the fish flesh thoroughly in the grill over the coals and ate with our fingers, and the white meat was juicy and sweet. We ate cans of beans out of the can. We ate candy bars and dried fruit.

The canoe was drawn up into the heart of the rock atoll, safe from any ideas it might get of wandering, a single bed of green lush cattails to its landward side. Canoes or boats come alive and get ideas of their own sometimes. So you chain them with three chains to rocks, or stakes, or trees. We were about four miles from the mainland by the stepping-stones of islands. The canoe was our life-line. Without it, we could starve to death, helpless to move. Where were we? I had only a rough idea. It didn't matter. We were somewhere in the archipelago of islands; the shore lay roughly to our right hand as we traveled. But what was "shore"? Shore, when it is endless in a true wilderness, loses its meaning.

As the wind rose in the night, bringing rain, we remained.

"Why do you always take a place right in the middle of the tent, Mom, and leave us crowding the sides?" The rain gave them an answer, and they thought it, and me, most unfair.

On another day we threaded endless similar islands to the left and to the right. We paddled; there were too many reefs to dare use the motor. We turned out to open sea to get more depth, then found we had got out too far. The islands would lure you out only to drop you far at sea, abandoning you to murderous reefs.

When I saw a big square barn on the sea, we turned toward it and I made a check mark on my map called simply Fish Camp. Nobody home there.

On the lee of a farther island we pitched the tent and scraped a slightly flyblown pike from the fish bucket for supper. Why bother to carry old fish with us, the kids had wondered. There seemed to be endless pike for the catching. But I wasn't sure about that. I liked to have a fish or two ahead for security. It didn't have to be the biggest fish in the world, or the choicest. If the wind rose, the easy fishing might vanish abruptly.

The wind rose mightily at once. The spruce trees sighed. The white waves curled into the narrow neck of the island. Jean slept outdoors on a boulder thirty feet above the tent. The ends of Jean's hair, escaping from her canvas tarp anchored to the rock by several basketball-sized stones, straggled in the winds of the north.

"I'm going to sleep outside, too, Mom," Ann announced, and taking her sleeping bag in the broad daylight of the night, crept under the tarp, also.

"Get out of here!" objected the older girl. "Go back to the tent with Mom!"

"Jeanie, a girl doesn't have to sleep with her mother *forever*." I heard familiar homey sounds of protest.

"Mom," came a call from the rock presently, "can we have one of the rifles to sleep with?"

"Sure. I think you probably should. Come get the .22."

"Can we have both guns?"

"No," I said. "Do you think I'm going to give up all my guns? I'm keeping the .30–06 for myself." But there was little to worry about out here. There are no rabid wolves or hungry bears when you are on a small island surrounded by a stormy sea, and human callers are most unlikely.

The storm made the island very cozy. The sociable gulls collected and screamed. These sacrosanct garbage collectors knew perfectly well that no man, white or native, would harm them, and that the presence of man, more often than not, meant fish upon the rocks. Perhaps also they hoped in their wild bird brains that any man here on the rocks would himself conveniently die. The animal kingdom, unlike man, is not burdened with moral scruples regarding the use of dead benefactors for a meal. We exempt animals from moral responsibility, and do not expect moral behavior from them. We do not judge the gulls.

Next day the girls, wearing bright orange life preservers, swam in the icy water a few feet off the island. Like the gulls they thrived, with enormous appetites.

"Come on, Mom. Jump in. The water's fine."

"Be careful, be careful," I called as the children cavorted from reef to windy reef.

All the islands we visited showed traces of man that dated back perhaps a hundred years. On the flat rock ledges where we came naturally to camp, we saw clues that man had come naturally to camp here before. We used the scattered stones from old tent rings to build our fireplaces. We used the fireplaces of more recent visitors, and our campfires burned the charcoal they had left. Dead branches bleached white by the passing years had once been chopped by an ax at this spot. Ann found a bed of dried spruce tips used by some long-ago wanderer. The spruce needles themselves had disappeared altogether but the skeletons of the branches showed where the unknown hunter once laid himself down and called this island home, even as we did.

Jean: "Look, family, I built our fire up by blowing on a spark."

Ann, patiently: "We know it, Jean. We could hear you."

Ann dipped long wooden matches into melted wax and put them one by one into our same old wide-mouth jar with a screw lid. We had the same battered casting rod and lures as last year. We had a five-gallon can filled with clear gas, a small funnel, and a two-burner folding Coleman stove whose purpose was to supplement our campfires at unfavorable locations or when food might be needed especially fast.

On such frail devices our lives would depend from here on. But we were well equipped with the basic essentials. Each of us carried knife and waterproof match container on her person. We had bought a lot of canned foods and a supply of can openers at Yellowknife. We found you can't have too many can openers. They rust fast outdoors. What would you do if they all somehow got lost — horrid predicament to imagine!

"Always remember, girls," I instructed my daughters in survival techniques, "the main thing is the can openers. With these handy little instruments you will always be safe and happy any place in the world."

I will jump ahead of my story here only to remark that, after those two summers of cans, none of us have been able to look a can in the face again.

Jean kept rousing me at half-hour intervals all night long. There was almost no time of darkness. She wanted to recommence traveling. The wind, however, remained brisk. Out to sea it roared. White breakers spilled over the narrow harbor reefs. I refused to get up, and was called fat and lazy. Finally about 4 A.M. Jean shot a seagoing duck with the .22, back of the island. She came charging to the tent and demanded that I get up and go with her in the canoe, through a strait of obviously tricky water, to retrieve the duck as it floated away.

Summoning what spark of life I could at four in the morning, I said feebly, "No, and that's final." My voice was only a gasp. How often the mother alone wishes she might magically summon a deep bass voice, a really ugly authoritarian one, for these occasions. Jean kept at it. "You don't even have to dress, Ma. Just hop into the canoe in your long underwear. Then you can go right back to bed. I want my duck, and I intend to get it."

"No!" I tried to summon great vocal and moral energies.

"Mom, Mom," cried Jean. "You get up. Don't just lie there. My duck's drifting away. Mom, I sat up all night to get it."

I roused slightly. After she had killed it I did hate to lose it. But it would be crazy to pursue the duck and thus get separated from the little island: Ann and our equipment were on the island. We were on the sheltered lee side of the island, looking across a narrow strip to open sea. But what if we got swept away? An empty canoe is an easy victim to the wind. It acts just like a big sail. The island and our small camp might never be found again by anyone for the next hundred years.

"Where do you think you are, Jean? Playing games on some millpond? Never get separated from your camp outfit, your food supplies, your tent! A mistake could mean all our lives, don't you see that?"

"If my father was here, he would get my duck."

"I'm not so sure."

"If you won't go help me with the canoe," shouted Jean in anger, "then I'll *swim!*"

A mistake might have happened even with a more professional expedition than ours. Trivial incidents of insubordination and ensuing tragedy have dogged many famous expeditions, disaster unfolding step by step.

"You will be thankful some day," I told her, "but I will not let you or me or anyone else go after that duck right now. I'm not going to risk our lives for a duck, and that's final."

In advanced old age Jean would probably remember her strong feelings as that duck floated away from our island, and my preventing her from swimming after it in arctic waters — but at least she had a fair chance of living to an old age as the result. Swimming is something most people say can't be done here, although the children were doing it in the shallows for fifteen minutes or even half an hour every day now, plunging in and out. A doctor said he believed the human heart would stop within twenty-five minutes to an hour, for the person who is immersed simply freezes to death.

With a deep grudge, her .22 rifle between her knees, Jean moped on the arctic island in the slow dawn. The waves crashed monotonously as she watched her duck drift away.

"Something will eat it, Jean, it won't really be wasted. Please, nail down the tent for me, will you? Be a sweet girl." One side of the tent, which was pitched crazily on a rock, was puffing and flapping in the wind. We had had no soil to peg it to, and it was threatening to get loose and fly away. At that very moment one of its hollow metal leg sections, twisting in the wind, went rolling away into the water. Jean came to herself at this and ran immediately to retrieve the tent-leg from the elements.

"Will you promise to get up, if I let you sleep two more hours?" she bargained with me heartlessly.

"We will travel at once, any time," I said, "as soon as the wind drops."

I snoozed lightly, listening to the wind and the crash of the sea, and to comfortable crunching sounds as Jean competently brought more rock anchors to hold the tent.

"Time to get up, Mom. The wind's dropped," she kept saying.

"No, it hasn't. It hasn't dropped enough yet."

About 8 A.M. we started traveling. We canoed through the broken granites and gneisses of a part of the world which, so said my navigation guide, is "normally given a wide berth by experienced navigators." As we threaded our way up North Arm the skies were strewn with ducks; and the marble-veined islands, in the lively wind of early day, gave the illusion of being under full sail in a running sea. Because of centuries of facing these same directional winds, all the little islands were shaped the same way, their stone bows pointing into the wind just like ships asail. The granite and marble gleam orange in a fitful sun, and they seem to move forward just ahead of us in the purple sea as we push hard to overtake each one.

Too much gasoline is used in fighting a head wind. Where was shelter if the wind rose higher?

The wind dropped presently, and we lunched on an island embossed with luscious banks of green mosses, interspersed with the white "caribou moss" which is truly a lichen.

The island was like a ship, having a few trees in its center for a mast. When I stepped from our canoe's bow, dragging the chain, I felt the water heave against the shore. Suddenly, I thought of taking Grandmother out to lunch. It was like this: the parking problem, I mean, at a popular restaurant.

"Hop right out, baby," I found myself saying. Then my reverie dissolved, and Jean and Ann and I happily were on another island, ready to open another can of beans.

Ann went for firewood. "Mother, Mother, come quick, something terrible!" she screamed. With every hair standing on end I ran to the spot.

It was a dead dog. It had starved to death. Ann wept.

Another dog, very much alive, but put out to starve, was seen running back and forth on another island that day, barking and howling pitifully as we motored past. The naturalist Ernest Thompson Seton wrote about this in a book published seventy years ago. He related how the Indians left their sled dogs on these islands all summer so as not to have to feed the dogs. If such a dog survives he is claimed in the fall when he is again needed for work. Although even seventy years ago the Mounties were trying to halt this cruel practice, there are so many islands in the lake that the Mounties have not completely halted the practice yet, as we saw. Like Seton seventy years ago we were obliged to steer our craft far from rocks with dog prisoners, else the pathetic animals might have come swimming out. It was impossible for us to fill the canoe with wild dogs, I tried to tell the girls. (They didn't believe me.) Further, it was impossible for a traveler to feed the dogs from his own rations, even if he took them aboard. (They didn't believe me again.)

We had made our way about thirty-five miles up the inlet, catching pike along the way. I have a humanitarian principle which I call "being kind to fish." I taught the girls how to smack fish over the head with a stick. I do not believe in letting fish dry out slowly and gasp to death. When I see people treating fish like this all over the United States, I almost feel I am drying out myself. Neither do I believe in keeping fish alive by dragging them behind the boat by the gills on a stringer; it is a terrible custom. One wonders by what perversity that custom got started, for it has no basis in reason. Science proves that animals which die a lingering death actually deteriorate in flavor because lactic acids accumulate in the flesh from the fatigue and stress of such a death. But instant death insures good flavor. Eskimos used to tell me that, only in different words. It is interesting that science steps forth to confirm the belief of the Eskimos who quick-kill all fish, there being no people with a more delicate sense of taste than Eskimos.

But the tough slimy old pike were too tough to bang over the head. Since we could not be bothered to carry a fishnet on this expedition, we had to figure a way to haul the hooked pike into the boat. Their razor teeth and heavy razor jaws would have cut the slender line. Or they would have broken our old rod if hauled with a straight lift out.

"I realize you kids want to use our .22 rifle, don't you?"

"Oh, gee, please, yes!"

So the way we managed was for one girl to hold steady with the .22 as the other girl played the pike to the surface. When the pike tired and could be held in position on a short line, the first girl shot it right in the middle, with a watery-sounding "whump!" Shooting pike in this way was quite sporting. It gave the girls the chance they wanted to use the .22 and they soon became a crack food-getting team. And teamwork was necessary: the rifleman must take care not to shoot the other people or the canoe, and not to cut the fishing line with his shot lest the fish swim merrily away.

We got to where the islands thinned out, and presently we rounded a turn into a deep narrow rock cleft which afforded the best natural harbor we had seen on this coast. It was not surprising, therefore, when farther up the cleft we found a full-size village of miniature gray weathered log cabins, complete with a tiny church and a variety of meat- and fish-drying racks on several rock levels.

The glasses showed the village to be completely abandoned but still perfectly intact. A whole boat lay neatly upside down on a ramp. The doors and windows of the tent-cabins and cabin-tents were shuttered. A few ancient iron traps hung by their chains. Children's broken toys were scattered about. Dog stakes surrounded with piles of manure testified that at least a hundred dogs had lived here, belonging to perhaps forty people in all. As I said to Jean and Ann from my reading, "Do you know that there are two and one half dogs for every human being in the Northwest Territories?"

As they didn't say anything, I added, "One of the marvels I have looked forward to seeing is the half dogs."

"You won't see them here. They've gone away," said Jean.

Yet here at this remote harbor you certainly got the feeling that they had been here only a short while ago. The deserted village demanded to be explored. Ann and I together climbed the rocks. Jean stayed with the boat.

"Listen! Do you hear someone jingling keys on a chain?"

In the stillness we listened. "It's the junco," I said. "It's just a small gray bird. There is nobody here."

"I feel as though eyes are watching us, Mom."

"A person gets that feeling," I said. "There is nothing more lonely or spooky than an abandoned place where people have once lived." I carried my big rifle slung on my shoulder as a matter of old habit.

How profuse, how mellow were the burgeoning wild roses in and around the village. A million roses spilled forth, while long, lush, green pasture grasses sprouted from pockets of soil created in this rock pile by the permeation of sheer rock with the organic waste materials of the human and dog populations. (These people had never built outhouses.) The interaction of the animal and vegetable kingdoms was demonstrated perfectly before our eyes: barren Precambrian bedrock flowered with a diversity of species.

"Whoever they are, they went away in boats," remarked Ann. The junco was hopping about, grabbing the black flies which lived in the manure.

"They were ichthyophagous. They were fish eaters," I said. "Unfortunately, they have no caribou. Not many moose either, by the looks."

"I found two old moose hoofs over there, Mother. It must have been a two-legged moose, I can only see two hoofs."

"Somebody took the other two on a trip sometime. They needed meat. They have gone away."

"Maybe," said practical, worldly Ann, "some of them are in Yellowknife. Maybe some of them are sitting at the Gold Brick Bar right now, who knows?"

"It takes a lot of money to buy meat and booze in Yellowknife."

"It takes money to buy fishing boats, and even to paint them, Mom. It takes money for nets and ammunition. Their biggest problem from now on will be money," Ann said. "Just like us, Mom."

Across on the opposite shore a distant silhouette of land could be seen from the elevation where Ann and I stood dreaming.

"This place is Ptarmigan Village. This is where we probably ought to cross the inlet, Ann," I told her.

"Mother, do we dare?"

We walked back to the boat. I slid the rifle into the slot in the bow, being careful of its 'scope.

"I'm asleep," muttered Jean. "It's warm here in the sun."

"She prowls all night and she wants to sleep all day," diagnosed Ann expertly.

"Can't a person do any sleeping or thinking around here without being accused?" growled Jean. "If we had got my duck we would all be eating a big, fat duck dinner right now."

"You mean a big, fat stinking duck dinner. All these flocks of bachelor ducks around here that look so good are sneaky fish eaters, Mother says so."

"I don't care. I'm hungry for *meat,* and I would boil it up in a bucket and eat the whole thing if I had it."

"The natives prefer the fishy ducks, as a matter of fact," I told the girls. "Like the eiders and scoters and loons, you know. They are fatter and oilier. They have this wonderful ability to make Vitamins A and D in concentration. Doesn't taste terribly good and they boil up like an orange rubber boot; the meat may be quite orange in color. But the farther north you go the richer the oils of all the swimming birds and animals, and the North is the home of the vitamins before they got into the bottle, you know. Always remember that. But the law says that visitors can't eat them unless it is a real emergency."

We put out to an outer island adjacent to the village and slept away the rest of the day in a flapping tent. I awoke to mosquito whine and stillness. "Crew! Get up! The wind has dropped!" The crew were loath to budge. They were sleepy at the wrong time.

Hastily we threw skillets and chains, pliers and tent poles, pots and pans and coils of rope into the boat. When we had checked our gas and motor thoroughly and set the auxiliary tank in readiness to hook on when the first tank gave out, we put straight out to sea.

Jean plied her motor with familiar skill and Ann rode forward hunched under the overhung bow with me.

"Batten down all the hatches," I directed. "Jean, put on your heavy clothes and your rubber slicker. Draw the hood tight around your face. Aim right for that white streak over there across the inlet. That's White Beach Point, and the only place we can get across. No matter what, remember, we've got to hit that point, for the coast falls away after that."

White Beach Point was an obvious crossing. The measured distance from shore to shore on my map was about eight and a half miles of open water.

But I had made the mistake of trying to cross North Arm too soon. We should have gone still a little farther up the coast. For we ran, not eight miles, but closer to eighteen or twenty miles of open water to cross on a diagonal in a head wind, according to our logged running time. But you must remember it was not easy to tell just where we were at the time: we were unfamiliar with the coast, and the coastline was confused by the archipelago of islands in whose midst we traveled.

We put out to sea at a steady throttle. We had a good seaworthy craft that could take a lot of sea, as we had often said. It was no broad, open sportsman's launch which would fill up with the first big wave, but a long, narrow, stable, seagoing freight canoe, and completely covered over at times like this. The outboard motor rode high on the stern and had an especially long shaft to enable its propeller to reach the water. We had two feet of freeboard, and we bobbed like a cork.

All went well for the first half hour. Then we gradually met a head wind.

It may be that a steady north wind had been blowing out on the lake all the time, but that in the shelter of the archipelago we had not realized this. That slight dark ruffling of water that we had scanned from afar with the glasses had given little indication of what was really going on out there. As we got more and more into the head wind we found ourselves unable to turn back. We found ourselves committed with our lives. The arctic blast funneled down across North Arm on a diagonal. We couldn't stop forward momentum or we could be done for.

As the bow smashed down upon the oncoming rollers, Ann and I were at first snug and dry up under the "wave splitter" of the *Jeanie Ann*. The canoe carried its one-thousand-pound gross neatly; in fact the weight helped. The "wave splitter" really saved us on this occasion. Ann and I tucked its canvas flap over our laps, sealing ourselves in. In addition, we wore arctic-type parkas that had nylon outer covering, and we kept our hoods drawn tight so that only our eyes and lower faces were exposed. Underneath everything our laps were also wrapped in fur: the old "bearskin" of so many uses. There was no place for water to get into the boat, we thought. Yet soon the residue of the bigger waves began to trickle down into the bottom of the canoe and collect in the stern, while Jean at the motor rode with her feet in water, veering as best she could into each blast, trying to outmaneuver the waves. The realization that water was getting inside and that we were slowly losing buoyancy, along with the sounds of the sea and the numbing shocks of the ice water pouring over us, was enough to fill the stoutest heart with terror.

Jean in the stern had it by far the worst. That was why she was there. Jean could do what Ann could not do, and what I could not do. She had great physical strength and I have not seen many who could match her resourcefulness in such pinches. She was drenched with waves over and over again during our one-and-a-half-hour ordeal; she took the wind in her face, ears, and eyes. In her stubbornness she had not put on her parka hood when we left shore, and now she could not take both hands from the tiller to do so.

Fortunately for us all, she was nearer seal than human. She was in top condition for the unexpected icy test. Her daily swims in ice water paid off now. I doubt if many people could have survived what she did. Had she let go the tiller a moment we would have been lost, as the pounding sea tried to wrench it from her hands. Our lives were in the hands of this half-drowned, half-seal fifteen-year-old girl. I didn't learn it until a year later but during all this test Jean kept singing at the top of her voice, in the teeth of the gale.

For no money or glory on earth would I cross North Arm again in a canoe. They were like drenched sea rats, those thoroughly frightened but brave little girls. They faced that day an untimely death in a watery grave, but carried on and did their best.

As the horrid voyage went on I turned occasionally, stiffly, in my parka, and tried to wave back at Jean through the roaring seas. The wind was too strong to exchange a shout. Even the motor could not be heard. There was really nothing to say. We all knew enough to see that there was a possibility we would end up at the bottom this time. I cursed myself for my poor judgment. It was my fault. Jean would never let go of the tiller if she froze there, and I knew she was slowly freezing.

Each was deep in silent prayer to God to save our lives. The shore we aimed at seemed illusory. It came no closer, but seemed to recede.

Desperately I watched certain distant dim rocks down the inlet. They were my check points. Yet each stayed about in the same position as time went by. That could mean only one thing: we were just barely holding our own, not making progress. Smack in the middle of the inlet, we were burning up fuel full blast, but the 9.5-horse motor could not buck it. With stomach knotted in fear, I asked God what to do.

"Relax and listen," came the thought. The gale dimmed in my ears.

I relaxed and listened for a few minutes. Then came the thought: "Why not change your course by just about five degrees? Maybe that will work."

Turning around stiffly from the waist, I waved Jean to alter the course to try to get a slightly different angle of attack on the wind. She got my thought instantly. I saw relief and faith flood her face for a moment. Slowly we began to win against the north wind's blast. I had my answer. Perhaps our time just wasn't up.

Within another agonizing half hour of alternating hope and despair we were gaining perceptibly on a sandy beach, missing White Beach Point itself but near it, and our terrible battle was won.

Eventually we came into the lee of a three-hundred-foot white hill which stood back from the lake at this place — it was the only exposure of Paleozoic rocks to be found on this shore — and our canoe slid into a strange and beautiful quiet in the blue midnight. I recall how we waited poised until the moment we touched ground upon the long, friendly, gleaming line of sand dunes. Sand beaches! That's why it was named White Beach Point, of course. We had crossed over the Shield! We found ourselves in a different geology: a nearly modern world. Soil-covered, it had a larger size forest, the transition or subarctic forest which would be our companion from here on down north through the Mackenzie Valley. Geographers classify this type of country as northwest, not arctic. By the same definition, all of Alaska and all of the Yukon Territory, other than their extreme polar plains, are northwest.

A white fog crept in the moment we touched and enclosed the beach. But we were safe. We had made it. Our timing was right.

Jean's hands were frozen and wouldn't work. Neither of the kids could pick up anything and they couldn't talk.

I had memorized exactly what I was going to do the moment we touched. I half fell into the friendly shallows and pulled a long chain behind me up the beach; then headed at a stumbling half run for the forest fringe, leaving a trail of water behind me as I stumbled. I was after tinder. I had a candle and birchbark with me that I always kept handy, nested up under the bow.

Up under the spruce trees I found dry dead twigs, and lost no time about it. Each step through the dunes roused clouds of sleeping midnight mosquitoes and sand fleas which followed me back to the lakeside. Meanwhile the kids, with the ax cradled in their arms, were slowly climbing out into the shallows and starting to unload and work. The merest glance around showed the whole beach was a paradise of driftwood: what we always called a woodyard in our family. All ours.

In no time at all we had a beach fire roaring twenty feet high. The fire warmed the entire atmosphere for yards around and made the bugs retreat. We raked out little fires from the big one and thawed ourselves with hot drinks made from the lake water and instant mix. For a long time we shivered uncontrollably as all the cold inside us slowly worked its way out through our skins.

Realizing that as Jean had had the worst of it we must take care of her first of all, little Ann was hastily digging holes in the sand with our short-handled camp shovel, to support tripods. Then Ann went to work and laid a twelve-foot pole across the tripods, making a drying rack. We stripped off our clothes and started laying water-logged parkas, socks by the dozens, and tied-together sneakers and dripping life preservers over the rack. And then Jean extended Ann's clothesrack with many tripods for forty feet along the beach. Presently the entire contents of the canoe were draped over it. Our rifles and their cases hung by their straps; so did our poor camera. The collection might have been seen for miles, for several days.

While I bailed out the canoe, the kids pitched the tent in the soft, malleable sand, an environment we had not met before and which at first delighted us all. Now they could drive tent stakes down at the proper slant, never meeting a stone. For the first time in a year of exploring our tent was pitched properly, just the way it looked in the catalogue pictures. We hooked the canoe to drift logs by forty feet of chains and cable run up the beach. We were in business again. There were no aftereffects from our arctic dousing.

In civilization both girls were known to teachers as "the sickest kids in the West." They were customarily so vulnerable to virus infections and so delicate that they could hardly hold their own, day by day, let alone attend school enough to make honor roll. They had never in their lives been able to take the full physical education regime.

"Please understand, Mom," they had so often said, "the physical education course is impossible. We just can't cope with it. They always run the hell out of us when we're half sick, and they don't believe we're sick when we tell them. Please, Mom, help! You know it nearly kills us each winter."

"But I've always been a believer in physical education and exercise for young people!"

"Oh, for heaven's sake, Mother," these frail students would reply. "They kill us in school. It's as regimented as the Marines. They simply kill us!"

Unfortunately those words were all too true, as it turned out. Winter after winter the compulsory school physical education program ended up costing us a good deal of money in drugs and doctors, with the result they always dropped it halfway through the term upon their doctor's prescription. The children were called neurotic sometimes by some of the authorities; but the real reason, I proved to my own satisfaction, was simply the filthy air in the city. The polluted air caused a large segment of children to be virus-sensitive and to get temperature rises each winter. They caught each other's infections along the way, of course, and too often the regimented physical education program in the schools aggravated or triggered these recurrent bronchial attacks.

But in the pure open air of the North there is a sudden and usually complete cessation of all old bronchial ailments. Besides that, a person can take a fantastic amount of exposure to the elements without experiencing aftereffects which would be inevitable were he in the filthy city. Such positive good effects of the fresh air of the West used to be a fact, also. Now, mostly, we have to go to the North to find the same effects. My conclusion? I am not against physical education. But I am for cleaner air to breathe. It will be a hard thing to get from now on.

I shall take a moment to add some theories about cold resistance here. Some studies on cold and blood chemistry have shown that a person can produce a certain degree of resistance to cold if he will hold as small a part of his body as one finger in cold water for a few minutes regularly each day. I tried to do this back in civilization, but was too cowardly to go through with it. Anyway, my experiment was nullified because the housewife is obliged to spend a great deal of time with both hands immersed in hot dishwater. But since the children usually managed one way or another to get out of dishes, they were far better prepared than I was to be arctic explorers; and from the beginning they felt the cold far less than I did.

I believe if hot dishwater and hot tubs are conscientiously avoided by the would-be explorer, acclimatization proceeds rapidly out in the pure cold air. Body shivering and teeth chattering subside, and most northern voyaging, with proper apparel for the cooler days, becomes fairly endurable. However, I should warn the next explorer — as many of our old mountain men so well knew — that cold immunity, and perhaps also physical strength, can be quickly routed by just one hot tub bath.

Excited by the dangers we had escaped, happy as larks, we had never been so much alive in our whole lives as we suddenly were at White Beach Point. Only a few times before had I known such tremendous happiness. Each of the girls felt it too. Perhaps it was a happiness reserved for those explorers who land for the first time upon a new shore. To have known it even once in a lifetime puts you in touch with something nearly divine.

In the blue small hours we settled down to dreamless sleep in our tent on the wild dunes. The insides of the sleeping bags had remained dry through all the crossing. Life was so good! We had dry packing underneath us to keep us off the sand, and we could hear the fog dripping upon our thin, eight-ounce canvas roof, while the sea washed beside us.

A black bear came out of the forest fringe and gazed with wonder at our camp and our long colorful clothesline as we slept. When he saw what was here, astonished, he dumped a pile of manure beside a tree. Then he turned around and circumspectly went back into the forest.

23

Where the Mackenzie River Is Born

WE will reverse direction and go back southward down North Arm to the open lake. After that we will proceed generally westward, for the Mackenzie River flows out of the west end of the lake.

We will cross many points and bays where milky green water washes golden shores. We will be exposed to the open sea as there are few islands henceforth. In some ways we will miss the sheltering islands. We will miss the pike fishing, too.

But we can swim a bit, with life preservers on. Even I approve of the bath on nice days in the safe, sandy shallows, although, as I told my family, it was not my natural habitat. The first time they pushed me in I protested, "Well, at least I got my bath over with for the summer." To my discomfort, after that remark they saw to it that I got an arctic bath nearly every day, building up a big beach fire as a preliminary to the savage ritual.

Before we departed White Beach Point, Ann built a sand castle with a wooden cross affixed upon its tower, and I realized it was a prayer shrine. All by herself on the beach she held solitary communion; gave thanks for our lives, purged herself of the terrors of the crossing, and solemnly made ready for what lay ahead. She knelt there much of a day, hands folded, while the sea gently lifted our partly beached canoe, the campfire crackled as Jean silently gathered more logs, and the half moon, lying on its back, sailed above a spruce-ringed shore. It was a time for saying nothing out loud, but doing a lot of thinking. Here the three of us were, for a moment in time, alone in a world brand new and freshly polished.

(I thought how in recent years I had seen sunsets in America, over the smokestacks, power lines, and billboards of her industrial complex, that looked like doomsday.)

It was midnight again. "Are you ashamed to build a sand castle to God, Jeanie?" I heard Ann ask, somewhat severely.

"No, of course not," answered Jean. "But, Ann, other people have their own ideas, you know, and building sand castles is not the *only* way."

"Sand is most appropriate here, Jean," replied Ann with certainty. We slept again.

With the .30–06 slung on its strap over each shoulder in turn, the two girls roamed the glorious open lands beside the lake. This was plainly good moose and bear country, you could see. The people of Ptarmigan Village must have come here for moose. "If you see a moose or bear, don't bother them. It's just that an explorer should be armed. Nothing will bother you around here," I told the kids. "You're perfectly safe, except from yourselves. So, just don't have an accident. You could always use the big rifle to signal me with. But remember, be careful. I'm giving you our only big rifle, and that leaves me with nothing but the .22."

Wringing the water out of my navigation guide I sat at camp and read: "Behind the shoreline are numerous lakes and extensive areas of marsh, separated by belts of spruce, pine, and muskeg. The shoreline composed of Paleozoic sedimentary rocks, seldom rises above 150 feet elevation. . . ."

No human footprints are on these far beaches but ours. There are no soundings given for these waters up the inlet, and no map names.

Our mighty driftwood fires are tremendous, compared to the thrifty ones we had had on the Precambrian side of the water. Here we build them between two logs, making a six-foot linear fire with supported "burners" for several cooking pots, and we can get fancy sometimes. The trees grow large. Some stranded beach logs have come all the way from the mountains of British Columbia. Their skeletons make clean, white tables to keep us and our equipment out of the sand. Sand works quickly into everything when you live in a sand world. It gets into rifle and camera mechanisms, and even now we can't close our pocket match containers because of sand, so they are no longer waterproof. We have cleaned up the rifles but they could become useless easily. The camera is presently a disaster.

"We'll rig a sail," we decided, at one of our lunch stops. "Save on gas."

With a skinny straight spruce pole mast and boom, we rigged the canvas boat cover into a simple triangle sail, the same canvas that also at times served for an extra tent windbreak, and away we skidded at a fair clip, with the wind pushing us. As we had little keel to hold to the water, we might get capsized. I was rather relieved when the fitful wind dropped. Dismantled, we motored on down the inlet.

We slept again and Jean stayed up all night, looking for gulls' nests that lay in the path of a square-sided orange sun that hung just on the horizon. The sun changed shape and grew hexagonal as it rolled along the rim of the world. Silhouetted against it was a stony point where wild spruce grew. A coyote or wolf, trotting through camp toward the lakeshore, got the surprise of his life when he perceived the human beings here. He sprinted back to the forest, kicking up sand as he flew.

"Mother, get up! A wolf just galloped through camp. Get up and look at these wolf tracks. Don't just lie there and *sleep.*"

I went to examine the tracks about noon next day. "He — she — was working the beach for stranded fish, maybe. It's hard living around here in summer, I bet. May have little ones, who knows? In case a wolf or bear gets tempted by our empty cans" — I turned to Ann (Jean was asleep) — "you just get to work now and seal all their ragged ends down and bury them with the shovel back from shore. We don't want all our neighbors on North Arm to end up with tin cans on their noses, do we?"

It was a lucky wolf who came through our camp and not through other camps that are occasionally to be found in this country. The men would have grabbed a rifle and shot the absent-minded wolf to get the government bounty. I don't believe in wolf bounty, myself. To me, the wolves belonged here.

The reason for the wolf bounty is that Canada is most concerned about her diminishing caribou herds. A hundred years ago there may have been as many as three million caribou. They had lived from the beginning of time with wolves preying upon them, yet apparently remained around three million, allowing for temporary fluctuations. Nature's cycles kept everything in balance. In 1949 a census revealed that the barren ground caribou herds numbered only 672,000, and by 1955 these had dwindled to 279,000 animals. This fantastic drop in caribou numbers coincides with the introduction of the rifle into these regions, starting from fifty years earlier. Recent studies have revealed other disturbing factors. Migration routes appear to have become erratic — a characteristic of animal populations which may sense their decline and coming extinction. The reproduction rate, further, seems abnormally low, down to 4 percent in some herds. In herds subjected to heavy hunting (by natives) the annual kill was admitted by the government often to exceed the calf crop. With further losses to predators, disease, and accidents, all Canadian caribou may be doomed to extinction within the next decade — so the experts have predicted.

In desperation the Canadian government has sought every means to save the caribou. One of the actions taken, perhaps the only positive one which satisfied the public, is an all-out wolf persecution. But the government either could not or would not take steps to halt the admitted killing of 100,000 caribou annually taken by the natives for food for themselves and their dogs. Treaty Number 10 (1906) and Treaty Number 11 (1921), the last treaty dealing with the Slave, Dogrib, Louchcaux, and Hare Indians and others in the Northwest Territories, had never taken into account the possibility of the extinction of the caribou by the natives themselves. However, it is not without precedent for the government to give its people an opportunity to review treaties from time to time. So possibly there is hope for the caribou in this direction.

But the incredible tragedy of the caribou is that in the last seventy years, like the buffalo, they have vanished because of the greed of the few. In this short span Indians and Eskimos armed with rifles have destroyed their own food supply. Nobody else has even seen a caribou.

Now the wolves also may be hard-pressed for food. If the trend continues the wolves too may be gone. Then there will be no more fur for parkas. As species which are interdependent upon each other diminish one by one, the wilderness becomes nearly empty and a place of death, where nobody can live at all.

Very recently, however, the Canadian Wildlife Service has begun to realize that the wolves' survival is threatened. A small number of individuals are trying desperately to promote reforms in the official policy toward wolves. Foremost in the new thinking are Toronto zoologist Dr. Douglas H. Pimlott, who has been conducting a three-year study of white wolves of the Arctic; and Canadian-born naturalist and author Farley Mowat, author of a remarkable and moving book called *Never Cry Wolf*. Among Americans, Lois and Herb Crisler have led efforts toward reforms and have written of their own experience with wolves in the remote Brooks Range of Alaska. But unfortunately, the interested biologists and naturalists can produce only a tiny minority vote against the weight of the official views of both countries: that man should kill wolves — and all meat-eating predators.

"Wah! Mew! Mew!"

Jean was still sleeping in the tent. "Jean, what's wrong with you? What is it?"

"Nothing at all, Mother," came the call from the tent.

"Oh, I see," I said, relieved. "It's the gulls. I thought you were wound up in your sleeping bag and strangling, or something." A mother's mind is never entirely at rest. Even though we lived with bears and wolves as good neighbors on every side, I started up at each choke or gasp as the girls slept or played.

"Ann, *stop* that running up and down the beach with a sharp stick in your mouth. You could fall down and drive it into your gullet."

"Really, Mother," with dignity, "I am not as apt to fall down as you are."

"Quite," I replied. "But I don't run around with sharp sticks in my mouth, and stop arguing the matter."

With many a stop and start we traveled onward on a day of sun-drenched blue sea and dancing wavelets such as the world has never known. In a bay we met a fishing boat — of ten tons, I later confirmed — and we motored up beside its goggled-eyed crew of three.

Everything smelled very fishy. Two men were paying out a long net from a small, power-driven winch. The net looked about fifteen hundred feet long; it was so long that their end flag, about ten feet tall on a float, was over the horizon of the world as seen from our low canoe.

The two men were just finishing the operation as we came up; they were wiping their hands upon their fronts, and a third man, turning toward us from the galley, was just in the act of opening a can of fish for dinner. A half ton of fish were below decks, which they had caught. Their boat looked like an awkward square box on glittering water. We stared, and they peered at us myopically. We tossed them a chain and suddenly at very close range looked up into the craggiest, most snaggle-toothed and hideous human faces we had ever seen. At that moment I think the girls instinctively shrank back. Instantly I wished we had never accosted them. They looked like pirates. But it was too late.

But these were just fishermen, of course, reason dictated. We hadn't ever seen any commercial fishermen in our lives, and apparently this was just how they looked.

"Hello there," I said bravely. "Is this Alexander Bay?"

"No, dis one Melver Bay," one of them, with a very dirty, greasy face, intoned in a guttural accent.

"Where you go?" his comrade asked us bluntly.

"We came from Yellowknife. We are going on down the Mackenzie River to Inuvik."

"You cross dat North Arm in dat t'ing?"

"Yep, we sure did."

This about doubled them up. The horrid, craggy, greasy faces broke apart in gargoyle caverns of mouths, and such guffaws came out that it appeared they might fall overboard. Grabbing each other with hilarity, they pounded one another on the back and howled with laughter. "Dey cross North Arm in dat t'ing," one of them roared, and the remark started them all over again.

"What's so funny?" I asked.

"You drown," they laughed, and all doubled up once more at the idea.

"Get hold of yourselves," I said. "We haven't drowned yet."

The men, I thought, might be of Cree blood mixed with long-nosed, long-trunked, bushy-browed Ukrainian. They looked like the rude Russians you might expect to find out on the steppes. Here they were, on the steppes of North America, making themselves at home, too. I got a feeling of Kamchatka, although I have never been there.

I also got a feeling that they were up to something that was against the law. I made a note to avoid these types in the future. I hastened to push off, never having left our own boat.

"Please tell the next people you see that you met us in Melver Bay," I tried to get across to them. But I was not sure if they understood.

("See if you can get some fish from them, Jean," I whispered.)

"What kind of fish do you catch?" she cleverly asked them.

"Oh, we give you feesh," one of the strange men said, and, opening the hatch, with his ghoulish smile handed over to us three choice big whitefish. They were humpies. They had a tiny head and a little sucking snout, like a pig, and their bodies were huge and flat with shining silver scales. These finer fish never bit on lures; we had no way to catch them. What a treasure for us: the three great flat shining-white opalescent beauties, layered in fat. How they would sizzle over driftwood coals! Jean called them the Porkers of the Sea.

Taking our wonderful whitefish we beat a hasty retreat, leaving the men slapping their sides in gales of evil, guttural laughter.

I shall call that fishing smack the *Seesaw*. It had its license number on its side, and being an author with an author's habits I wrote the number down.

In another bay we met other fishermen. The second occasion was upon a gray day, and we came upon them surprisingly deep in a lonely bay filled with reefs: a place where you would not imagine a large vessel could go. The encounter was eerie, a mirage-like experience. For, until we had come within a hundred yards, we thought we were seeing a floating packing box. At the very last, the four-foot box grew into an eight-foot box and then suddenly into a full-size fishing vessel. The dim gray bay muffled all sounds.

The second vessel was a mate to the *Seesaw*, so I shall call it the *Seasick*. Its crew of three had craggy, snaggle-toothed faces and guttural voices, and one of the men was opening a can of fish and tossing the can overboard as we drew near. We just said hello and left.

When we ate later Jean seemed weak and chilled. She had been dieting which meant fasting, day in and day out. She had developed meanwhile a kind of abscess on her head behind her right ear, and it was giving her an earache. Perhaps it originated from some infected bug bite. The thermometer showed she had a temperature of 101 degrees.

After half a day we found a place for a suitable camp. We stayed over and rested, while sulfa pills worked on Jean. Jean stayed in the sack, and was served choice fat broiled whitefish that was probably as nearly complete a food as any food can be, comparable to good steak. At such times I read to the children aloud. When I explored my nearly waterproof attaché case, I could nearly always find some little surprise tucked away underneath the many maps and the navigation book. The feeling of wholesomeness permeating these readings filled me, if not my captive audience, with warm nostalgia.

"How about this one, girls?" I read the title of an article — " 'Cooking Mouth Watering Brussels Sprouts Dishes.' Or, 'Petunias Are Her Hobby.' Shall we try that one?"

"What are petunias?" asked Ann.

"Oh, here's an interesting and stimulating subject, 'Is Education Wasted on a Girl?' "

"That was what Grandmother read in her youth," objected Ann. "Can't you find something more modern and to the point, Mom?"

"Education won't be wasted on *me*." Jean stated firmly from her sleeping bag. "Do you know something? There's going to be a lot of trouble spots in this world, and about fifteen years from now, do you know where you're going to find me? Right in the middle. Doing something to help."

"But what will you do, Jeanie?" from Ann.

"I don't know. Surgery, maybe. Or perhaps some kind of research in the biological sciences. Something like that. Is education wasted on a girl? Ha! This world's in such a shape there isn't a minute to be wasted. If anybody has any brains, and I know I got some brains, somebody has got to roll their sleeves up and go to work, and *help*."

I told her I was really glad she had that attitude. I could just see her rolling up her sleeves, at least.

I read to the girls about wildflowers then. " 'Favorite wildflowers for many wives are' " — I read aloud — " 'the cohosh bugbane . . .' Listen, kids, this might be useful sometime . . . 'the St. John's wort, the stripped pipssissewa, and butter-and-eggs toadflax . . .' They sure have strange names in Canada."

"Never heard of them."

"Perhaps we are north of them, my dears."

"Thank God," said Ann irreverently.

"There's a lot you haven't heard of yet. There is the monkeyflower, the single-headed pussytoes, the four-leaf loosestrife." The article continued: "But it is sometimes difficult for the wandering housewife to distinguish a wild flower from a weed."

I also found this blurb carefully tailored to fit a proper American concept of Canada:

" 'Have a fun-crowded vacation in uncrowded Canada,' " I read aloud as the north wind blew. " 'There will be puppet shows, and a series of delightful Sunday evening concerts with a distinctly maritime flavor. There will be poetry readings. And, out-of-doors, the season's traditional regattas, highland games, and harness racing will round out the busy calendar of events.' "

Alas, future advertising will increasingly manufacture an image of Canada to fit the American materialistic psychology. It is to be a Canada of the new luxury hotel, the late, late nightclub, the extravagant cuisine never again beyond anyone's reach. Never mind that Americans have an anxiety over physical ease and luxury that amounts to a national obsession. The point is that the Americans have the money.

Finally I found an article that was more appealing to our expedition members. Its title in large type on a front page of "News of the North," was: "Old Trapper Returns to Home in Barrens."

We were camped in the usual pile of bleached driftwood. These clean white logs waited like tablets; they tempted you to write messages on them. Jean got up, still running a temperature, and wrote with a charcoal stick, across one big white log, "I was here." Jean's temperature went down but the lump remained for a long time before being absorbed.

We camped above Foam Point, a very bad place. After that point the map became more filled in, with charting for mariners. The shore of Sabourin Bay was littered with boulders which could have admitted no craft but ours into the bay. We did it nicely, with inches to spare, weaving between the reefs.

A southwest-curving coast lay ahead, with many enormous, empty bays named Lonely Bay, Caribou Bay, Jones Bay, Jones Point, tremendous Sulphur Bay (marked as "milky water with numerous weeds"), Cranberry Island, Windy Point, Burnt Point, Moose Point, and Deep Bay. And at the end of the lake, where the Mackenzie River begins, is North Channel, a place nobody ever goes — that is, not if he can help it. It is marked on the map with the notation: "Strong current and many boulders." How to avoid getting swept into this current could be a problem on the day when you tried to find the right channel to take at the west end of the lake.

Now we came slowly into the fishing grounds. We could hear distant humming on the lake and there was often a tiny stream of smoke on the horizon. We noted that the ships disappeared whenever the lake got rough. Where did they run?

We had no place to run to; and on many days we could travel only three or four hours along the edge of the shore, because of the wind. The freight canoe could run ahead of the big swells, but the sight of them rising above us at the stern and snapping at our heels was still unnerving. One mistake could have turned us right over. Frequently we put to sea and then couldn't get ashore. As the wind rose we would search desperately every undulation of the shoreline ahead, only to find rocks everywhere again. Not Precambrian: just rocks. There were no creek mouths to lend shelter.

At last, on a certain day, we came in on a crashing sea to a very small indentation in the shoreline, only about the size of a big room, near Bloomfield Point. We jumped out into the water and struggled to thrust the boat up onto a pileup of logs which was wedged there. These logs were dangerous. Some of them were rolling. They could maim or drown. But every day we had to save our boat and ourselves like this, so we were learning some ingenious devices and some fancy footwork. And the enormous output of physical strength which it took to wrestle the boat to safety, or to launch her again day by day, had been strengthening us — or so I chose to believe. Anyway, we sustained no injuries.

At this place we got the canoe partly unloaded as the waves crashed about us; then Jean left Ann and me on the woodpile and pushed back to sea for a run. With the motor wide open she was able to run the bow of the canoe up on the logs. The stern was still left in the surf, so to keep it from being inundated we lashed it to tough limber willows on either side of the "room." Then we tied down the canoe at about a thirty-degree angle to the sea so she couldn't move.

The girls had thus discovered an engineering principle which freed us from the constant need to find good harbors. Our craft was too heavy for us to haul completely ashore as men would have; but three ties on the boat log pile preserved her at waterline; and once the angle we wanted was achieved, our boat was tamed for the night, athwart the wedged logpile. We could bail it out the next day if water got inside. We just didn't want it demolished.

Ann found a campground back in the bushes which obviously had been used by other knowledgeable persons who pulled light boats up upon these same log rollers. Ukrainians? Crees? Slaveys? Whoever they were they had cut a series of poles and laid them across ax-cut tripods, providing drying racks for the boat canvasses and clothing of seafarers. The racks had also been used to dry moose and bear meat. The camp was right on a natural game trail which led under dense spruce cover across a neck of land to a lagoon.

"Ug! This place is perfectly horrid," cried Ann, revolted by the sights and smells which suddenly assailed us. "Look at all the tin cans and eggshells and garbage around here!" The former campers had profaned the forest.

"Come here, you guys. A washtub. People washed clothes here."

"Don't be naïve, Ann," I heard Jean through the bushes. "Nobody ever washes in this country, haven't you been here long enough to know that?"

"Oh, I see," I said, coming up. "The washtub is here for boiling up moose and bear meat feasts."

A giant discarded coffeepot lay on its side in a refuse heap. Like the washtub, it waited to be pressed into service upon another day. There were empty pop cans and whiskey bottles about. The previous campers were supplied far more richly than ourselves.

We hated camping in the stench of this place, but no other choice remained, considering the high seas. We pitched the tent in a small clear spot between the alders, and then, as the girls pressed me to do so, we made preparations to receive as possible guest a black bear. We could not afford to take the chance that a bear might destroy our canoe or food supplies or gasoline while we slept; and fresh piles of manure all over the place testified that it was literally a summer retirement center for big, fat, vigorous, enterprising bears. The animals lived most of the time entirely on berries. But they like to hang around, waiting for new people who might move in and leave garbage of the kind they had previously enjoyed at glad intervals.

"What are you going to do, Mom?"

"Decoy the bear," I said. "If he comes we must draw him away from the canoe and gas cans. We'll set up a booby trap with our pots and pans on this cut stump over here, see? Go get me our old greasy skillet, Ann, and the last of the bacon with it. That will draw him, if he comes. Now, it's just fifteen measured yards from the tent door. That's right where we want him. Not too far. You can't kill a bear far off. Now, we'll make a little blind with the sail, so if he tips over the pots and pans I can crawl out and shoot him right from the tent, and he'll never see me. I don't want him to ever see me," I added sensibly.

"Let me, Mom! Can I shoot the bear?"

"Not this time, dear. If you hunted, you should start with moose first. Bears call for an old expert like your mother. Bears are tough to kill."

I was actually slightly aghast at the boldness of my plan. But the action was justified in self-defense, to save our outfit. Common black bears are one animal that is far from extinction, and I quickly convinced myself that one little black bear out here would scarcely be missed if we should happen to eat him up, as I was sure we could.

"Oh boy," cried the girls, "fresh meat!"

"Shh, that's bad luck," I shushed them. "Don't say it so loud. Bears are spooky about remarks like that. Now, we must all go into the tent and to sleep. The rattling and banging of the pots and pans will wake me if he comes. Just go right to sleep."

"Supposing the 'scope is knocked out of line?" was my main qualm. I didn't know how to "sight it in." After years outdoors? How disgusting. Anyway, it couldn't be too far out at this range. I would get him when he turned sideways at plumb center, back of the elbow, and one or two shots placed through the thin ribs should do it. I had shot a black bear at this range before with only a .30–.30 and open sights. We were languishing for fresh meat. Our three weeks on Great Slave Lake were meatless. So were all our others. I could almost taste fresh steaks and chops already, and alder-roasted ribs; and fresh liver would be great, too. Of course, the sheath knife and saw and ax all needed sharpening. It would be a hard job for us girls to butcher a bear alone but . . .

But no bear came. That is typical of bears. It is typical of the wilderness reverie, the wilderness dream. We three slept in a pile of people in the tent. Jean shifted in her sleep with the lay of the land, and sack and all, it was she who ended up half out the tent door sound asleep behind the "bear-shooting blind."

The kids rose groggily quite early when we heard the wind drop. After a gut-busting struggle to wrest the boat off the slippery log pile, we left.

The bays passed by one by one until we were adjacent to Long Island. There we had a hot meal between rains. (In this land the weather may switch from icy showers to arctic winds to sweltering heat all in the same day, so the traveler is hard-pressed to know which of his equipment to grab for first.) We plowed onward resolutely. However, it is not resolution which pays off; it is strategy.

We hit reefs right at the entrance to twelve-mile-wide Lonely Bay and the motor stopped. Madly we paddled for our lives to the nearest headland, just in time to avoid being swept out to sea in an offshore wind. While Ann and I hung on in a margin of wild rice and willows, Jean opened the tool kit. She checked the sediment bowl, carburetor, starter, fuel mixture, rubber gas hose, and spark plugs, and tightened the swivel. Jean worked in a bobbing boat. Finally, for no particular reason, the kicker started.

Proceeding carefully into the bay — we didn't dare cut out across it — we lay to behind the next point as a tremendous sea over rocks was running beyond that point. We were all disappointed not to make it all the way to Garbage Bay (as I shall call it) that day, for Garbage Bay was where the fish packer was stationed, and where all the fishing boats in this area of the lake turned in their catch.

We had to find Garbage Bay. We had to get gas. The authorities would soon be getting restless as to our whereabouts. There would be communications there. We had seen a few other ancient villages on the lake, but all were deserted. The only habitation was the mobile packer that was said to be working in Garbage Bay.

I awoke to the wooden sound of the boat going thump-thump-thump on the beach. Jean heard it, too. The boat had somehow worked around from its thirty-degree angle on its brace-and-log tie. "The canoe's got a rock under its belly, Mom."

"Well," I decided reluctantly, "we better all get up."

We all got up and adjusted the matter, wearing just bras and panties and sneakers, so as to keep our clothes dry. Then back to bed or to loaf for the better part of the day. The girls swam, washed hair, and dressed for company, since our entrance into the society of Garbage Bay could not be far off. When it began to rain softly, I grabbed up bundles of damp woolen socks from my drying rack, gathered them tenderly, and rolled them into the small emergency pack, with condensed foods and headnets and things. My principal daily function in the expedition was that of Sock Dryer, or if you like, High Custodian of the Long-Handled Underwear. Since nobody else cared about that position, it was left to me.

"I was thinking, Ann," I heard Jean nearby, "how do people lose freedom?" I was protecting our foods from raindrops by inverting the dishpan over some of them on the clean moss.

"I'll think about it for a day or two," replied Ann, and she meant just what she said.

"I was thinking about it while we were trying to get around Lonely Bay," said Jean. "Skipper and I," (she referred to her motor), "have lots of time to think about things."

"Here's what I think happens," said Jean. "They pass laws, that's all. They keep on passing them in their state legislatures and in the national congress. Just pass them everyplace. Well, since they have no legislature to un-pass them, can't you see what happens? Every power group that wants something special gets its own laws passed. Soon they have legislated *everything* out of existence. You can't even go to the bathroom without special legislation regulating it. It's real easy to lose freedom, Ann, just give any nation a hundred years of legislation. They just keep on making more laws, and whisk! — before you know it freedom for anybody to do anything is gone from all the world."

In a way, she seemed to be right. Modern life had got so complicated that it might reach a point where everything in fact bogged down in a quagmire of laws and restrictions — but all of it, as Ann sharply pointed out, was due in large part to overpopulation.

We used to have many of these philosophical conversations as we followed the long shores in our adventuring. We decided that we were almost glad, by the way, that we had not shot that black bear. Had we done so it would have meant one bear less; and within forty years, some scholars warned, there might possibly be no more land wildlife left on earth, because of man's multiplication and his predation. We would not contribute further to the destruction of this now-threatened nature, if we could help it. For in our view nature was somehow linked with freedom and with all joy and goodness.

"Our children will curse us," one statesman-scholar told us plainly. That day has even now arrived for many children, right in America.

Two days later, after another icy drenching in our best and thinnest clothes, and having dried out by a bonfire built over water on a drift pile in the back of a cluttered bay, we reached people.

Garbage Bay turned out to be a wonderful natural harbor. About a mile and a half deep, the harbor lies out of sight of the lake behind a steep, forested hill, and is shaped like a comma. Its waters are deep and still, completely protected from the outer surf.

Rounding a bend, we saw the barge deep in the bay, surrounded by green hills. This barge, worth an estimated eighty thousand dollars, had been converted to a floating, mobile packing plant, owned by one of the four or five companies which worked Great Slave Lake. The company would tow the barge here and leave it for the season. About fifteen ten-thousand-dollar, ten-ton fishing smacks, many independently owned, worked out from here and sold their catch to the packing company. The fishermen dwelled in shacks and tents along one shore of the bay. Some had their families with them. They brought their food straight across from Hay River when they came out each spring. More food and supplies could be obtained on order once a week when the company fish-hauler came out.

I met one red-haired wife from Germany; she and her husband and five sons were here for the fishing. They had pitched a good tent. Although they had lived in Canada ten years, they still remained German nationals. We met a few full Indians, and learned that one resident Indian family lived at the bay all winter to trap. One of the young women, extremely attractive, told us she was of the Slave Tribes, more commonly called Slavey, and that these were the tribes we would meet right on down the Mackenzie to the Eskimo territory.

Aboard the packing barge the girls and I were given welcome by the husky Indian foreman and were served supper by the husky female Indian cook from Ontario, who was named Geranium. The dozen men living on the barge — the resident fish-packing crew — ate regular galley meals aboard, slept in company bunks, and were on a salary to the company. All were Indian, but were largely "outside" Indian, not residents of the Northwest Territories. We were invited to take our meals aboard a few days and rest ourselves up, but we must pitch our tent ashore to sleep, commuting by our boat each day. This we did, sleeping on a greensward made hideously corrupt by the accumulated refuse of previous frontier campers. Two outhouses back in the trees served the fishing community.

All were wonderfully kind and hospitable to us. As a special accommodation we were allowed to buy gas and food from the company's own stocks. The first thing I did was to get our rifles hung up to dry on the engine room's warmest wall, and presently they were cleaned of their sand by a young man who had had Army training. Meanwhile, other men poured oil into our propeller shaft, and checked our motor. We all enjoyed the break in the monotony that a rare visitor from the outside afforded. In return for our board and this hospitality, the girls found jobs packing fish. The floating packing plant produced its own ice. Wooden fish boxes were assembled by hammer and nails on the spot. Working with heavy gloves, learning from the experienced barge crew, the girls soon were grabbing gutted fish from the trough with good speed and packing them properly in shaved ice in sixty-pound boxes, which they hefted with the best of them along the track. There was plenty of work. The girls also tried at times to help Geranium in the galley at washing and drying dishes, although this task was less to their liking.

We were waiting on the weather outside the bay. We planned to make our getaway as soon as feasible, not wanting to impose too long.

I was in the warm galley when Jean came in as wet as a seal. What had she been up to this time? Well, it seemed that each evening the girls enjoyed a cruise in the garbage scow which dumped the fish offal of each day's catch for the banquet of the wheeling gulls along the bay's opposite shore, where people didn't live. But on this particular evening when Jean went joy-riding the scow was loaded with a number of young wild Indian companions; and Jean enjoyed the unusually exhilarating experience of being deliberately capsized, along with some garbage.

Not one of the young people wore a life preserver. They went out of the bay, pushed by an eighteen-horse outboard motor, at a time when everybody knew the surf was wild. The pilot then deliberately headed for the stoniest point he could find, one which had a reef of rock stretching out to sea. As Jean crouched with the others in the six-foot broad open boat, huge waves filled it, she said, and she knew it was foundered in the breakers, helpless. But the Indians were laughing their heads off. Presently everybody had to abandon ship. Never one to cry uncle, Jean only yelled, "I hope the rest of you can swim as well as I can." Everyone was dumped helter-skelter into foam and rocks. As the waves rolled back for a moment, leaving them afoot on the reef, Jean yelled that they might as well at least try to save the motor.

In the end the motor was lugged ashore through the sea-swept reefs by the laughing, howling, hilarious crew, and the sunken garbage scow secured by a chain ashore. It was reclaimed upon another day.

"Jean, you are too wild," I decided. "You have simply got to stop such wild carryings-on."

"I'm not wild, Mom. I just got taken for a wild ride. Can I help it if the young people around here get wild ideas of fun?"

"See that it doesn't happen again," I reprimanded her. But I felt my reprimands were somehow inadequate for the situation. Dear Jean: half drowned as usual, very happy, and rather garbagy. Jean the summer she was fifteen. Jean and Ann, headed for the Mackenzie country.

It was a lively young bunch, that fish crew. They liked to tease our coquettish cook, Geranium, so stout and jolly. Though she weighed about two hundred and forty pounds she was little more than a young kid herself, temperamental and high-spirited. Shrieks and giggles rang frequently from this barge as one or another of the mischievous crew seized our fat cook in the alley and tickled her, and a battle royal was on. Off for a few hours' lark in the woods between her culinary duties, Geranium could leap and run like a deer.

On this particular summer the fish-packing barge had got its first toilet aboard. Until now, the workers had just hung over the sides, at some peril, to fulfill the wants of nature. But although the law stipulated that the toilet bucket was to be decontaminated and emptied ashore each day in a pit dug for the purpose, the toilet remained in actuality but a formality for the record. It was only a board seat built in a little shelter, with a shaft which dumped sewage from the barge into the bay in time-honored custom. This had been going on for twenty years, presumably, before our travels brought us here. On shore right nearby, the people living in tents and shacks meanwhile continued to dip their household water by the bucket. Or the more careful ones got water out at sea. It was a matter of everyone doing as he wanted, in nearly complete freedom. In this way, even a very small population unfortunately can destroy its living environment quite easily.

I was in the galley and two of the crew were teasing Geranium, as usual, about her supposed boyfriends. To make her angry the most frightful thing they could say to her was that she was in love with a "Mountie." "Oh, yes, oh yes, I not give *you* a single look, you come my way." She tossed her head blithely. "You come by, you see yellow stripes hanging on my door." Then Geranium stepped out on deck, tossed overboard another consignment of tin cans, decayed cabbage heads, potato peelings, and steak scraps with gravy, and returned to her slimy dishwater. The water for the dishes and for drinking was pumped from directly under the barge and used without treatment. I had a feeling that it was time we were traveling on once more.

Just then someone came into the galley and said clearly, "One of the boats didn't come in this weekend."

"Which one?" Our idle chatter ceased and we all listened in shocked silence.

"They don't be sure yet. May be the *Seesaw*, what we hear."

We all waited for confirmation of the rumor.

"Who see the *Seesaw*?" it was asked around.

"I saw the *Seesaw*," I volunteered helpfully. "Wrote its license number down, too. Let's see here . . ." I opened up my little pocket notebook, as the fish packers — with fishy hands and slopping coffee mugs — crowded around. (All the boats were out again, and there was little to do until one by one they came in with their catch.)

The law officer came in from the inner packing area of the barge. He worked with the group on the barge daily; but like us he slept ashore in his own small padlocked government tent-house. Nine-teen-year-old Lucky Larne was the only Government Fisheries Inspector the government had sent out here.

Lucky Larne was a slim little fellow with freckles, a freshman in college, working his way through college by a summer job. The young Canadian had a man's boots to fill here, but such was the shortage of trained men that apparently no one else could be found for the position. Not only had he to inspect every single incoming fish for parasitic infestation — often working a sixteen-hour day, and more, seven days a week — and put the government stamp on each box as it was sealed, but he had a certain problem to maintain the law all alone in an area where he was the only representative of the law and where he might be expected not to be overly popular. He chose not to wear the official government revolver which was supplied him, and everybody amiably called him "Lucky."

"Where did you see it?" he asked now.

"We saw the *Seesaw* in Melver Bay." Ann looked toward the slim boyish officer. She had been helping him check parasites in fish every day, having elected herself to be his constant companion, an attention which it was clear he did not mind in the least. If he wondered at this dedicated scientist of but thirteen years, he said nothing, and answered all her questions thoughtfully.

"You sure it was Melver Bay, Ann?" he asked.

"Oh, yes, because they said so. Mother thought we might be in Alexander Bay, and she was just asking them . . ."

"And they said it was Melver Bay," I repeated.

"They're not supposed to be in either of those bays," said the boy officer curtly. "They were too far up the inlet. Did you actually see them fishing there?"

"Sure we did. We saw them set a net there," I said.

"Fisheries Department has caught over two hundred violations on the lake this summer," the young officer told everybody glumly. "Including use of too small mesh in a good many cases. Some of you don't seem to know the law changed this year to allow nothing smaller than the five-and-a-half-inch mesh." There were some half-voiced sentiments from his listeners I didn't quite catch. "The fish grow very slowly here, and we have to stop them catching the smaller ones, and they should know all along they can't fish far up North Arm."

Alas for the *Seesaw* and its snaggle-toothed owners. Word came in a day later that the empty boat had been found drifting far out on the lake, with not a soul on board. There was absolutely no trace of the three fish pirates we had met, and nothing was ever seen of them again. They vanished. Our experience meeting them still seems like a mirage when I think of it. Later the Fisheries Department saw to it that the illegal net and all others bearing the *Seesaw* flags were picked up.

"But what do you think happened?" I asked several on the barge and around the shore, as the news of the fishermen's disappearance went out on the radio to the Mounted Police.

Several people said the fishermen had been seen quarreling. However, with no rails on those square box boats, and the winding of the winch and all the nets to handle, it would be easy, it seemed to me, for a man to skid on the fish scales and fall overboard in those heavy rubber boots, and drown in his own nets — that is, if a man was to keep at the fishing game long enough. All here knew the risks well.

How could all three of them drown, though? Well, that wouldn't be so hard as you might think, either. None of these people knew how to swim. One man overboard and you could have a mix-up, handling the nets, the winch, and the motor all at once. There was no ladder or rope alongside by which a man overboard could climb aboard again. If all went overboard for some reason nobody could catch the boat. Freezing, if not actual drowning, would soon occur. As the fishing boats came in that day and each fisherman came aboard the barge to clean his fish, no one could think of anything but the disappearance of their comrades. But nothing was said, as the fish scales flew.

You rarely hear of violence among fishermen, no matter how snaggle-toothed they may be. "Did you ever know of a fisherman killing somebody? Did you ever know of any committing suicide?" Jean asked at the gut trough, as one man expertly wielded a blunt-ended gut knife.

"No," he told her in deep guttural accents. "Too busy working." His blunt ugly face and voice like gravel were like some fish you might, in a bad dream, pull up from the bottom of the sea. Like such a fish, he didn't give out information from the deep, and as I happened by the gut trough at that moment, I made a sign to Jean that perhaps it would be better policy not to question any of the gutters further.

"I work right with him all day long," Ann was saying to Jean, as I came up. "*Oooh*, doesn't he have the cutest freckles?"

"Who?"

"Lucky, of course. Who else?"

Jean only grunted. It was the first time in all their lives that the older sister was losing out to the younger one in getting the solicitous attention of a young man. Jean had been the unchallenged queen of the Slave River and the lake last summer. She had walked off with all the prizes. She was the only girl.

Lucky Larne was a fine man of the kind we can only call Canada's finest. He was strictly business. He showed Ann why some of the fish were rejected for export to the United States but were consumed in Canada; the American laws were very touchy, he said.

"We can all really trust Lucky," Ann told us. "He is a true Canadian and you know what that means."

We did. He would carry on through all odds. He was the Canadian who considers honor a thing beyond price.

"How does a girl attract boys, Jeanie? You have always had a deadly fascination for them."

"Well, in the first place," cautioned Jean, flattered, "keep your voice soft and gentle, like a little bird. Like Mother, when she talks to Gerald." I perked up an ear. "You have always had a very shrill scream, Ann. You have to be gentle and feminine. Whether you feel like it or not. . . ."

"What about my voice when I talk to Gerald?"

"You are just a little cheeping bird then, Mother."

"What about when I talk to Bumbles?"

"If you want to know the truth, you sound like a dictator."

It was remarkable how the kids got the gist of things, better than I knew myself, by the tone of my voice.

Summer was getting away. So when the weekly fish-hauling boat came to Garbage Bay, I made what I now believe to be a most wise decision; the girls and I asked for a ride on it and a tow for our own boat. The *Seaworthy* stayed at Garbage Bay only a few hours to load fish. When she left, we said good-bye to all our friends and went aboard with our sleeping bags and purchased supplies, and put to sea on a tranquil summer night.

The *Seaworthy* wasn't going where we wanted to go, exactly. She was going to Hay River, back to the south shore of the lake. But as I considered all the innumerable lonely bays and points of the north shore, I realized time was short. If we got to Hay River, from there we could follow the south shore quickly to the Mackenzie in a more conventional way. But we left the wild northern shores reluctantly, for that was the best game country we would see.

The trip across took about five hours. The lake was pink glass; the sun sank at 10:45 P.M. but hung around not far away and rose again at 3:05. The night's tranquillity was interrupted only by fussing between the kids as to who was going to steer the twenty-ton packer. (The Indian pilot didn't care who steered. He enjoyed instructing them by turns.)

Our engineer was a seventeen-year-old white boy who was born on Heckla Island in Lake Winnepeg back east. His people were fishing folk. He hated wolves bitterly, I learned. When he was nine he was called to help search on the ice of Lake Winnepeg for his uncle. His uncle had disappeared when he went out to tend nets, pulling a hand sled. When the body was found the opinion among the fisherfolk was that it seemed to have been pulled down by wolves. (Could a heart attack have caused the actual death?) At any rate the wolves had half eaten the body, and the boy hated them. Although they are long since extinct in the United States, wolves exist in every Canadian province: you don't have to go to the NWT to find wolves. The boy engineer was a child of hardship and poverty. Yet poverty among the fisherfolk with its tales of wolves seemed less dreary, somehow, and more stable in its emotional aspects, than the massive, frightening poverty of contemporary urban ghettos.

When I expressed surprise to our engineer that he held such a job at only seventeen, he told me that boats on Great Slave Lake were more often operated by boys than by grown men, because grown men refuse to operate many working boats, so ramshackle and decrepit are these vessels. The companies also use boys so as to avoid the union.

"Me, young?" The boy's pale face grimaced tiredly. There were circles under his eyes, and he had not yet sprouted a beard. "There's lot of boys running boats on this lake. Some younger than me, maybe. We got a job to do, we do it. I didn't get to sleep in four days," he said.

Just as our engine stopped in port at 4 A.M. the nose ring by which our canoe was towed gave way. It had been threatening to do this for over a year, since it first came from the factory. Because of the chronic weakness in the nose ring, it was a wonder that we hadn't lost the *Jeanie Ann* in the middle of Great Slave Lake, somewhere in that clouded and golden arctic dawn. Now, in port, we snubbed the canoe up by its thwarts, and all fell asleep in the bunks, secure in the knowledge that the town of Hay River lay right up the beach.

But I couldn't sleep long. I felt that the girls and I had better move while the calm lasted. So I brought the canoe alongside, and from the deck of the *Seaworthy* into the canoe the tired seventeen-year-old engineer helped us stevedore our motor, gas cans, and cargo.

I trudged sleepily to some offices nearby and asked that the Mounted Police be notified we were here and that we were embarking again.

"Do you wish you were going down the Mackenzie?" I asked the boy engineer as we shoved off.

"Might be all right," he answered. "But it's kind of a small vessel you have there. Well — take care of yourself."

It was just twenty-eight miles westward along the south shore of the lake from here to where the great river commences, and as Ann said later, "You couldn't miss it." But the south shore of the lake along here was exposed to the predominant northeast winds and there was absolutely no shelter when the wind blew. There is really no easy way to get to the Mackenzie be it north shore or south. As we chugged along the shore I anxiously scanned the weather. Sure enough, the day soon grew gray and miserable, the wind rose, and the journey turned perilous.

The coves were shallow miles out from shore and filled with acres of seaweed. A perfect mess was what this shore was. We were in rising swells, a half mile from the low, muddy shore, yet scraping bottom. Every few minutes we had to stop so that Jean could pull the motor out on its hinge and untangle seaweed from the propeller. After many dozens of stops, she learned to "buzz" the weeds out of the prop, using power, and thus could sometimes avoid the stop.

A nasty situation was developing as we tried to run before a wind, "surfing" the swells which pursued us. There were ominous sounds of a real blockbuster of a storm commencing to seaward. At least I was getting hard stomach muscles. They had been tight with fear and apprehension so many times that I had lost about two inches from around my waist — I was doing natural isometric exercises without even knowing it!

Finally, in a blow, we rounded the last stony point and escaped Great Slave Lake. We passed over a series of shallow bars and saw big dim islands and channels of all kinds under the rainy sky; and the water began to flow out of the lake. The Mackenzie River is twenty miles across where it leaves Great Slave Lake, and dotted with islands. In early spring an ice jam holds a long time, preventing navigation in these messy island shallows. We weren't on the best channel but it would all get together somehow.

Behind us as we made our exit the wild whitecaps of Great Slave Lake — exciting and challenging to the last — rose in gale force, and we entered upon the great, fabulous, seldom-seen Mackenzie River.

24

Sea Gulls in My Sleeping Bag; or, How I Conquered the Mackenzie

SLOWLY through the low, wooded islands the water flows our way and the great river is born.

The Mackenzie is 1,171 nautical miles in length, if measured from a line joining Pointe Demarais and the eastern extremity of Big Island, to the seaward end of the buoyed channel in the Delta in the Beaufort Sea, states the *Great Slave Lake and Mackenzie River Pilot*. Another figure frequently given is that the Mackenzie is 2,514 miles long, measured from Finlay Forks, British Columbia, if you include its largest tributary the Peace. But it is its great volume of water flow which, as much as its length, ranks it with the six greatest river systems of the world.

The river is flowing west as it leaves Great Slave Lake. As soon as we know definitely that we have really found the source of the Mackenzie River we put ashore out of the south channel and hurl ourselves triumphantly into the wet growth, and pitch our camp in the muskeg there, under a fine rain.

We have plenty of food for our great adventure. We have gifts and exchanges of equipment from encounters with people along a thousand miles of Canadian shores. A lost ax (something like the tenth ax) has been replaced by a fine sharp one, given us by a man named Earl Mackenzie. A Nova Scotian originally, he was at Garbage Bay. Earl has a log cabin home on some big lake which is tributary to the Mackenzie River a few miles down from here.

I pick up Mackenzie's ax and walk into the woods. I remember the old man's sea-blown eyes with their red lids, their brightness catching the glint of the sea and the wild waves. In his eyes suddenly it is the distant North Atlantic that I see. He is a man who has lived all his life with the elements, and he is a very kind man from Nova Scotia.

It is a hard business for a white man to try to make a living in the Northwest Territories. The country has no living to offer. Outside white men have not been allowed to trap here since 1936, unless they were resident before that date. In that case a man and his descendants are permitted trapping and hunting privileges on a par with the Indians. There are not many such men left. Our friend Mackenzie told us how he survives by being a sort of independent trader for the band of Indians he lived with. He fished with them under the ice in winter, ordered their nets, helped them build their boats, and marketed their winter fish. His grown son drives a winter tractor train from Yellowknife overland to serve the settlement at Great Bear Lake in winter. They are in competition for a living with the native Indians; but the Indians have it easier under the laws, and the Indians are subsidized by government dole.

I can hear him say now, "That's a fine little craft you got there. That little boat is seaworthy. Why, I would go any place on earth in that boat you got." I carry Mackenzie's sharp fine ax into the woods, and feel the smooth, worn ax handle that a friend has given me from his own hand.

At once we get the feeling and the smells and the look of the great Mackenzie Valley. It is classed by geographers as a northern kind of extension of the Great Plains region, or Northwest. The murky, slumbering river, on its way to the Arctic Ocean, flows between the arctic rock Shield on the east (from which we came) and the high, wild Mackenzie Ranges on the west.

The valley itself has a benign climate most of the way north in summer, and is forested with spruce all the way. It has more hours of sunlight the farther north you go, until you reach the point where the sun's warmth is counteracted by the cool breath of the three million square miles of polar icecap lying beyond: a cool breath which begins to be felt north of Fort Good Hope. At Fort Good Hope the lowest temperature recorded was minus seventy-nine degrees in February. But each post along the Mackenzie River records summer highs in the nineties.

Many people, including several politicians, have fancied that vast agricultural possibilities exist for theMackenzie Valley. The frost-free period, measured at Fort Resolution beside the Slave Delta, varies from forty-five days in poor years up to ninety-two days in very good years. The number of frost-free days fluctuates too widely. Summers are not predictable; nor can you always find arable soil. The Mackenzie Lowland is swamp and muskeg, poorly drained, cold, and sour; while the upland soils farther from the river are cold and sandy, and altogether without organic materials — not the friendly, developed soils which will grow crops.

What is the economy of the Mackenzie, then? What about trapping? For trapping too, the Mackenzie District offers slim pickings. The fur empire may have been fabulous once, when it was controlled by a few daring "gentlemen trading out of Hudson Bay"; but in living memory trapping throughout the Northwest Territories has accounted for only 10 or 15 percent of the total Canadian catch. The catch of the Mackenzie Valley is chiefly the stunted northern muskrat; and some beaver, mink, marten, wolf and fox are taken. White foxes are the chief catch of the Barrens east of the river. The catch has been decreasing each year for fifty years as the whole North has been overtrapped and overhunted.

Even in the beginning the great North of so many legends was a land of more shadow than substance. Sir John Franklin, in the most expensively equipped expedition backed by the British Admiralty of its time, starved to death with one hundred and twenty-nine men — with evidences of cannibalism — in 1847, just north east of here. The men, forced to leave their vessels *Erebus* and *Terror* when those ships became hopelessly imprisoned in the polar ice pack, straggled in groups, pulling sleds, across the sea ice and across the equally inhospitable mainland of the frozen continent. How many of the ill-fated explorers reached the mainland we shall never know. Eskimos queried by McClure and McClintok seemed evasive. Possibly some of the explorers were killed by the Eskimos. We shall never know. But the times were hard then, as they are now. The land has not changed.

In the years following Franklin's effort it has been said that some seventy-eight expeditions took place: they caused the North American Arctic gradually to take its place on maps of the known world. The Northwest Passage, which men had sought for three hundred years, was accomplished by ship by the Norwegian explorer Roald Amundsen — discoverer of the South Pole — only early in this century. The passage is not generally ice-free and Amundsen's voyage has not been duplicated many times since. It is a saga of the North.

The lands we penetrated by way of the Mackenzie River that summer had caused the death of many great men; but perhaps that is the way all lands treat their original explorers. Many lesser men also died here whose names we shall never know. It is difficult to convey to the outsider the distances and the intrinsic poverty of the one and one-half million square miles of this land. The trapper must cover enormous distances to find a single fur animal in his traps or rifle sights. (I myself, in the arctic Brooks Range of Alaska, have seen as much as four months in midwinter when nothing stirred, when not so much as a moose passed by the cabin.) It is a world that has always required from a hundred square miles to possibly four hundred square miles to support a single large family living off the country.

It is breakfast time, and we are seated on the tarp spread across the peat hummocks around a smudgy, punky fire. Our camp is only a few steps from the river's edge.

"Jean, dear, take Mackenzie's ax and go chop a birch into sections, will you? Cut two support logs for my grill, and I'll make pancakes. Ann, please go to the canoe and fill the primus stove with clear gas, and *please don't spill*."

Jean chopped lackadaisically, accomplishing little. I sat in my long-handled underwear — my second skin. I could hear the metal dipper clanking in the pail, and birdsong from the trees all around us. And for thirty minutes the sound of distant rhythmic chugging was carried to us on the fitful breeze. Then it was gone, leaving us to wilderness solitude.

That was Klinker over there. Or, maybe Captain Anderson or Captain Grey. It was one of the tug-and-barge trains coming up the

Mackenzie and over the shallow bars around the other side of Big Island into Great Slave Lake; and the stubborn, churning tug was just out of sight behind the islands a few miles across the Mackenzie River.

"We should have crossed over yesterday," I was saying. "We should have got on the track, where everybody goes."

But it was luxurious for the moment just to lie back, munching on pancakes and tough chewy broiled beef, in the dank muskeg and Labrador tea, and let the smudge fire cure you like a sausage, and sink into the somnolence of mosquito whine and birdsong and wilderness, and feel this empty land.

Just then an outboard motor's bark broke into our world.

We rushed out through green horsetail fern, pushing aside rotting alder limbs and pulling on clothes as we ran, and peered out through the leafy screen to see a boat loaded with cleanly scrubbed young white men pulling in to our shore.

"It's the Helmericks party," said a clear young voice. Then, as long legs leaped ashore: "We've found them, Jim. Hey, you chaps, they're here some place. Hey, we've been looking all over the place for you chaps for a week," said one of them, shaking hands with me. "Now, if that isn't just like a woman, hey? What are you doing over here? Don't you know you're on the wrong side? But simply nobody comes to this side, you know."

"You are Fisheries," I said. "Engaged in biological research. We heard by the moccasin telegraph you were in Great Slave Lake. We sure are happy to see you all."

They had been out on reconnaissance with their small kicker, when by chance one fellow had seen our canoe drawn under the trees. Their research vessel itself, an elegant white forty-two-foot government yacht, was not far away. They had amused their imaginations as they scoured the lake's west end, seining its waters for specimens. Failing to find us in the lake, they followed us into the Mackenzie, hoping to find three gorgeous mermaids. (They were disappointed.)

We served them all coffee from our primus stove back in the woods, then promptly enlisted their cheery services to break camp. Down came the tent in a flash. Sleeping bags and gear were assembled with the help of the extra hands. Then they took Ann in their boat to lead the way, and Jean and I followed on through the islands, across the Mackenzie. We found the sleek Fisheries vessel anchored just off Brabant Island, a known rendezvous of travelers here on the commercial navigation track, and a site, incidentally, of some excellent fishing for pike and arctic grayling.

A second smaller cabin cruiser, operated by an American couple in their fifties, also lay anchored here for the day. They had taken a run to Hay River, coming up from highway contact at Fort Providence. It was a sociable camp. At Brabant Island the Fisheries researchers pitched our tent for us on one of the frame floors which waited there on a firm, clean beach. And in an elegant dinner served aboard the government vessel that evening they shared with us their last steaks.

"How's Lucky Larne getting along? Did you chaps see him at Garbage Bay, and how is he doing there?"

"He's up to his neck in fish," replied Jean. "Tons of work."

I turned to the older man who was a Fisheries old-timer. "Seems to me that Fisheries might send another man out there," I said. "You must be well aware that he is outnumbered, in more ways than fish."

"The Indians drown him yet?"

"They would if they dared to," the older man allowed, smiling kindly, however, as he said it.

"I stayed right by Lucky's side all the time we were there," offered Ann of the young officer.

"I'll bet he was glad to have you for a protector, sweet Annie," the fellow kidded her.

So shorthanded was the Department for scientific personnel that the vessel was manned by college undergraduates in various fields of study who were simply hired for the summer. These boys did the field work for the government biologist; he laid out the summer's work and analyzed and classified the materials and records brought in, representing different places in Great Slave Lake and different levels in the water.

"Would you like to go see the breeding grounds of the sea gulls?"

At sundown Jean and Ann set off with some of the younger college boys through the tundra of Brabant Island in the middle of the Mackenzie. Large herring gulls congregated there in many hundreds, and the girls wandered, fascinated, among the feather-strewn and messy ground nests. It was a marvelous sight: the low lingering sun, the parent birds wheeling and screaming above the spruce trees, and the little ones huddled in their nests upon the tundra. But for human beings to invade the nesting grounds was unwise. The college boys, unfortunately, had not read *Argen the Gull*, a new, scientifically written book for children, or perhaps they would not have walked through the nesting grounds handling and playing with the appealing baby birds. According to *Argen the Gull*, herring gulls are cannibalistic toward offspring not their own. The birds grow hysterical, and mixing up families in the nests might cause many infanticides.

That evening, unknown to me, Ann and Jean each lifted up a soft, gray, floppy young gull and brought it back all the way to our camp.

Later the girls said the reason they took upon themselves the decisive responsibility of abducting two of the babies, contrary to anything they had ever done before, was to save their lives. On the basis of this argument we were to be saddled for the second time with unexpected hitch-hikers which would demand all the girls' instinct for motherhood as we traveled onward toward the Arctic. The two gulls would have to be hand-fed; when young these birds absolutely will not eat by themselves. They are passive. They need a mother.

The college boys involved in the gull abduction must have thought it a capital joke on me when Jean and Ann hid the gulls in their jackets and prepared to hide them in their sleeping bags that night. And when we embarked the next day the girls nested their gulls in a grass-filled bucket inside the canoe still without my seeing them — and covered them up snugly out of sight. (There had been a certain restlessness in the girls' sleeping bags all that night. Neither girl had slept a wink.)

Soon the wind picked up and our glorious day vanished. We were faced with the usual struggle for our lives. Mile after mile the little motor churned along beside a low, swampy shoreline, as the Mackenzie broadened out to what is called Beaver Lake: a big, shallow muddy nothing, infested with banks of seaweeds curling like snakes. Each time Jean cleaned the weeds out of the prop our forward momentum ceased. Just as we were in a most precarious position of exposure in the weed banks Jean called to me, "Sorry, Mom. Please excuse me, but we better look for some place to tie up, I guess. We're about to run out of gas."

I had assumed that of course our engineer and the helper always filled the tanks before setting out each day. Not to do so was inexcusable. But thoughts of seagulls had driven from their minds the coming dangers of Beaver Lake and the Providence Rapids, which lay above Fort Providence and through which we must soon pass. It is a well-known rule of boat safety that gassing up should always be done ashore. It is a ticklish business to stand up in a boat and funnel gas into the tanks. Especially when your funnel is as small as ours was. It seems the Hudson's Bay Company had just run out of standard funnels at the time we outfitted. So we accepted innocently a funnel which held but half a cup of gas at a time, almost as dainty as a housewife's kitchen funnel. But the Bay Company in all was very good to us. As we continued on down north we remained, therefore, "good loyal customers of the Bay."

I can't recall how, exactly, we successfully tested our loyalty to the Bay in the midst of Beaver Lake's weedbanks in a blow, using that microscopic funnel; but we did gas up, and we survived the day. And, having passed the mouth of Earl Mackenzie's river along the course, and having weaved through the Providence Rapids nicely, we presently left the ferry *Johnny Berrens* to our stern, and with it the last road in a thousand miles. After an eight-hour run we reached a high and lofty island soaring majestically above the river just above Fort Providence and within sight of it. We landed on the island to camp.

"Mom, we've got a surprise, and promise you won't be mad."

"They're awfully cute, see if they aren't."

It was then that I looked into the bucket.

"You know, Mom, we believe we can keep them alive and raise them."

We pitched the tent and lashed the extra ten-ounce canvas over the side of it to give protection and anchorage against the northeast wind. In the middle of the night the wind and rain spatters stopped and the extra canvas was removed to prevent suffocation of the inmates. At that time thousands of mosquitoes surged suddenly forth from the beach. In my troubled sleep I pulled my headnet over my head. I felt girls crawling in and out over my face, carrying gulls. The gulls couldn't sleep outside because something might eat them outside the tent's safety. And they had to be force-fed clusters of lovely, gelatinous fish eggs. These got tipped over.

Fortunately I was a sound sleeper during my conquering of the Mackenzie. (Sound sleep of nights is a reward of the truly conscientious and honest explorer.) I only knew it dimly when the two gulls in the little tent emerged from their bucket, and strolled over our inert bodies, and "plopped" all over the sleeping bags, leaving lime trails, and screamed like diesel horns for feedings.

So it was that we had come two hundred and fifty miles from Yellowknife to the first town. We awoke to a late Sunday morning. We could see Fort Providence across the river, using the binoculars, as the mist lifted. The children, however, were not all eager to make calls at Fort Providence.

"Just like dead," Ann put it, as the binoculars scanned the town.

"Very typical," I mused. "Girls, it makes me remember the Alaska river towns twenty years ago. The best way is always plan to camp right above any town before actually going into town."

"Why?"

"Why, for one thing, there's no way to take a bath or clean up there, and you don't want the people to see you. There's no place to sleep, so you need to be all rested before you hit town. There's not even any place to camp. No rest rooms. Nothing to eat. It's best to get those things all attended to at your own camp, and then go into town fresh as a daisy. This party doesn't look very fresh this morning. Let's try to clean up somehow, for all those people over there: the police officer, the teacher, the Roman Catholic priest, the Anglican father, and the respectable Indians."

Eventually we motored over the swift current from the island to town and tied up at the RCMP dock. It was breakfast time, and

Ann and Jean and I were wearing mud-caked boots and floppy raincoats; the girls carried their birds hidden under wraps. We checked in at the Mounted Police office, reported our progress, and picked up the mail which was held for us there.

But the only people we actually ran into to talk with on that rainy Sunday were some middle-aged American motor tourists who sat over coffee at the Snowshoe Café. We hesitated to knock on the doors of private homes — the tidy little government houses — and of course what usually happens at these villages is that nobody ever comes out.

Travelers who have passed through towns in present-day Alaska and in the Yukon Territory tell us there is a frontier type of friendliness exceeding every dream they may have harbored of the old West. These "frontier traits" are not evident as you go down into the Mackenzie country. Nor were they always true in the Alaska of old. When a village is truly isolated from the mainstream of life there is virtually no eagerness to meet with travelers and outsiders. The more physically isolated the village the more this holds true.

Perhaps this hearty spirit of frontier life, of friendliness and mutual protection, is nearly lacking in the NWT because there is not enough of a white community to generate it. The vigorous entrepreneurs of Alaska and the Yukon want to know what is happening in their communities. But the entrepreneurial motivation is lacking in the Northwest Territories. There, villages are still very much dominated by missionaries who began coming here in 1858 — only shortly after Sir John Franklin. As the missionaries see the matter, their duties to their wards do not include being hearty boosters of the country to outsiders. And they are here on special duties which cause them to be bound close to the village, often to have little interest in or awareness of outside things. Even the missionaries, however, get around locally better than the public school teachers. Frequently the missions maintain their own boats and guides for summer travel. But teachers, flown in and out from these posts, not only live isolated from the outside world but are helplessly inept in the hostile wilderness which surrounds them. They stay cooped up in their houses the year round. Turnover of teaching personnel is just about seasonal, because of the melancholy and inertia induced by confinement: there is rarely the same teacher at any village two years in a row.

Today, as many as three hundred Indians will live in many villages which historically housed only fifty to a hundred Indians; and often in the past they were not in their town cabins much of the year. Today the Indians just wait around a lot of the time for the dole. Three hundred Indians here is overpopulation. They are suffering from malnutrition, living on cheap starches such as flour and beans. They are hungry and cold. The surrounding country cannot support them, even to the extent that it once did.

I asked the police officer a few questions about Fort Providence, before we left. Was the river safe to drink? The officer said that the residents at Providence bought their water at two cents a gallon, hauled by a water truck, after the water was run through a treatment plant and chlorinated. Water was piped direct into the new government houses, where government personnel paid two cents a gallon. This was an expensive rate to pay here in a world of water. The majority of the Indians whom the teachers and missionaries served did not drink this water. Nor did the Indians have any bathhouse or clothes-washing facilities like those enjoyed by their well-meaning mentors. These facilities, which were lacking in all Mackenzie River villages we saw with the exception of Inuvik at the end of our journey, would be to the American mind the most immediate need of a populace which has now been assisted by the white man for over a hundred years. A hundred years of being unwashed, yet dealing daily, praying daily, with washed white men! The white man appears to be superior in each daily encounter, because he knows, and everybody knows, he smells better! How much nicer it would be for everyone if every village in the North might be equipped with a public bathhouse, with government men to maintain it, I often thought.

That night we camped below Fort Providence on one of a pair of tiny rock atolls which guarded the entrance to big, misty Mills Lake.

"I've got a surprise for you," I told the girls.

They unwrapped the burlap package I passed them from the canoe.

"*Meat!*" came joyful cries.

We hadn't been able to buy any provisions in the village on Sunday, and the next stop, Fort Simpson, lay one hundred and sixty miles ahead.

"It's moosemeat," I told them. "Fresh a few hours ago. Only, soon as you eat it, forget it, because it's illegal."

"Where did you find it, Mom? Not those American tourists . . . ?"

"Of course not, silly. Only certain people know there's moosemeat in that town, and in the summertime, too. But tonight we eat!"

Confined for three stormy days on the little atoll, we were running out of both moosemeat and wood (the primus stove was on the fritz) when the clouds finally lifted. I can see us now: Ann in her rain parka singing to herself as she probes the Mackenzie waters for fish egg clusters. Jean standing alone at the head of the island in the soft rain, feet planted apart, thumbs in pockets, watching for the tug to come by. When finally it comes, she waves — we all wave — and Jean relapses into her solitary mood.

Beyond the last atolls we could see the opening of Mills Lake. It was eleven miles long and ten miles across, and curved westward. It must be calm for us to traverse it, for it was shallow, weed-cursed, and mean as any swamp can be, if the buoyed navigation track was not followed accurately right down the middle.

Once, they said, a young American girl had set off through here alone in a canoe. When her parents were at Fort Providence she saw her chance to leave the road and civilization behind, and grabbing the first Indian canoe that could be taken, she pushed off for the beyond. She had no provisions. She didn't even have proper clothing. Perhaps she hoped the wilderness would envelop her forever. It almost did: her escapade was nearly suicidal. We learned that the fourth day of her voyage a party of Indians coming up the Mackenzie under power found her and brought her back to her boring old parents. There is no escape in the wilderness, unless you have proper equipment to sustain you as we did, or at least some maps and some elementary knowledge of what you are doing. Yet I can certainly understand the impulse that led the girl to set off upon the river.

Everything that I knew about the river ahead I learned from seeking out the Indians at the villages. The Civil Service people from outside, serving for a limited time here, just did not know what river life was all about; nor could they be expected to.

"Are there many trees for the fire?"

"Ah, yes, there are many trees for to build the fire. It is good country all the way down. Many muskegs but always the stands of spruce. You will have not trouble at all."

Or, "Watch out for them rapids below there. Some fellow drown there sometime." The Indians could tell you — and told you truly and gladly — where to catch fish. The Indians could tell you which cabins along the Mackenzie banks were inhabited at the moment, and which abandoned.

The Mackenzie Valley was an alluring land, all the way. It had managed up until now to support a whole people. God knows how it did it, but it still did. It was a far friendlier river than the muddy, churning, lonely Peace and Slave that we had followed the year before. The cleaner water and stabilized riverbed, with firm footing on the banks, filled us with joy. The old Mackenzie never grew tedious. Life on the river out under the sky with nature was at once engrossing, challenging, and soothing to every sense.

Small Slavey camps, catching fish, were occasionally to be seen. The families lived in white wall tents which gleamed from afar, hinting of human habitation. After the last road the farther north we went, the happier and friendlier to us the Indians were.

Right down the channel we went through Mills Lake. The water was glassy calm. Not a moment was to be wasted, for safety's sake. A mirage appeared in the evening sky over the thin pencil line which was the horizon of the earth; it looked like a small, misshapen box.

Presently my binoculars saw smoke. But Radium Line tugs are

smokeless. Finally we came abreast of an antiquated, shaking, smoking tug with what appeared to be a solitary family on board; they were pushing a small barge carrying their household things and two cars. It turned out that an entrepreneur from Fort Simpson made this run to transport people with cars out of the North or from one post to another.

Our camp this night was very different. It was far back on some unnamed little tributary of the Mackenzie. The water was deep and clear there, like a pane of black glass. Delicate, thin, jointed weeds rose from the black depths; it was an absolute fairyland. We fished, but no fish popped here. The beauty and the silence affected us: we talked in hushed tones. We had found an old Indian campsite complete with handy hooks and racks, and at dusk we pitched our tent and built our fire under the poplars. Strangest of all, there were few mosquitoes. There were only mushrooms for the fairies and elves. As we slept, one or two secret bank beavers came out, and worked at cutting down the poplars around us all night long.

Ann was most strongly moved by this place. She went into a sort of rapture. She has often remarked since that the feeling was quite beyond words to convey.

"It was just some old Indian trapline," I say.

"But, Mother, there was something strange! Even the beavers were so spooky. Why was it so silent?"

Jean didn't go for the spooky, silent places, off the beaten track. Their richness was oppressive. There are a million such places, rich-green, hypnotic, mirrored in water. Enchanted by the winding, dreamlike labyrinths, always longing to know just where they went to, we followed and camped again on another black-and-silver-watered hidden forest aisle. We found campsites which had not seen anyone for at least ten years, apparently. Why had the clock stopped? Even the birds in the trees did not sing in the painted secret places.

"Why are the birds still, Mother?"

"Because it is midsummer, I think," I replied uneasily. Over my shoulder, just before I turned around, I sensed shadows of prankish spirits. If I were an Indian I wouldn't come back here alone.

We became so fascinated with exploring the bypaths of the Mackenzie that later Captain Klinker told me that the tug captains lost track of us during this period. It was more than a month, and they were a little concerned.

They needn't have worried. The expedition moved at its own pace. The kids spent nearly six hours each day at camp work and gull care. They did just about everything themselves except that I did the cooking and dishwashing. I also advised, cajoled, proselytized, picked up a good deal, toted loads, and arranged loads, exactly as any mother does at home. And just as at home, the young committed each day the utmost sacrileges. They kicked sand into the pancake batter and went barefooted and hurt their feet. They wouldn't wear their woolens, they ignored their toothbrushes, and they threw knives and tools carelessly on the ground; I had to fight the housewife's unending battle against the loss of our equipment. They did not hoard birchbark or candles, and never considered the problem of starting a fire on a wet day. They played and fussed along the way, and they swam in the brawling blackwater creeks and along the white Mackenzie sands, with their big happy herring gulls.

Once the glasses picked out what looked like a big black log down the shore; but it had branches on one end of it which moved. I gave the girls the camera and sent them out to chase a big black bull moose for their exercise. The moose was wary. Of course they never got near him, but they had fun trying. I baby-sat with the gulls.

One day, when there was a wind, Jean was dragging her laundry behind the boat. The lack of modern laundry facilities was becoming an acute problem. And we had been twenty-three days without a bathtub.

Ann and I sat in the bow brushing our teeth.

"*Stop that!* Your spit is blowing back at me!" shouted Jean. Moments like this broke the monotony of a thousand miles of river: Jean spiritedly responded to the teeth-brushing up front by speeding up and steering the boat in erratic loops, despite Ann's and my protests.

I can see us now. Ann is busy at mixing up the powdered milk as we travel down the middle of the Mackenzie; she is thoughtfully stirring it with her comb. At the helm, Jean is tossing our extra spark plugs up and down.

"Jean, please be careful. Can't you think of anything more constructive to do?"

"Just passing the time, Mom. Skipper and I have to sit here a lot of miles."

"Then, haul in your laundry before we lose it, and *anyway, please stop juggling the extra spark plugs, will you?*"

"Don't shout at me, Mother. You're making me nervous!"

At the place called the Upper Ramparts, or "Head of the Line," the river abruptly narrowed between steep cliffs. You sensed an excitement, a speed-up of the current. Jean said that it was as though the devils that lived under the river were trying to wrest the propeller out of your hands. Here the whole Mackenzie cut into hundreds of feet of unconsolidated glacial material and squeezed down to half a mile wide to plunge through sixty miles of rapids to Fort Simpson. We had a good fast ride there, but no fear of rocks sticking out, since the river is perhaps a hundred feet deep or more.

On our left hand the flat-topped Horn Mountains rose up for a thousand feet. Over in that direction was the Yukon Territory, classed (like most of Alaska) as northwest, not true arctic. The Northwest is characterized by spectacular mountains and deep, gashed, linear valleys. The fact that what little agriculture exists in these valleys must be government subsidized, still does not make it "arctic" with the geographers, though arctic it may be to explorers, and colder than the Arctic may be some of its winter temperatures. Jean kept looking up to the mountains, wide-eyed. She gazed up to the high windswept rocks, the sere short pasture grass of the mountain sheep — Stone, Dall, and Rocky Mountain bighorns — and she watched the storms' shadows moving across mountain slopes and mysterious valleys.

"Hey, you guys," she said once, "you know, I think I like winter the best. I'll bet winter is the best around here."

Some people do, in fact, think winter is the North's best season. However that may be, certainly winter is its true self here; and to

the hunter of earth's high latitudes, winter can be the season of great travels, great adventures, even great feasts.

We came to the point where the mighty Liard River comes crashing out of the high country to join the Mackenzie and swell it to twice its size. Here we would find Fort Simpson.

"Keep to the left side of the river, the left side," I kept reminding Jean at our tiller. "Get ready to cross the mouth of the Liard as far into its mouth as we can get. Or we might get swept past the whole town."

Fort Simpson occupies an island which has been built up at the confluence of the Liard with the Mackenzie. The current is swift. Two fellows had drowned when their boat hit some driftwood and overturned here, just a week before we came. And periodically, like the town of Hay River, the whole town of Simpson gets flooded by an especially powerful spring breakup and has to be rescued. The taxpayers of Canada in the cities to the south and east pick up this tab. Every spring they pay about fifty thousand dollars to rebuild twelve miles of washed-out road which connects Simpson to its airport on the mainland. This is all a part of the great northern game. Canada's North continues increasingly to drain her economy, and the North is unable to put anything back into it. The basic problem is that a permanently frozen subsoil or permafrost exists, probably all over the Northwest Territories. (Not all of it is likely ever to be surveyed.) The permafrost dates from the last Ice Age; it inhibits crop development because soil temperatures cannot rise to the level necessary for fruition.

Fort Simpson is an old place. It was named for a great Hudson's Bay explorer — either the powerful factor who built trading posts, or his brilliant young nephew. The first Simpson had his nephew murdered by Eskimo guides. It was not clear today which "Simpson" Fort Simpson was named after. (Personally I should prefer the young nephew to the old murderer uncle.) At any rate, we found its population today somewhat over three hundred persons; and half of them were actually outside whites — more whites than we would see again! They were, of course, employed in administrative duties — educational, medical, and so on — serving the Indians of a region covering tens of thousands of square miles, as well as Eskimos brought to them from northward. The government had boosted Simpson to the level of an important administrative center. When we visited there, there was a rapid turnover among the government people. Over 80 percent of them were new each fall.

25

Mackenzie River People

BEFORE we reached Fort Simpson we met two white men.

It was a bitter, rainy day when we put in, half frozen and in filthy rags, at the little Indian Village at Jean Marie River. I had it in mind to try to buy whitefish from the Indians. But, unknown to me, a solitary bachelor teacher was living in that village: a man in his forties, who had earlier studied for the priesthood. He had chosen to live away from his own kind, in an undeveloped part of the world, and to give a service of himself. He had served alone there for a year. Numbly stumbling up a path, I came upon the lone man surrounded by adoring and adorable little Indian children.

"I've got my two girls in the canoe down at the landing," I introduced myself to the surprised misogynist. "We are making a voyage of the Mackenzie. . . . But they're shy types. You see, we haven't seen a tub for several weeks, and they refuse to get out of the canoe. For another thing, they have some sea gulls on their laps which they refuse to let go of. . . ."

The Indian children were chanting, "White man here! White man here!"

They thought I was a man, or perhaps they had no other word for me. "They're singing my song," I said nervously.

He didn't say much, just looked sympathetic. He accompanied me silently down the mud path between barking dogs, followed by swarms of grinning children, and abruptly addressed Jean and Ann, in a surprisingly cultivated, very British tone of command:

"Come now. Time to get right out of there." He said the words with all the authority of several thousand years of British Empire behind them, and out they climbed at once, obedient to him.

"Well!" I said. "That's a relief, anyway."

That night the lone government teacher cooked a glorious meal, and we spread our bags out in the classroom which adjoined teachers' quarters, and slept beneath a civilized roof. The three dirty wanderers had tub baths. But we had to delay washing our clothes, for no dryer had been furnished with the teacher's washing machine — one of those occasional oversights on the part of government planners.

We have said that there are not many true resident whites in the Northwest Territories. But we were forewarned by the outside teacher that we would be able to meet old Whiting, age seventy-three, along the Mackenzie, if we watched for a small sawmill and a much larger pile of sawdust.

True to arctic summer habit, all awoke late at Jean Marie Village, for of course we had talked into the wee hours the night before. We stayed for part of that day so the sun could dry out our stuff, including the waterlogged life preservers, spread out on the dock. Consequently, it was early afternoon when the teacher bade us farewell with a final meal. Away we went, Ann at the throttle today, and the Mackenzie a dream between its green, wooded banks.

It was just three miles down to Whiting's Sawmill and teatime. We climbed there to a homey two-room frame house on a steep hill.

Whiting, an American, had come to the Mackenzie country in 1918. We found him an energetic, rebellious, stubborn seventy-three, with a warm, womanly little Indian wife beside him, and five children under the age of sixteen. The old man was expansive and garrulous. His arctic family were quiet and unobtrusive, saying little. Since his wife was not much beyond thirty-five, it seemed probable that he, like many such men I recalled in Alaska, might have outlived several Indian wives.

In the friendly cabin on the hill we had coffee and fresh saskatoon berry pie. Beside the house some nice potato plants thrived. Whiting told us he had even raised watermelons of a certain strain along the Mackenzie banks (I never saw them!), letting them ripen later in a root cellar. He told us that over a thousand cases of canned peas were eaten each year by the inhabitants of Fort Simpson downriver, but he knew positively that the Mackenzie country could grow all its own peas if only the government would include an agricultural campaign and train the Indians to work the soil. As it was, the government only offered formal classroom studies, which Whiting said were of little use out here and left the Indians half literate with no livelihood other than a future of waiting around to collect their government relief checks: truly a most demoralizing situation. The debate about Mackenzie Valley agricultural possibilities is perennial; but his argument seemed most reasonable on that beautiful sunny day.

"It's a shame they don't use this country right, it's a fine country," the old man contended. "The natives have even forgotten how to make moosehide moccasins, how to make snowshoes and dogsleds. Do you know, they are now ordering them all from outside, with their relief checks?" (This may or may not have been accurate.)

The old man had raised beef cattle for many years at various sites along the Mackenzie River, apparently with some success, selling beef at Simpson for fifty cents a pound. But after the government brought in frozen buffalo meat for the hostel to sell at the native cooperative store, Whiting was forced out of business. And after the government bought out the Yellowknife Transportation Line, he could no longer get tugs and barges to stop by his place for the small amount of lumber he had to sell. The old man was bitter. You could see his point. He couldn't make a living. No matter how hard he worked and planned ahead to stay independent, everything he tried seemed doomed to failure. He despised the government and its minions — he who had lived in the Mackenzie for thirty years before the government even knew there was a North.

"My sympathies," I said, having heard such tales before. "I lived many years in the North — well, about a thousand miles north of here, I guess, and another country, but it's all the same. You have a nice little place here."

"Want to buy it?" he asked suddenly.

"Well, I wouldn't say that, but . . ."

"Come, now, how much do you think it's worth?"

He was not speaking of property boundaries. The ground was not owned by anyone. I was certain he had no title. He just meant the shack, the sawmill equipment, and the cleared and fertilized garden plot.

Glancing around, I took a wild guess. "Two thousand dollars?"

"*Sold!*" the old man cried. That was the day I nearly had myself a house on the Mackenzie, like it or not.

"Hey, now, hold on! But you have a nice little place here anyway, wonderful view, wonderful freedom."

"Come fall," he said, "soon as we dig the potatoes, we're moving up to town. Up to Providence on the highway. I've tried everything since 1918. But I'm an old man now, I'm through fighting her at last. The North." He did not say whether he would go on fighting the government. He was probably ready for an old-age pension.

"What do you think of the economic future of this country?" I asked. "What do you think about the future of the Indians?"

I was very interested in old Whiting's ideas for helping the Indians and his prognosis of their future, inasmuch as this subject has been a constant plague and object of speculation to government planners for years, and a problem on the conscience of everyone. Literally millions of words have been written on the subject. But the intractable North, land of the Indians, is not amenable to quick or easy change just to accommodate the theorists. Old Whiting — over saskatoon berry pie, picked wild and baked in a woodstove oven by his wife — said that in his mind the government practice of building hostels (steam-heated boarding schools, actually) at such principal settlements as Yellowknife, Simpson, and Inuvik, was ultimately entirely unsatisfactory as a solution to the Indian survival problem.

At present, the children of the North are educated and boarded at northern hostels but have no future because they were born into a habitat which is not life-sustaining. The government recruits these youngsters from remote, primitive villages, educates them to a certain degree, then flies them back to the same villages from which they came. Then they are simply left! Many children sent "home" are unable to adapt again, either psychologically or physically, to the village. They go directly onto relief, to subsist. It is an endless, futile cycle. A cycle of pitiful human misery. A cycle of perpetual taxpayers' expense, also, for those who support it.

Whiting believed that the boarding schools should be built in southern cities such as Edmonton and Vancouver, where the children would be in constant touch with the mainstream of life as they grew up, where they could be specifically trained in skills not available in the North and where they could be integrated as modern citizens in a modern world. He emphasized the urgent need for trade schools and job placement. For, after all, he said, employment — the capacity for independent survival — must be the primary service we give youth. Little else matters, really.

Much later I read an analysis of Alaska's problem by Dr. Diamond Jenness, an anthropologist whose arctic researches in both Canada and Alaska go back before 1923, and who has watched the administration of Indians and Eskimos develop through the years in both countries. He has concluded that the younger, oncoming generation must be offered opportunities by their governments to get out of the North and stay out!

"They must either migrate farther south to earn a living wage," says Dr. Jenness, "or else continue today's heart-breaking struggle . . . through the oldtime pursuits of hunting, fishing and trapping, and resignedly trust to social security payments and services to keep their heads above drowning level." * Yet it is sad to think of our North American Arctic as empty of people and empty of possible livelihood. Despite our hundred years' experience with these lands, we keep hoping that some day the right answers will turn up, if we will but search farther. To this end the Department of Northern Affairs and Natural Resources continues to move more money northward as fast as they can get it, and they were moving

* Diamond Jenness, *Eskimo Administration: 1, Alaska*, p. 57. Paper published by The Arctic Institute of North America, New York and Montreal, 1962.

the capital of the Northwest Territories north to Yellowknife at this very time.

But until some of the answers come, it hardly seems reasonable that governments should continue subsidizing such poverty and misery. Our North American Arctic has an intrinsic poverty only equal to that of Asia. It should be made clear, however, those who recommend the depopulation of the Arctic, or certain regions of it, make no suggestion whatsoever that such coercive methods be used as were used to solve Asian problems. The government can and should offer employment programs and the opportunity to get south; but it should be left up to the individual whether he goes south or stays north.

Through fast water and boiling rapids Ann and Jean saw Fort Simpson on its island in the distance. We crossed the muddy Liard mouth, the glare of the evening sun in our eyes, and went straight to tie up at the RCMP dock.

A young Mountie's wife dined us in the Mountie's apartment on bacon and eggs, banana pie, fresh strawberries and coffee, as the sunglow lingered. Then the girls and their gulls and I were delivered by police car to the Anglican hostel; there we could lodge for a dollar a person a day, and use the washing machines and dryers and other such luxuries.

A kindly woman at the hostel, Mrs. McPatches, gave us some clothes collected by the mission. Our own clothes, in their second year, were in such condition that there was little to be done but discard them. They had been through war. That is why, in this narrative, I call her Mrs. McPatches; and she took us to her heart as the patched-up orphans that we were.

We spent three days in all in the mission at Simpson, resting up a bit and getting our clothing and gasoline supplies in order for travel again. I drove out to the airfield to meet the plane. It came Saturday and Tuesday afternoons, and I hadn't seen one for some time. The carful of assorted Canadians included a new bride-to-be (last winter's teacher) and her swain; and a broad Indian woman, mother of ten, who was to depart for Hay River for a holiday, and to visit relatives. When I asked confidentially who paid the bills for the Indian lady's holiday flight, the answer came: "Oh, her husband works for N.C.P.C. and two of her boys work for D.O.T. and some other relatives work in the field, that is building the outhouse for P.W.A." All work was government work. Indians with capability can get some employment. Consequently this lady could take her holiday out of here; and it was good to see her happy, beaming face.

The waiting station at the field was a frame shack. I believe it had no provision for heat at fifty degrees below zero. The rest room was a single-seater in a dark, doorless woodshed. All around was the bush.

It was on this drive to the airfield that I also met the Norths. This couple could be representative of more truly north-oriented people with a hopeful future here. Mr. North had been trained in agriculture, but being unable to get employment in this line, he had made a career of teaching and administration in the far northern schools. Having spent the past six years in the arctic delta town of Inuvik, the Norths had come as far south as Simpson only for the past year. By September first they would return to Inuvik, where he was to become school principal.

Sad to say, the police took the gulls away at Fort Simpson. I insisted on it. Being the gulls' grandmother, I felt that I could hardly either abandon them in the wilds or murder them before the eyes of my children. Yet the gulls were much more than a mere nuisance. They were an actual menace for explorers, because these particular explorers could not keep their minds on their business with gulls always in their laps in the canoe, gulls dominating every expeditionary decision, gulls interrupting everyone's sleep each night. The fact was, we were all getting terribly birdy. But when I appealed to a Mountie for help, he resisted.

"I really don't see how we can take children's pets away from them. After all," he worried aloud, considering all ramifications of the problem, "what will your children's opinion of us be from this? Don't tell me! You know very well, yourself! It will sink to a low which they may never forget. What about our image, I say? What will our image be with the children in America after this?"

"But there is this *law*," I urged. I tried to speak calmly. "Wild things in the first place are not to be expropriated from nature to be the playthings of human beings. Please help me. I am a mother alone with children *and* sea gulls in a canoe. All our lives hang in the balance."

Reluctantly, then, the police took the birds away. Good-bye, dearly beloved gulls: we hope that the game warden at Simpson and his children raised you properly. (Many a time the kids all but fell out of the canoe, and what with you for pals, they paid no attention whatever to their steering through the Mackenzie rapids.)

Within hours the gulls were forgotten. The girls picked up a normal interest in life and their surroundings, with the result that our chances for survival increased several fold. Refreshed and eager, wondering what lay ahead, we headed down the Mackenzie. After that point the river is divided into two kinds of water: the muddy Liard water coming in at Fort Simpson takes up the left hand or west side of the river for nearly the next two hundred miles.

Added to the muddy Liard that very day was the muddy torrent of the unfriendly, stump-strewn North Nahanni, as well as the sizable Root River flowing in from the western mountains.

On an adventurous impulse we decided to go up the Root River a ways.

"I doubt if we can get very far up it," I said, "but I guess we can give it a try."

Practically all of the major streams coming into the Mackenzie come from the Mackenzie Ranges. I knew from the book, as well as what I could see, that these tributary rivers had a fast runoff. None were held to be navigable for more than fifteen miles.

At Simpson the Mackenzie takes a really decisive turn to the North. Up until now there had been a question in our minds as to whether we might find our way westward to the North Pacific Ocean: the river tries ceaselessly to do this with all its might. But the more it twists and squirms westward, the more strange mountains rise on the left to bar its way. It was here and subsequently, as the river plunges along the edge of these ever higher ranges, that Alexander Mackenzie faced the great disappointment of his life. He had hoped for a noble trade route to the Pacific. But the river which bears his name just can't find a way through the Rockies.

It is inevitable that any voyager beyond Fort Simpson will raise his eyes and gaze in fascination at the mountain walls. Composed of several little-known mountain chains having a north-south alignment, these mountains are still largely unexplored. The largest in Canada, they cover an area of around seventy-five thousand square miles, and have unknown peaks to fourteen thousand feet, and labyrinths of canyons known to be deeper than the Grand Canyon, full of dark caves and the wailing of mysterious winds.

There is a clear-water river coming out of these mountains which has a legend: the South Nahanni. To find it one has to fight up the mighty Liard about a hundred miles, so unfortunately we could not. The legend has it that early in the century the McLeod brothers from Fort Liard found gold, but then disappeared mysteriously in the valley of the Nahanni. Their skeletons were later found without their heads. Other men, following the McLeods, had their cabins burned to the ground and their heads taken. Naturally a good deal was made out of this; and eventually the South Nahanni River became known as Headless Valley. There are hot springs there also, and a waterfall twice as high as Niagara. One certain thing is that it is a country of unbelievable beauty and desolation. But even the Indians and Eskimos are said to fear to go there. Fort Liard and Nahanni Butte up the Liard have long functioned as trading posts — but legends persist.

Now this Root River came out of the same general country, but it has no legends. It is just the swift, muddy old Root River. But our party must be careful in our navigation that we did not make a legend out of it.

We had swum on the Mackenzie beaches and sunned from 7 A.M. till noon; so it was five in the afternoon when we came upon the Root River entering the Mackenzie and turned up it. Sundown, perhaps 9 P.M., found us encamped on a long open gravel beach on our private river, building a fire of pungent drift, in full view of the unexplored ranges. The swift, glacial-gray mountain river surged beside us. Every inch of progress we had made up it had been a fight. The savagery of the river repelled me. I was glad to get ashore where we did.

"This is grizzly country," I told the girls. "The bears may be hungry, so keep an eye out. The mountain grizzlies are not the same as black bears. Sometimes they'll come boldly."

On the beach we had perfect bug-free comfort and a view. The kids chose the camp. But the natives wouldn't have picked this place. They would have taken the heavily timbered cutbank right across. The bug-ridden cutbank offers better fishing (you can't set out a net from a river bar), better hunting (you might get your grizzly by shooting right across the river to the bar), better sod for tent stakes, shelter from winds and storms, and a far more snug boat-tying berth in the cutbank. Neither in Alaska nor in Canada in all my years had I noticed natives camping on a river bar like ours. But we liked it. It was all nice country. We had plenty of food.

At pancakes and coffee and grilled canned meat early next day we heard a motorboat coming up our Root River. But just as we began to think that we were going to see another human being so far off the track, the sound faded away.

We never discovered who had made the sound. "Did this river have any tributaries where he might have gone?" I asked the kids.

"Gee, I didn't notice any, Mom. I don't think so."

I recalled how I have always been a little bit superstitious in solitary places. Suddenly the Root River this morning (and such a gay, bright morning it was!) didn't feel good.

We finished breakfast in leisurely fashion and the Franklin Range seemed so close we longed to reach it. But to fight farther up this river was no good. The river might get narrow after the next turn or so, and we would find ourselves boxed in. "This is as far as we go, crew," I told my stout-hearted companions, whose faces fell.

An explorer often has to turn back or change his tactics, I told them. The Explorers Club in New York, made up of fine, eminent men bearing long strings of scientific degrees, is known for the extreme antiquity of some of its members. They frequently live to be older than the general population.

"Take your father, for instance. Of course he's a year older than me."

"He wrote that he's a year younger than you are, Mother," countered Ann.

I got up from the delightful cooking chair Ann had built for me. She had gathered two side supports of dry driftwood from the river bar, which had convenient knobs on their ends to form the curls of a natural armchair. Then she laid three small crossbars across the arms for a seat. The result was a seat six inches off the hard beach where I ensconced myself with kettle and grill at the small cooking fire. I could reach my pots and pans on either hand — the day we almost touched the Franklins.

"If only we were men, not girls, we would at least try to push back into those mountains," grumbled Jean, as I began to pick up things. "*Men* wouldn't just stop here!"

But left to ourselves we females are usually like this. Our exploration up the Root River incorporated no legends, no particular adventures, no material profits. We seem to be peace-loving creatures, if nobody stirs us up.

We tootled on down the fast turns and spills of the Root River and into the Mackenzie again. We passed an Indian frame house. The sign on the door, deciphered through the glasses, said: "Not at home." A mellow, diffused haze lay in the stillness over a giant land. From horizon to horizon stretched the smooth water; green islands seemed to float in the sky, and shores that turned out not to be shores but more islands.

"Look, it's Indian summer," Ann said.

Moose tracks, bigger than cattle tracks, were imprinted along the bank when we stopped for lunch. The river was dropping.

Ann slept in the warm sun atop the canoe's load. Jean motored, challenging a masculinized world, with one booted foot up and her back supported at one side of the boat by an upthrust paddle blade. She reached for a hollow metal tent pole, thrust it down into the water, and took a long, cold drink, using the pole like a big soda straw.

"Don't drink out of the tent pole! It's a four-mile current; you'll hurt your mouth."

"Stop shouting, Mother. I've been doing it all summer. What's wrong with . . . *ooops!*"

The hollow tent leg was hurled from her grasp, and down it went to the bottom of the Mackenzie River. I tried to glare ferociously.

"Now look what you've done," said Jean. "You made me nervous."

After that the tent had a wooden leg, chopped by Mackenzie's ax.

That Indian summer day was followed by a storm. We watched it for two hours, as it built up over the Mackenzie. Thunderheads formed but there was not much lightning — too far north. The storm slashed over the river, half green water and half brown from the Liard, the North Nahanni and Root rivers pouring in. Luckily we just got the edge of the downpour. It passed and we went ninety miles farther that evening: all the way to Wrigley.

There were one hundred and thirty-five Indians at Wrigley, and twice that many howling, hungry dogs. The one white man, the Bay trader about nineteen years old, received us rather crossly after store hours, opening up for us. The few goods he had to sell looked exactly identical to the ones we already had from the Bay in our canoe, except that he had less supply than we had.

Asked about other people, visitors, the news of the countryside, and so on, he admitted grudgingly (under probing) that there were, in fact, two other whites here besides himself. Just below town, he said, there were "some crazy missionaries" eking out a miserable existence without any church; he was certain we would not care to see them.

"What kind of missionaries?"

"I dunno. Some independents. Don't belong to no regular recognized church. They call themselves the Only True Helpers of God, something like that. We don't have a resident priest here now. Our priest, he comes up the river couple times a summer, but these crazy Only Trues sneaked in here meanwhile when his back was turned, and none of our people like it one bit, I can tell you."

"Come on, kids," I said. "I guess we'll visit the Only True Helpers of God."

"Can't we just go on?" they asked miserably.

"Don't you ever get tired?" I asked.

"I don't like to see people," said Jean.

"Stop being ridiculous," I reiterated. "We've traveled maybe a hundred miles today, it is late. Can't you see the wind's blowing out there on the river now? Besides, missionaries in the field in far lands are just something you don't pass by, if you are in the far lands. Besides, they may need some help, by the looks of it."

Parking our canoe just below town, we climbed to a little two-room log and tarpaper cabin upon a steep hill, and there they were: the Only True Helpers of God.

What they were was a perfectly sweet, terribly young American couple from Cleveland, with two little babies, living there in that cabin which they had managed to build on the bank of the Mackenzie River with their own hands. Their earnest faces made you think of that little band of Christians who through long history have brought the faith to far places, always in the face of insuperable odds and cruel enemies. The wife was a trained nurse. She brought the only medical services available in this part of the world. The husband made their living as best he could, in ingenious ways, and between times assisted the Indians as a brother would. Whatever you believed about the sect they called themselves, you could see that the poor missionaries in the field were not poor, not lonely — but rich and free. They knew what they were doing without any doubt at all.

Perhaps that's what we had in common: we were all in the same tippy boat of adventure — whereas most other people were complacent. The evangelists lived in a world of ideas, whereas the majority live in a boring, materialistic world which too often has little to offer for the spirit of man.

At once we became their guests for that night. We set to work at a practical exchange and transfer of our canned and dried foods, with the result that we were able to set a magnificent table. Jean and Ann and I were very happy to be able to let them have some of our cans of milk, juices, and vegetables — for we found that the family had nothing but starches in their cabin. In addition, there was a brand-new baby only three weeks home from the Fort Simpson hospital; it had come here in its mother's arms in the family boat. Luckily, besides being a trained nurse, the young mother was fortunate in being able to supply natural mother's milk for the baby, thus automatically eliminating many problems.

From the Rightfields we learned that most of the Indian men were presently absent from Wrigley and from other such villages on the Mackenzie. American oil companies had been moving fast, the last seasons; they flew the men even as far as distant British Columbia for summer labor. While this employment seemed a good thing inasmuch as it brought good wages, the Indians were apt to spend most of what they earned, we were told, at gambling, drinking, and having a big time. So many Indian heads of families brought home nearly nothing from a summer's work. While these heads of families were gone and the usual government family allotment cut off, the women and children at the village were often desperately hungry. To fill the gap missionaries were urgently needed to help on the spot. Missionaries have been known to give up their own food and supplies and share them with their people during such emergencies.

At the time we arrived here we witnessed that peculiar northern phenomenon: the moving of a whole town.

Wrigley was about to get a government-built airfield. We had seen machinery working atop a Mackenzie River cliff as we voyaged past. The forest had been removed up there, and the land leveled. But since the only place the field could be built was four miles upriver from the town of Wrigley and on the opposite side of the river, it was necessary, in order to get town and airfield together, to move the Indians, house by house, to a new site near the field. This process, already started, was supposed to be finished a few weeks after fall freeze-up.

"It's going to be kind of cold moving, isn't it?" I asked.

"No," the missionary couple explained, "moving after freeze-up is a lot easier. We just build the new houses and then move into them. Or some of the shacks may be pulled by tractor over the river ice."

"How do the Indians afford to move?"

"The government takes care of it, and moves them."

"How about yourselves? What will you do when they all move away four miles?"

"Oh, we'll follow."

"Does the government build you a new house, too?" I asked, somewhat wryly.

The Rightfields looked a little unhappy, but they mustered a smile. "My husband," said the new mother, "will build us a new home at the village site, if the Lord be willing. And we shall, of course, continue in His blessed work."

Since their log and tarpaper house was much too tiny to hold guests, I should explain that to enjoy the company of these good people we pitched our tent nearby on the boulders right beneath their hill. We attached our canoe to their dock and locked it tight in its snap-down canvas, then covered it all over with a strip of wire mesh fencing supplied by our hosts. We had been warned that the loose dogs of this village were so starved that they might rip the canoe contents apart as we slept. (This had happened to previous house guests of the missionaries this summer.) Also, unfortunately, the True Helpers admitted, there were some individuals among the Indians who, distrusting unorthodox missionaries and unknown guests, might be tempted to steal everything from the canoe during the night. The heavy wire mesh prevented this — although I heard dog feet (and perhaps Indians) on top of the canoe all night that night.

"Are you all alone in the Mackenzie? Have you no others in your group to turn to in time of need?" (It seemed possible, though they did not mention it, that the Bay trader might have refused to sell food to them.) I asked about this at breakfast with Mrs. Rightfield early next day. Her husband had left very early that morning with his boat to haul some drums of diesel fuel downriver for a fee, she explained.

"Yes," she said, "there are some Only Trues, a very wonderful couple we hope you will visit, at Fort Norman down below. I wonder — would you mind taking a few little things I have for them, in your canoe? They belong to the faith. They are true Christians. They are working there. Well, also, I don't suppose you will get over to Great Bear Lake, it's far out of your way. . . ."

"Wow! Mom, Great Bear Lake!"

"I really don't know how on earth we'll get to Great Bear Lake," I said, "but we would sure like to. It's almost all we've talked about — I mean in addition to Great Slave Lake, of course, which we saw earlier — since we thought of this trip. Ann, honey, run down the hill and get my attaché case from the canoe, with my map of the river to Fort Norman, and also the map of Great Bear Lake. I want to figure where the next missionaries live."

"They'll be real happy to see you, especially if you can get to Great Bear Lake," said the young missionary eagerly. "I haven't been there myself. You can stay with them there, I'm sure. They hardly ever see any visitors over that way. I'll write them you hope to get there."

So it was that we went on our way, bearing messages, greetings, and little gifts from the Rightfields to their fellow Christians at Fort Norman and at Great Bear Lake, in case by some miracle we could reach that latter great inland sea of the Arctic.

"To reach Bear Lake," I was calculating out loud as we loaded that morning, and Jean checked the motor, "involves actually going *up* the Bear River ninety miles. It's such a swift river our motor could never make it. Also, there are eight miles of portage around unnavigable rapids right in the middle. About the only way I can figure it, kids, would be if we caught some kind of a ride with some bigger vessel."

But that seemed very chancy indeed.

The Mackenzie changed color under the sky: today it was muddy gray and frothing. We met Reggie Rightfield in mid-river as he was returning home from his 5 A.M.–5 P.M. sortie downriver. The people to whom he had delivered the Caterpillar fuel, he said, were white men at an oil camp. I pricked up my ears. They had fed him a dinner that was just like Christmas, from which he was still licking his chops.

Wishing Reggie Rightfield well on his way, we went bucking the waves on down the river as fast as we could, licking our own chops in anticipation. "They asked me all about you girls. They heard about you already," Reggie told us. "You know they got dinner cooking for you already? All they asked me was questions about you and your canoe trip the whole time I was there. Oh, my, do they ever feed good in that camp!" Another thing we had in common with the poor missionaries was that we were terribly hungry all of the time. Anyway, the kinds of foods oil people eat are not found every day at Hudson's Bay trading posts for Indians.

How curious, the different faces of nature. The friendly dream river of the golden day when we met old Whiting gives way to today's beast to battle; and the very thought of human companionship awaiting us somewhere ahead — past the Ochre River, past the Blackwater, down at the junction of the Dahadinni — becomes pure bliss to contemplate. They say it's an *oil company!* That's what they say. They are from the great outside. They have come into our country to drill test holes for oil, and they are very rich. Nobody knows if they struck oil or not; they just drill away. And they're not telling anything. Sometimes when they find oil, they just let it lie there in reserve for years and years, and never touch it. Take it off income tax. They don't want other companies to come in on the field. Even the workers themselves, the roughnecks, hardly know what's going on. It costs them two and one-half million dollars to drill this test hole. Will they win? Will they lose?

Their name is Shell. They are an international company based in the Netherlands. All these companies are international. This is the American branch of Shell. Well, are there Americans there on the Dahadinni, then? Well, no, not exactly. They are a Canadian subsidiary contracted to the American Shell. Something like that. Anyway, they are all Canadian men working there. No, there are no women.

"Steamboat's a-comin', Mom!" Jean broke my thoughts.

The river was painfully narrow right where we met the vessel, which was pushing a couple of oil barges up the river. The barges lay low in the water. Water was flowing right over their tops, I could see through the glasses. Full of oil, they were. Full of oil from the Mackenzie oilfields below Fort Norman, discovered in 1920, developed in World War II.

"I'll cross over in front of them to the other side," yelled Jean.

"No, no," I yelled back. "It's against maritime law! You can't cross their bow; we're coming down on them fast."

"Oh, they're not moving, hardly at all. Do they think they can hog the whole river? I'll show them!"

"No!" I protested hoarsely.

"But they'll wash over us where we are, Ma!"

"Mother, you really are a terrible sissy," said Ann. "What do you want Jean to do, climb out on the bank?"

"Just stay as close to our shore as you can get," I instructed. "About six feet from shore, that's it."

"Ma, it's just the old Y. T. *Husky*, that's who she is. You know the *Husky*."

"No, I don't."

"Don't you remember? Look, some of the fellows are waving at Jean and me."

"Well, they're waving at me, too, then," I cried, and started waving gaily.

Suddenly we were bottled up by the old *Husky*, close to the rock shore. Just like a cork against the sides of a bathtub. She came around the bend, chugging up the current. As she passed I perceived that an enormous wave was rolling toward us. Nothing to do but meet it, turn into it as it hit us. Up, up, reared the wave. I did not know if the fellows laughing on board were really laughing or felt some degree of conscience. Right over the bow of our canoe crashed the icy wave, right over Ann and me, like Niagara Falls.

The plucky canoe righted herself in an instant. We of course were deluged with ice water. On top of this, we ran into a squall as we turned the river bend. Drenched rats, we scrambled ashore. There was no shelter at all: just this bathtub effect for miles ahead. The river here is flowing down a rock chute.

The storm passed by. A yellow sun broke feebly through and gulls floated on the foam. We pressed onward; travel was a bit treacherous, but nothing could quench our high spirits.

Two chilly hours later we found the oil camp.

26

Sports Day at Fort Norman

IT was a bluish arctic summer evening when we saw the line of oil drums and tractors along the shore. Three men met our canoe and helped us tie up at the oil camp. Other men could be seen walking around a muddy bulldozed clearing, wearing dun-colored work clothes. An oilfield is a tough place and very workmanlike. It has no place for women.

The question is, if you happen to be of that fair sex and come along in your canoe, just how do you conduct yourself? I had formulated a policy. Linger a day or two if invited. Enjoy the situation. Don't overstay. Probably the same rule works if you have young, nubile daughers in your canoe.

"Come on over to the cook shack and have some coffee," came the hoped-for invitation. I glanced jubilantly at my crew. We were in.

I will say briefly that we stayed there a couple of nights and were given for our guest room a giant six-bunk empty box trailer, where we used our sleeping bags and had electric lights. Such trailers can be seen on giant wheels or giant sleigh runners at many construction camps. We liked the calm Canadian oilfield workers, the pilots, and the foremen, and talked with many of them in the big semi-trailer which served as dining area and social headquarters. There wasn't a rough word used in our presence, it almost goes without saying! (The girls' washroom in an average American high school is probably rougher nowadays.) Perhaps I am a little old-fashioned, but it seemed to me to their credit that there was not even a strip-tease photo or a girlie picture in this camp. The atmosphere was not American. My girls drove with the cook on his fork lift to get water out of the Mackenzie in big milk cans. Then, having made friends with one of the capable oilfield "roughnecks," Jean drove a bulldozer with him; she quickly learned to operate it by the lamps at midnight, becoming briefly what I can only describe as a kind of wholesome Canadian "bulldozer queen."

The oil camp was in the process of dismantling when we arrived. It was real lucky timing that we got to see it at all. Had we passed but a week later, there would have been nothing at all on that point where the Dahadinni River joins the Mackenzie, but an empty, dreary, bulldozed area of raw earth. Beside the river lay the dismantled oil rig in sections. The drill bit had been sunk to twelve thousand feet, without results. Even the garbage, thrown everywhere around, would soon be bulldozed under, according to the regulations followed by legitimate oil companies.

"Now don't go barefooted around all this filth and scrap metal," I tried to warn the girls. (They had had tetanus shots earlier.) We had seen before that Canadian men working in the bush in summer do not build outhouses. Everybody just used the bush — everywhere. The bush, pushed back in windrows by the bulldozers, was an impressive jungle of branches, tin cans, vegetable peelings, heaped mud, wads of toilet paper, and human excrement, immediately surrounding the trailer encampment.

"Just look," I tried to tell my daughters, "do you see any of these sensible, experienced men of the world going around *barefooted?*" Eventually, in fact, the girls did see my point. The oil camp is memorable to me because it was the one place where I was able to get them to keep their shoes on. The Arctic in general completely failed to curb the delight and pride they took in going barefoot.

I myself never saw the actual drilling site. It was back behind the river, two hours' tractor drive, or ten minutes by helicopter. But the girls saw it next day. They simply asked, "May we polish your helicopter bubble for you?" and were given rides by its weary and charming pilot; and they also saw the adjacent three-thousand-foot field which had been bulldozed for the use of conventional aircraft nearby.

While we were at the base camp the helicopters came and went, shuttling personnel between the drilling site and base camp, settling down on the cleared ground near us with a shimmering whir of rotor blades. You had to take care you didn't walk into one of those long slim blades. They are longer than you think. As they whirl just above a man's height, they are safe on a perfectly level airport; but if a whirlybird settles on uneven ground and you happen to be standing nearby on a slight elevation, a careless moment on your part could end in your neat decapitation.

I was interested to learn that helicopters of the kind that can settle on both land and water, while essential to this kind of operation, are miserably complicated. They require two skilled full-time mechanics on the ground for each two kept in the air. The mechanics are shipped out by conventional aircraft to wherever helicopters operate. At this camp we had identical twin brothers working as special mechanics.

I was privileged to behold here on the banks of the Mackenzie the rather new Nodwell Transporter. It was a seventy-thousand-dollar tread vehicle which was capable of carrying up to ten tons of heavy equipment over swamp and muskeg so soft that a man could not walk there. The foreman said there were just fifteen of these things in the world at that time. He explained that the Transporter worked by distributing its load over giant treads in such a way that only two and one-half pounds were carried to the square inch. It was this Transporter which had carried the tremendous drill bit inland to the drill site, and had returned it piece by piece to the riverbank.

"But how do you determine the drill spot to begin with?" I wanted to know. The sites are chosen by company seismologists, using seismographs and mobile trains of bulldozers and tractor vehicles, and sleigh runners during the wintertime. They go "seismographing" right overland through the wilderness, carrying cook shack, bathhouse, and bunk shacks with them as they go: their entire heated quarters and their total equipment. These arctic caravans are among the world's most remarkable phenomena.

During the winter when the ground is solidly frozen the caravan pushes through subarctic scrub with little resistance; for this scrub is shallow-rooted. It breaks off readily in the low temperatures if it is not rooted out. The permanent scarring of the landscape which results seems to concern nobody. It is such a new ability of man, this hewing of roads into the North — roads that are always quickly abandoned — that any one person concerned with the land cannot help but wonder what effect this cutting up of the once-inviolate wilderness will have on its future. Here is one of the last great wilderness areas left in the world. All others are long since gone. But the growing numbers of seismograph roadways are quickly parceling the wilderness into blocks. This may limit the game in its breeding ranges; it also hems animals in at the mercy of their natural and human predators, hastening their extinction. The caribou, especially, may be the most hardy of animals, but they do require one thing: their privacy, with large undisturbed tracts to roam over. I would venture to guess that seismograph roads may be a factor in the annihilation of caribou from Canada.

The invasion of man here seems to contribute nothing. He comes, he slashes, he retreats, leaving a truly desolate land behind him. This stripping of the land is going on over tens of thousands of square miles of this part of North America. We believe the wilderness could make a comeback if the problems were sufficiently studied, or possibly even if it were simply left alone for a while. Even now, oil explorations seem to be falling off, as a matter of fact. But our future needs for wilderness are quite incalculable at this time. To destroy all wilderness within a generation is madness. For our experience has been all over the world that once it is destroyed, the wilderness can never be returned to its original condition. And yet even today, arctic and marine seismic crews are busily exploring some of the last untapped spaces on our planet.

Still, had our canoe party been able to witness that oil-drilling operation during the preceding winter, we would have had to admire man's courage and ingenuity as he digs for the almighty dollar. For the first ten days in January, the average daily working temperature was minus 60.5 degrees below zero Fahrenheit.

Days were so dark that the helpers on the recording crew had to wear miners' headlamps. Daylight lasted one and one-half hours. The survey crew dealt with this darkness by painting their stadia rods with luminous paint, then beaming auto headlights on the rods. Battery packs supplied power. Wind does not blow at below minus fifty degrees, so at extreme subzero temperatures, exhaust from the vehicles made clouds which hung in the air, obscuring the surveyors' line of sight.

It was an eerie world. Air drills were used exclusively, since water would freeze. Gear boxes froze. Kelly hoses and metal parts became brittle, breaking in half. The thump of frozen tires was a common sound. The men found that dynamite freezes completely at minus forty-five to minus fifty degrees below zero. When they punched the frozen powder in, the action produced a very audible bang, suggestive of a partial ignition; they had to make new investigations into the safety limits of using frozen dynamite. At minus sixty degrees they found it was impossible to start a frozen Cat, so the Cats had to be left running twenty-four hours.

Supply lines of course presented vast difficulties. During the summer of advance exploration all the heavy equipment, explosives, fuels, and major supplies had been barged in over the thousand miles from Hay River and road connections there. Everything else was flown in to the airstrip on the prospect.

Constant radio communication was essential. The recording camp maintained contact with the Edmonton office through a one-hundred-watt transmitter; the bulldozer camps kept up nearly constant communication with the recording camp, using thirty-watt A.M. transmitters; and recording, shooting, reel, personnel, supply and fuel tank trucks also had their radios.

Camp problems all but insoluble were solved. Fuel oil for the stoves became viscous and full of ice crystals. Brittle trailer hitches and frames continually broke. Thawing water lines for the kitchen and utility trailers was a constant chore. (Up to two hundred men could wash clothes with the electric washers and dryers.) Even the propane had to be heated to insure a steady flow.

If something had caused the power to go off and the stoves to cool, these men could have frozen to death as did Franklin's men when they were forced to abandon their powerless ships.

The attitude of these overwintering men, therefore, was that nature here was something to combat with all their strength and by every means available. In their experience, nature was the enemy.

It was a most unprepossessing beach we came to rest upon, after we left the oil camp. We could still hear occasional distant helicopter hums, a distant agitation or a kind of flitting, as puny as that of mosquitoes.

The gay mood of visiting changed to a kind of despondency, once we rounded the bend. When isolated arctic camps of people encounter different groups, the event often leaves the participants restless for a number of days. But in our case the restlessness lasted only a few hours: we had the great advantage that we were traveling and continually seeing new places. Our experience was unique in that only we, of all the people we met that summer, were seeing the whole Mackenzie from end to end. The people we visited, on the other hand, were largely unaware of each other and isolated at the same time from the very country they lived in. They were all flown into the Arctic and then out again directly. All they ever saw was their own work, their small quarters, their immediate associates, their little airfield, and the horizon of surrounding bush which closed them in. Yet it was so simple to get around. All you really needed was to get a little independent camp outfit and a small boat, and go down the current. It showed you the country as nothing else could.

Now we were on our own again on the shore of the Mackenzie. Rounded boulders and gravel, wet sand, sloping banks, soggy driftwood, and gray waves rolling toward us. For the moment, civilization had spoiled us, it seemed. Nobody felt like pitching the tent. Nobody would work together.

Ann wandered off down the beach, strewing fishing tackle and headnet, and pulling her sleeping bag as she went. The fishing rod was jackknifed. The lens of the camera nowadays kept falling out on the ground with a depressing "plink." Presently, far down the beach, Ann set carefully to work with the damp wood and built her own campfire. Jean then built her own fire a quarter of a mile away in the opposite direction; and each tended her own fire. So I built my own fire, too. We were tired of looking at each other. Three campfires blazed on the beach. (If a boat had come by she would have thought it was a distress signal. Nobody came, fortunately.)

What was Ann always daydreaming about? Of course I didn't ask her. She was growing up. Only much later she hesitantly revealed that the summer she was thirteen her principal companion was a handsome, twenty-year-old millionaire who took her that summer to what she said were called "the isles of Greece" and adorned her in beautiful gossamer gowns as his dearest love. But you don't tell these things easily. It sounds too ludicrous out loud.

For myself, I laid down the old tarp and the black "bearskin" before my fire, and prepared myself a comfortable rest. I knew the girls would pitch the tent when they got around to it. The necessities of survival would attend to that. A bulldog fly whizzed past me. Such flies can take real bites of flesh and blood. But the bugs this summer had scarcely bothered us as we stuck to the river.

I yawned and stretched, and decked my back in canvas against the flies, and lay down in the smoke stream.

You can hear all kinds of voices in the whiny insects' wings. You hear voices in the river and in the forest. But most of all, the voices are inside yourself. Subterranean layers you never knew you had. Snatches of old tunes you haven't thought of since childhood go around in your head for days. You have to use mind control. There is always this unstoppable babble because the mind refuses to be a vacuum. It must contrive some activity, if there is nothing there but long hours under the sky. Then it is that gradually you succumb to nature's enticing lullaby. The lullaby goes that nothing in civilization is really important anyway. And after a while, if you stay in the wilderness, you will believe it.

The babble of words and tunes, the impressions of missionaries and oil camps, of long Mackenzie River rapids, of Radium Line tugs traveling with their laundry hanging out in the breeze to dry and Indian tents beneath scalloped cliffs; all faded off. . . .

I saw Gerald. Suddenly I found that I was hand in hand with him walking on some shore somewhere, and the ground was all covered with golden fall leaves. I saw the white trunks of birches in an open parkland beside a great mysterious lake or sea, of exactly the kind I have always liked to explore. In my dream Gerald was handsome and a distinguished intellectual. Even though he was exploring this beautiful terrain, I saw he was wearing the same correct charcoal suit; and he wore his necktie, of course. Presently we came to an old summerhouse on the shore, and it seemed that I had known all the time that it was there. We walked inside to look. But alas, the place had no furniture. As we looked it over, we saw that it had cracks in its walls and ceiling, through which the fall winds blew.

That was all of the dream. I was still holding Gerald's hand when I sat up sleepily, reached for a stick, and stirred my little campfire.

Could the old summerhouse be patched up, somehow? I wondered. After all, summerhouses must be expected to show a bit of wear after half a lifetime of living. You get to work at repairs. I decided to write Gerald right away.

It was an interesting coincidence that Jean, at her own campfire down the beach, was also writing a letter at this very time.

Dear Gerald: (she wrote)
I am sitting on the lonely bank of the old Mackenzie River, wondering where my destiny will take me. As you well know, this has bothered me for some time.

I think at last here I am at peace with myself — almost. By the way, please keep body of the enclosed mosquito as a special souvenir from me.

It's all I have to give you right now. It doesn't cost much air mail.

Well, I wrote my father recently about going over to Alaska with him. I won't know how it will turn out until I can mail it. I hope he will reply at one of the Forts before the Arctic Ocean. It probably won't work out, but I thought it would be worth a try. I just can't stand the thought of returning south any more. Everything is so difficult and ugly there. I hope he won't think I'm fat, and I am trying once more to lose weight before he sees me.

If I did go live with him, I sure would miss you a lot. You know that you have always been my father image. Yet I think I should get acquainted with my real father. We are getting farther north each day on the river now and I might be able to fly over to Alaska on some airline that flies north of the Arctic Circle from Canada to Alaska, but I do not know if there exists one. Or, maybe Dad would come from the north coast of Alaska where he is and get me flying floats, if he wants me.

I want to be loved by my father and respected by him. I know I am very ornery and stubborn. I'm always in trouble. As Ann said, "Jeanie fights the whole world instead of accepting it as I do." Perhaps she is right, but the main one I fight is myself. If I was a man I know what I'd do. Probably enlist and go to fight. But a girl can't have men's and boys' respect or admiration by her feats of great strength or bravery, so just what can a girl do, I ask you?

I am getting to the age where I realize that this is one of the most important things in life: to have your father know you are alive and respect you. Oh, well, guess I'm a pretty mixed up kid at times. . . .

After a while the girls wandered back. Somehow they liked Mother's campfire the best. "What's for dinner, Mom?" Jean broke a five-hour silence hungrily.

We were motoring down the rushing, bubbling current, following the familiar friendly channel markers the big vessels followed. Ann had the motor. Shore targets of black and white Ann kept to her right hand. Red targets she kept to her left. The river plunged ahead and the purple mountains soared. Jean lay atop the load rewriting for the third time the difficult letter to her father — bush pilot, guide, polar resident, who lived in a house where caribou wandered by, a house that faced the drifting polar ice pack, over in Alaska.

"Mom," Jean spoke up, "do you think it would be all right if a person took just a year off from school? I would live on the north shore of the continent. I would see the polar pack every day. You know Dad is as far north as a person can go, Mom. It's five hundred air miles north of a school."

"It's really hard to say," I said. "I mean, I suppose you might. Seems to me nobody is going to know the difference a hundred years from now, if you look at it from the long-range view. You just put your proposition up to your dad, and see what he says."

"Sure you wouldn't miss me too much, Mom?"

"Well, of course I would miss you, terribly. But you have the right to know your dad. And I would never be the one to stand in the way of any person seeing Alaska while they are young."

"I'm going to go to Alaska, too, Mom," Ann said, and repeated firmly, "I want to go to my father!"

We had camped up the clear, cat's-eye waters of the Keele River, and we headed out over its shallow, tinkling gravel bar into the muddy Mackenzie about 3 P.M. When we had drifted down a few turns we heard a motor's hum. Often, in the wilderness, you can hear this sound for an hour or more before your glasses focus on the tiny speck that is the boat, followed by its wake of white foam, moving against the background of brown Mackenzie water and massive embankment.

Today it was a single young man in a small, sixteen-foot canoe powered by an eighteen-horse motor. We saw him creeping along the cliff base using his motor judiciously against the powerful current. Little spumes of dust rose from the cliffs at intervals as piles of gypsum dust and rocks tumbled down chutes into the river.

As the young man passed close by we saw that he was young and tanned and, like ourselves, an adventurer on the river. He had holes in his shirt, but was clean. He was somewhat bearded so he was clearly a white man; and he wore (here is the real giveaway to adventure) one of those nearly useless, big, broad, thick skinning knives at his belt ready for anything that came along. Like a slab of bacon, perhaps. This way he always had his knife right on him in case of emergency, too — not a bad idea, really.

"Let's go ashore. Have a cup of tea," I hailed him. "Turn out, careful there, Ann, he doesn't have a whole lot of freeboard."

"Where do you want tea? Look at the cliffs."

"What did you say?"

"The cliffs. The cliffs. No place to drink tea right here."

"Right upriver a few yards. There's a little tiny beach. It's right between the cliffs," yelled Jean.

When the two craft had made the tiny beach we found he was a young teacher from British Columbia, and not a Canadian but an exchange Australian; and like my girls, he was lightly clad and barefooted.

"How far down the river have you been?" I immediately asked, eager for river news. "How did it go down that way?"

The barefooted Australian was efficiently starting a fire of dry little sticks for tea, as he replied, "Oh, it's nice down there. But now I have to hurry back to British Columbia." His speech was rapid and clipped.

"Wow! Think you'll make it up this current in time for school?" asked Ann.

He thought he probably would, if he just kept pegging away at it. He had been down all the way, past Inuvik at the head of the delta, out through the delta island, across giant Mackenzie Bay in the Arctic Ocean, clear to Tuktoyaktuk — the cargo center for the eastern Arctic. He had practically commenced a northwest passage in that canoe.

"See any ice?"

"No, the ice is all out to sea, near the North Pole, looks like. You never find ice in Mackenzie Bay this late, you know."

"How about the wind? Would you think that we could make it? I haven't seen Tuktoyaktuk in years. It would be nice if the girls could see some Eskimos."

"Well, I would not advise it now. Fall winds beginning to come up."

"Mother," Ann reprimanded me severely, handing the Australian more little sticks for the fire he tended, "you promised us *ice*."

"Sorry," I said. "I'm doing the best I can."

A passing shower caught us at that moment, all of us barefooted, in the niche of warm sand beneath the big gypsum cliffs. Everybody leaped to batten down the hatches of both canoes, then dove under our canvas tarp; conversation was scarcely disrupted. There was so much to catch up on when we had the rare pleasure of meeting another river person, another vagabond, that we were only dimly aware of the shower. We sat under the canvas with our feet sticking out in the rain and drank the scalding, convivial tea with our fellow beachcomber.

"I got quite a surprise the other day," he told us. "I was running up the current close along the shore, you know? Then I saw these sea gulls were after something that was lying half in, half out the waterline there. Well, do you know, it was a human body lying there? Pretty much of a mess from the birds, too. Quite a mess it was."

The body had belonged to one of a couple of missing Indians from Fort Norman, whose boat had disappeared on the Mackenzie the month before. The Australian had continued to Fort Norman and brought the coroner back, and together they had brought in the body.

"He is a good man. The coroner, I mean. You will like his wife also. Of course you have to allow that these people are missionaries, if you don't mind that. I'm not religious myself. These people call themselves the Only True Helpers of God, I believe it is. Never heard of that one before, did you?"

"They're our favorite brand," Ann piped up. "Try to stop and say hello for us to the Rightfields. They belong to that kind, too. They are just below Wrigley."

"Do you think he would be able to repair our primus stove?" Jean asked. "The missionary at Fort Norman, I mean?"

"Oh, sure, he can fix anything. He'll help you out, don't you worry about that. What do you think of the plight of these Indians along here, that the missionaries have been working on seventy years?"

"A cynical conclusion is nearly inescapable, isn't it?" said Ann rather formally.

"Yes, but you Americans are always champions of the underdogs, aren't you? So I wondered what you would think of this country. One has to ask oneself how it is that all these good missionaries, plus the government doing its good works, too, for the last twenty years, could have done so little to alleviate the actual misery of the natives here."

"The problems are enormously complicated," I said. "We have just about the same problem of poverty among the Indians and Eskimos in Alaska; that's a quarter of the total population. And despite the fact that we spend tens of millions of dollars every year we can hardly make a dent in the poverty."

"Actually," put in the Australian, "this degree of poverty is about on a level with the highlands of Bolivia and Peru; or I have heard another comparison of it — like the fellahin in the Nile valley. Well, it's too bad, a sorry situation. But well — the rain has stopped. I really must be on my way," he said then.

The rain had stopped indeed. Whirlpools fifty feet across churned at the base of the long line of cliffs, stretching upriver and downriver as far as the eye could see.

That night the two girls and I camped upon a great sandbar that rose out of the river. It was an enchanted desert isle. It had no vegetation and no insects. It had fresh breezes and wondrous empty space for miles around. The river, like a woman's hair, divided at the head of the isle and washed smoothly down either side. At first we thought the sandbar might have been used for a landing field, for great parallel tracks ran down it, like tracks made by some large aircraft. But after some thought we realized the tracks had been made by drift logs at flood time. Our party was a close unit once again as we gathered pieces of drift and built our fire and pitched the little tent in the lingering sundown.

We are on an island once again on the Mackenzie. Jean sits filing the cauliflower ears on the blades of the number two propeller, which she has taken off the shaft. There is always the slight possibility that she will lose the pin and will not be able to put the propeller on again. It is ninety degrees in the noon sunshine, and we have our own ringside view of any vessels which may come along the highway of the river, as we sit here right at the middle of the world, right on the main channel. What friendly vessel will it be?

We complete our toilette and get all ready for visiting the next fort. Suddenly our activities cease as we hear one of the most glorious sounds to be found in nature: the trumpeting of distant sandhill cranes over the Mackenzie.

The cranes! They are flying low over the dunes. They are restless. They may have young ones. An hour later, as we have been forewarned by the wary cranes, into our world comes a clattering tin can of a vessel, about forty tons, with seven boats tied alongside her and piled atop her deck. I am utterly happy as we look out from our family island at this ramshackle, quivering treasure of an affair of boats, clanking along the old Mackenzie under an azure sky.

Later we reached Fort Norman. It occupies a commanding position on the high north bank, at the eastern entrance to Great Bear River. (Fort Norman used to be at Old Fort Point in the old days. These towns have moved more than once during the centuries.) We shoved in between small boats and driftwood, and tied up at a crude quay. A forty-five-ton vessel named *Old Bear* lay there. Above us rose a green, grassy hill, upon which the pretty Indian village was scattered. As soon as we were tied fast, a couple of white men came out of the vessel's deck.

"Come aboard *Old Bear*," the captain called. "Better have a beer. What do you think of this hot weather, eh?"

"Sure has been hot," I called over. "Is it always like this around here?"

"Hottest summer on the Mackenzie in thirty years,"replied the grimy captain. "Hot as hell, and dry. Come on, have a beer." -

"What's going on around here? I see a lot of people out on the hill."

"Don't you know, it's Labor Day?" he said. "You're Yanks, aren't you? The Yanks have their Labor Day later in the summer, I heard. We call it Sports Day, too, and don't nobody do no work at all, but just take a little drink — if they can get it. Well, if you change your mind, come aboard *Old Bear* any time."

"Thanks, but I probably better check in with the Mountie first, and let him know we're here."

"Oh, he don't care," said Captain Blum. "Somebody will tell him you got here, you can be sure of that. He's up at the Scout Cabin, directing the games. Got a loudspeaker and music up there, can't you hear it? There ain't nothing to drink up there. You climb that hill and what do you get? Soda pop. Fort Norman's all dry — or supposed to be. The missionaries, three kinds of 'em in this town, keep the Indians dry. Least that's what they think. Keeps them Indians making up home brew all the time, cause home brew is all the Indians can get ahold of."

"By the way, what port are you from?" I called, as the kids and I started trudging up the tractor road to the village.

It was then, over my shoulder as it were, that I learned that of course the *Old Bear* traveled the Bear River! She spent her life taking gasoline and fuel oils up the Bear River, and then sacks of ore down the Bear River again from Great Bear Lake. She was the sole vessel which knew that dream river, the river whose water, coming from Great Bear Lake, was the most beautiful, clear water in all the world. The game little tug belonged to the government's Radium Line of proud vessels, though you scarcely would have known it, so much smaller, shabbier, and older was she than the smart vessels of the mainstem Mackenzie. Yet *Old Bear* exemplified the very essence of the whole great Radium Line. She alone knew the fountainhead for which the line was named.

The first radium-bearing ore in North America was discovered on Great Bear Lake. It was this apocalyptic find, made by Gilbert La-Bine in 1936 — and its ores subsequently barged one hundred and eighty five miles across Great Bear Lake and ninety miles down the Bear River into the Mackenzie, then fifteen hundred miles upriver to railhead — that made possible the Manhattan Project and the two atom bombs dropped upon Japan. The radium ore brought an abrupt end to World War II and unleashed a new terror upon mankind. Canadians and Yanks worked together in those days on the Bear River to bring this ore to the outside world. In 1954 (the first year for which statistics are available) fifteen and a half million dollars' worth of uranium came from here. By 1956 production had fallen to nine million. All production of uranium ceased here in 1960 because of the distance to the markets.

Today Captain Blum's *Old Bear* was the river's only commercial traveler, hauling a little silver ore out. Captain Blum had used to command a stern-wheeler, *Older Bear;* but the government took it from him in the mid-1940's and stashed it in the tundra beside the Bear River (you can see the stern-wheeler there to this day). They had the present-day *Bear* built just for Blum, or at least had him hopefully in mind, we may be sure, for after the war was over everyone went away to other things, and he was the only man left who cared to go on memorizing all those two hundred turns of the river. The government, having Blum in its employment, has never felt the need of putting up navigation markers on this river.

It is not, however, a river that many captains would be interested in sailing. It is one hundred and fifty to three hundred and fifty yards wide, but in only a few places is it more than two feet six inches deep. So the twin screw, diesel-powered, forty-five-ton tug *Old Bear* was specially manufactured to have a draft of exactly two feet. It goes without saying that a nice precision is needed for a captain successfully to bring the *Bear*, with its cargo on a barge, over the multicolored rocks of the Bear River for a total of thirty-four summers without a single disaster. Blum had trained a couple of Indians to spell him at the wheel so that he could catch an occasional catnap during the season, but actually there was no one but himself to whom such responsibility could be entrusted. Navigating the Bear River would not be nearly so tricky if it were not for the current. The water flows at eight to ten miles an hour; in places the river is a veritable cascade. Climbing up it is one thing; slipping down again, around the tight turns in such a current, with a forty-five-ton vessel and its barge, is something else again.

Captain Blum was a happy man. Nobody supervised him; he did as he thought best. The clear, icy, beautiful waters of the Bear River were at once his home and his calling. To Captain Blum, the Mackenzie Lowlands had too many missionaries, and too hot a climate for a man to endure.

It was Sports Day at Fort Norman. We joined a holiday crowd of ancient Indian men leaning on canes, mothers with babes on their backs, and twinkling old crones who rocked as they sat in groups on the grass beside the clipped ballfield. The annual softball game between the Norman team and the crew of the visiting *Old Bear*, with assorted players from Fort Franklin, was just ending. Fort Norman was the winner, for the first time in several years.

The whites at the village numbered half a dozen or so: the bachelor Bay trader, the unmarried, pretty nurse, the frosty, correct Mountie and his helpful wife, and the missionaries of three denominations. All these were helping with the games and refreshments under the trees. The women had baked many cookies. Jean and

Ann and I bought hot dogs with mustard on buns from the Scout concession, and we bought bottles of lukewarm pop. I found the Only True Helpers of God and shook hands all around with their tiny group of Indian converts. It was a real old-time river village.

That was a lucky day. The captain of the *Old Bear*, being in an affiable mood on Sports Day, told us that we could bring our canoe and camp outfit on board the flat barge so as to return with him up the Bear River and into Great Bear Lake. There would be a transfer to truck at the foot of the rapids. Then he and his crew would transfer to *New Bear*, another similar vessel (only newer) which traveled the river above the rapids. Departure from Fort Norman was scheduled for 7 A.M. next day, Captain Blum said.

In the meantime, there was no thought of sleep on the part of the merrymakers at Fort Norman. Fortunately, we had arrived in town already rested. We were ready. A northern town plays hard when it plays. Old animosities between missionaries and converts, between missionaries and missionaries, between teachers and traders, between teachers and natives, are put aside during the day of games, races, and feasting. This is a great thing. It is only too bad that in frontier life it can't happen more often.

The day was perfect; a day such as you have never seen, unless you have seen the Mackenzie under the full blaze of the summer sun. Not a leaf moved. On the hill the grass was exquisitely green. Small boats pulled up on the shore looked like bright toys. Chained, slant-eyed huskies lay panting.

While Sports Day progressed I kept an eye on our canoe: it held all our worldly goods, and there were all kinds of strangers in town. The missionary mended our stove, as the Australian had said he would. Great Bear Lake, the missionary said, had a truly arctic climate. Fuel was scarce there. The missionary and his wife often went to Great Bear Lake in summer. They ran the supposedly unnavigable rapids, both up and down, with their powerful motor, and camped with a tent. They loved this country. And they had eight converts now in about ten thousand square miles, and had hung electric lights in Fort Norman's main street in winter for the first time.

Jean and Ann went with the crowd to a church basement for movies. They moved on with the crowd to play darts and quoits. Late in the day everybody attended the native drum dances. It occurred to me that as many of the crew of *Old Bear* were feeling their liquor, I would be wise to get our *Jeanie Ann* aboard the barge some hours in advance of our scheduled departure. *Old Bear* was not in the passenger business; this was the one chance we would ever get to go up to Great Bear Lake.

The sultry day passed and the arctic sun swung toward night. About 11 P.M. a storm could be heard rumbling ominously, coming up behind Bear Rock toward the village. Bear Rock, a landmark in these parts, is a conical, parapeted peak of limestone. Little Christmas trees march part way up it. High on its side, fifteen hundred feet above the Mackenzie, hot springs gush into a natural limestone basin; generations of Fort Norman youngsters have gone there to swim. Fitful heat lightning flickered over Bear Rock, as the *Old Bear*'s cook and engineer and I loaded the *Jeanie Ann* aboard the barge. I got all our stuff, including the repaired campstove, stowed under deck canvas in a pile, just as the first rain drops fell.

At 1 A.M. I was still sitting on the barge in the dim gloaming. The ship's engineer scanned his watch in the darkness and the stout cook yawned.

"Good heavens, I didn't know it was so late," I said. "I wish I knew where those kids of mine are."

"They'll be all right," the engineer assured me. "People in these parts has respect for women."

There was one other white girl at the fort, a contemporary of Jean and Ann. The drum dances were going strong on the hill, virtually the whole village joining in. The local girl showed the Indians how to do the jitterbug which was something like their original drum dances.

"Jitterbug? You mean you still dance jitterbug around here?" Ann was saying. "Boy, are you all ever behind the times. I'll show you some new steps." So Ann proceeded to put Fort Norman on the right track. From midnight until about 4 A.M., it seems, Ann had nearly the entire populace doing the Jerk, the Popeye, the Watusi, the Swim, the Alligator, the Monkey, the Pony, the Shimmy and the Frug.

When I crawled fully clothed into my bedroll, exhausted, the engineer and cook were still there. They pulled a piece of deck canvas over me, for it seemed certain that it would really rain soon.

"Will the girls and I have this whole barge to ourselves? Why isn't there any cargo?"

"Oh, the cargo is right here. Right under the deck," I was assured. "Fifteen thousand gallons of fuel oil. It's in nine separate tanks." The engineer hopped over the side of the barge onto the attached vessel and disappeared inside. Only the stout, greasy, whiskery old cook seemed to be around.

"Are you sure you're comfortable there?" he asked. "Everybody having fun, don't you know that?"

"Do you think it's going to rain?" I asked.

"Weather's due for a change, that's for sure. I'll tell you one thing, this is the last summer they'll get me to work on this old tub," he confided. He was overheard.

The engineer appeared again, with his bottle. "Won't do you no good to take your complaints to the company, I told you that before," he told the cook. "Do you think they're going to get a new ship just because some old fool of a cook don't like it?"

"Don't you call me an old fool," cried the cook in falsetto. Summer lightning flashed across the deck. "This is the last summer they'll get me to cook on this old wreck, I told you. With the galley right next the engine room — why, a cook gets cooked alive, just cooking there. So much heat escapes from that engine you wouldn't believe it. Such a clatter and racket from that engine any cook could go deaf. I won't stand much more of it, I'm telling you."

Snuggling down in my bedroll I hoped I could sleep out the rain, the lightning, my worries over my kids at the drum dance, and the inebriated arguing at my shipboard bedside. I only wished the girls would get home to their sleeping bags. The cook continued complaining bitterly.

"Look," I said wearily, "why aren't you both inside your quarters?"

"Well," said the cook coyly, "I didn't want for the Indians to cause you no trouble here." At that point the engineer vanished for the night.

I looked around. A couple of lovers from the village, mere shadows in the darkness, slipped across the deck of the barge. Shadows of other couples could be discerned climbing onto the barge, which was vastly freer of mosquitoes and less public than the beach. The unsavory cook sat beside me, leaning close. Cook: "It's starting to rain. It's cold out here."

Me: "What's the matter with your bed in the boat?"

Cook, sadly: "Indians. It's full of Indians. Everything full of Indians around here. Dear me, I don't see any place for me to sleep this night."

"Just go away!" Deep in my sleeping bag I tried to ignore him.

"You got sleeping bag?" came an Indian woman's voice. I awoke from a light doze just in time to wrest my children's sleeping bags from a couple who had started to drag them down the deck.

"Say, now, you stop that!" The cook rose gallantly to the occasion. "Now you just let them sleeping bags alone here. Them is private property."

The night became a struggle to defend my sleeping bags, upon which the whole expedition depended. I was almost glad at moments, as it turned out, that the cook had stayed. As each couple crept aboard the barge, each in turn would seize an unused bag as their own discovery; and they paid little attention to me as I began to nod in spite of myself. I might have lost my possessions if it had not been for the embattled cook, sitting cross-legged beside me with his bottle.

Finally the rain, so long pent up, hit hard. The hand-in-hand couples sprang for cover. They crawled under deck canvases and lay on the cold steel deck. At this, the disgruntled cook went around kicking the unfortunate bundles.

I was quite relieved when the rain drove the cook into the vessel, where I believe he sat up the remainder of the night. More couples came and clamored to get inside, but no more could fit in: the *Old Bear* was full. It seemed as though most of the village had come to the boat. Probably only the missionaries and a few converts re-

mained at the proper recreations which had been provided for them.

"Why don't those kids come home?" I worried. Then I stopped and thought it over. I decided that actually it was fortunate that my daughters were among the most indefatigable of the dancers that night. Home that night was not the best of places for them.

By around 5 A.M. the decks were cleared of people. Dawn had come; the rain pattered on the shining deck. I dozed fitfully, only hoping my girls would get on the barge before she embarked. They did. We moved over to the mouth of the river, and there we picked up the girls and several crew members on a path.

Suddenly I looked around and it was full morning. The rain had stopped. Fog was lifting from the river. Everything was wet and glistening. You could hear the splash of clear, icy mountain water; and the throb of engines began.

The vessel was still, to my surprise, full to bursting with Indian girls and women who had not gone home from the party. When we started up the river I doubt if anybody knew exactly who was on board. Indian women peeped out from every pile of deck canvas, from around corners, from bathroom and lifeboat. They were in the crew quarters and engine room. (Some young girls had come down from Fort Franklin originally, and of course these were returning home.)

Suddenly I recalled the previous afternoon. When I had come aboard chatting with the minister, I had thought it a little odd that the engines started up when we were tied to the dock. All the time the minister and his wife and I were aboard the engines idled. When we got off they stopped. Starting the engines, at a signal from the lookout on the bridge, informed certain persons in the vessel that administrative or missionary visitors were coming.

It seemed likely, as we started chugging up the Bear River, that there were some bad headaches that morning. My kids and I had had as little sleep as the others and we had not had a square meal since our own camp on shore above town a day ago. We stared groggily at the river of our dreams as the fog lifted from her.

The color of the water, after the muddy Mackenzie, was remarkable: it was brilliant green. As it swirled under the tug and barge it looked just as though we were floating over vivid green mint jelly.

It was ninety miles upriver to Great Bear Lake, and fighting a ten-mile current, we made a gain of five miles an hour along the riverbank. Not counting an hour or so at the portage, our traveling time to Great Bear Lake was nineteen hours. The return trip took around four hours.

Although a number of people are able to see a little of Great Bear Lake in the summer fishing each year, they all come in by air. It is not inexpensive. In fact it costs almost as much as an African safari because of the lake's remoteness. Very few are invited to ride *Old Bear*. It is almost unknown for Captain Blum to take outside whites on board. I believe the reasons he did so in this case may be attributed to the happy mood of Sports Day. It may be that he had more or less forgotten his impulsive invitation, and was surprised that the cook and engineer had helped me load our things aboard. And as a matter of fact, I do not think it likely that he will ever bother with tourists again, goodhearted man though he tries to be to everyone, year in and year out.

27

Great Bear Lake

I stood on the bridge with Captain Blum, watching the water. Schools of swift, beautiful arctic grayling sprang lightly out of our path. Their big dorsal fins were like those of flying fish. We passed deep, icy, green pools, where shafts of blue light filtered down into the darkness.

Boulders as big as trucks lay in many of these pools. Their tops could turn a small boat over instantly if struck. Their tops could hang up the hull of the barge we pushed before us, loaded with fifteen thousand gallons of oil. White water marked the subterranean boulders. But here the markers were deceptive: the white water churned not where the obstacle lay but as much as fifteen feet below the object, because of the swiftness of the river.

Old Captain Blum was an artist. He pushed steadily up the wild river boils, crossing and recrossing the river. All two hundred crossings were carried in his head; the river had no markers. Creeping up to the lip of each rock bar, he would hang poised there for interminable seconds before making each crossing. (I would have made a mistake each time and crossed too soon.) The thin layer of water Blum needed under the hull to cross over the three hundred yards or so to the cutbank shore was all but unbelievable. You had to go with him to believe it was possible.

In the galley the cook scrounged in his cupboards for something to feed us. He just couldn't find anything; and it was all but dinnertime. He was desperate. "I don't know what they expect me to cook them to eat when there's nothing to cook," he whined to himself. At last he seized on a little can of minced ham, and baked up rock-hard baking powder biscuits; they had no baking powder in them and therefore did not rise. That was all he had. There was coffee. The cook sighed. This sure was a nervous job. The gallant *Old Bear*, veteran of the wildest river on the continent, the craft upon which all of enormous Great Bear Lake depended for cargo from the outside world, had given away her crew's provision at Fort Norman's annual Sports Day down on the Mackenzie — and perhaps she should be acclaimed the nobler for that.

The thin Indian women had come begging with buckets and gunnysacks and baskets and had carried away our larder to their families. Others, even more gregarious, had neglected to return to Fort Norman and were still with us. These women did not appear at meals in the galley, but remained shyly hidden, probably mostly in the crew quarters, as their presence was against company rules. In a way, we had some of the same problems, being vagabonds hitching a ride; but we had our complete camp outfit with us, including our own boat and grubstake. So anywhere that we could float, we were at once independent and self-sustaining as the poor Indian women were not.

Almost exactly in the middle of the trip up Bear River is the St. Charles Rapids, lying adjacent to the landmark of Mount St. Charles. Around this rapids during World War II the Americans built eight miles of single-track dirt road for trucking cargo and personnel to the point above the rapids where navigation can be resumed. The Americans had also built an underground oil line around the rapids. Now, years after the Americans had left, all fuel oil was pumped out of *Old Bear's* barge through the pipeline, and directly into a barge waiting with the vessel *New Bear* eight miles away.

Bear Camp was the farthest that *Old Bear* could go. Here the crew would hasten over the portage in trucks and transfer to the other vessel. After that it was just a matter of fitting some pipe attachments together and starting up the pumps, and soon the cargo of fifteen thousand gallons of oil would be eight miles above the rapids and in the *New Bear*'s barge.

(I wondered vaguely how the forty-five-ton *New Bear* and its barges had originally been deposited above the rapids, as well as a third vessel which alone worked Great Bear Lake; but I never solved this puzzle. I simply accept the fact to this day. It occurred to me that my friend Bumbles would have enjoyed going over the technological accomplishments in the Bear Lake area, and would immediately have come to terms with them, if he had been there.)

At the foot of the rapids three of our crew loaded our stuff aboard a truck, and we rode atop the load along the eight miles of wilderness track. At the other end we helped stevedore our things aboard the new barge for the second and even swifter stage of the river.

Meanwhile, the crew had stopped at Bear Camp for a brief meal. Our good captain would have invited us to share this meal, but the man who ran Bear Camp, being married to an Indian woman himself, was of no mind to feed traveling outside whites at his camp. I felt that I was suffering from racial discrimination, but there was nothing I could do. Therefore the girls and I waited with rather nagging hunger pangs until the end of our nineteen-hour journey to the lake; the way events worked out, we did not have a real meal in three days.

"Rain's stopping," the Captain said to me as he turned the wheel. We were struggling up the cascades of the upper half of the river. "Why don't you go inside my cabin, and you and your daughters get yourselves some sleep? It will be a nice day tomorrow."

We climbed to the Captain's cabin, pushed open its small door, and laid our sacks out upon its tiny floor. (After all, the one bunk belonged to the Captain.)

After an indeterminate time the twilight grew so thick around the vessel that he couldn't see to navigate. I could only imagine it outside myself, the sheer wildness of that mountain river. At long last fog and the darkness of a cloudy night brought the clatter of the engine room to silence. With heavy steps the tired Captain came in; and shortly he fell into whistling snores beside us in the little room. We had tied up in the woods, where some tributary comes in. There aren't many berths for a tug to hang onto along that Bear River shore.

The children and I first saw Great Bear Lake at seven in the morning. I woke in my sleeping bag and realized that the Captain was gone; we had been traveling for some time. When Jean and Ann and I got out on deck we were just at the last bend of the river, as the whole wonderful lake opened out before us. The water danced and sparkled under a brilliant sun. And simultaneously a crescendo of loud music seemed to burst upon our ears. We reeled, as quite suddenly we were buffeted by the arctic wind whistling down off the lake. We hung onto the rail to balance ourselves.

The privilege of that moment, my first view of a virgin lake, is something I shall always treasure. After our nineteen-hour trip through rain and overcast the day was glorious, just as the Captain had predicted. We had achieved our farthest quest: lonely Great Bear Lake — sunny, blue, dancing, vast. Twelve thousand square miles of pure, sweet water. Absolutely clear and beautiful. But oh, so cold! It was an inland arctic sea, with its blue horizon ruffled considerably under the arctic winds. Here, at continental tree line, the Indians stop and the Eskimos begin; that is, if you can find any people there. There never were many people even in the beginning, and there aren't now.

As we came into the lake we saw on either hand the green moors with caribou moss and the delightful populations of tiny arctic flora we loved. Out toward the prairie horizon, the dark tiny spike spruce dwindled into the mysterious Barrens.

On this giant shore, Bear River Landing's little government docks and oil tanks and one or two parka-clad government men looked small and absolutely alone. Opposite us, four miles away across a bay, we could see the ramshackle houses of Fort Franklin. The only other settlement we knew of was Port Radium with its silver mine, one hundred and eighty-five miles eastward.

Captain Blum dumped us on the docks in these wilds, took unceremonious leave and at once moved off downstream again. He just slipped quickly around the bend of the foaming mint-green arctic river and was gone. The barge had been loaded with sacks of silver ore. The vessels *Bear* are instructed not to stop all summer long except when visibility fails: on a cloudy night late in the season perhaps, or in fog or a quick freeze on the Bear River's deadly course.

The two girls and I donned our parkas and pulled up the hoods, and rapidly stowed our cargo inside our twenty-foot *Jeanie Ann*. A white man, working about the government warehouse, eyed us dourly. His Indian woman waved shyly from the steps of his house.

"What do you want to do first, girls — eat or go fishing? Now that we're here, I'll leave the choice up to you."

Weak with hunger, they said they thought we could compromise. In order to eat we would have to canoe along the shore and find a place. Out of the wind, if possible. But while doing that, why not just drop our single line overboard on the way?

Now I must report that we never actually fished on Great Bear Lake. What happened was that the trout hit our spoons only incidentally when we put a line out. Before we knew what had happened, there were violent explosions out of the lake, and we had several enormous, aggressive trout flopping all over the canoe. As it would not have been ethical to take more than we could eat, we made our way ashore at once to attempt to cope with the first three fish, which together weighed perhaps twenty-five pounds. Thus we never actually got to go fishing, because things happened so fast.

They were rainbow-hued and spotted, and their bellies were shaped like half-moons. They were the kind of fish you can put into an oven and roast, or into a big bucket and boil, and they will float in their own yellow butter because they are so rich. In civilization you simply don't see fish like these. Their flesh was meltingly sweet, and deep orange in color like salmon. They were spawners and in the pink.

A whole people can actually live on fish of this quality, for nutritionally speaking, they are equivalent to prime beef steak. The village of Fort Franklin depended nearly entirely upon fish for survival, taking — so the Hudson's Bay Company man estimated for the Fisheries Department — about ninety tons a year in their nets to feed one hundred and thirty-five persons and their dogs!

But the Fisheries Department's studies showed that the fish grow very slowly here; they had long ago refused to open the lake for commercial fishing, and still stood adamant upon this decision. The entire twelve thousand square miles of this noble lake can be used for sport fishing and tourism only, except for the take of the local Indians for their needs.

The kids and I set up our tent, and we sat on the beach boiling fish in a five-gallon bucket, within sight of Fort Franklin across the bay. It seemed strange somehow that while communication by radio went on constantly between the three tugs of the Radium Line and their docks, the village which lay within sight across the bay was not connected in any way with this modern commerce. Fort Franklin remained isolated and roadless, its one hundred and thirty-five persons living almost as they would have in the Stone Age.

I showed the kids how to search along the ground for the little dead willow sticks, scarcely larger than a pencil, out of which we built a campfire. Sometimes the dead roots of the willows can be found sticking out of hummocks, and these may grow as large as a fist. These creeping ground willows supply the sole natural fuel of the Barrens, aside from the crisp clumps of a kind of heather, called *cassiope*, or *tripe de roche*, which can be burned, although with great labor and difficulty. If you explored far afield it would be essential to know how to survive with the sparse fuel that the prairie offers, in case something happened to your imported burner and its special fuel supply. Because of the lack of sticks this land north of the tree line has become the land of the tallow soapstone lamp (or blubber lamp on the seacoasts), the land of much *quak* (the Eskimo name for raw frozen meat or fish), and the land of the round snow house.

In the four days we were at Great Bear Lake we saw only its extreme west end. We had not the time, the gasoline supplies, or the preparation, this season, to voyage around this lake. Its shoreline is about 1,360 miles long. The lake is shaped like an elongated starfish, its five arms extending from the central body to five points of the compass. Each enormous arm is fully as large as the central body. The water level fluctuates almost not at all (unlike that of its sister lake, Great Slave Lake to the south). It has never been sounded. Average depth is believed to be around five hundred feet, and probably some holes are much deeper. There are practically no geographical place names on its shore.

The lower arm, into which we came by tug from Bear River, is Keith Arm. McVicar Arm lies just east; a tourist lodge commands its narrow entrance. The peninsula which separates them is called Grizzly Bear Mountain, and you can be sure it contains real Barren Ground grizzlies in their natural state. As for Smith and Dease Arms, the two enormous northward seas, they have no people, and the map says nothing about them. These arms stretch from the Temperate Zone into the Arctic Zone.

This leaves only the eastern McTavish Arm for a sprinkling of summer fishing lodges, all served entirely by air. They operate for ten weeks of the year: from late June or early July to the first week of September. The reason that fishing is concentrated in one arm of the lake only is that the lake has no islands or sheltered bays except in McTavish Arm; and you can't operate little fishing boats here unless you can seek out shelter from the winds of the open sea.

We could see considerable activity in the air from the spot where we had pitched our wind-flappy tent. A luxury flying boat, a Camsel, went over. It belonged to one of the fishing lodges, which were mostly American-operated and American-patronized. Sitting at our boiling bucket of fish we could imagine the plane filled with our fellow countrymen and their guides.

"I wonder, Mom," mused Ann, "do you think a person with a little boat could navigate around this whole lake in one summer's time?"

"You might spend the whole summer sitting on the shore trapped by the winds," Jean commented. "If you tried it, better take enough food!"

"Maybe the freeze-up would catch you before you could finish the trip. Then what? Who would rescue you, Jean?"

"You would have to take care not to get lost around here, in the first place."

I was pleased that the girls were beginning to think with the judgment of veteran arctic explorers. I had been working hard on this for a couple of years. I hoped their experiences in making valid geographical judgments would carry over and be of general help to them the rest of their lives. But most of all, I hoped that perhaps they would learn to believe in a dream. Some other time they just might carry out such an expedition around Great Bear Lake; who knows? If not, they would dream of something else. Their dreams would be good ones.

In the evening a motorboat approached us and put ashore to visit. It was the young Hudson's Bay trader from the post at Fort Franklin and his wife.

"My wife saw some smoke over here yesterday, and she thought she saw a little fire — with flames!" he said. "We have been watching with the glasses. We wondered if some people were stranded over here. Usually we don't see people on these shores. We extend our welcome to you."

They were an attractive couple in their twenties, and had got married two years before when they happened to meet at Fort Franklin. He had been there on assignment from the Bay company and she was teaching the little Indian children. The couple had not been to the outside world but had been virtually alone during the whole first two years of their marriage.

"Please come over and stay with us as long as you like," they invited us. "Excuse us right now. We have to get on with the fishing. But do come on over soon. We'll be expecting you."

They were putting up a few hundred pounds of fish to be frozen for the winter ahead. When they arrived, Ann was away on a four-hour exploratory hike; and by the time she returned the northeast wind had risen and the Hastings had long since finished up their evening's labors and returned homeward.

We were prevented from accepting their invitation the next day: the wind was too strong. We stayed in our cold, flapping tent, unable to move from the spot, living on cold boiled fish. Even the girls, who usually disdained the interior of houses, thought fondly of a warm interior, and as for *tuniktut* (white man's food), we were all ready for anything warm served up at a table.

When at length we reached Fort Franklin, carefully lifting our propeller blades from the water so as not to tear the many fishnets which laced the approaches to town, we were met by a swarm of children spreading like a tide across the shore.

"Good heavens, children," I expostulated to my own. "Did you ever see so many kids in your life?" Later the trader told us that of the population of one hundred and thirty-five people, the average age here was *fourteen years old*.

As we drew up to the Hudson's Bay dock the white, snow-laden clouds of a polar-looking August evening hung low over all; they looked ready to unload an early deluge of snow. The Indian people who met us, thin as shore birds, were small and dark, showing that here there has been very little infiltration of outside blood.

I was thinking uneasily that perhaps we should honor the prior invitation issued through the Only True Helpers of God. But the friendly Bay couple were most firm in their recent personal invitation. They met us at their dock and hustled us promptly inside to their fragrant supper table, saying, "Well, good to see you made it across. We've been watching rather anxiously, you know."

It was not to be our destiny to stay with the missionaries here as we had originally planned, although of course I went to call and had tea. As it turned out, their missionary cabin was far too small to accommodate house guests under its roof.

We stayed two nights with the Hastings, during which we were grateful to have warm shelter and good friends. A cold rain was followed by a shrill west wind that howled about the eaves of the solidly built little trading post. Wicked whitecaps rolled upon the cobalt lake, holding the embarrassed house guests fast.

"What a wonderful opportunity," I said to the girls, "for you to do our laundry."

And I went calling about the village: to the bright Chinese nurse, a fellow member of the Commonwealth, over from Hong Kong; to the French priest and the monks who helped him — "I met you at Pauletuk, over east," he said. "Do you remember the many ptarmigan we ate together that day? Do you remember, now? It was on the Feast of the Assumption. Your husband shot them — the ptarmigan — beside the mission on the prairie." And I met an American woman anthropologist who had come to study the changing cultural patterns of the Indians. They wore the scantiest of thin, thin dresses and coats and trousers, she said. The Hudson's Bay Company brought such thin clothing here, in imitation of fashions worn in the south. The Indians suffered greatly from cold, as well as from hunger. But no, there seemed to be no joint arthritis, most common affliction in Canada southward in the cities. There was no rheumatism despite their thin, starved bodies and their body shivering.

"The suffering here is extreme," said the anthropologist. "It must be terrible in the wintertime. There are no caribou skins any more. They killed them all off, you know. Yet, even if there were caribou, one wonders if they would really go back to wearing furs again, for you see they are convinced they will be laughed at by the white man if they do not imitate his fashions of clothing. They think I'm ridiculous because I'm all bundled up in woolen trousers, and it is only summer now.

"Oh, what a ridiculous, fantastic situation!" she expostulated. "Now, we the whites, who of course live our lives comfortably enough in the south, have actually convinced these people that they should dress scantily like us, while they live in their *arctic* climate!"

Outsiders and government persons have frequently expressed to me their disgust with the apparent "laziness" of the natives and their unwillingness to "get out and trap." These outsiders perhaps have never trapped, themselves. (I was a partner in a trapping enterprise in the far North for one year. We made three hundred and fifty dollars total.)

Before the white man came the Indians and Eskimos gathered together in small villages or camps during the worst of midwinter, which coincides with the legal trapping season. In those days they could at least enjoy community association in their miserable lot; they could share their sparse food as well as share their fears and worries. But commercial trapping forces each man to go alone with his dogsled, endless miles away from the village. The women and children wait in the village and have no man to chop their wood or to bring the comfort of his mere presence; and the man for his part never knows when he goes on one of these long, lonely trips if some evil spirit may follow him, or if he will ever return. The Indians have been trapping commercially in order to obtain rifles, tools, and cloth for more than a hundred years now. And this way of life separated families and made the North into a place of such sheer unhappiness for the superstitious and fearful natives as an outsider can hardly understand. Unless he has trapped himself with his own trapline a hundred miles or so long, he'd better not speak.

The priest was trying to get a "native cooperative store" started at Fort Franklin, to sell the Indians' pelts and handicrafts, to bank their credit, and to be their buying and shipping agent. But it needed professional management desperately. There are but seventeen coop stores in Canada at this late date, and they do not do very well; they are plagued by mismanagement and undercapitalization, and have a hard time surviving in competition with private traders (like the Hudson's Bay Company) offering more liberal credit.

I was placed in a delicate position at Fort Franklin. I was enjoying the generous, friendly hospitality of my likable Hudson's Bay Company hosts, and yet couldn't help feeling compassion for the Indians at our doorstep whom a combination of circumstances, induced by the white man and in which the Bay Company still played a major part, had reduced to the ultimate degradation and poverty. My host gave his views of the situation this way:

"I would like to tell you," he said, "how certain parties come in here and erode all the labors and investment of years of an established trading post. That priest here — he is setting all the Indians up with a desire to trade at the coop store. But do you think this is fair? Is it right that a man's own government should compete with private business? Well, our Indians I am sure will continue to deal with us anyway. We stock the things they want and need. By the way, there wouldn't even be this village of Fort Franklin except that the Company, you know, founded the village while the people were still roaming around, and we induced them to settle here."

Undoubtedly well-developed coop stores could do a lot to help the natives in the NWT. It would be one more little hope on the side of developing a life habitat in the arctic lands where a population might be able to exist. But when government steps in with its

financial backing, acting as unpaid middleman for the native population, it works to the detriment of each local trading post; and in
Canada there are hundreds of these posts where the Bay Company
has the sole monopoly — so it is big business which would suffer if
the government set up more coops, and on its own historic domain.
In fact the young Hastings believed that probably if the government went too far in establishing coop stores on public lands (not
tribal lands) it would eventually be proven a violation of federal
laws. As we arrived in Franklin arrangements were just being completed to engage a salaried "manager" for the Indians' coop store,
at two hundred and fifty dollars a month and expenses.

How did the young trader and his wife adjust to their isolated
and uneventful life, so empty of the entertainments of the world?
The government, in its struggle to keep these posts manned, is
giving a great deal of attention to this problem. The Hudson's Bay
Company also now utilizes some of the governments's studies, or at
least is aware of their results. The government and the company
ask themselves, "Where death by freezing lurks behind the double
windowpane and man lives in a box surrounded by broken, bleak,
majestic waste . . . " what can we do to make him stay, attend his
job, and like it?*

The pattern of the northern settlement is a sprinkling of wooden
houses showing scarcely any color contrasts, one or two radio masts,
and one or two moving figures as you approach, "which," adds a
government bulletin, "are always the Indians." You are struck
with the absence of noise, except for specific sounds such as a sled
dog wailing, or perhaps the sound of machinery which is swallowed
up immediately by the vast sky and earth. The immense backdrop
of silence is always there.

The physical struggle to move in cumbersome clothes from
Point A to Point B, cursing the wind, sand, sweat or bugs, as the
case may be, hoping that one's journey each day will not end in
some terrible disaster (says the bulletin) never ceases. I will add
that the ever present threat of danger is compounded in modern
times when personnel are airlifted over the Arctic from post to

* J. S. Willis (General Superintendent of Public Health Services, Canada),
Mental Health in the North. A government bulletin.

post. The inhospitality of the aerial view, combined with the vulnerability of the small plane in fog or storm, may be more alarming to the novice traveler than more primitive ways of moving about.

Because arctic personnel are bound to their posts by a schedule of duties, and because they do not have the experience or skill to look after themselves, they find themselves dependent upon help from the Eskimos (or Indians) for anything more than a short journey. The public health nurse must get a native guide to take her in the official motorboat to the next camp, in order to give inoculations. The priest, the Mounted Policeman, must have their dogsled drivers to assist them.

Thus a psychiatrist finds that the climate, by driving the white men indoors, emphasizes the isolation. Because the settlement is very much spread out (to lessen the danger of fire) various groups within the same village tend to become isolated from each other. The weather, and the necessity of perhaps a three-mile walk in it, discourages visiting. In the winter months of near darkness the range of physical activity is drastically cut down, with the result that apathy sets in.

Symptoms which often develop in people based at these settlements are motor retardation, greatly increased hours of sleep, lack of attention to personal appearance, untidiness of quarters, and a disinclination to take on extra work or odd jobs — despite complaints of not having enough to do. A progressive narrowing of the individual's field of attention occurs. There is a loss of interest in events outside the camp or in any outside visitors who may come along; then a decline of interest even in other individuals within the same camp. Under severe cold the individual's attention becomes restricted merely to keeping his body warm and putting food into it.

One third of the men in an antarctic IGY Station experienced marked and unusual difficulty with memory or concentration. This condition usually developed after several months on the ice — absentmindedness, wandering of attention, and mild fugue states. The individual would recall leaving his quarters, but nothing thereafter, until he found himself later in another part of the camp wondering how and why he got to that area.

The government in Canada now tries to give employees a longer workday than eight hours; it gives them a sixteen-hour workday if possible, because experience seems to prove that this is the best way to maintain mental health in the North. People are asked specifically to overwork themselves at their posts in order to keep busy. Both Canadian and American arctic counseling stress that family life is very important, and wherever possible government tries to staff home units for normal family life. (I have never been in the Arctic when I have *not* been living family life, which has certainly been a primary ingredient of my contentment there.) There must be adequate privacy for individuals within living units. There must also be the opportunity for community life, and this means construction of social or recreation halls. There must be adequate provision for cleanliness, including modern electric appliances. There must be aesthetic satisfaction in the home and surroundings.

But all these things are frightfully expensive to achieve during the brief summer season in the North, far from all supplies. The reality lags behind the ideal. The settlements we visited still all consisted of ten or twenty buildings (or far fewer) put up more or less at random by four or five different agencies, built of wood and stuffed with items ordered from the mail-order catalog. And there was no recreation.

A wholly different approach has been tried: sending the worker out alone and housing him in a smaller, cheaper type box for a shorter tour of duty. But after the first few months many workers show signs of wear, as most ask themselves, "Why am I living like this, when in civilization I can have fun, and friends, and have everything so much better?" One wonders what the Indians and Eskimos really think of the white man, as they see his discontented numbers come and go from the eternal village.

The needs of defense, of modern air travel, and of the effort to help and even support the native population have vastly increased the numbers of outside personnel sent north, so that now there is a double problem. The first problem is how to help the natives; the second is how to keep the white man and his family mentally healthy and how to maintain him physically on his accustomed level, after you have got him north as a helper.

It is therefore not surprising that a good deal of thought is being given to just how to remake these old trading villages: in fact, how to remake the whole environment. One new plan is to build a number of housing units like apartment buildings in close proximity, so that distances to utility services can be shortened and operating costs cut drastically. It is also believed that people would be happier in this type of apartment. The idea is to put wood aside and use concrete or other fireproof materials. Thick walls would be built between units, to eliminate noise and insure each family's privacy. Not more than ten to twenty families are envisioned in one housing block; they would be separated by a shopping center or school from the next block of families.

Since there must also be a way for the individual to escape from his family, it has been suggested that sizable areas of ground might be covered over in the center of the arctic village. This area would offer room for strolling outdoors, for sitting, for playing games, for courtship and gossiping and the like. The space would be heated in winter. It would be a pseudo-park area covered against the outside weather like a huge greenhouse. The planners point out that real outdoors arctic life and sports also should be encouraged; but they recognize there is a limit to the amount of time that the residents of such villages will be able to endure the outside climate, wearing today's modern apparel.

What the planners haven't solved, however, is the question: Will the Indians and Eskimos, whom these people have come to serve, be left outside this cozy arcade with its assorted delights? Or will they too be taken inside in a giant conglomerate togetherness?

There seems no end to the problems. You hear that "this is a period of transition." But just how can we all make this transition, and to what? Although the government planners have come up with some interesting visions, villages by the hundreds remain almost exactly like impoverished and primitive Fort Franklin, with minor differences.

How did the young Hastings manage to come to terms with

their harsh environment? Well, they lived very much as all Hudson's Bay personnel have lived for a hundred years; and they seemed to like their life, with all its disadvantages. Each day, no matter how bitter the weather, they made the supreme effort of getting outdoors for a couple of hours for a walk or visit, or for fishing or some kind of contrived recreation. Generally speaking, in fact, the Hudson's Bay people and the missionaries, who have mostly lacked the material advantages that government tries to give its people, have persisted somehow in having probably the best mental health records of all arctic groups.

Asked if she thought the teachers and weather people and health people really liked living in those new apartment buildings down the river at Inuvik, young Mrs. Hastings was quite horrified.

"No," she told me emphatically. "I talked to several of the teachers, and they just hate it. People don't like to live in a complex of many boxes," she said. "They are terribly unhappy there, and they all leave as soon as they can, for they have no individuality."

The Hastings enjoyed the autonomy of "being on their own"; and perhaps that is the great attraction which draws certain types of people to the pioneer life to begin with. Destroy the lure of pioneering and adventure, and what kind of people can you hope to attract here, except for malcontents?

But it is a complicated problem, how to keep people happy in the North to do the jobs which must be done there by someone. The Hastings, using their five-hundred-power binoculars, found a new interest right in their own back yard; and that interest — a two days' visit to be discussed for many weeks afterwards, no doubt — was Jean and Ann and me.

We hoped our stay as their unexpected house guests enlivened their lives, and we certainly were grateful to know them at remote Great Bear Lake.

28

Oil Camps and River Dredges

WHEN the wind dropped we watched our chance and scooted across the bay to await the arrival of the tug for a return down Bear River into the Mackenzie.

We pitched our tent and waited. The Indians had a saying, "Great Bear Lake is boss." According to what I had heard, Great Bear Lake has only ten or twelve "good" days in the whole summer, and this was one of them. Even so, we shivered as we waited in the unheated tent. Even the long underwear was not enough, and I thought fondly of my old caribou parka. The only thing to wear north of the trees is caribou. In summer you wear the summer parka, which is just one layer; in winter the outside parka goes over it. You need fur trousers, fur stockings, and boots of seal or caribou, as the case may be. But no one has them today. The art is virtually lost. Lacking caribou furs and without even the means for a good campfire, the only thing you can do is crawl into the sleeping bag and stay there.

Awakened by the throbbing engines of the tug, we plunged from the frost-rimmed tent in chill fog about five in the morning to catch the vessel *Bear*. She wouldn't wait long at the docks. It was an experience all young people should have: to rise on an empty stomach, shivering with cold; to break camp in frantic haste and labor like a slave at some outlandish adventure in the wilderness. We give them everything but adventure, everything but the chance to face the challenge of wild but honest nature.

Jean motored us precariously down the fast current. To my dismay, when we got to the docks it seemed that the Captain had all but forgotten our existence. He seemed surprised to see us again, and not the least anxious to wetnurse us on the return trip. Prayerfully we crossed behind the idling tug, and the scowling Captain on the bridge, seeing us, cut back her engines so that "them fool wimmen" (surely such were his thoughts) could get aboard and not hold up the day's operations. We had no time to put on our frost-laden life preservers. I was afraid of drowning clumsily right before the Captain's gaze. Afraid of power failure, afraid some mistake in our operation would pull us under the barges waiting below. But somehow we made it once again, and the deck hands rallied to haul us and our equipment aboard from the wild river. Our backs were nearly broken, all of us, for pulling a heavily loaded freight canoe four feet up out of such a river is no easy task.

We wandered into the warm galley. "Hello, old friend, how are you?" I smiled brightly at the cook.

Soon we were at the halfway mark at the rapids. But this time the *Bear* was to turn right around and go back up to the lake, so we were left with no transport for the lower half of the dangerous river.

"Oh, I think you can navigate it from here down," the Captain said calmly. "You just go around one side every time you see white water."

The woman anthropologist somewhere behind us was voyaging the entire ninety miles of the Bear River, including its rapids, by canoe, with an Indian guide. Certainly we could manage, especially since we were below the worst rapids. So we set off. First we shed many layers of clothing, for suddenly the heat was intense, after our time on the arctic lake. Then we had a thrilling ride down on those magic waters of the Bear. We skimmed swiftly over water like sliding sheets of glass, so clear that the rocks and boulders of the stream bed seemed just beneath our hull. We thought surely we would collide with them, but we never did. Schools of arctic grayling popped and played on all sides of the boat, and loons dived at a more discreet distance. The sun was warm and golden. Whenever no rapids were in sight, we sunbathed.

We reached Fort Norman late in the afternoon, and stopped

briefly to have tea with our missionary friends and to bring them fresh trout. Then we left with an armload of groceries from the Bay store.

We camped below town, just around the bend, at the base of forested and boldly scarped Bear Rock. Supper was cornflakes, canned blueberries and canned cream. It was surprisingly hot, there at the Arctic Circle. The water from Bear River in the Mackenzie was fresh and clean to drink.

The next day dawned hot and lazy, and we were late starting. That was a mistake. By 3 P.M. the sky clouded over and the Mackenzie ruffled up. We were on a straight, windy piece of river which had seen a capsizal and drowning this very week. We battled a perilous forty miles, soaked with icy spray, to the inhabited camp at Norman Wells. At ten-thirty at night, finally we struggled ashore. But Norman Wells offered no particular welcome or warm congratulations; not even physical comforts. Although up to two hundred whites worked the forty producing oil wells and the refineries, here there was no hotel for travelers; in fact no way for travelers to purchase food or lodging. Money itself was of no value to the traveler here; nor did people swoon for joy at his arrival. Rather, boat travelers may have been regarded, for all I know, as undesirable persons. It was a company town. It disregarded anyone not doing business with or for the company.

Originally during the war, the American people spent four hundred million dollars to develop this town; and from here laid oil lines across the wilderness to Whitehorse, Yukon Territory, to fuel the staging route to Alaska from which the Alaska Highway (four fifths of it being in Canada) subsequently developed. The defense of Alaska depended upon Norman Wells for its fuels. However, the pipeline which was to carry the oil was built with an eye to tight budget appropriations and was too small in bore. It clogged and was abandoned directly after the war was over. The Norman Wells field produced two million barrels from 1942 to 1945, the duration of the Canal Project. The Project left a recoverable reserve of thirty-five million barrels to supply "local needs," and today the field is worked by Imperial Oil, which is actually owned by Standard of New Jersey.

As the oil is right on the surface here in the Mackenzie oilfields, no pumping is needed to bring it up. All the field needs is control, containment, and shipping. Even in winter oil seepage can be seen in the river through cracks in the ice, I was told. Pipe is laid across the ice surface in winter. By summer the tugs and barges of the Radium Line tote oil steadily from wells on Goose and Bear Islands to tanks on the mainland.

We had been advised by the Australian and others not to expect any hospitality at the company town. Yet people all along had been so wonderful to us that we threw aside suspicion and, since the night was dark and windy, found ourselves coming wearily ashore, dripping wet and cold, at this arctic town of local ill-repute.

We climbed a long boardwalk of steps up over a hill and found an airlines man who allowed us to creep into the dampened beds of a shack which was held for the use of the airlines pilots. (The oil officials had turned us down for a bed.) Garbage was piled high by the door, the paint was peeling from the shack, and we went to bed supperless — but were glad for a place to lay our heads.

The next day no breakfast was offered, either. Sagging with fatigue from our irregular and skimpy eating habits, we struggled to assemble our soggy equipment and depart, so that we might make camp by ourselves and eat downriver soon. None of the government departments or company departments permitted the feeding of outsiders at their mess. Had it been a small camp probably the men would have yielded individually to the instinct for charity; but in this larger town with its social protocol and strict status lines, no one dared risk such a violation of rules.

But just as we were shoving off we were rescued from starvation by a Scottish widow who hired as cook aboard a retired little vessel. This retired vessel was not in the water; it had retired so far that it was actually set up in the green grass on the hillside overlooking the river. A D.O.T. crew used her to board and to live in because of the lack of other accommodations. This good Scottish widow raised such an uproar about what she called the disgrace of sending three females off without a meal from a camp containing two hundred men (some had family homes), that her foreman, growling ominously, allowed us to climb hand over hand up the unpainted wooden ladder to the unpainted old vessel propped in the hillside weeds; and there this widow fed us a hot meal on board, to our everlasting gratitude.

Having fed, we departed the forty producing oil wells and their unfeeling masters as promptly as we could. One of the great psychological hardships for the explorer is the condition his clothing gets into, the disreputable appearance of his person in an age where appearance counts almost everywhere on earth. I had long been wearing hand-me-down things, originally intended for the Indians: baggy men's work pants and shirts, long underwear, and bulky shapeless parkas, which fit badly and were extraordinarily unflattering. Only my great loyalty to the arctic cause enabled me to go on, looking the way I did. The girls, on the other hand, disciplined themselves to thin, form-fitting clothes for appearance's sake. On cold days on the river they froze; but at arctic camps they came into their own. The girls were growing up fast — so fast that it was paralyzing.

Downriver from Norman Wells the whole Mackenzie River water tasted of oil for a long time. We wished that like the river tugs we could take on fresh water and store it. The tugs got their water principally from three fresh rivers: the Bear, Willow Lake River, and Thunder River. Sometimes they bought fresh water at Norman Wells, if they had to: there was a big fresh lake inland right back of Norman Wells. Fresh good water was all behind us now, as the muddy oily Mackenzie, grown to about four miles wide as it flowed around Olgivie and Judith Islands, and Perry, Stanley, and Patricia Islands, carried us onward toward Carcajou Ridge and Carcajou River mouth.

The old river was getting ready for a big drop: the San Sault rapids. "These rapids are considered the most difficult and dangerous section of the Mackenzie to navigate" says the *Great Slave Lake and Mackenzie River Guide.* "Passage through the rapids should not be attempted without an experienced pilot. The rapids are formed by a rocky ledge, that extends into midstream from the east bank. At high stages of the river, the rapids are drowned out; . . . at low stages, the rapids are shallow and less turbulent, but contain numerous eddies."

Of course it was late in the summer runoff and the river at this stage made a series of drops. They cannot be navigated by a small boat or canoe at any time. The missionary of the Only True Helpers of God at Fort Norman had told me, however, exactly how he hugged the shallow west shore and bypassed the snarling lines of rock teeth with his small boat. Here was the one place on the river where a small boat must *not* follow the regular navigation markers. To try to go where the big vessels went out into the middle of the river, passing between the rock reefs, meant certain swamping and disaster for the small boat.

A fierce east wind warned of the approach of fall days. The wind told also of the new climatic belt we were about to enter — for even the warm Mackenzie valley cannot extend its tropical kindness indefinitely into northward latitudes. Our tent seemed near collapse, when that wind blew. I wondered one day how it managed to stand at all; it was pegged in loose gravel, and one by one its hollow pipe sections twisted out of the joints and went rolling down the beach, to be retrieved at a lively sprint. The girls on windbound days had developed the usual arctic adaptation described in the manuals: they learned to sleep away such days (when it was nearly impossible to cook) without food or drink. They curled up like cocoons in their down sacks; we got up only to make tea, or to chase the tent legs. (The primus stove worked only sporadically. Its pressure valve leaked air.)

Tea is the great restorer in the wastelands of the world. Drinking gallons of hot weak tea can brighten the darkest day. Even muddy tea helps. In one Canadian government manual I read a statement which I fully believe: that only this drinking of large quantities of hot tea keeps the Indians and Eskimos, especially the small children, from becoming severely dehydrated. Dehydration is as great a risk in summer travel along the river as it is in winter when travel is by dogsled or snowmobile.

When evening came and the wind dropped, Jean wandered off down the big river island we were camped on. She didn't announce her plans — just disappeared. When she got into such moods she did not carry knife, matches, or gun. Doing much of the heavy camp work and bearing the major responsibilities of motoring as she did each day, Jean had the position of man of the family; and she felt that she might do as she wished in her spare time, abandoning Ann and me to the menial camp chores if she wanted to. It bothered me, but it was hard to know how to deal with her. On this particular stormy night Ann shoveled and buried logs for toggles to hold our boat fast, since it was a very poor shore. I built a big fire. We needed Jean's help, but she wasn't with us. Eventually, about eleven o'clock that night, when it was black, Jean came in from her long beach walk. Since our boat was blown up on high ground, we had a rough time to launch her from the island the next day, but we made it.

"Why do you act that way?" I tried to ask Jean, when she was feeling more friendly another time.

"Well, I never *see* you all day long anyway, in the canoe," she said. "You just sit up in front staring out ahead, with your parka hood always up. All I ever see is your parka, or you turn only to yell at me once in a while. You don't even look like Mother any more — just some object far away."

Jean had never read any of the arctic manuals that I had studied, so that reply interested me. The manuals point out that in winter in the Arctic, the wearing of the parka, combined with the roar of the wind or thunder of machinery, cuts off communication between man and man, so that the tendency of each is to withdraw into sullenness. Deep inside the thick parka, without the daily visual and physical contact we take for granted in other climates, each person feels hopelessly shut off and alone. Jean's withdrawal at this time may have had something to do with the fact that she was fifteen years old. But it may also have been brought on by the aloneness of our venture, by parka wearing, and by her resolve to leave me and go to Alaska, alone. I am sure that her moodiness was accentuated by the monotony of river life, the poor food, the lack of companionship with others, and the abnormally close confinement of the family crowded into a small tent. Jean feigned fearlessness as her defense, and she feigned hardness as her choice of a survival mechanism. Ann on the other hand sat nearer me in the canoe, so we could talk through the days; besides, Ann had far fewer head-of-the-family problems than Jean; so she had but few of Jean's symptoms.

Our expedition's conflicts, such as they were, were just the kind which beset any party on an expedition of comparable rigor and duration. The stresses generally evaporate once the expedition is over and the threats and dangers of alien territory are removed. I do think, however, that the climatic difficulties cannot be overestimated in this part of the world. Although I lived north for a dozen years, as have many Alaskans and many northern Canadians, I think it is only reasonable to admit that psychologically, for the white man, there are enormous difficulties in the colonialization of the far North of our continent.

Following the abysmal, cold, foggy, dripping loneliness of Patricia Island (or Judith Island; I'll never know which island it was) — loneliness of the kind that eats into you until a kind of emotional glaciation takes place — my two girls and I pressed cautiously northward. The waves were subsiding. The wind shifted and eventually died into a pink, glassy sunset. It was the evening of August 13.

Although it was late in the day, I decided we should push on with it, regardless of dimming light, to take advantage of the precious calm. I asked Jean to cut the motor as we drifted, and I pushed my parka hood down. "Quiet everybody. Just be perfectly still, and let me listen. . . ."

Often I can hear a rapid farther than I can see it. I hear it singing to itself somewhere ahead, a melodious, harmless humming and babbling. After a few minutes of scanning, the binoculars will reveal a pleasant-looking line of foam and bubbles stretching partway across the river. This we must studiously avoid by motoring past one side of it. Tension develops as we approach on the quickening current. It is not easy, unless you are forewarned by other travelers, to see clearly at a glance which side to pass on. During the approach, as the vista changes moment by moment, one has to make an effort not to become panicky.

We crossed above the San Sault — the current was already

quickening — to investigate two house barges we saw hung up on the cutbank where the river turned. But they were empty of people. No life around.

Unfortunately the siege of wetness had fogged my glasses at the one place on the whole Mackenzie where unclear vision might be fatal. We should never have crossed where we did. The rapids around the corner were too near. Right here the river turns sharply and, out of sight and earshot of the small boatman, the deadly rapids and reefs begin.

Because a drowning occurred here a few seasons past, the government has put a sign forty feet tall on the hillside near where those barges were. This sign warned the small boatman to leave this side of the river at once. But having set aside my binoculars, I had not seen the sign from across the river; and in fact I never did see it even when we got near, because it became hidden in the hillside's undulations.

"Look, Mom! Real pine trees on that hill! Can you smell 'em?"

"Wonder what they're doing here all alone, just one stand of beautiful pines?"

But I had no interest in pine trees at the moment. I only knew that the river was big and we couldn't see around the next corner. "Jean, hug the shore tight. Make it back up the river a mile. Then we'll cross back over to where we belong, using the islands. We've got to stay on the other side. The missionary gave me directions."

The missionary had also told me there were men working the river with a dredge, in the middle of the rapids. The men of Dredge 462 were expecting our arrival, and it was to find them that we had taken some risks. I had no idea how we would get to them, but I was determined to do it this evening while the calm weather lasted. They must have experienced the same recent storm we had. They were the loneliest crew on the river, for unlike the other vessels their own was stationary. They worked for the Department of Public Works and their job was to keep the rivers clear while some of their fellow tugs placed markers throughout the eight thousand miles of commercial navigation routes in the North.

Keeping in mind the waiting hospitality of the dredge, we gathered courage. We worked our way down the west side around the frothing reef, staying so close to shore that our propeller often banged the bottom. It took nerve; but if we could find the friendly dredge whose lookouts were watching for us, that would be the reward. A red buoy means that you are supposed to keep it to your left when you are going downstream. But the missionary had told us to leave it to our right instead. It was meant for the big vessels, not for us.

At last in the pale blue evening we spotted the dredge operation: a neatly painted white tug and white house barge beside a black iron monster. They were anchored alongside a sizable island below the first big rapids. We made for it through sneaky fast water, banging bottom all the way, in the gathering dusk. Shallow channels tried to pull us every which way over gravel bars, but we averted this peril by alternately applying power and hoisting the whole motor out of the water.

It was a glad moment when we were taken aboard the houseboat from the boulder-strewn shore in the gloom. We must have looked awful: frightened, half drowned, wind-burned, our hair uncombed since before the storm. I had on two pairs of torn pants and three shirts and two parkas. As I started shedding layers, my hair fell over my eyes and I couldn't even see our excited hosts.

"Fellow got hisself drowned going through them rapids one time. Hope you didn't make that mistake. We was afraid you would follow the markers," said a voice.

"He thought that he was a hundred-ton rig," said another.

"I told you, Jock, I would advise we take down our markers for the tugs if we knowed we had females coming in a little canoe. We could have drowned them."

The lights and voices and warmth were making me giddy.

"Guess they come around the west side. They must have, Jock, to get through, you know."

Many hands helped us to a bench at the galley table, and poured the hot coffee.

"I'll not forget the time I come around there in low water in a small boat," said Kork McCorna, the captain of the *Radium River*

Muck. He was half Indian and half Scot. His father before him had been a Mackenzie River captain, and Kork McCorna had with him this summer his own young son who hoped to become a river captain in his turn.

"How many times did you crack your propeller on the rocks? Ha, ha." Tensions were beginning to relax.

"Oh, three or four times maybe. Mother thought this boat ought to climb right out on the bank, if she had her way."

"Mother thinks our boat is a mountain climber. She's scared of water."

"Three or four times? Ha, ha. My propeller cracked them rocks four hundred times," said the Mackenzie captain. "And after two summers of it, you have not even nicked your propeller blades? That's what I call good navigation."

It was the best compliment our expedition ever had. We tried to accept it modestly.

There were actually three vessels hung here in the fast water alongside the island. There was the houseboat, where the men lived in separate private rooms (they had rooms to spare) and had their meals, cooked by a professional, a Czechoslovakian, in the galley. This houseboat was moored to the shore and never left its mooring. Each morning the work crew went out from it to work.

Then there was the tow vessel, *Radium River Muck*, and each day she towed out the black iron dredge and placed it wherever it was to work; and Dredge 462 was, in a manner of speaking, the third vessel.

Luxuriously comfortable in her interior appointments, as though to make amends for the monotony of her assignment, the *River Muck* was designed and constructed especially to spend her whole life in this one bad piece of the Mackenzie River. Captain Kork McCorna could move the vessel only a few yards, back and forth, back and forth, towing the dredge on its barge; that was all he did. Yet it took all the craft of a veteran captain to maneuver the *River Muck* in the Mackenzie's most perilous waters. Each evening the captain brought the dredge back to shore again. The crew were brought to the houseboat for lunch by an extra high-power scow. It was rumored that Kork had formerly had a bit of difficulty with the bottle; but out here, where he couldn't move far, he couldn't get liquor.

On the tug, in addition to Kork McCorna and his elderly engineer and little son, there was the rotund, bespectacled foreman of the dredge operations, and his diverse crew.

We were there two days. The girls and I went out on the dredge and climbed to the high cab where the boss man of iron pulled the levers that extended the legs of the dredge to grip the bottom of the river, and the levers that guided the tremendous steam shovel to swivel in a mighty arc, and take ferocious bites of boulders from the bedrock of the river bottom; and other shrieking, grinding levers, and handles, and gears. We even took a trip on the "dumper." A blond young college boy who attended Brigham Young University in Utah took apart our rifles and binoculars and cleaned the fog out of them. The Czechoslovakian cook baked us a special cake.

Many in the crew had worked summers here before. The dredge and tow vessel were assigned here permanently, because the rapids kept bringing down such an amount of gravel that the channel had to be continuously scraped out. Operating from a record of the lowest water level recorded, they dug each summer nine feet below it. They lined up red targets from shore, to mark the site precisely.

A sample of the conversation on Dredge 462, year after year, might go like this:

"How many ton of gravel do you calculate we moved today, Percy?"

Percy: "Moose and Mac? Did you happen to count the trips out with the dumper?"

"Four or five trips, I guess," comes a sonorous, mooselike voice.

"The shovel can get one and one-half ton in a bite, just keep her biting."

"Naw, we always just count it in square yards."

"Anybody know where I can borrow a 9.5-horse propeller?" asks the cook, popping over from the stove and looking at Jean and Ann. "I sure could use that propeller of yours to mix my cake batter tonight."

"Well, I never thought about it in tons before," comes the background conversation.

"Oh, hell, who cares how many tons of gravel?"

"Say, somebody, I saw a whiskeyjack, a Canada jay up on the shore this evening," says Ned, after a lapse in the conversation.

"Did you see any girls?"

"Anyone for cribbage?" says another dryly.

Presently Percy's small group clusters around playing cards. And Moose puts on a record: a mournful song of lost love.

When we left them there, the girls and I presented them with a poem we composed in their honor — for we thought they were the finest bunch we had been privileged to be hosted by in the whole Mackenzie.

The San Sault rapids are the last ones before the Mackenzie leaves the mountains and enters the arctic coastal plain. Here the river narrows to a width of half a mile as it passes between the Lower Ramparts, a series of sheer limestone cliffs rising two hundred feet from the water on both sides. These last rapids, though turbulent, arc not to be feared; for the water is deep and no rocks stick out.

Immediately below the Lower Ramparts and about forty miles below the San Sault, Fort Good Hope lies on the east bank of the Mackenzie, at an expansion of the river. We stopped there for an hour to explore the village paths. But the only people who came along were a small group of churchgoers carrying food for a pot luck supper, and having wished us a pleasant good evening they went their way. The mission garden plot at Good Hope was impressive in both size and antiquity; generations of missionaries had tilled here. We were also impressed by the historic old church filled with relics and works of art.

Of more immediate interest to us was a racy-looking motor schooner with a tall mast which was tied up at the police dock there.

The policeman who manned it was up at the village visiting with the Fort Hope policeman. This schooner smacked of the sea and of the lower Mackenzie's broad expanses. Waiting on board the schooner was an Eskimo, who served as translator and guide for the visiting Mountie.

"Oh, girls!" I whispered, the moment I laid eyes on that broad, copper-colored, friendly, intelligent face, and caught a glimpse of wolverine fur fringe.

"You see he is an Eskimo. Go ahead, just talk to him for yourselves. He will give true advice about the river. I have never known anybody who doesn't love the Eskimos!"

Everybody loves the Eskimos because they are extroverts. By contrast, the Indians too often remain a mystery. It is as if the Eskimo's character were influenced by the broad open lands north of tree line where he lives; but the Indians of the dark forest seem to many outsiders withdrawn and secretive. The difference in cultures is remarkable. However, we should also remark that the Loucheux Indians, who go clear to the Mackenzie River mouth in the Arctic Ocean and who meet with the Eskimos there, have in many cases intermarried with Eskimos in recent times, so that it is becoming most difficult to tell the Loucheux from the Eskimos.

Having collected our mail from the Mountie, we went at once from Fort Good Hope into the sunset on the smooth river.

"The Eskimo tells me there are some white men, another oil exploration crew, just below town," I had said to the Mountie. "Do you know them?"

"Not very well," replied the Mountie shortly, and changed the subject. He would not have told me about the existence of the oil people in the isolated world of Fort Good Hope, had I not discovered it already; and even then he apparently hated to have to admit it.

We found the seismographic camp three miles below town at the junction of the Hare Indian River, which had a fresh water supply. The oil company had built three miles of road connecting Fort Good Hope to their camp: the only road ever to be built here in the hundred years of Fort Good Hope's existence. It was a worldwide company. The first organization in the plateau area of the Mackenzie, this company figured its cost of seismograph operation to be one thousand dollars per mile. Equipment at the base camp included six large tractors and an assortment of trucks and huge mobile living units. Supplies were trucked to the mobile exploratory camp which moved continuously about the frozen country, as far as one hundred and thirty bulldozed miles from base camp, while all the time keeping radio communication with the Edmonton office fifteen hundred miles south.

It seemed inconceivable that Fort Good Hope could totally ignore the economic and other effects of visitors of this magnitude upon their country. But Fort Good Hope fastidiously turned its gaze away from these newcomers — simply refused to admit their existence. (Though privately this topic was foremost in their minds, beyond doubt.) Here you see the psychology of the isolated arctic village, explain it as you may. It doesn't like strangers.

But we may have solved a bit of the mystery of reticence in this case.

Tethering our boat to a drift log on shore, the girls and I climbed the embankment toward the big trailers and heavy equipment. We were quite unnoticed. We saw nearby an Indian encampment of several tents. The Indians had set out their fishnets; in fact it appeared that a goodly proportion of the Indians had left Fort Good Hope and their benefactors of the centuries, to set up camp right beside the affluent newcomers — dogs, tents, fishnets, fish-drying racks, women, children and all.

At the oil camp itself, however, we found only two men in residence this evening: the cook, and the maintenance man called Jeepers. They welcomed us heartily and fed us well in the mobile cook shack; and we slept in an empty giant trailer in bunks that night.

But gradually the reasons for the Fort Good Hope's aversion to the seismograph company became more clear. We sat at table with two men so chewed up in appearance that they could have qualified for a leper colony, so spotted and pasty were their complexions, so scrofulous their whiskers, so drooping and slouching their posture. And they affected pointed-toed shoes; and while one of them, the young man, bit his fingernails to the quick, the older man's nails were polished, long, and pointed!

The cook of the pointed fingernails had been with the company as long as ten years. He had been going on these junkets into the

North, he said, for a long time. He had a wife and child "at home."

As for the young chap, named Jeepers, with long-lashed girlish eyes and a silly laugh and rotting teeth, he was the most illiterate, albeit amiable of wandering bachelors. What a difference from the wholesome, instinctively courteous men of Dredge 462. Yet these men were very kind to us and gave abundantly of the hospitality they had to give in the wilderness.

Jeepers of the long eyelashes had stayed at this site all alone the previous winter with no communications to the town three miles distant. He could have frozen to death, had he fallen or met some accident alone. He had taken on this lonely vigil for his company (which was just now in the process of setting up operations for the forthcoming winter here) with matter-of-fact courage. (Girlish eyelashes and all.)

Jeepers told us that during the winter when he had no soul to talk to he had fancied he might like to become an author and poet. Here is a sample of the several little things he wrote:

LONESOME NORTH

As I sit here in this Indian camp,
The weather, oh, so terribly damp,

It makes me sad and blue,
Sitting here, thinking, sweet thing, of you.

Came up here intending of making a buck.
Things didn't go so good, ran out of luck.

The rain kept coming and the mud got worse,
Oh, God, what a place, it makes you curse.

There are Indians and squaws and lots of dogs;
This place has millions of rotten logs.

You can work and sweat and swear all day,
But you sure as hell can't make it pay.

You can smoke cigarettes 'til you're blue in the face
And all you see is this dark-skinned race.

There shacks and house are oh, so torn,
It makes you wish you had never been born.

By Jeepers

"Well, that's real nice," I said. "Will you give me another one?" and he generously did. He had a lot of them.

NWT TRUCK DRIVERS

By Jeepers

All the truck drivers are jerks.
They take a big Mac when they go to work.

When they leave the camp, they're allway stuck,
But I think there just running out of luck.

I have to go and pull them out with my truck,
And all I get is only one buck.

My truck has no heater and all bent up.
The windshield is oh, so frozen and cold,

All I can see through is a small hole.
I dam near freeze my hands and feet,

But still the mechanics hasn't got it fixed.
Well, now Spring is here
And now I got my heater and gear.

Ha, ha, and now they ask me, "Am I warm?"
"Oh, yes," I say, "just right for this storm."

"Trouble around here, is," said Jeepers, "them Indians always sneaking around the Mack trucks and the tractors, and trying to strip them down and steal things off of 'em, and such. I got a gun, now. But I don't never fire no gun in my life," he giggled, and batted his eyelashes without thinking, as it was a habit he had.

"Them Indians. That's right. Nothing but trouble," said the scrofulous old cook. "Makes a fellow feel kind of spooky, specially when the nights get dark. Last night I went out by the trucks, you know we ain't got no toilets yet, and two bullets from a rifle come whizzing right by my backside, pardon me, m'am. Sure hope them Indians don't shoot someone, specially me."

"Why doesn't the company employ some of them?" I asked.

"Oh, them Indians no good. Company can't do it," replied the older man, the cook. "I been on lot of expeditions in the North, and they never can depend on the natives."

"That's too bad," was all I said.

How often, throughout my years in Alaska, as here, have I sat like this inside some comfortable white man's camp, and heard the white men describe the unreliability and pitifully backward ways of Indians or Eskimos who were meanwhile starving nearly to death and desperately in need of a chance to improve themselves, just outside our very doors. Throughout the long history of Alaska, in the fishing and mining business, all the companies have brought in their white labor force from outside by contract: scarcely any effort has ever been made to employ or train the deprived local population.

As we talked in the midnight lamplight Ann had slipped outside to the arctic rest room.

I ran out after her as fast as I could go, and just then I actually saw the shadowy form of an Indian disappear behind the row of Mack trucks.

"Hurry, hurry!" I cried to Ann, really worried. "There is a little trouble in this camp, and you might get shot." The poor girl hurried as best she could, while I stood guard.

Why were some of the Indians firing stray shots toward the seismograph camp? What was their grudge?

It wasn't only unemployment. In the morning as the cook cooked our pancakes and poured coffee for us and himself, and Jeepers nervously chewed his fingernails and smoked cigarettes, we learned more.

Just as we were eating, a third white man belonging to the camp ambled in for breakfast, for he had been at one of those nearby Indian tents all night.

It seemed this one had really "gone native," as they say. I have never run into anything quite to match this young man. After a few months in this lovely country he had allowed himself to become physically dirtier than any person I have ever seen. It appeared he had not bathed in half a year or more; he had let his beard grow ragged and untrimmed halfway down his chest, and his hands were filthy. But his toenails were his most arresting feature. They stuck out of open sandals and had grown so long that they dug into the earth, and their color was a hideous green streaked with river mud. For his long toenails he was naturally known to his two very nervous companions as "Bear Claw."

From the breakfast table conversation it appeared that Bear Claw did not rate well with the two men of the pointed shoes. They considered his fraternization with Indian women to be the most filthy personal habit which they could imagine. In fact, as they had feared it would from the first, Bear Claw's intimacy with the Indians had at last outraged one of the Indian husbands, with the result that rifle bullets were flying around the camp, endangering the lives of everyone.

But Bear Claw thought he was a great guy. Really the greatest.

That morning, as we said good-bye to Bear Claw and poor, silly, witless Jeepers and the unsavory cook, our roster of diverse characters of the far North was nearly complete. We had met every kind of person, from the poorest Indian trapper and lowest workman to flyers of the Queens' Flight.

Suddenly we realized we had but two hundred miles to the village of Arctic Red River; and it would be but eighty miles beyond that to reach Inuvik, and our long river exploration would be over.

29

Five Hundred Miles North of School

BROAD reaches of water, empty of people, on the lower Mackenzie. Winds: likely. Sun: forty-five degrees at high noon. The air:
sweetly crisp. But now, beyond the Arctic Circle, we heard the roar
of heavy machinery.

We drifted slowly on the giant, sluggish river, toward what
looked like a conglomeration of settlements: like big long white
houses ahead on the shore. But the map showed emptiness. It was a
bunch of Radium Line tugs, and Y.T. barges 196 feet long and 40
feet wide, and tankers able to carry 275,000 gallons of oil, or 1,200
tons in weight. Some portable silver oil tanks gleamed in the sunlight. Stevedoring was going on. Another oil company setting up,
or pulling out, that was what it was. Atlantic Oil.

I checked my map again. The junction of the Ontaratue River
with the Mackenzie. (We have passed the Travaillant River, and
the Tieda River — well, I think so, anyway. Could have easily
missed seeing one of them.)

"Considerable changes in depths are reported to have taken
place in this vicinity during recent years" (if it is the vicinity I
think it is) "due to shifting sandbars; main channel is reported to
lie westward of the recommended track, as shown on Chart
6385. . . ."

Suddenly Jean and Ann were yelling, looking through the glasses
at the far bend of the river. Yes, that was her. Our oldest and first

friend among the Mackenzie River tugs. It was the old *Radium Royal*.

"Whoopee, won't he be surprised to see us! Hi, Klinker!"

It was, indeed. There he was, somewhere right in the middle of the doings, Captain Klinker. A thousand miles from where we saw him last but just the same. He was walking along the shore amidst all the piled cargo.

"How you girls been?" he asked, just as natural. Just as though he expected us here beyond the Arctic Circle, among the thousands of miles of forest on every side, among the lakes blood-red with iron rust, and the endless ponds and sloughs choked by the green fringe that bordered them. And over to the eastward the Barrens, its grim black monotony broken by pingos and polygons, drumlins and eskers. But on the highway of the great river all the people stayed faithfully; and when occasionally they met each other, it was with the feeling that everything that man builds here, and every hitch he serves, is only temporary, after all, in the face of such giant nature.

"You girls been minding your mother real good?" Klinker asked.

"Jean hasn't. We are going to go to our father over in Alaska."

"Well, maybe," I said. "If he gets the letter. We are hoping now for a reply at Inuvik, it's our last chance. Too much traveling for mail to catch up with us, maybe. . . . I told them not to get their hopes up too much. How you been?"

"Tired," the veteran river captain replied. "We been working pretty steady. Sure like them new 1500 Caterpillar engines. Lot better than the old 900 we had when you were with us last year on the Slave. Lots of trips back and forth. We can do twelve thousand mile without an overhaul in a season. Come on, git yourselves a hot shower and then the cook will fix you up."

"We are so happy to see you, Klinker," cried Ann. "I can still hardly believe that you are here, can you, Jeanie?"

"Oh, it's me, all right. I'm always around some place. You keep looking and pretty soon you find me. Some of the captains been wondering where you were most of the summer. We didn't see much of your tent. What do you think of this hot weather we been having?" We were following him aboard. "Shower's right down this way. Hey, Shiny, do we have some spare trousers maybe, we could let 'em have? Looks like they're about to come right out of their britches. This is my new engineer, Shiny."

"How do you do?"

"He just come over from Germany, speaks with a little accent yet. We nicknamed him 'Shiny.' "

"Oh, we got some pant and shirt for you, I think of something," Shiny said. "I ask some of the other boys, excuse me please."

"Well, it seems to me," I said, "that the heat kept the mosquitoes down, you know. Bugs haven't been bad along the shore, really. Most of the scars I have on my shins are from old days. . . ."

"That might be it, the sunshine," Klinker said. "They're usually kind of bad, you know. Early this spring, before you ladies come north, Shiny used to fuss when we would have to stop at some of these little towns to unload, they poured into the engine room — the mosquitoes, I mean — course some of the town did, too — and you couldn't see to oil up. The bugs got into the oil, got into everything. Well, you're from Alaska, I don't need to tell you."

"I hear they're spraying a lot of places by airplane in Alaska," I said. "But I never have approved of it. Kill the birds and fish in the wilderness, which depend on the mosquitoes to raise their young — and what have you got left? Just an empty wilderness. I'll take the mosquitoes just as they are, if I have to choose."

I went to sleep, after talking with a lot of people, in the company bunkhouse in one of the executive bunks. But the girls hung around their dear Klinker all night, and drank coffee on the tugs and became a part of the all-night stevedoring. Jean had become quite a tractor driver, or thought she was. She had started out with a small fork lift, weighing about four thousand pounds, and worked up during the summer.

Not to be outdone, Ann lifted a drill bit right off the ground. The way it happened was that some of the fellows promised Ann that she could become a riverboat hand if she could lift the drill bit. According to the way the story reached me later, she shoved her thirteen-and-one-half-year-old shoulder under a part of it and it actually tipped a little. To show how heavy it was: a fork lift was engaged in lifting five drill bits, and the lift lifted itself but the mining equipment was so heavy it stayed right there on the ground. I believe this is somewhat the way Paul Bunyan stories must have got started in America.

"Mother, what do you think of this plan? Jean and I — that is, if we don't go to our father — would like to ride on a tug and barge train back up the Mackenzie and Athabasca rivers this fall, instead of flying south."

"Company wouldn't take you," I said. "These aren't people boats."

Ann waved this aside for the moment, as she spun her dream. "But, Mother, there is just one serious problem. Jean and I would have to have two separate boats."

"So you each could be queen of your own vessel, perhaps?" I put in.

"Well," Ann admitted, "she and I just don't get along. I've tried all my life to get along with her but she's impossible." (They were in reality inseparable friends.)

"True, true, but if you and Jean each went on a different boat, which boat would be left over for me?"

"Oh, you could fly, if you wanted to. Anything you like. We'll meet you later in Edmonton at the Mac."

"I am afraid your sister is going to be terribly disappointed if the Alaska thing doesn't work out," I said to Ann, seriously worried.

"Oh, Mother, you can't even imagine!" Ann turned serious at once, in our mutual concern over Jean. "You know Jean takes everything so hard, and she has got her heart just set on our father, and nothing else will do. That is why I got the idea of going on the tugs, and Jeanie could have her own tug and crew, well, just in case Father doesn't work out."

"I see, Ann. That was very kind of you. But how about you? How do you really feel about Alaska?"

"Oh, I would love to go, Mom. But I'm kind of a little scared, too. We could go for a visit — really, I think I should go along with Jean, as she might need me there more than she thinks — but for myself, I could take it or leave it, I think. I think probably we should both come back and go to our own school, because, for one thing, we've got to get educated."

"Ann, you are a wonderful girl," I said.

Along the river came the Y.T. *Saline,* and the *Marjorie* came in at the oil camp. The girls: "It's the *Charles.*"

"No, it's the *Ekileu!*"

"It's the *Charles,* stupid."

"No, the *Charles* couldn't be back from the Arctic Ocean so soon." A couple of barges got away down the river, and the *Marjorie* went chasing them.

And as four hundred barrels of fuel oil in the big quarter-inch plate iron shore tank were being drained, somebody forgot to open the valve on top with the result that the tank caved in.

Atlantic was pulling out. As Jean said, busily, "We've got ninety thousand gallons to pump into the barge beside the riverbank here, and a lot of big red ten-ton trucks to move, and other things."

"Well, come on," I said. "They will have to get along without you, because it's a lovely day again, and even if you girls didn't get any sleep, we've got traveling to do."

"Mother, do you really think a letter will be waiting at Inuvik?" she almost whispered.

"Our big problem is to find Inuvik," I replied, "and not float out to sea lost in that delta which covers about five thousand square miles or so. Trouble is, the only map the government could seem to get me was made a few years before the town of Inuvik was invented, and I don't know what channel it's on."

Yes, here would be the toughest part of the trip, in its way — the vast delta. But Klinker drew in the town for me on the map I had and told me how you just follow the markers. The only trouble was that the river forked a number of times, and actually many of the tugs did not go to Inuvik at all but directly out to Tuktoyaktuk right on the Arctic Ocean to the delta's east side.

A canoe traveler could get into a lot of trouble if he got mixed up in that mess. The main channels of the Mackenzie and Peel rivers may be followed through the delta in twisting, meandering courses, although from the air they are hard to distinguish from the numerous, intertwining tributary channels. Between the channels are innumerable lakes and cutoffs of all sizes and shapes. So much water covers the surface that from the air the delta looks like strips of land separating bodies of water. The delta is slowly building northward; shallow water and sandbars are found ten to twenty miles out from the island-studded river mouth, actually in the Arctic Ocean.

We said good-bye to Captain Klinker and the other men, and we never saw them again.

The gracious sun smiled down in a flawless arctic sky. The river was four miles wide. We were burning five types of gas now, each can being a sort of surprise package. We were burning what Canadians call purple gas (tractor gas which is dyed purple mainly to show that, unlike auto gas, it is tax free); yellow gas, and 180 octane aviation gas manufactured for four-engine planes. Apparently we didn't get our mixture right, for they were to prove expensive gifts indeed. They were to be our undoing.

We were in hand-me-down clothes, and I had burned up my parka one day when the wind swept the campfire to a dry drift log on which the parka lay drying; and Jean had much earlier in the season left her parka on a gull rock off the coast of Great Slave Lake. Our poor camera had ended up in six inches of muddy water in the bottom of the canoe one night following a storm. But nearly everything we had brought at the beginning of two years had been used, although not always for the purpose for which it was originally intended. We bailed the boat with the dishes and ate out of the funnel. Band-Aids held the fishing pole joints together. I had fallen down on the little finger of my left hand and broken it early this summer, but it never bothered me; it only grew a little crooked. It was a country that kept you so awe-inspired that you could break a leg and walk away and never really know it, I think.

All this time we had never let our boat get away as we slept. We were adept as foxes at survival techniques. We would roll a two-hundred-pound log down the beach to tie to; and the girls could operate winches, cranes, and bulldozers, and hook on 196-foot barges and back and turn (with the captain, of course) neatly with 275,000 gallons of oil. They were absolutely amazing the way they knew the registered tonnage of every vessel on the Mackenzie

River; and they talked of different things now than the average American girl or boy.

Trouble was — they didn't want to go south. Trouble was, they would now always belong to two worlds — and this is at once the special privilege and the burden of northern people. Because you can never forget the North. It pulls you back to it, time and again, when you have fallen under its spell.

I can see us now, floating down that turgid current northward. Ann, fiddling with the loose wooden matches in her jeans pocket, scratched her thumbnail against one, and it suddenly ignited, setting her pocket afire. (What country boy hasn't done the same?)

As she hopped around, slapping the blaze out, I yelled at my eldest for the umpteenth time, "Jean, for God's sake, this boat's full of gas! Do you want to blow us all sky high?" Then I realized it was little Ann I was yelling at.

"Ann, you make us all nervous," lectured Jean.

"I feel nervous," said Ann. "I feel terrible, if you want to know." She too was beginning — rather late — to feel the stresses of the teens.

Little did we know that the last camp was almost at hand. It is always that way. I have seen this before. The last day dawns just like any other, and you never have the slightest inkling that this will be the last camp. Then suddenly, you are catapulted out of the reverie.

One day, after a late lunch on the beach, the motor simply refused to start. Jean thought the *stop* button was stuck on *stop*. Anyway, the cause was beyond us. We couldn't figure it out with all our combined brain power.

As it was less than a hundred miles to Arctic Red River, there was nothing to do but start paddling. But it was hard to move the heavy, unwieldy boat, with its load of useless gas and the useless motor, against rolling waves and a headwind.

The wind became worse but there was no place we could stop. The river channel became a tunnel of wind. "Jean, you and I take turns, and we'll have to line the boat," I said. "I'm sure we can do it, as I've done it before. There's a good bank for lining, too."

"Can I have a turn, too?" asked Ann, not to be left out.

"Nope. You're too lightweight for lining."

In lining a boat, you untie your tow rope from the bow and attach it to a thwart about one third down the length of the boat, and this technique usually helps hold the boat offshore. One person walks off the miles down the beach towing the boat, while the other person uses an oar from the stern for rudder. He may also have to fend off with the paddle, as there are always occasional rocks and snags.

Soon Jean had struck a steady pace, pulling the boat with the chain snapped around her waist. She walked the boat mile after mile, her head bowed to the wind.

With our power suddenly gone, the world was more hostile, far more chancy — but we were happy. The original Mr. Mackenzie had nothing on us.

Far ahead, the binoculars showed a violent sandblast hanging over that enormous, unending shore. The river might become choked in sand; we were far off the traveled channel. Yet the only shore possible for us was the one chance had dumped us upon. Where would it lead, into a sand trap or spongy muskeg quagmire?

The thin lemon slice of moon came up in a pale green eastern sky; one bright star — was it Venus? — seemed to hang off her prong. The wild river, running north through sand dunes into a late sunset, blazed green and red and gold.

At last, a cleft! Safe shelter for camping. Bowed into the sandblast, we shoved the canoe into a narrow, muddy brook mouth. The willows on the riverbank bent in the wind and slashed about us. We built our cooking fire in a frost crack, out of the wind, behind the mountain shoulder, and pitched our tent in the one sheltered spot in miles. Was our position desperate? Not at all. The country was ferocious but we were fit for its tests. Perhaps there is no such comfort on earth as to bed down on such a night, with one's family in sleeping bags laid on fur, after a hot meal.

In the middle of the black night we heard a Radium tug pursuing the channel in the distance, and we saw her lights.

It did not snow, as I had almost felt it would that night, but the next day dawned hot and positively tropical again. We were to be given the grace of a series of such golden, serene days. We pushed our advantage, as you can imagine: soon we were out in the main current and paddling steadily right down the middle of the river from target to target, watching anxiously for the slightest ruffling of wind. The sun was so hot that we striped down and soon began to get brown.

We came abreast of a white wolf who trotted on long legs down one shore. We watched him for several miles as he kept pace with us, his shoulders standing high and handsome. He looked extremely white because he stood out, a symbol of approaching winter, against the world of brown mud and sand. Presently a crack opened in the cliff beside his course, and he vanished up a gulley about his business.

Far ahead again the glasses picked out what I believed at first were two adult swans and their cygnet. But I had never before seen swans walking upright with long strides on sand dunes. And they usually nest inland on the lakes, not on the river. I was left to wonder if we may not have seen that day, at a great distance, a family of the nearly extinct white whooping cranes—a thousand miles off their known route of migration. The two adults spied us from miles away and all three flew soundlessly into the distance. Few people have seen the wonderful white whoopers in their arctic breeding grounds.

We camped again, upon a high sloping gravel bank, the river forty feet below. A tinkling spring flowed from the cleft above and splashed down over stones beside the tent, singing and talking with almost human voices. Snow water. Back in the forest a lynx screamed.

The pattern the river made on its beaches was familiar to us. A line of big white logs that catch the sun's rays and gleam for miles is at the edge of the water. Fifteen feet up the beach from the logs comes a sinuous windrow of smaller stuff. Polished rocks of grapefruit size seem carefully inlaid to please the camper's eye. Then come alternate bands of smaller gravel with plateaus of intermediate pebbles, all neatly graded. Thus the river paves its curves. But beauty in such loneliness cannot expect a camper to come along very often. The river creates beauty to please itself.

A camper naturally pitches his tent facing the river and his parked canoe, hauled out on rollers and chained to rocks below. He overlooks his great, free domain from on high with his binoculars always at hand. A camper sleeps on the clean gravel with his feet downhill toward the river. It is comfortable unless he makes the mistake of lying where a plateau falls off a few inches abruptly in the middle of his back.

As evening settled over the lower Mackenzie we sat on high, eating bacon and eggs and canned fruit. The river turned pale violet; the moon rose. Ann made little wooden boats filled with oil and equipped with wicks of string; then she lit the wicks and set the boats sailing down the river glimmering in the night.

"Shall I leave my teddy bear here?" she asked next day, as we packed to leave what was to be our last camp. "You know, it is about time I left my teddy, because I am grown up now."

For a few moments she toyed with the thought of saying a final good-bye to him right here, to leave him propped up looking out over the Mackenzie from a high perch, with the tinkle of the spring in his ear. It would have been nice to remember him like that. (He was so dirty, so completely unsanitary, to go on living with.) But the move from childhood into adulthood is not any definite step. It is made easier if the steps are so gradual you don't notice it.

"Oh, no!" I cried. "Please don't leave Teddy here. I couldn't bear it, Ann!" In the end, therefore, Teddy went along in the canoe as usual. He disappeared eventually but none of us will ever remember just where.

That was our last camp.

We saw the village of Arctic Red River in the distance, with the white Gothic towers of the Oblate Fathers shining in the sun. How slowly the current and our paddle strokes carried us toward it! Couldn't some of those people there see that we were without power? It would have been nice, I thought, if someone started up a power boat and came out and towed us in.

But there was no sign of that. Eventually we reached the town situated where the Arctic Red River comes in, up which remote Fort McPherson lies; and we saw that, while the official building of the RCMP and the Hudson's Bay Company crowned the hill, most of their charges — the Indians themselves — had forsaken their musty cabins during the summer season to pitch tents on the beach, right beside the water and their fishnets. In so doing, they had at the same time forsaken the few outhouses back up the hill. As the result we saw that the beach was an unsanitary mess, just as we realized that we were nearly dead with thirst. But we did not dare to drink the Mackenzie water within miles of that village.

A walk up a dirt road to the official building brought us to the only white men (at that time) in a town of about two hundred natives. Having asked for our mail and received it from the Bay man, we prevailed upon the Mountie who was with him for a glass of pure water from his house. This, like the mail, was handed us formally, and in almost absolute silence. Neither of the two white men had a word to say apparently. Their faces as they looked at us were a perfect blank. As it was apparent that we were not welcome there and that our problems with the broken motor were of no interest to them, we left them upon their hill and returned down the path to the waterfront.

"I wouldn't stay here at this town one minute if they paid me a thousand dollars," said Jean, deeply offended by the silence technique which had been used upon us.

"What a greeting after two hundred and ten miles," bristled Ann. "Did you ever see anything to match it? Let's get out of here."

"Yes, we've got to go at once," I agreed. "We have plenty of food. We don't need them. But most especially, do you notice this weather? It can't last. We had better travel all night and push our luck somehow! Or we may be in trouble later."

Even the Australian had said that Arctic Red River was a peculiar sort of town. But wait:

When we arrived back at our canoe, having let more than an hour slip by in climbing up and down the hill to the buildings, there was one of those arctic men whom I have known before, a native, but tall and big like a white man, showing white blood. He had been waiting for us. Shorty McDonald was his name.

"Perhaps I can help you with your motor," he offered. "I will look at it, anyway, if you like."

He took off the case as we waited beside him. "Oh," he said. "Too bad, too bad. I am sorry for you. I cannot fix him. For you have burned out the head complete. Nobody can fix him, I think." He clicked his tongue in pity.

"Guess we burned too strong gas, that aviation gas, ha, ha."

"Oh, too bad, too bad. That aviation gas too strong, you burn the motor up. You have to send outside get new parts."

"Shorty, I'll give you twenty dollars and the remainder of our grubstake — there's a fishing pole, too, you can have, and a primus stove, all this stuff, except the binoculars, the rifles, and the sleeping bags. How would you like to tow us with your big boat to Inuvik tonight? You can have all this canned food and all our cans of gasoline besides."

"Sure. I go tell my wife. I going to my tent. Be right back."

"I hate to have to travel tonight, I would rather wait until tomorrow," I said. "But I got this feeling we better travel tonight, in any case."

"Oh, sure," he said. "This damn good weather. It no good if we wait for tomorrow. Tomorrow maybe bad. You been to Inuvik before? You will like it. Many white people there," he said.

"Kids, that's a good man for us," I said. "He knows what he's doing and he will take us through the delta, where I sure don't want to get lost this time of year with no motor." I had already mentioned Shorty McDonald to the Mountie, I might add, and was assured that he was a good man for a guide, so that I had, besides my own judgment, an official opinion.

Shorty was a Fort Norman fellow, he later told us. He married a Loucheux Indian and thus joined Loucheux society when he came here. He selected a young man quite Japanese-looking, about seventeen years old, for his helper on the trip.

"It isn't a very friendly village, is it?" I said to Shorty. We were loading his thirty-foot narrow plank riverboat with our duffle. We donned our heaviest apparel and prepared to tow the *Jeanie Ann*.

"No, it never was a very friendly village," he said. "I don't know why that is. It's always that way, don't make no difference who is here. Whatever people is here, they not friendly. Even the Indian people not friendly to other Indian people," he told me. "White man change every year, and they not friendly, too. I don't know why that is, this town."

He put on a wolverine-trimmed parka and drove us through the winding, intricate delta waterways of the East Channel all through the chill night. I bedded down with Ann amongst the gas cans, canvas, fur rug, and sleeping bags. Jean talked to Shorty and kept him well entertained all night long with her philosophy of life, much of which he probably did not understand, because of the vocabulary.

At one point we stopped and Shorty built an instant beach fire by throwing a gallon of gasoline onto a pile of sticks we had tossed together. We thawed out with hot canned food and coffee as the grotesque shadows leaped around us.

When we reached Inuvik it was seven o'clock in the morning and broad daylight; but we were all so weary that we just went to sleep for a while in the warm sun in the bottom of the scow, tied up to a bigger scow just above town, and waited for the town to wake up. The name Inuvik in Eskimo means Place with People. At nine-fifteen a raven, coming by to see if we were dead, uttered a loud squawk and then alighted nearby. Then the Fisheries Department Eskimos had to move the scow we were tied to; so we all got up. Shorty, I soon realized, was anxious to get to the bar with the twenty dollars he had coming. So I gave it to him and let him go, and the girls and I started sorting foods and duffle, all to be disposed of.

A D.O.T. channel marker vessel, the *Dumit*, a native word which means Roadway, welcomed the girls and me aboard from our waterfront labors, and we showered and had a noon meal there. The engineer of the *Dumit* diagnosed our motor again for us, cleaned it of water, and oiled it so that no further corrosion would take place during its winter storage. Deckhands helped Jean and Ann hose out the mud and filth from the canoe; and the Y.T. Company agent promised me storage for the canoe and motor over the winter, until the Bay would take them for resale. As storage space is precious in such an arctic town, this was important.

When our equipment was disposed of we faced the immediate problem of where to stay until we could get air passage out. It seemed strange no longer to be able to camp, to be dependent on shelter. It gave us an empty and rather frightened feeling, this giving up of our camp outfit. The trip of two years was ended, the canoe and duffle hauled away, and all we seemed to have to show for our monumental journey was a broken camera, some mud-spattered maps, and my portfolio of numbered field journals giving off a strong odor of swamps and fungi, and redolent of campfires and birdsong.

The whole first day was spent merely coping with survival problems. It is difficult getting around the northern town without a car, because everything is spread out over a distance of several miles, so that accomplishing each errand becomes a frustrating task. Most roads are dusty or muddy. There are almost no signs on any of the wooden or sheet-metal buildings. At the community coin Laundromat I spent five hours waiting my turn with our filthy clothes behind a considerable lineup of Eskimo women with theirs.

That Laundromat was the best thing I had seen. It was run and partly supported by the government, and included a dry-cleaning facility and community showers for those travelers and hunters who poured into the village from the surrounding arctic wastes. Unwashed natives can take the first step on the road to self-respect by meeting some of the white man's standards of hygiene. Every Mackenzie District village should have this kind of community facility, I would say.

Our food we put on the vessel *Dumit*, courtesy of her captain, so that it could be guarded for Shorty — but unfortunately we had to take the food off again when the *Dumit* was due to pull out late that day.

Our lodging was supplied by an international oil company. We found that no lodging whatsoever was to be had in the town. A large convention of visiting Russians filled the entire Mackenzie Hotel facility; and the large Anglican Hostel was booked full of the Carruthers Commission from Ottawa, including the Minister of Northern Affairs and Natural Resources, who had come to make government inspections and hold a series of forums and conferences here at the "show place of the Arctic." The time of year set for such tours is always early fall, as the mosquitoes have died but the snow hasn't yet come. As a result of these conferences the capital of the Northwest Territories was moved five hundred miles northward from Fort Smith to Yellowknife; the transition taking effect in 1967, Canada's hundredth anniversary of nationhood.

I should add that at this time the town of Inuvik contained not less than thirteen hundred white people from outside, living in beautiful houses which boasted every imaginable comfort. There was even a Navy barracks for the training of an encampment of one hundred and sixty men here; apparently the Navy Department was supposed to help support the other government-supported facilities of the arctic city and keep the city going.

At any rate, our lodging problem was most acute. Finally I found the oil company offices in a shack which was being painted and was not yet furnished; and there, after babbling my pitiful tale, I was rescued. A kindhearted agent would do his best to help a lady and her children in distress so long as what he called "the brass" didn't know about it.

"The brass, the big shots, are flying in from Edmonton," he warned. "Our company has these trailers just setting all empty out on the hill above the river, see? You could put down your sleeping bags in one of them. Fifth one from the right is not locked. But don't nobody know that in Edmonton. We keep that one that way for guests. No plumbing, no lights, no stove. The weather turning cold. But if you don't mind, at least you will have a roof overhead while you are here."

"Sure. Fine. I'll take it."

"Well, there's just this one complication, remember. The brass, see? They will want to make the rounds and inspect all the trailers and equipment. If you wouldn't mind waiting until after eight o'clock this evening to move in, I think I can have the brass moved along by then."

The brass, however, arrived late. It was not until the following morning, while I was still lying unhappily in the sagging bunk, that through our door I heard the voices of the brass, guided gently along on tour by our secret friend. After they passed, we were in the clear.

Even in our difficult position, we had decided that we must stay for a few days so as to try every resource to contact the girls' father in Alaska. What would we have done without the free lodging? I shudder to think. We could not afford even to eat many restaurant meals here, at the end of our long journey, with our diminished resources.

Each day we went to the Mounted Police station to see if a letter had arrived. Each day Jean returned homeward to the trailer in a desolated condition. All summer long as we had voyaged north she had dreamed of this goal: that surely her father would fly his plane on floats along the Arctic Ocean shore from Alaska and get her here.

We had hoped to be able to reach him direct by radio from Inuvik; by this date the Radium Line vessel which was to be our contact in Alaskan waters had already left Alaska and returned up the Mackenzie. We tried some Dew Line stations, all of whom knew him. Somehow, our family had been heard of everywhere throughout the two countries, the mere matter of the border making little difference in the Arctic.

Again, Jean rose early from her sack, and barefooted as the days grew colder and colder slipped away, saying nothing. She could not stand being spoken to by anybody. She couldn't bear my voice or my suggestions or my physical presence, couldn't be reasoned with. I let her go — failing other means to cope with her. I turned down a chance for the three of us to get free air passage on an oil company executive plane south to Edmonton, on account of Jean. There would be other oil company flights, but only this one was an empty. We continued to plod back and forth for mail each day but nothing came.

One day, at the fledgling Arctic Research Station, I ran into an American girl from an eastern college, who happened to know several people I knew both in the United States and Canada.

"Come on," said Eleanor, "I'll take you into the bar and we'll have a beer, and you can talk with some real people."

We sat with beers and soon many people joined us. One of the nicest surprises of my life was that a thin, ragged white man with an Eskimo wife came and sat down, and said to me, "Connie, don't you remember me? Well, I wasn't married then. Please meet the wife. We live on an island out in the delta. Don't you remember, now? I give you and your husband your first meal when you come to Canada from Alaska the summer of 1947. You had built runners on the bottom of that canoe, to pull it over ice when ice blocked your way, remember now?"

"Oh, yes — why, you're Mike McConnell! Oh, this is wonderful, seeing you! Yes, that was our canoe, the *Little Willow*. You ought to see the one I got now, the *Jeanie Ann*. Named for my two daughters, Jean and Ann, you know. How's the muskrat trapping?"

"Well, not good, not good," Mike said. "The wife and I come into town so I can do a little carpentering this summer. We raising minks and cabbages out on the island. You should come out. . . ."

"Would you say the trapping is not so good as eighteen years ago?"

"That right. Delta is getting trapped out, you know. Too many people. It was once the world's greatest muskrat area. Oh, I remember that day you come along through the delta from Alaska, threading your way like that. I give you your first white man food in my tent." We both laughed.

"It sure tasted good," I said. "But made me sick later. I was used to only meat and fish. Oh, those were the days! Will there ever be days like that again when we were all young?"

But at once I thought: "Yes, there are days like that always. My kids will talk about these days which are real great to them."

Then a day later I met other wonderful friends I never dreamed were in Inuvik. "Do you remember, Connie, we met you in Aklavik? First you came by canoe and then you came in with your little plane sometimes. From Alaska. Don't you remember? We're Dave and Mary Jones."

"Oh, good heavens," I said. "How wonderful seeing you again. But do you live here in this place?"

"Sure," they said. "Lived here since they built it. Been in the Arctic straight fifteen years now. Working with the oil company nowadays."

"You've simply got to come over and stay at the house," said Mary. "Oh, if we had only known. We have a lovely place. . . ."

"But we can't." I demurred. "We're too dirty and terrible to be in such a nice place. . . ."

I was trudging along the road toward the trailer when a police car stopped. "Mail just came in. Got something for you!"

It was from Alaska, air mail. In the trailer I found the girls huddled in their sleeping bags because it was so cold in the unheated trailer that you could see your breath. Their combined spirits were at the lowest.

Jean took the letter from me and dejectedly, hopelessly, opened it. I heard her breath expel in a long gasp. Then she composed herself and read it haltingly aloud.

"Dad can't come and get me himself," she said. "Too busy with his other family but also mainly the arctic business. He says to take the airlines over to Alaska through Whitehorse and Fairbanks, and wait for him at the trading post at Bettles where he has a charge account, and he'll try to get over the Brooks Range, weather permitting, and pick me up there on skis. They're flying skis already on the north coast in Alaska. It may take a week or ten days for me to make connection with him, if I leave right now. . . ." Jean could hardly believe it.

He was so busy he hadn't been able to write. . . . He had been hosting the director of the Royal Game Preserve from Kenya. Then the owners of *Time* and *Life* came for a vacation, and immediately following came an A.B.C. television crew with the actors and everything, to shoot a film on the ice; and the children's dad was guide and packer for them all. . . . Anyway, he wrote Jean a cordial welcome to the lodge beside the polar ice pack.

He pointed out that she would be out of school a year if she came to his home. It was five hundred and ten air miles south to Fairbanks and school. She might stay on permanently if she decided to take all her high school courses by correspondence. This posed some problems as she would be giving up all of the usual American teen-age way of life, he pointed out — a way of life for which he personally had no admiration. He would like to see Ann sometime, too, he said. The girls would be expected to work hard at the lodge if they came. There would be dishwashing, for instance.

"There aren't any doctors, Jean," I mused aloud, although Jean was past hearing me, as her thoughts raced ahead. "But then, frankly, I have got awfully tired of paying doctors. . . ."

"He said he will have my furs made for me right away," she said. "He said he likes girls also to wear dresses and very fashionable slacks inside the house. From Bonwit Teller and Saks Fifth Avenue, he said."

"Now," I said, "speaking of Saks, you girls climb out of the sacks, right now, and stop this moping. . . ."

"Gee, you're lucky Jean," said Ann. "You always get everything. I wish I was going." None of us could know how soon Ann's wish also was destined to come true.

Ann and I flew south to Edmonton, collected our car there, and then drove on southward still. After we left Inuvik, Jean stayed for a while with the Dave Jones family as she awaited her flight to Alaska, which had first to service one of the arctic islands. When the flight finally left Inuvik, she went with it.

Just a month later Ann also flew to Alaska. She had got sick as soon as we arrived south — the old viruses — and as she had missed her whole first month of high school, I gave up on her for the time, and sent her also to her dad on the far polar shore to see what he could do about it.

Bumbles and I saw her off at our town airport. Her cough started improving right there. Her father would have to find furs for her on short notice, as it was already around thirty degrees below zero on Alaska's polar plain. But he could do it; he was always resourceful at digging up good furs, and he knew an old Eskimo seamstress who had helped us all for many years, and she still sewed well.

In Alaska, Ann was met at a remote trading post north of the Yukon by an airplane on skis. As it landed it scattered clouds of snow along the staked runway and taxied up in a no-nonsense way. Then her father stepped out of his plane, enormous and rosy-cheeked and beaming, and enveloped in otter and wolf and mink — his usual costume for the latitudes where he chose to dwell. He bundled his little girl into his big furry arms and carried her away three hundred miles north of the trees to the shore of the Arctic Ocean.

"I have always been a little suspicious of these mother-daughter teams," I had told the girls once. "Those teams that keep on doing things together forever." There is a time to write finis.

It is natural and probably healthy that the parent always loves the child a great deal more than the child loves the parent. The young person is too busy living, is too involved with life every minute, to find time for looking backward. I was the same way with my mother: to look back at your parent is not very exciting. It brings no progress for anyone. It is not the way of youth, or of life.

When the kids came flying back out of the sky, well — Bumbles and Gerald and I, and Grandmother, too, would all rejoice. Just to see them come out of the North again as the wild geese fly, was really something. But wild geese you can't hold. You have to let them go.

I have a half-burned scrap of a diary of Ann's among my mud-spattered maps and river charts. The first page has a drawing of a large Mounted Policeman, holding up his hand; and it says in bold print: "Keep out! This is a private diary." As an afterthought, it warns: "Can't you read?"

The rest is lost; I rescued this remnant one day when she threw it into the campfire in a pique (the girls were to keep diaries with the sincere intention of helping me write this book). Now sometimes I press it to my nose and sniff the ashes and the campfire smoke once again, and suddenly it is the old Mackenzie that I see. Or maybe for a moment I hear the lapping waters of the treacherous Slave or the mighty Peace. Then I see us and our brave little tent somewhere along that wild river, and I know that we used our time well.

CANADIAN RIVERS

FIRST SUMMER